MANAGING WATER QUALITY:

ECONOMICS, TECHNOLOGY, INSTITUTIONS

MANAGING WATER QUALITY: ECONOMICS, TECHNOLOGY, INSTITUTIONS

Allen V. Kneese *and* Blair T. Bower

Published for Resources for the Future, Inc.

By The Johns Hopkins Press, Baltimore and London

Preface and Acknowledgments

This book is a substantial revision and extension of a 1964 volume *The Economics of Regional Water Quality Management*.[1] In the four years since its publication public concern over water quality in the United States has continued, and, if anything, grown more intense. Two laws of major national significance have been passed—the Water Quality Act of 1965 and the Clean Water Restoration Act of 1966. Both laws emphasize federal government enforcement action against waste discharges, coupled with subsidies for the construction of municipal waste treatment works, as the major thrust of federal policy. The 1965 act also requires that each state set water quality standards for its interstate and boundary waters. This requirement raises the question of what the rational basis for a particular standard or set of standards may be—one of the matters we examine in this book.

Since *The Economics of Regional Water Quality Management* was written, considerable research has been done on water quality management, a substantial portion of it under the auspices of Resources for the Future. The present book makes use of the results of this recent theoretical and empirical research.

The new work underscores the shortcomings of conventional approaches as means of achieving economically efficient management of water quality. They are not pointed toward systematic balancing of costs and returns to achieve optimum net benefits from the use of water resources, including their use for waste disposal, and they are unlikely to achieve a least-cost solution for even a single water quality objective. Continuing growth of population and economic activity makes these deficiencies increasingly serious, as the residual waste loads of ever-larger conurbations put mounting pressure on watercourses. New approaches

[1] A. V. Kneese, *The Economics of Regional Water Quality Management* (The Johns Hopkins Press, for Resources for the Future, 1964).

v

to water quality management are called for; and steps to encourage them need to be taken by governments at the federal and other levels.

While this book has important implications for current policy, it ranges beyond what may be immediately practical. It reports on research that points to promising directions for future study as well as to ways of dealing with present problems.

Before listing those who made specific comments on this book, we wish to acknowledge once more our indebtedness to all those who contributed to the preparation of its predecessor, *The Economics of Regional Water Quality Management.*

Discussions with and encouragement from a number of members of the RFF staff were very helpful to us. We wish to note particularly the contributions of Michael F. Brewer, John V. Krutilla, Charles W. Howe, and Edwin T. Haefele.

Useful comments were also received from a number of outside reviewers. Special acknowledgment is due Alvin L. Alm, U.S. Bureau of the Budget; J. Hayden Boyd, Department of Economics, Ohio State University; N. H. Calvert, Water Resources Board, England; Lyle E. Craine, Water Resources Committee, University of Michigan; Otto A. Davis, Graduate School of Industrial Administration, Carnegie-Mellon University; L. Michael Falkson, Environmental System Engineering Department, Cornell University; Irving K. Fox, Water Resources Center, University of Wisconsin; Fred H. Hubbard and Edwin L. Johnson, Federal Water Pollution Control Administration, U.S. Department of the Interior; Jon C. Liebman, Department of Sanitary Engineering and Water Resources, The Johns Hopkins University; Alvin R. Morris, Federal Water Pollution Control Administration; Donald E. Nicoll, Administrative Assistant to Senator Edmund S. Muskie, U.S. Senate; Edwin E. Pyatt, Department of Bioenvironmental Engineering, University of Florida; James M. Quigley, formerly Commissioner, Federal Water Pollution Control Administration; Richard Schmalensee, Council of Economic Advisers; Joe B. Stevens, Department of Agricultural Economics, Oregon State University; J. W. Thursby and James F. Wright, Delaware River Basin Commission.

ALLEN V. KNEESE
BLAIR T. BOWER

Table of Contents

NATURE OF THE WATER QUALITY PROBLEM

I

Introduction

1

Deterioration of water quality is not a new problem. To some extent it has existed ever since people began to congregate in cities. But man's impacts on the water environment and on water quality were quite localized and limited until the industrial revolution. Then, the growing concentration of both factories and people gave new dimensions to water quality problems, first in Europe and later in the United States. In recent decades, with the increasingly rapid growth of the economy, the problem has become so large and complex that water quality management must be regarded as a modern problem calling for new approaches.

In the United States water quality deterioration first received attention as a public health problem following outbreaks of typhoid, paratyphoid, dysentery, and other water-borne diseases. During the first quarter of the present century, water treatment processes were developed and applied to insure that potable water could be made available to the rapidly growing urban populations. The rivers and other watercourses still received the waste discharges, but it was some time before they could no longer assimilate the residual wastes. The conditions that brought early action on the smaller European rivers did not develop here until comparatively recent times. Wide recognition of the water quality problem in the United States and large-scale efforts to control waste discharges date essentially from the end of World War II.

A distinctive feature of the modern problem of water quality is the fact that the economic institutions on which we customarily rely to balance costs and returns—the interaction of market forces in a private enterprise system—do not perform this function satisfactorily for waste disposal. In deciding how to dispose of its wastes, an upstream firm or city is not forced to take into account the costs imposed by its effluent discharge upon downstream water users or the value of other uses of the water that may be foreclosed by its action.

3

Because of these aspects of waste disposal, market forces have been supplemented in a variety of ways. Appeals have been made to civic responsibility to minimize waste contribution to watercourses. Damaged parties have occasionally resorted to adversary proceedings in courts of law. Enforcement actions have been brought against waste dischargers by public agencies. In recent years the federal government and a number of states have offered financial inducements to encourage waste treatment, particularly by municipalities.

Action along these lines has accomplished a great deal. Major streams like the Ohio, Delaware, and Potomac are now in much better condition than they were fifteen years ago. The traditional approaches will undoubtedly bear further fruit, and the time may soon come when comparatively small amounts of floating and suspended solids will be discharged to watercourses. This will be a major accomplishment, and doubts that the means of attaining it were not always the most efficient should not detract from it.

Even so, serious water quality problems will confront the nation. They will be particularly severe in densely developed regions where basic treatment processes can no longer keep up with the heavy waste loads generated. In such areas there is need for carefully planned systematic attacks, if the problem is to be handled in an efficient manner.

The situation is beginning to be reflected in various ways in research, planning, and deliberations by public bodies, and in policy decisions. In the contemporary situation, disjointed and more or less ad hoc approaches to control at individual waste outfalls are likely to be inefficient.

THE ISSUES

The contemporary problem of water quality management, in our view, raises three main issues: First, how do we determine the quality of water we want to maintain in our watercourses, both surface and underground? As a part of this problem, we must decide the degree of certainty with which we want the specified level of water quality, i.e., 100 per cent of the time—which is virtually impossible in most cases— 98 per cent of the time, 95 per cent of the time.

Second, what is the "best" system of management measures for achieving the specified pattern of water quality? Research has shown that there is a wide variety of alternative measures potentially available to improve water quality. Devising the best system must be done within the context of over-all water resources management, as noted more explicitly later.

Third, what are the best institutional or organizational arrangements for managing water quality? What sort of organizational form and range of authority should a management agency have in order to use information on alternatives provided by engineering-economic analysis and to implement an effective and efficient management program?

All these issues are related. For example, the choice of quality level must depend on the cost of achieving that level, and the cost, as will be seen in later chapters, largely depends on how effective the management agency is. However, this categorization does help to isolate the most important issues.

What Levels of Quality?

What qualities of water are appropriate for the many uses of watercourses? What limit should be put on the use of watercourses for waste disposal now and in the future? How can a proper balance be achieved between this use and other valuable, and often conflicting, uses, such as municipal water supply and recreation? Removal of the most blatantly offensive material is but a beginning step in improving water quality. It is one thing to remove fecal solids from a stream and another to assure that residual organic wastes do not interfere with fish life by causing periodic reduction of oxygen levels. It is one thing to remove oil from an industrial effluent and another to assure that residual phenols do not impose increased treatment costs upon downstream municipal water users. Many wastes have little effect on the appearance of water but still cause costly and widespread damage. The proliferation of products, such as the wide variety of paper goods now produced in a range of colors, contributes to the amount and complexity of waste discharges. These wastes can reduce the value of water for recreation, impose treatment costs on successive users, damage facilities of various kinds, and make it necessary to turn to alternative sources of water.

Decisions must be made, for the conflicts among water uses are becoming stronger as economic development and a growing population increase the demand on watercourses. Demand for water-based recreational opportunities is growing at an especially rapid rate, outpacing the increase in population and per capita income.

It is true of every known waste removal technique that, as complete removal is approached, costs mount rapidly. Therefore it becomes increasingly important to consider carefully what is the appropriate level of water quality, to control waste loads in the most effective and efficient ways, and to search for alternative ways of improving water quality.

How Can a Given Level of Water Quality be Achieved at Least Cost?

What is the preferable combination of alternatives to achieve any given level and pattern of water quality? Or, to put it slightly differently, how can we determine the economically optimal regional system for managing water quality? This question increases in urgency as the costs (waste reduction and damages) associated with waste discharges rise.

Treatment of wastes in individual municipal and industrial plants is but one way of managing water quality. Industries can substantially reduce the generation of wastes by modifying or changing their production processes, by recovering raw materials, by going into by-product production, and by reclaiming wastewater. Water can be stored in large reservoirs during periods of high flow and released during periods of lower flow, or wastes can be held for release when streamflows are high. A variety of measures can be taken to enhance or make better use of the assimilative capacity of water bodies. Oxygen can be introduced artificially into streams, lakes, or estuaries, or pipeline distribution systems can be used to take advantage of the naturally occurring assimilative capacity. Even the location of economic activities is an important determinant of the costs of waste management and the provision of water supply.

Moreover, water quality improvement is only one output from a water resources system. Such a system is composed of individual and collective structural measures such as reservoirs, treatment plants, levees, groundwater recharge facilities, irrigation facilities, and power plants, and non-structural measures such as flood warning networks, zoning, standard setting, withdrawal fees, and effluent charges. Efficient water quality management can only be achieved with explicit consideration of other outputs from water resources systems—energy, water supply, irrigation, navigation, water-based recreation opportunities, flood damage reduction.

Individual measures are those applied at the sites of individual production units, such as industrial plants or irrigated farms, and at individual cities—e.g., a municipal water or waste treatment plant. Collective measures are those which are applied to, or service, several production units—e.g., a waste-handling facility or a reservoir serving several industrial plants or municipalities.

In this book we use the term "management" to denote this "bundle" of activities. To be more specific, as shown in Figure 1, management involves the whole range of activities from data collection, research and analysis, through operating water quality monitoring networks and treatment plants, evaluating performance of system units, setting standards and charges, and so on.

What Institutional and Organizational Arrangements Are Needed?

Defining the level of water quality to be achieved and the optimal combination of measures to achieve it, within the context of over-all water resources management, will be of no avail if there is no adequate

Water Quality Management

PLANNING
*(economic projections and en-
gineering-economic analyses of
alternatives leading to decisions
on what structural and non-
structural measures to put
into use when and where)*

Research
and
Data Collection

IMPLEMENTATION
*(design and construct facilities,
including monitoring networks;
set standards; establish inspection
procedures; devise procedures
for levying charges)*

OPERATION
*(pushing buttons, closing/opening gates, making
inspections, operating reservoirs and
treatment plants, levying charges)*

Figure 1.

organization or institution or agency to implement the system and carry on the bundle of activities involved in water quality management.

Recognition of the limitations of civic responsibility and of law and adversary proceedings in controlling the quality of watercourses has resulted in recourse to administrative regulation of waste discharges from cities and industries, usually on the basis of some sort of general standards. In recent years the federal government and some states have provided financial assistance to local communities for the construction and operation of waste treatment facilities. Also the federal government now provides low-flow augmentation for water quality improvement on a nonreimbursable basis from federal multipurpose reservoirs (provided certain standards of waste treatment are met).[1] Are these the best methods of proceeding toward optimal management of

[1] A proposed change in this policy is reported in Chapter 14.

water quality? Or should serious thought be given to revising governmental organizations and policies now used in controlling water quality? As we hope this book will make clear, engineering-economic analysis suggests that deep thought should be given to new institutional arrangements for planning and implementing water quality management systems. Much attention abroad to "regional" approaches to water quality management reinforces this view.

OBJECTIVE AND PLAN OF THIS BOOK

The objective of this book is to help shed light on these vital issues through the economic theory of resources allocation and case studies of a number of actual situations.

A central concern of economics is the allocation of scarce resources to alternative ends. In ordinary instances, the market may be expected to perform this task in a reasonably satisfactory fashion. But because of the special circumstances[2] involved in the development and use of water resources, the market, as already stated, cannot be expected to allocate water efficiently or to generate efficient means of management. Economics, which has been called the "science of choice," can help to devise decision criteria which public or co-operative agencies can use in making decisions about the management of water resources. Even where all relevant values cannot be quantified, the "economic approach" often provides a useful way of thinking about the problems and a useful way of organizing data for decision-makers.

The book is organized in five parts. Part I consists of the introduction and three chapters that provide background information on some of the scientific and technologic aspects of water quality. Chapters 2 and 3 identify and classify the major wastes entering the various types of watercourses, describe their effects on receiving waters and on various water uses, and illustrate the methods and costs of treating intake water for subsequent uses. Chapter 4 sketches some of the factors that affect the generation of wastes and describes some of the more important methods of reducing wastes generation and of handling wastes after generation. It also describes ways of increasing or making better use of the assimilative capacity of water bodies, which are possible substitutes for waste load reduction, at least over certain ranges.

Part II, consisting of Chapters 5 through 9, outlines the theory of economic resource allocation as it relates specifically to waste disposal problems at individual points of waste discharge, and presents two case

---

[2] These "circumstances" are external economies and diseconomies, economies of large scale, and collective-good aspects. Each of these concepts is explained in some detail in subsequent chapters. It should also be noted that "reasonably satisfactory" is not meant to imply that the market has no other imperfections.

studies as illustrations of the theory. The major focus is on the problems presented by the offsite, or external, costs imposed upon subsequent users by wastes discharged into watercourses from individual outfalls. The concept of external cost is explained in Chapter 5.

It should be noted that throughout the book we maintain a rather careful distinction between "waste discharge" and pollution. Under some circumstances a waste may be discharged into a watercourse without measurably deteriorating the water quality or, even if it does so, without causing damage to subsequent uses. In such cases the terms pollutant and pollution—with their connotations of adverse consequences, are not appropriate. Thus we normally use the terms waste discharge, water quality deterioration, and damages associated with waste discharge. When we do refer to water pollution it is meant to imply that damages are associated with the water quality deterioration. "Water pollution control" is used to describe only one element of water quality management—the regulation of waste discharges at individual outfalls.

Chapter 6 deals with the problems of assessing the value of offsite costs of waste disposal and causing the waste disposer to consider such costs systematically in his decision-making. Chapter 7 addresses the question of how to deal with situations where not all values affected by waste disposal can be assessed in a commensurable way. It is in this connection that quality standards for water bodies are discussed. Comparisons are also made between effluent standards and an economic incentive technique, "effluent charges," for implementing quality standards, on the basis of criteria of economic efficiency and equity. To lend concreteness to this discussion, two case studies are presented in Chapter 8. In the first the suggested criteria of cost assessment and redistribution are applied to a water quality problem in the Ohio River Basin. In the second a study of the possible use of effluent charges to implement a water quality management program in the Delaware estuary area is discussed. The final chapter in this part, Chapter 9, presents a summary discussion of policies for controlling waste discharges at individual outfalls.

In Part III the focus shifts from individual outfalls to a broader concept of regional water quality management. Because there are substantial economies of scale in certain means of water quality improvement, alternatives to treatment or other means of waste reduction at individual points of municipal and industrial discharge may contribute to a "least cost" regional waste disposal system. Efficient quality management on a regional basis would often require that a system incorporating the available scale economies be planned and operated through some sort of a co-operative or collective arrangement, or by a public authority.

We also take this opportunity to point out some of the broader interdependencies among water quality management, water resources management, land use management, and waste disposal generally. For example, hydroelectric operations, especially for peak power production, and regulation of streams by a series of low dams for navigation often have an adverse effect on the waste assimilative capacity of receiving waters. Locating an industrial park and its effluent outlets immediately above a municipal water intake, or along a watercourse of high recreational value, may create costs that more than offset the benefits from the new industry. Burning wastes instead of discharging them into streams can improve water quality at the expense of air quality.

Chapter 10 establishes criteria for planning and operating an economically optimal system of regional waste disposal. Consideration is given to the many devices for managing water quality that may be available in any given region. These include—in addition to waste reduction at individual points of waste discharge by means of process change, materials recovery, by-product production, waste treatment, and combinations thereof—treatment in large regional plants of wastes collected from numerous industries and municipalities, treatment of the stream itself via oxidation impoundments or mechanical reaeration, and in particular instances other alternatives as well. Methods are discussed for incorporating in both system planning and system operation those values which cannot be, or are not, made commensurable with others. Optimum system planning and operation are also greatly influenced by the probabilistic character of water quality levels, and this is discussed. A mathematical appendix to Chapter 10 summarizes the economic principles used in the book.

In general, it is found that while a system incorporating regional scale measures presents a much more complex planning and operating problem than the simpler system analyzed in the previous part, it requires no new economic principles. It does raise truly fundamental questions of management, however, because the potential net gains from the more complex systems can be realized only if there are regional agencies with the requisite powers.

In Chapters 11 and 12 some cases are described and analyzed within the framework set forth in Chapter 10. Two instances of regional water quality systems analysis in the United States are reported in detail in Chapter 11. The first involves the Potomac estuary and includes relevant material from the Corps of Engineers' study of the Potomac Basin and from a study supported by Resources for the Future. The second concerns the study of the Delaware estuary done under the Federal Water Pollution Control Administration's Comprehensive Water Quality Studies program. Each case well illustrates in quantitative terms the gains to be achieved from a systematic consideration, evaluation, and incorporation of a range of alternatives into a regional water quality management system and clearly poses the institutional challenge to realize these gains.

Chapter 12 relates the economic principles discussed in this study to the operation of regional water quality management systems in the Ruhr industrial area of West Germany. The Ruhr area water associations are the only organizations in the world which have planned, built, and operated regional systems for water quality management. Of equal interest, they have developed comparatively sophisticated methods of assessing costs and levying charges on effluents. While not ideals to be imitated slavishly, these associations do represent interesting and unique organizations which have gone some distance toward implementing what we call "the regional approach."

The discussion of the Ruhr provides a bridge between the largely engineering-economic-systems orientations of Part III and the institutional cast of Part IV.

Part IV deals with the organizational approaches to regional water quality management in several highly developed countries of the western world. One concept central to postwar legislation in a number of European countries is that water quality management is best carried out by regional (river-basin) agencies having broad water resources management authority. This idea has been less strong in North America, but Canada is heading in this direction,[3] and the United States now has one agency—the Delaware River Basin Commission—authorized to develop a unified approach to water quality management as part of over-all water resources management. Others are in prospect.

Chapter 13 describes and evaluates on the basis of broad efficiency criteria the organization and authority of the *Genossenschaften* (water associations) in the Ruhr area of Germany, the French basin agencies, the River Authorities in England and Wales, and the Delaware River Basin Commission. While the analysis of organization and legal authority is important and useful, it should be noted that only the *Genossenschaften* have operated long enough to be evaluated. Having adequate powers does not always result in efficient performance.

Finally, Part V recapitulates the main points made earlier and attempts to draw out their implications for policy in the United States. First, we suggest criteria for regional water quality management agencies —criteria that are based on the technological-economic characteristics of

---

[3] This is reflected in the recommendations of the National Council of Resource Ministers and the operations of the existing Ontario Water Resources Commission. With respect to the latter, see "Ontario Manages Water Resources from a Single Agency," *Engineering News-Record*, Vol. 178, No. 22 (1967), pp. 36–37, and Ontario Water Resources Commission, *Annual Report* (1966).

water quality management and that represent necessary, but not sufficient, conditions for achieving economically efficient water quality management. Then, we point to the need for new initiative in federal and state water quality management policies. We conclude by suggesting a series of changes in public policy at all levels of government that we believe would lay a sound groundwork for efficient water quality management in the United States within the context of over-all water resources management.

The Nature of Waste Discharges and Their Effects on Receiving Waters

2

A complete description of the physical, chemical, and biological aspects of water quality, as a function of natural and man-made factors, and the technological measures available for changing water quality can easily fill several extensive volumes. Chapters 2, 3, and 4 are designed as a brief introduction to these matters. The aim is to provide a background for consideration of the economic and institutional aspects of water quality management.

The subject matter of these three chapters is schematically depicted in Figure 2. Chapter 2 describes the major types of wastes and their effects on receiving waters. Because each type of receiving water has characteristics that, to some degree, result in differential impacts of the same waste discharge on water quality, no attempt at complete coverage is made. Chapter 3 describes the relationships between source water quality (quality in the watercourse) and various water uses, including intake water treatment methods and costs. Chapter 4 considers various methods for improving water quality, subsumed under the two major categories of reducing wastes prior to discharge and improving or making more effective use of the assimilative capacity of watercourses. The relation of these various methods of region-wide water quality and water resources management will also be indicated.

MAJOR TYPES OF WASTES AND THEIR SOURCES

The many substances having an impact on water quality that enter surface watercourses and groundwater aquifers as a result of man's domestic, industrial, agricultural, and recreational activities can be grouped in various ways. One common classification differentiates between physical substances (e.g., radioactive, inorganic, organic) and

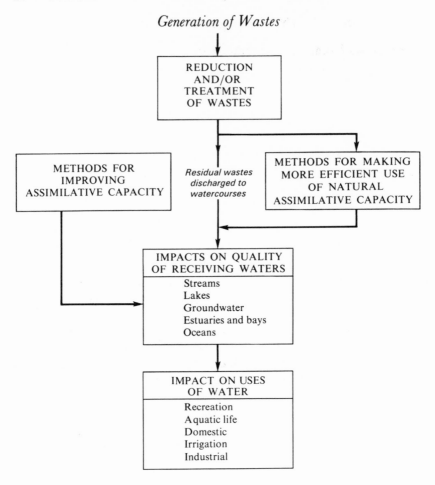

Figure 2.

biological substances (e.g., bacteria and viruses). In addition, the quality of a waste discharge can be measured in various ways. Some of the common measures are biochemical oxygen demand (BOD), chemical oxygen demand (COD), alkalinity, acidity, color, hardness, taste, odor, turbidity, and electrical conductance.

For the purposes of this book, however, the most useful classification of wastes distinguishes between nondegradable and degradable substances, based on their behavior in receiving waters. Nondegradable wastes are usually diluted and may be changed in form, but they are not appreciably reduced in weight in the receiving water. Degradable wastes are reduced in weight by the biological, physical, and chemical processes which occur in natural waters.

Nondegradable Wastes

The sources of nondegradable substances—mainly inorganic chemicals, such as chlorides, synthetic organic chemicals, and inorganic suspended solids—are many and widespread. Industrial waste discharges frequently contain inorganic or metallic salts, synthetic organic chemicals, and other materials which may be toxic or corrosive, may impart color or taste to the water, and/or may produce odors. Domestic water use results in a small increase in the content of chlorides and other dissolved salts. The return flow from irrigation is generally significantly higher in dissolved salts than the applied irrigation water. The discharge of copper, zinc, uranium, and other compounds in drainage from mine tailings can have very adverse impacts on water quality, and acid mine drainage is an acute problem in some of the major coal-producing areas. In the heavily industrialized sections of the country and in the major irrigated areas of the West, industrial operations and irrigated agriculture may be major sources of chlorides and other dissolved salts.

Natural geologic formations, such as salt deposits, may result in high concentrations of chlorides and/or dissolved solids in watercourses. Another instance of deterioration of water quality by a natural source is from seawater intrusion in groundwater aquifers near coastal areas (following a change in the hydraulic gradient because of pumping from the aquifers). Similarly, the quality of water in inland groundwater aquifers can be adversely affected by excessive pumping where there are hydraulic connections with brackish or saline aquifers.

Suspended materials, which can be considered nondegradable in the sense that they are essentially not changed in weight in receiving waters, consist of sediment from natural and accelerated erosion from land surfaces and stream channels and colloidal material[1] from clay deposits and in domestic and industrial waste discharges. Suspended sediment usually settles out, but colloidal matter does not, except under unusual circumstances. Both suspended sediment and colloidal matter cause turbidity in surface waters. This not only makes the water less attractive, but can damage fish life. Turbidity may also inhibit the growth of algae and other aquatic plants, which may or may not be undesirable.

Agricultural activities generate both nondegradable and degradable wastes. Storm runoff from agricultural land carries silt, clay, fertilizers, and weedicides, as well as organic material and bacteria, into watercourses.[2] In contrast to the sources of wastes described above, which result in waste discharges concentrated at one or a few points, agri-

---

[1] Colloidal material is intermediate in size between clay particles, which are larger, and inorganic molecules, which generally are smaller.

[2] See S. R. Weibel, "Pesticides and Other Contaminants in Rainfall and Runoff," *Journal American Water Works Association*, Vol. 58, No. 8 (1966), pp. 1075–84.

cultural activities generally result in dispersed waste loads, except in the case of feed lot operations. In predominantly agricultural regions, for example the Missouri Basin, these dispersed waste loads may be the major sources of nitrogen, phosphate, and pesticides, as well as organic wastes.[3]

Actually the classification into degradable and nondegradable waste loads is a simplification. Some types of substances, such as radioactive materials and some of the organic chemicals, are degradable to some degree. Viruses also appear to be in the in-between category. Some radioactive wastes decay rapidly; others extremely slowly. Some of the synthetic organic compounds, such as alkyl benzene sulfonate (ABS) detergents, are not strictly nondegradable, but they resist attack by stream biota. On the other hand, the new detergents based on linear alkylate sulfonate (LAS) are degradable, both in streams and other watercourses and in waste treatment plants.

One other point with respect to nondegradable wastes merits mention, namely, the problem of identifying the substances in the receiving water. With respect to many of the complex industrial, agricultural, and pharmaceutical chemical compounds, not only have techniques not yet been developed to identify them, but the concentrations involved are often on the order of a few parts per billion, rather than parts per million as with chlorides or suspended sediment. Further, the extent to which there are synergistic or antagonistic reactions is not fully understood as yet. Viruses also present identification problems because they can exist in a dormant condition outside living organisms and be reactivated under proper environmental conditions.

Degradable Wastes

Degradable wastes—the substances that are reduced in quantity by the biological, chemical, and physical phenomena characteristic of natural waters—include organic wastes of various kinds from domestic and industrial operations, bacteria, and thermal discharges. The most widespread source of degradable organic materials is domestic sewage. In terms of total quantity, industrial discharges represent the largest source. The highly unstable, putrescible, organic waste can be converted to stable inorganic materials (bicarbonates, nitrates, sulphates, and phosphates) by the bacteria and other organisms found in natural water bodies. If the water is not too heavily loaded, the process, commonly but somewhat deceptively known as self-purification, will proceed aerobically by the action of bacteria utilizing free oxygen and will not

[3] See R. C. Loehr, "Municipal and Industrial Pollution Now and in the Future," *Public Works*, Vol. 95, No. 6 (1964).

produce offensive odors. If the receiving waters are loaded excessively, the process of degradation will proceed anaerobically by the action of bacteria not utilizing free oxygen, and hydrogen sulfide and other gases will be produced. Both of these processes are utilized in waste treatment plants, which, in essence, systematize, control, and accelerate the processes that take place in natural waters.

Bacteria are omnipresent in natural waters. Except for a few types, i.e., the pathogens, the vast majority are beneficial. The primary waste discharges that are sources of bacteria are from activities of warm-blooded animals. The coliform count is the most common index of such waste discharges.[4] Total bacteria count is also used as an indicator of water quality in relation to such discharges. Both coliform count and total bacteria count serve as crude proxies for the actual substances of concern, namely, the bacteria that cause infectious diseases—primarily typhoid, dysentery, and cholera. Bacteria may be considered degradable since they tend to die off rather quickly after leaving the body.

Thermal loads are classed as degradable because the heat is dissipated in receiving waters, primarily by evaporation in surface water, and by some combination of evaporation and conduction in groundwater. The primary sources of thermal loads are the generation of electrical energy and the cooling operations in the petroleum refining, pulp and paper, iron and steel, and chemical manufacturing industries. Thermal discharges are particularly troublesome when industrial operations are concentrated along a stream or an estuary.

EFFECTS OF WASTE DISCHARGES ON RECEIVING WATERS

Nondegradable Wastes

Given the weight of a waste in a discharge and the volume of the discharge, the concentration of a nondegradable waste over time in a stream or lake is relatively easy to predict because dilution is the dominant process when the substance is in solution. Prediction is more difficult for estuaries because of the complex hydraulic characteristics resulting from tidal action and topography. Inorganic chemicals may precipitate out in lakes, reservoirs, and, under certain conditions, in flowing streams. Suspended sediment will settle out to some degree in receiving waters, particularly in sections where there is a major decrease in stream velocity, although the spatial pattern of deposition cannot always be accurately predicted. For a nondegradable waste discharged to

---

[4] *Escherichia coli* or colon bacilli, the harmless bacteria which inhabit the intestines of warm-blooded animals.

a groundwater aquifer, predicting the concentration over time at various distances from the original discharge point is complicated by variations in transmissibility, both vertically and horizontally, and by the physical processes (such as adsorption) and chemical reactions which are possible. In all of these situations the weight of the discharged substance remains essentially unchanged, although the form may be modified in the receiving waters.

It should be emphasized that, while the prediction of concentration of a nondegradable waste in a specified water body is relatively easy for a known weight of waste and given volume of receiving water, prediction of the actual time pattern of concentration resulting from a waste discharge is far less simple. This is true for two reasons. First, with respect to the receiving water, there is uncertainty about the quantity of water available for dilution, i.e., hydrologic uncertainty.[5] Hydrologic events are stochastic variables, hence the quantity of water available is known only in terms of a probability distribution. Second, where the source of the nondegradable substance is an industrial operation, there often is significant variation from day to day (and even within the day) in the quantity of waste discharged. Despite these difficulties, procedures have been developed which enable reasonably accurate prediction of time patterns of concentrations resulting from defined time patterns of discharge of nondegradable wastes.[6]

Degradable Wastes

Predicting the time pattern and spatial pattern of concentration of wastes presents considerably more difficult technical problems when the wastes are degradable than when they are nondegradable. This is particularly true for organic wastes, but it holds to a lesser degree for

[5] For discussions of hydrologic uncertainty see M. B Fiering, "Synthetic Hydrology—An Assessment," in A. V. Kneese and S. C. Smith (eds.), *Water Research* (The Johns Hopkins Press, for RFF, 1966); and M. A. Benson and N. C. Matalas, "Use of Regional Analysis in Synthetic Hydrology," *Water Resources Research*, Vol. 3, No. 4 (1967).

[6] Examples of these procedures are: for surface waters—the calculation of chloride profiles in the Ohio River, in "Chloride Control Considerations for the Ohio River," a staff report prepared for the Ohio River Valley Sanitation Commission in 1957; and the calculation of total dissolved solids in various rivers, in E. F. Eldridge, *Return Irrigation Water, Characteristics and Effects* (Portland: Public Health Service, Department of Health, Education and Welfare, 1960); for groundwater—Wen-Hsiung Li and R. P. Canale, "Dispersion from Sources in Non-uniform Seepage Flow," *Journal of the Hydraulics Division, Proceedings of the American Society of Civil Engineers*, Vol. 93, No. HY3 (1967), pp. 65–79; R. W. Nelson, "A Sequence for Predicting Waste Transport by Groundwater," *Water and Sewage Works* (Reference Number, 1966), pp. R/85–R/94; and R. H. Brown, "Hydrologic Factors Pertinent to Ground Water Contamination," *Proceedings of 1961 Symposium*, Robert A. Taft Sanitary Engineering Center, Technical Report W61–5 (1961), pp. 7–16.

thermal discharges, for certain types of radioactive wastes, and for those synthetic organic pesticides which decompose to some degree. With respect to organic and thermal waste discharges, the primary concern is not the fate of the wastes *per se*, but the effect of their degradation on water quality, in particular the dissolved oxygen concentration in the receiving waters. Because of the importance of organic waste discharges in relation to total waste discharges and because of their widespread occurrence, we turn to a relatively detailed discussion of such wastes. An understanding of the phenomena involved is essential for the discussion of the economic, technological, and institutional aspects of water quality management in the remainder of the book.[7]

A measure of organic waste load is biochemical oxygen demand (BOD),[8] which indicates the amount of oxygen drawn upon in the process of decomposition of the waste. The amount of oxygen demanded and the rate at which it is drawn upon are functions of the type and quantity of the waste and of other factors, among which the most important are the chemical characteristics and the temperature of the receiving water.[9] Toxic substances, for example, may appreciably reduce the rate of decomposition by inhibiting bacterial action, and in extreme cases of toxic concentration a body of water may become bacteriologically "dead." At higher temperatures, when the oxygen saturation level of water is relatively low, bacterial action is accelerated, wastes are degraded more rapidly, and dissolved oxygen in the water is drawn upon more rapidly. The imbalance between available oxygen and oxygen demand may proceed to the point where septic (anaerobic) conditions result. Such conditions are most likely to occur in summer and early fall when streamflows tend to be low, and temperatures high.

The rate at which BOD is exerted combined with the rate at which oxygen is restored determines the level of dissolved oxygen (D.O.). In

---

[7] This is not meant to imply that the problems associated with radioactive and pesticide waste discharges are not important. In particular locations they are. However, the analytical approach is the same for all types of wastes. Where nonorganic degradable wastes are important, what must be developed are techniques for predicting their degradation in receiving waters. With respect to pesticides for example, see R. W. Okey and R. H. Bogan, "Synthetic Organic Pesticides: An Evaluation of Their Persistence in Natural Waters," *Proceedings, 11th Pacific Northwest Industrial Waste Conference*, Engineering Experiment Station Circular 29 (Oregon State University, 1963), pp. 222–51. With respect to radioactive wastes, considerable research on their degradation in natural waters has been done, particularly at the Oak Ridge Laboratory of the Atomic Energy Commission.

[8] Accurate determination of the BOD of a waste requires careful laboratory work. See D. G. Ballinger and R. J. Lishka, "Reliability and Precision of BOD and COD Determinations," *Journal Water Pollution Control Federation*, Vol. 34, No. 5 (1962), pp. 470–74.

[9] Other characteristics of the receiving water affect the process indirectly, primarily through their effects on plant life and photosynthesis.

flowing water the combined effect of an organic waste discharged at a specific location and reaeration in the stream results first in a decrease and then in an increase in D.O. as the waste is carried or moved downstream. This phenomenon is illustrated by a characteristic curve known as the "oxygen sag."[10] Two such curves are shown schematically in Figure 3. The variables affecting the shape of the curve can be described by standard equations, the development of which is given in the appendix to this chapter.

Other things being equal, factors that reduce the rate of BOD lengthen and flatten the oxygen sag, while those that accelerate BOD have the reverse effect. The shape of the oxygen sag is also affected by the rate of reaeration, which depends largely on channel characteristics as they affect turbulence and the area of the air-water interface, the net photosynthetic oxygen production, and the velocity of streamflow.

The role of photosynthesis, as a producer of oxygen, in the dissolved oxygen balance of receiving waters is a complex one. Photosynthesis depends on light and nutrients available, stream velocity, amounts and types of waste loads, water depth, and water temperature. Most of the photosynthesis in water bodies is performed by aquatic green plants called algae, which range in size from tiny, single-cell plants to various types up to several feet in length.

The contribution of photosynthesis to the oxygen content is complicated by the problem of respiration. An important factor in the assessment of this contribution is the P/R ratio, the ratio between oxygen production and community respiration, where community includes aquatic animals, plants, and bacteria. Directly downstream from the discharge of an organic load the P/R ratio is usually very small, i.e., on the order of 0.01. The peak production of oxygen occurs in the early portion of the "zone of recovery" (see Figure 3), where the P/R ratio may be on the order of 3.0 or more. Downstream a significant distance from the waste discharge, as the dissolved oxygen content of the stream approaches the level prior to the waste discharge, the P/R ratio tends to approach unity. The wide variation in the P/R ratio which has been found in various streams[11] complicates the analysis of the impact of organic waste loads on dissolved oxygen.

---

[10] The oxygen sag and the equations relating thereto were first formulated in H. W. Streeter and E. B. Phelps, *A Study of the Pollution and Natural Purification of the Ohio River—III: Factors Concerned in the Phenomena of Oxidation and Reaeration*, Public Health Bulletin No. 146 (February 1925). Subsequently various modifications have been made, one example being H. A. Thomas, Jr., "The Dissolved Oxygen Balance in Streams," Lecture No. 4, Boston Society of Civil Engineers Seminar on Waste Water Treatment and Disposal, 1957.

[11] H. T. Odum, "Primary Production in Flowing Waters," *Journal of Limnology and Oceanography*, Vol. 1, No. 2 (1956), pp. 102–17.

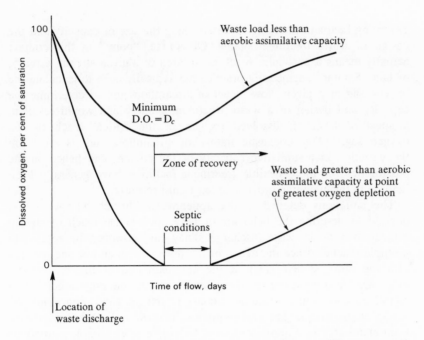

Figure 3. Schematic primary oxygen sag curve for two different organic waste discharges, assuming waste enters a stream that is fully saturated with oxygen.

A further complicating factor with respect to organic waste loads and photosynthesis involves the diurnal variation in dissolved oxygen. The diurnal variation may be of particular importance for certain types of water uses, such as fisheries.[12] Thus the analysis of water quality based solely on longer time periods, i.e., weeks or months, may—in certain instances—be inadequate as a basis for optimal water quality management.[13]

The low point on the oxygen sag (e.g., D_c, in Figure 3) has been a

[12] See the discussion of water quality in relation to fish in Chapter 3.

[13] The diurnal variation of dissolved oxygen in streams traditionally has been assumed to be one in which the D.O. is high during the day, with a peak between 2 and 6 p.m., and low during the night, with the minimum usually around 6 a.m. However, empirical investigations of various streams have disclosed considerable variations from this classical pattern. For example, study of the Sacramento River [C. G. Gunnerson and T. E. Bailey, "Oxygen Relationships in the Sacramento River," *Journal of the Sanitary Engineering Division, Proceedings ASCE*, Vol. 89, No. SA4 (August 1963), pp. 95–124] showed that this "classical" curve was approximated only about 37 per cent of the time. In 5 per cent of the cases the curves were inverted; i.e., with a nighttime maximum and a daytime minimum. Thus, there still seem to be some significant unexplained interrelationships involving the production and consumption of oxygen in biological systems, which in turn affect D.O. levels in water bodies in relation to imposed waste loads.

governing factor in planning or determining the size or capacity and the design of waste treatment plants. Of course, "point" in this context actually means a particular reach or an area of a given stream, estuary, or lake. Sanitary engineering practice has typically been to calculate the oxygen sag at a given "low" level of streamflow and to determine the capacity and design of a waste treatment plant which would result in a specified level of dissolved oxygen in the critical reach of the oxygen sag.[14] The stochastic nature of streamflow and its effect on the variation in assimilative capacity of the stream, and hence on the possibilities for more flexible treatment facilities, have generally been ignored in this planning process, at least until recently.

The equations detailed in the appendix to this chapter were first devised to describe the behavior of D.O. in a single reach of stream subject to a single waste discharge. They can, however, be applied to multiple reaches, since the deficit at the downstream end of one reach is also the initial deficit (D_a) at the upstream end of the next reach. Such straightforward use of the equations is possible only under highly simplified conditions, including a constant oxygen saturation along the length of the stream. The basic equations describing D.O. behavior have been elaborated in a number of ways to handle more complex situations including both multiple reaches and multiple points of waste discharge.

Consideration of waste disposal and water quality management on a regional basis requires methods for tracing the effect of waste discharges on long reaches of streams, in lakes, and throughout estuaries and groundwater basins. Where wastes are discharged to flowing streams from closely spaced outfalls, the level of D.O. at any given point is a function of the rate of reaeration and the exertion of BOD from the various sources, and of course the factors that affect both. (The same is true for lakes and estuaries.) At a given downstream point the BOD from the farthest upstream sources may be almost completely exhausted, while that from less distant sources will still be exerted at a high rate. A dissolved oxygen profile for a long stretch of such a stream will show deep valleys below large waste discharges or closely spaced small discharges and peaks at or near the D.O. saturation level at other locations. Figure 4 shows a dissolved oxygen profile of the Ohio River obtained by computer simulation for given conditions of flow, temperature, and waste loads.

Among the complexities that beset the calculation of oxygen levels, especially for long reaches of a stream, is the fact that BOD proceeds in two stages. When an organic waste is discharged into a stream where

---

[14] For an illustration of this "critical period" approach, see Federal Water Pollution Control Administration, *Willamette River Basin Water Quality Control and Management* (1967), pp. 28–29.

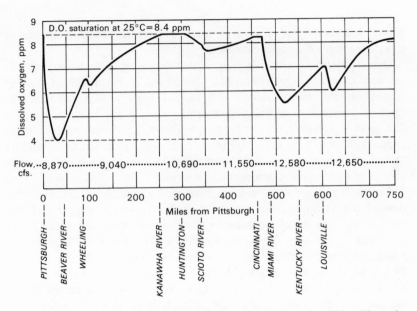

Figure 4. Dissolved oxygen profile projected for the Ohio River for 1980 on the assumption of medium growth, 70% waste load reduction, temperature of 25° C., $k_2 = 0.1$ (reoxygenation coefficient), $k_1 = 0.435$ (deoxygenation coefficient). *Source*: R. L. O'Connell, J. B. Cohen, E. C. Tzivoglou, "Future Stream Flow Requirements for Organic Pollution Abatement, Ohio River Basin," U.S. Public Health Service, Robert A. Taft Sanitary Engineering Center, Cincinnati, mimeo.

dissolved oxygen is near saturation level, there is an immediate and major draft upon the D.O. content of the stream, as the organic wastes are degraded by bacterial action. Thereafter the D.O. level tends to recover. Farther downstream, corresponding roughly to a travel time of five to seven days, a "second stage" BOD occurs, as the nitrogen embodied in the organic wastes is converted to nitrite and then to nitrate by aerobic nitrifying bacteria.[15] The second stage is more diffuse and does not by itself reduce the D.O. to as low a level as the first stage does.

Tracing the fate of an organic waste load in an estuary is even more difficult because the estuarine environment is complicated by tidal action, the large expanse of air-water interface, more complex hydraulic characteristics, and generally complicated patterns of inflows. In addition,

[15] For an excellent discussion of the two-stage nitrification process see F. E. Stratton and P. L. McCarty, "Prediction of Nitrification Effects on the Dissolved Oxygen Balance of Streams," *Environmental Science and Technology*, Vol. 1, No. 5 (1967), pp. 405–10.

photosynthesis may play an even larger role in the oxygen balance of an estuary than of a flowing stream.

Despite these complexities, significant advances have been made in developing models which interrelate the many variables involved, such as streamflow and temperature—with less or more consideration of the stochastic nature of both—and multiple waste loads, and enable prediction of regional profiles of D.O., temperature, and other water quality characteristics. These analytical models, virtually all of which depend on the use of computers, have provided the bases for economic optimization studies of water quality management systems.[16]

To cite one example, Thomann developed a mathematical representation of the Delaware estuary water quality system, composed of two subsystems: (1) the biochemical oxygen demand subsystem; and (2) the dissolved oxygen subsystem (see Figure 5). For each of the sections into which the estuary was divided, mass balance equations were written for both subsystems, assuming steady-state systems, i.e., invariant with time. These consisted of two linear differential equations based on the hydrological, physical, and biochemical characteristics in each section. The result was two sets of thirty simultaneous equations.

By matrix manipulation a set of transfer functions was obtained from the coefficients of these equations. This set of transfer relationships yielded the transformation of a waste load input in any specific section to the dissolved oxygen level in any other section. Since all of the equations in the system are linear, the solutions could be linearly superimposed. Thus, the total effect at any section was found by adding the effects in that section caused by inputs at any number of sections in the estuary.

Then the assumptions of a stationary system were removed, i.e., the parameters in the equations were permitted to vary with time, and a digital computer was used to solve the equations. Comparisons between the model results and actual data provided verification of the model and simultaneously the more accurate specification of the variables in

[16] Examples include: R. V. Thomann, "Mathematical Model for Dissolved Oxygen," *Journal of the Sanitary Engineering Division, Proceedings ASCE,* Vol. 89, No. SA5 (1963); R. A. Deininger, "Water Quality Management: The Planning of Economically Optimal Pollution Control Systems" (Ph.D. Thesis, Northwestern University, 1965); A. S. Goodman and W. E. Dobbins, "Mathematical Model for Water Pollution Control Studies," *Journal of the Sanitary Engineering Division, Proceedings ASCE,* Vol. 92, No. SA6 (1966), pp. 1–19; J. C. Liebman and W. R. Lynn, "The Optimal Allocation of Stream Dissolved Oxygen Resources," *Water Resources Research,* Vol. 2, No. 3 (1966), pp. 581–92; D. P. Loucks and W. R. Lynn, "Probabilistic Models for Predicting Stream Quality," *Water Resources Research,* Vol. 2, No. 3 (1966), pp. 593–605; D. J. O'Connor, "The Temporal and Spatial Distribution of Dissolved Oxygen in Streams," *Water Resources Research,* Vol. 3, No. 1 (1967), pp. 65–79; and E. Hurwitz, R. Beaudoin, and W. Walters, "Phosphates, Their 'Fate' in a Sewage Treatment Plant-Waterway System," *Water and Sewage Works,* Vol. 112, No. 3 (1965), pp. 84–89.

Model of Dissolved Oxygen System, Delaware Estuary

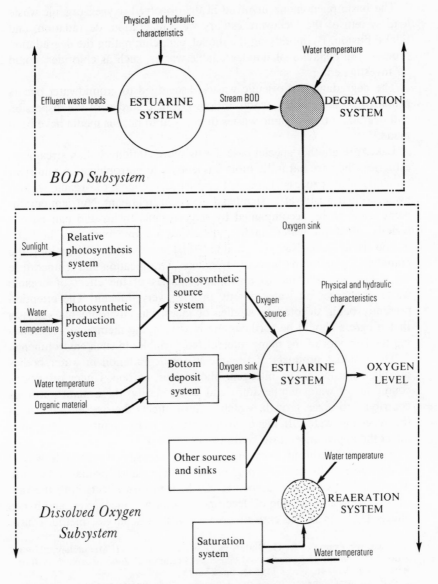

Figure 5. Source: Adapted from *Delaware Estuary Comprehensive Study* (Philadelphia: Federal Water Pollution Control Administration, 1966), p. 38.

the equations. The verified model was the basis for analyses of various combinations of inflow to the estuary, waste discharges, and additions of supplemental oxygen, and variations in reaeration and degradation rates.

The basic phenomena involved in the dissolved oxygen-organic waste load system of the Delaware estuary were reaeration, degradation, and tidal diffusion. By modifying the model, e.g., eliminating the degradation process, the behavior of nondegradable wastes, such as chlorides, could be investigated.

The degradation of organic wastes discharged to groundwater occurs primarily by anaerobic decomposition. Detailed studies of the dispersion and degradation of organic wastes discharged to porous media have been made.[17]

Lakes are another special case. Being more stationary than streams or estuaries, they are naturally more susceptible to eutrophication (nutrient buildup). This process is speeded up by the discharge of organic wastes, even residual wastes after significant levels of treatment. Nutrient enrichment tends to be accompanied by oxygen deficiencies and can have a serious effect on water quality, as evidenced by conditions in Lake Tahoe (California-Nevada),[18] and Lake Erie.[19] Eutrophication, the complex circulation patterns of large lakes, stratification and temperature inversions, all combine to make the analysis of the effect of organic waste discharges on water quality in lakes very difficult. The attention presently being devoted to studies of lacustrine environments suggests that progress should be forthcoming in developing methods for simulating the behavior of the many interrelated variables in such environments.

The residual products of organic waste degradation in water bodies are plant nutrients, i.e., nitrogen, phosphorus, carbon. Under propitious conditions of water temperature and water clarity, these plant nutrients contribute to algae growth, which in turn affects the oxygen balance in the receiving water. If algae are present in large quantities, they may affect the appearance, taste, and odor of the water.

As can be deduced from the previous discussion, degradable wastes in the form of thermal discharges are of importance primarily because of their effect on water temperature, which in turn affects both the rate of reaeration and the rate of decomposition of organic wastes, and hence affects D.O. As in the case of organic waste discharges, methods have

[17] See, for example, R. G. Butler, G. T. Orlob, and P. H. McGauhey, "Underground Movement of Bacterial and Chemical Pollutants," *Journal American Water Association*, Vol. 46, No. 1 (1954), pp. 97–111.

[18] P. H. McGauhey *et al., Comprehensive Study on Protection of Water Resources of Lake Tahoe Area* (Engineering Services, Inc., 1963).

[19] "Lake Erie Dying but Not Dead," *Environmental Science and Technology*, Vol. 1, No. 3 (1967), pp. 212–18.

been developed to predict the dissipation of thermal discharges in water bodies.[20]

Summary

While simple classification systems for types of wastes and types of receiving waters comprise a convenient point of departure for discussing the technical background for water quality management, they obscure, to some extent, the highly complex phenomena and interrelationships which are involved. A vast number of substances enter watercourses. Some result from man's activities and others are of natural origin. Their effects are interrelated in many complicated ways. For example, water clarity is an important precondition for the production of algae. Thus, streams with high turbidity are not likely to have the taste and odor problems that often accompany prolific algae growth. Consequently, when measures are taken to reduce turbidity, thereby increasing the clarity of water, algae production may increase with resulting taste and odor problems that previously did not exist.[21]

Lakes, reservoirs, and estuaries, like flowing streams, are subject to the deposition of sludge banks, which if suddenly dispersed produce a "shock load" of oxygen demand. But these bodies of water also have special problems of their own. Stratification, the formation in essentially stationary bodies of water of thermal layers which prevent deep circulation, complicates the analysis of water quality in lakes and reservoirs. Plant nutrients also take on special significance because they tend to accumulate over time in relatively stationary bodies of water and contribute to the depletion of oxygen in the lower levels. In a tidal estuary, wastes may be moved back and forth within the estuary for long periods of time rather than being dispersed into the ocean. Thus, residual wastes may build up with resulting water quality deterioration.

Much has been done to develop generalizations about the effect of waste discharges on the quality of various types of receiving water. However, the accuracy and precision are less and the uncertainty is greater in relation to predicted behavior of these phenomena than in many fields of scientific and engineering analysis. Therefore, it is important that any estimates of behavior based upon simplified models be checked with empirical data. Nevertheless, much progress has been

---

[20] For example, see J. E. Edinger and J. C. Geyer, "Heat Exchange in the Environment," *Cooling Water Studies for Edison Electric Institute*, Research Project RP-44 (The Johns Hopkins University, 1965); *Heated Discharges, Their Effect on Streams*, Publication No. 3 (Pennsylvania Department of Health, 1962); and J. M. Raphael, "Prediction of Temperatures in Rivers and Reservoirs," *Proceedings ASCE*, Vol. 88, No. 2 (1962), pp. 157–81.

[21] See R. D. Walker, "Role of Silt in Water Pollution," *Journal American Water Works Association*, Vol. 58, No. 11 (1966), pp. 1483–88.

made in developing mathematical models of waste transport, dilution, and degradation processes in receiving waters. Several models are now operational and capable of predicting, with a reasonable degree of accuracy, the sequence of results over time and space of the discharge of wastes. Such models are essential for economic optimization analyses of water quality management systems, and as tools for water quality management organizations, both of which are discussed in subsequent chapters.

APPENDIX TO CHAPTER 2

EQUATIONS OF THE "OXYGEN SAG"

The two processes involved in the oxygen sag are biochemical oxidation and reaeration.

Biochemical oxidation is indicated as a first order reaction of the form:

$$\frac{dL}{dt} = -k_1 L_t,$$

where L_t is the unsatisfied first-stage BOD (ppm), t is time (days), and k_1 is a rate constant (days^{-1}) which is a function of the characteristics of the waste and the water temperature. If L_a is the initial ($t = o$) first-stage BOD[22] of the waste load, L_t is computed as follows:

$$\int_{L_a}^{L^t} -\frac{dL}{k_1 L} = \int_o^t dt.$$

The result of the integration is:

(1) $$L_t = L_a e^{-k_1 t}.$$

Reaeration is also indicated as a first order process. It is a function of the difference between actual dissolved oxygen concentration and saturation concentration, as follows:

$$\frac{dC}{dt} = -k_2(C_s - C_t),$$

where C_t is the D.O. concentration (ppm) at time t, C_s is the saturation concentration (ppm), and k_2 is a rate constant (days^{-1}).

The rates of the two reactions are combined and the resulting equations written in terms of the D.O. deficit ($D_t = C_s - C_t$):

$$\frac{dD}{dt} = k_1 L_t - k_2 D_t.$$

---

[22] The first-stage BOD involves primarily the oxidation of carbonaceous material.

Substituting $L_a e^{-k_1 t}$ for L_t and integrating gives:

(2) $$D_t = \frac{k_1 L_a}{k_2 - k_1} (e^{-k_1 t} - e^{-k_2 t}) + D_a e^{-k_2 t},$$

where D_a is the deficit and L_a is the BOD concentration, both at time $t = 0$.

If a plot of D_t versus t is made, the result is the typical oxygen sag curve, as shown in Figure 3.

The time at which the maximum deficit occurs (t_c), can be found by taking the derivative of equation (2) with respect to time, setting the result to zero, and solving for t_c. The resulting expression is:

(3) $$t_c = \frac{1}{k_2 - k_1} \left\{ ln \left[\frac{k_2}{k_1} \left(1 - \frac{(k_2 - k_1) D_a}{k_1 L_a} \right) \right] \right\}.$$

At the location corresponding to this time the deficit is:

(4) $$D_c = \frac{k_1 L_a}{k_2} e^{-k_1 t_c}.$$

The Relation of Water Quality to Water Uses

3

The preceding chapter has described, in summary fashion, the types of waste discharges and their effects on the quality of receiving waters. We now turn our attention to the effects, both direct and indirect, of water quality on various water uses—recreational, domestic, agricultural, and industrial. Even under natural conditions water may require modification for certain uses. With increasing population and rising production of goods and services, there is a concomitant increase in the production and discharge of wastes, and these have varying impacts on the quality of receiving waters. Some of these relationships between water quality and water use are illustrated in this chapter.[1]

AESTHETIC AND RECREATIONAL USES

Aesthetic enjoyment of bodies of water is obtained primarily through visual perception. At a minimum this means water bodies should be free from obnoxious floating or suspended substances, particularly solids from domestic sewage, and objectionable colors, such as those resulting from some industrial waste discharges. Absence of foul odors is likewise a prerequisite for aesthetically pleasing water.

For recreation activities involving water contact, the water not only should be aesthetically pleasing but should contain no substances toxic upon ingestion or irritating to the skin and should be reasonably free from pathogenic organisms. Most efforts to relate water quality to recreational use in terms of water-contact activities have been oriented toward the last condition, i.e., density of pathogenic organisms. The wide range in standards which have been established, for example, from 50 to 3,000 bacteria per 100 ml, and the variety of ways in which the standards are specified, i.e., arithmetical mean, geometrical mean, or median

[1] For a comprehensive discussion of water quality in relation to various uses, see J. E. McKee and H. W. Wolf, *Water Quality Criteria*, Publication No. 3–A (2nd ed.; California State Water Quality Control Board, 1963).

of monthly samples, maximum concentration, or percentage of samples which may exceed a stated concentration, indicate the lack of firm knowledge of the relationship between water quality and effect on bathers. McKee and Wolf state:

> Insofar as this survey has been able to determine, all of the bacterial standards for bathing waters as promulgated by state, interstate, and local agencies have been established arbitrarily on the basis of esthetic considerations and ability of compliance.[2]

No such standards appear to be based on sound epidemiological evidence showing a direct relationship between contact with contaminated water and bacterial infections.[3] Certainly the possibility of infection exists, more so in fresh water than in saline water, but there is great uncertainty about the level of probability.

In the main, nondegradable wastes have little impact on aesthetic and recreational uses. The exceptions are toxic substances, of course, and suspended sediment in concentrations high enough to impart unattractive color to the receiving waters and/or to coat surfaces coming in contact with the water.

AQUATIC LIFE

The utility of water as habitat for aquatic life is of importance for some recreational uses of water, as well as for commercial fishing. The value of water for fishing, for example, can be reduced or destroyed by waste discharges which do not render the water repulsive or even necessarily unattractive to human beings. The determination of the effect of waste discharges on aquatic life is anything but easy.

The effects of discharges of various substances on fish and other aquatic life have been the subject of many investigations. Unfortunately, there has been a wide variation in the results of these investigations, even where the investigators were dealing with the same substance and using the same species of fish. This wide variation stems from several sources: the method of handling the fish prior to the investigation, the

---

[2] McKee and Wolf, *op. cit.*, p. 119.

[3] McKee and Wolf (*op. cit.*, p. 120) describe the results of an extensive bacteriological and epidemiological study of more than forty popular bathing beaches in England carried out over a five-year period. The waters of most of the beaches were subject to contamination with sewage. The study committee concluded that: (a) the risk to health from bathing in sewage-polluted sea water is negligible; (b) where risk exists it is probably associated with chance contact with intact aggregates of infected fecal material; and (c) public health requirements are met reasonably well by preventing the contamination of bathing areas with undisintegrated fecal matter.

phase in the life cycle of the fish, the effects of water quality variables other than the one under investigation, the time pattern of exposure to the waste, and the method of measuring the effect.[4]

The impact of the discharge of a particular substance on fish life varies with the physical and chemical composition of the water. Higher temperatures, excessive acidity or alkalinity, and low dissolved oxygen, all of which can result from man-made discharges, increase the sensitivity of fish to toxic substances and in extreme instances can themselves result in fish kills. The combined influence of several substances acting simultaneously may result in greater damage to fish life than the sum of the individual effects taken independently. Conversely, certain combinations of salts act antagonistically to reduce the deleterious effect which would occur if each were acting independently.

Perhaps the most important factor in determining the tolerance of aquatic life at a given stage in the life cycle to the concentration of various substances is the time-concentration relationship. Thus, while a single short-term exposure to high concentrations may show no damaging effects, repeated exposures to the same concentration or continuous exposure at a much lower concentration may result in death. However, with gradual exposure many organisms can develop tolerance to concentrations that would otherwise be toxic.

Different patterns of concentration over time and in space of a substance discharged into a water body can have significantly different effects on aquatic life. Generally it has been considered that a "slug" discharge with its associated impact on water quality is more deleterious than a steady uniform discharge with adequate mixing in the receiving water body. This is not necessarily true. If the receiving water quickly recovers from a slug discharge, fish and other aquatic life may not suffer so much as they would from a steady discharge of a less concentrated waste. Where the hydraulic characteristics of the water body result in varied concentrations across a given cross-section or in a longitudinal direction, fish may be able to avoid or move away from the locally high concentrations.

Not all waste discharges result in adverse conditions for aquatic life. A modest level of domestic waste discharge can benefit fishing waters by promoting the growth of algae, which in turn enter the food chain. (Extensive algae growth can, however, be toxic to fish life.) Similarly, thermal discharges under some conditions may improve the environment

---

[4] Some of the indexes used to measure effect are frequency of gill action, the pattern or absence of feeding, response to stimuli, and the efficiency of utilization of food for growth.

for aquatic life, including fish, by increasing water temperatures during winter periods.

DOMESTIC WATER USE

The amount and character of water treatment before domestic water use are related to the quality of the water intake.[5] When water contains organic substances from domestic sewage that are only partially decomposed, it must be treated with larger amounts of chlorine or other disinfectants (ozone, for example) to kill the bacteria.

When the available water is corrosive, saline, hard, or contains unusually high concentrations of iron and/or manganese, special treatment may be needed. Modification of the water quality can be done in a central plant or by the individual user. Generally it appears to be less expensive per unit of water to modify water quality in central plants than in individual residences and commercial establishments.[6] Alternatively, individuals may use the water without additional treatment and incur the costs of larger quantities of cleaning agents, bottled water, and more frequent replacement of pipes and fittings. It should be noted, however, that little rigorous evidence is available on which to base a limiting standard for drinking water with respect to total dissolved solids. A search for the origin of the oft-used standard of 500 milligrams per liter (500 parts per million) produced no evidence about its birth.[7]

Water treatment costs are further complicated by the stochastic, i.e., probabilistic, nature of water quality. Because many water quality variables are related to streamflow, and because streamflow is a stochastic variable, the water treatment plant faces a variable quality of supply. In some cases the variation in cost of chemicals for water treatment can be directly related to variation in water quality.[8] Not only are treatment costs a function of several water quality variables, but treatment designed to improve water quality with respect to one variable may also have positive effects with respect to another variable. Similarly, the same water management measure, i.e., construction of a reservoir

[5] See R. L. Woodward, "Relation of Raw-Water Quality to Treatment Plant Design," *Journal American Water Works Association*, Vol. 56, No. 4 (April 1964), pp. 432–40.

[6] Since all domestic uses of water do not require the same level of quality, another alternative is to provide two separate distribution systems delivering two different qualities of water, for example, one low and one high in hardness and total dissolved solids. This was found to be the least-cost approach at Coalinga, California.

[7] P. H. McGauhey, "Folklore in Water Quality Standards," *Civil Engineering*, Vol. 35, No. 6 (1965), p. 71.

[8] See G. K. Young, T. Popowchak, and G. W. Burke, "Correlation of Degree of Pollution with Chemical Costs," *Journal American Water Works Association*, Vol. 57, No. 3 (1965), pp. 293–97.

to regulate streamflow, may have different impacts on different water quality variables and hence on treatment costs.[9] It should also be pointed out that there are significant economies of scale in intake water treatment.[10]

Although the nature of the basic water treatment processes has changed relatively little in several decades, substantial improvements have been made in the processes themselves. For example, the efficiency of sedimentation has been increased by use of polyelectrolytes, filtration by use of activated carbon, and disinfection by use of ozone and various chlorine compounds, to mention only a few. Further developments are in process, with respect to methods both for the detection and for the removal of various substances in water for domestic use.

IRRIGATION

Delineating the effect of the quality of water used for irrigation is possibly more complex. Although water quality deterioration is reflected in crop yields, the extent to which crop yields are reduced is a function of a host of interrelated factors. These include: type of crop; type of soil; climatic conditions; irrigation and cultivation practices; extent of drainage; the concentration of the soil solution, which generally is several times higher than the concentration of the applied irrigation water; and of course the quality of the irrigation water, including the possible compounding effect of the presence of one ion on other ions. Salts affect plant growth adversely by: (1) physically preventing water uptake by plants (osmotic effects); (2) directly affecting the metabolic reactions of plants (toxic effects); and/or (3) indirectly through changing soil structure, permeability, and aeration.

As a consequence, the effect of water quality on irrigation use cannot be defined in terms of a single water quality variable.[11] Therefore, water for irrigation use is generally classified in relation to several variables,

[9] For example, the construction of reservoirs on the upper Missouri River has reduced the concentration and quantity of suspended sediment at the Missouri River intake of the St. Louis County Water Company. This in turn has reduced the cost of removal of suspended sediment. However, the increased clarity of water has led to taste and odor problems which did not exist before. In addition, the costs of BOD removal have increased, because some portion of the BOD load formerly was removed in the reduction of suspended sediment. See H. O. Hartung, "Missouri Basin Water Resources" (Paper presented at American Society of Civil Engineers, Environmental Engineering Conference, Kansas City, 1965).

[10] See L. Koenig, "Cost of Water Treatment by Coagulation, Sedimentation, and Rapid Sand Filtration," Journal American Water Works Association, Vol. 59, No. 3 (1967), pp. 290–336.

[11] There are a few exceptions, such as boron. Thus, traces (less than 1 mg/l) of boron are essential for all plant growth, but concentrations of only several mg/l result in drastic reductions in yield even for crops tolerant to boron.

such as total dissolved solids (TDS), specific conductance (at 25°C), per cent sodium, and boron. Although not often considered in the past, water temperature can have important effects on irrigation water use. Regulation of streamflow by the construction of reservoirs has resulted in both increases and decreases in the temperature of applied irrigation water. Depending on the crop and the season, such changes in water temperature may improve or reduce crop yields.[12]

To illustrate the interrelationships among the various factors, water with high total dissolved solids, i.e., 1,000 parts per million (ppm) or more, can be used for irrigation of all types of plants, including salt-susceptible ones, if drainage is good and if sufficient water is applied for leaching. The basic alternatives for the irrigation water user are to accept reduction in crop yields or to incur the costs of providing additional leaching water and drainage facilities, or some combination of reduced crop yield and additional facilities. Removal of dissolved solids by treatment is economically infeasible, except for crops with a very high value.

INDUSTRIAL WATER USE

The range of water qualities utilized in industrial operations is very wide, depending in part on whether the water is to be used for processing, as boiler feedwater, for cooling, or for sanitary purposes.[13] For example, in the canning of fruits and vegetables, water is used as follows: for conveying the raw product from the reception areas into the plant; for cleaning the raw product; for conveying the product from place to place within the plant; for conveying wastes from the production line for disposal; for making syrup or brine; cooling the containers after cooking; and in the form of steam for peeling, cooking, cleaning, and the production of power. Quality requirements also vary from industry to industry, and from plant to plant within any given industry, as a function primarily of the production process and the product mix.

McKee and Wolf[14] have defined various in-plant water quality targets for various uses in various industries. For each use there is a water quality recipe that specifies limiting concentrations of such variables as hardness, pH, temperature, and total dissolved solids. These targets do not apply to water in the stream, lake, estuary, or ground-

---

[12] See P. J. Wierenga and R. M. Hagan, "Effects of Cold Irrigation Water on Soil Temperature and Crop Growth," *California Agriculture*, Vol. 20, No. 9 (1966), pp. 14–16.

[13] For a more extensive discussion of industrial water utilization see B. T. Bower, "The Economics of Industrial Water Utilization," in A. V. Kneese and S. C. Smith (eds.), *Water Research* (The Johns Hopkins Press, for RFF, 1966).

[14] McKee and Wolf, *op. cit.*

water aquifer, as intake water can always be treated. Further, the targets are in most cases just that, and not inviolable *requirements*, except for a few critical production processes or operations in those processes. For most combinations of production process and product output there are more or less continuous functional relationships between in-plant water quality and process performance or between in-plant water quality and product output quality. A target represents the location (or point) on these relationships (or curves) where the slope begins to increase rapidly, i.e., process performance or product output quality begins to decrease rapidly with a small decrease in in-plant water quality. Usually the alternative exists of using water of a lower quality with a consequent reduction in performance or in product quality, just as the use of lower quality water in irrigation may decrease crop yield, instead of upgrading the quality by treatment.

Feedwater for high-pressure, high-temperature boilers requires perhaps the highest quality requirement of any industrial use. Concentrations of total dissolved solids for such use are established in terms of parts per billion, rather than the usual parts per million. The quality specifications for low-pressure boilers are much less stringent.

Next to high-pressure boiler feedwater, the targets for process water, which comes into contact with the product, are the most demanding. But even so, as noted above, desirable water quality varies considerably among different combinations of production process and product output. Some combinations must have unusually soft water, while others need, or can use, comparatively hard water. For example, low hardness is critical in canning peas, low chloride concentration is critical for bleaching paper.[15] A poorer quality water can be used to manufacture tablet backing than to produce photographic paper.

Cooling water can be of almost any level of quality, with respect to total dissolved solids and even BOD. Ideally, cooling water should have a low and relatively constant temperature, contain a low concentration of scale-forming materials, be of good sanitary quality, and so on. However, it is possible, with treatment and/or other adjustments, to use virtually any quality of fresh water (or sea water) for cooling purposes.

Water used by industry for sanitary purposes, which includes drinking water, must meet the quality standards for potable water. The same considerations discussed under domestic water use are relevant.

---

[15] However, even for the one water quality variable for a single process an industry source gives the range of "desired" chloride concentration as 10–150 ppm. H. F. Berger, "Evaluating Water Reclamation Against Rising Costs of Water and Effluent Treatment," *Tappi, The Journal of the Technical Association of the Pulp and Paper Industry*, Vol. 49, No. 8 (1966), p. 80A.

Because of the multiple uses of water within an industrial plant, often the most economical procedure is to withdraw water from several different sources and provide different degrees of treatment for the different in-plant uses. Some large plants use river water, groundwater, and re-claimed sewage effluent, applying various degrees of treatment from none to virtually complete demineralization (total dissolved solids concentration less than 1 ppm). Such practices are becoming standard procedures in the major water-using industries. This diversity in responses to water quality in available water sources makes generalization about industrial water utilization patterns difficult. However, recent studies are contributing greatly to an understanding of industrial water utilization and waste disposal.[16]

The effect of water quality on industrial operations is reflected primarily in the extent and cost of water treatment to provide the desired water qualities for the various in-plant uses. Some of the common types of treatment are listed below:

Sedimentation	Coagulation
Filtration (sand, diatomaceous earth, carbon)	Aeration and deaeration
	Dealkalization
Chlorination, ozonation	Demineralization
Iron, manganese removal	Neutralization
Silica removal	Softening (lime-soda,
Slime and algae control	sodium zeolite, hot-process phosphate)

Even for heavy water-using industries, it is economically feasible to take virtually any quality of water and produce water acceptable for any uses within the industrial operations. In most cases, the additional costs represent less than one-tenth of one per cent of total production costs.[17] Differences in plant location, production processes, and product mix can produce a great variety of water quality requirements and consequently a wide range in intake water treatment costs within a single industry. This is illustrated for U.S. petroleum refineries in Figure 6, in terms of replacement costs of treatment facilities per barrel of crude charge capacity.

---

[16] Studies under the sponsorship of RFF include: P. H. Cootner and G. O. G. Löf, *Water Demand for Steam Electric Generation: An Economic Projection Model* (Resources for the Future, 1965); G. O. G. Löf and A. V. Kneese, *The Economics of Water Utilization in the Beet Sugar Industry* (Resources for the Future, 1968); H. D. Mohring and J. H. Boyd (petroleum refining); B. T. Bower and N. A. Olson (fruit and vegetable canning).

[17] See W. R. Walker, *Industrial Water Use in North Carolina*, Water Resource Paper No. 13 (University of North Carolina, 1964); and Löf and Kneese, *op. cit.*

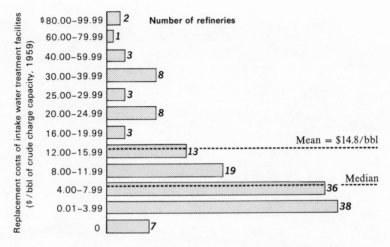

Figure 6. Frequency distribution of replacement costs of intake water treatment facilities for U.S. petroleum refineries, in dollars per barrel of crude charge capacity, 1959. (Based on original data from the American Petroleum Institute.)

SUMMARY

Determining the effects of various levels and time patterns of water quality on different uses is a critical component of water quality management. For some uses, i.e., municipal and industrial, the effects are directly ascertainable in terms of costs, i.e., for water treatment and/or decreased process efficiency or product quality. For agriculture the problem is more complicated because of the interactions among various water quality variables and between water quality and agricultural practices as they affect crop yields. Still more complicated is the determination of the effects on aquatic life, water-based recreation, and aesthetics. Nevertheless, if efficient water quality management is to be achieved, continued effort must be devoted to developing techniques for measuring these effects.

Managing Waste Loads and the Assimilative
Capacity of Receiving Waters

4

The quality of water bodies can be improved by reducing the waste loads discharged to them, by increasing or making more effective use of their assimilative capacity, and by combinations of the two. If the focus is on water quality management in streams, and if there is no problem with floating materials, reducing waste loads and changing assimilative capacity are technical substitutes for one another. Assimilative capacity can be increased by altering the time patterns of streamflows, by altering the time pattern and/or locations of waste discharges, by artificial reaeration, or by some combination of these measures. If the assimilative capacity is known, intake water treatment can be a partial substitute for waste load reduction.[1] Indeed, if water were not useful, offensive, or altered in quality while *in situ*, intake water treatment would be technically interchangeable with waste load reduction. Flowing streams, of course, are much more amenable to procedures for changing assimilative capacity than are groundwater aquifers or even reservoirs and lakes.

Improving the water quality of receiving waters by reducing waste loads can be accomplished in two broad ways: first, by reducing the generation of wastes; and second, by modifying the residual wastes. Within these two broad categories a variety of techniques are available, as indicated in Table 1. The dividing lines between methods that reduce waste generation and those that affect the residual wastes are not always as clearcut as implied in the table. Materials recovery, for example, is in a sense a change in production process because it involves a change in the mix of raw product inputs; process change may be necessary before

---

[1] See R. J. Frankel, *Economic Evaluation of Water Quality, An Engineering-Economic Model for Water Quality Management*, SERL Report No. 65–3 (1965), and R. J. Frankel, "Cost-Quality Relationships in an Engineering-Economic Model for Municipal Waste Disposal," Conference Preprint 150, ASCE Water Resources Engineering Conference, Mobile, Alabama (1965).

in-plant water recirculation is possible; and product output changes may require some changes in production processes. Nevertheless, the distinctions are worth preserving as a basis for discussion. Also listed in Table 1 are ways of managing the assimilative capacity of receiving waters. The various alternatives in both categories are depicted in the generalized flow diagram of Figure 7. For example, following generation, waste materials may be recovered, used for the production of by-products, reduced by waste treatment, temporarily stored prior to discharge, conveyed to another water user,[2] or discharged in various possible ways into one or more receiving water bodies.

Although Table 1 and Figure 7 are oriented primarily toward industrial plants, they are for the most part relevant also to municipalities and urban areas. Thus, "municipality" could be substituted for "production process" in Figure 7. This would require only slight modification of the diagram, i.e., elimination of the line to "materials recovery, etc." and of the line indicating direct recirculation.

Industrial wastes play such a large role in water quality management that an understanding of the factors that influence the generation of these wastes is extremely important. This is not to say that the magnitude of wastes generated by domestic and commercial users is insignificant. On the contrary, with expanding population, particularly in urban areas,

Table 1.   Methods for Improving the Quality of Receiving Waters

METHODS FOR REDUCING WASTE DISCHARGES

Methods for reducing wastes generation
1. Change in type of raw material inputs
2. Change in production process
3. Change in product outputs
4. In-plant recirculation of water

Methods for reducing wastes after generation
1. Materials recovery
2. By-product production
3. Waste treatment
4. Effluent reuse (including groundwater recharge, wastewater reclamation or renovation)

METHODS FOR INCREASING OR MAKING BETTER USE OF ASSIMILATIVE CAPACITY
1. Addition of dilution water
2. Multiple outlets from reservoirs
3. Reservoir mixing
4. Reaeration of streams
5. Saltwater barriers
6. Effluent redistribution (including regulated discharge)

[2] For example, sewage effluent from a city may be treated in a waste treatment plant, and subsequently used to irrigate golf courses or be conveyed to some industrial plant where it may be used directly in cooling or some other operation.

Flow Diagram of
Water Utilization, Waste Generation, and Waste Disposal

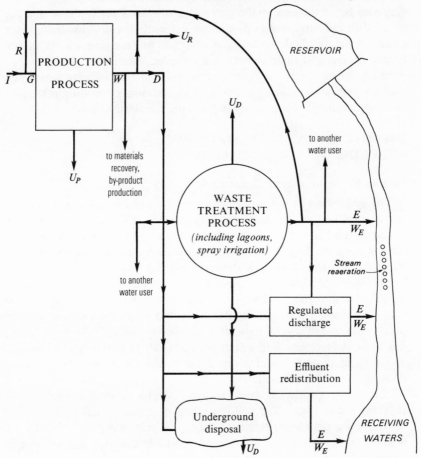

Figure 7.

I = Intake water.

R = Recirculated water.

G = Gross water applied for all in-plant uses.

U = Consumptive use or net depletion of water. $U = U_P + U_D + U_R$, where U_P = consumptive use in the production process, U_D = consumptive use in the wastewater disposal system, and U_R = consumptive use in the recirculation system.

D = Wastewater discharge from the production process.

E = Final effluent from the production unit (available for reuse). Where a lagoon or spray irrigation system is involved, the final effluent (if any) consists of seepage, lagoon discharge, and/or surface runoff.

W = Waste load generated in all operations of the production process, for example, pounds of BOD, Btu's of heat.

W_E = Waste load in the final effluent ie., pounds of BOD, Btu's.

Degree of recirculation $= R/G \times 100\%$.

the absolute quantity of domestic wastes generated is bound to increase. And with the widespread adoption of garbage and paper grinders, there may also be an increase in the generation of wastes per capita within the home. But industrial waste discharges currently account for the greater share of the residual materials discharged to receiving waters in the United States, and their control is a complex, multi-faceted process. In contrast, treatment is the only general method for reducing waste discharges from households, barring significant changes in consumption patterns. Accordingly, the primary focus is on industrial wastes.

IMPROVING WATER QUALITY BY REDUCING WASTE DISCHARGES

Factors Reducing Wastes Generation

The generation of industrial wastes per unit of raw product processed or per unit of final product is a function primarily of the type of raw materials used in the production process, the technology of the production process, the product mix, and sometimes the extent of in-plant water recirculation. Thus there is a wide range in the wastes generated per unit by different industries, and also by different plants within a single industry. To illustrate, a German study reported ratios of high to low waste discharge (in pounds of BOD per unit of product or raw product processed) within several industries as follows: about 25 for paper mills, 2.5 in malt factories, 6 in starch factories, 50 in pork slaughterhouses, about 10 in tanneries, and about 20 in textile factories.[3] Similar variations occur in U.S. industries.

Shifting to a different grade or type of raw product is one way of reducing waste loads. The sulfur content of crude oil has an important bearing on a petroleum refinery's waste. In pulp and paper, the type of wood used is significant. In fruit and vegetable canning, the size, shape, per cent of solids, and resistance to damage and bruising in harvesting and processing the raw product affect the waste load per ton of raw product processed.

Changes in production processes, however, have the major impact on wastes generation, although it should be emphasized that technological changes have not been, and are not usually, instituted because of water quality problems. In fact, most changes in production technology have been stimulated by factors unrelated to water problems, and have been

---

[3] See W. Bucksteeg, "Problematik der Bewertung giftiger Inhaltsstoffe im Abwasser und Moeglichkeiten zur Schaffung gesicherter Bewertungsgrundlagen" (Problems in the Evaluation of Toxic Materials in Effluents and Possibilities for Obtaining Secure Evaluation Standards), *Muenchner Beitraege zur Abwasser-, Fischerei-, und Flussbiologie* (Bd. 6; Muenchen: Verlag R. Oldenbourg, 1959).

developed without explicit consideration for their effects on water quality. On the other hand, where various stimuli to management, such as sewer charges, have been used, they have often resulted in process modifications, as is discussed in Chapter 8. As more systematic means are developed to bring to bear on industry the broader social costs associated with the discharge of waste materials into the environment, the generation and control of wastes will receive more prominent consideration in process design, and perhaps even in product development. Studies of several industries make clear that even comparatively small design changes can have a substantial effect on the generation of wastes.

In the pulp and paper industry the proportions of the total output produced by different processes have shifted significantly over the past two decades (see Table 2). The largest and most significant shift has been from the sulfite process to the sulfate process, which, by making the recovery of chemicals for internal reuse economic, can reduce the waste load in terms of pounds of BOD per ton of product to about 5 or 10 per cent of the previous level. The development of save-alls to recover waste fibers which formerly were simply discharged into water courses was stimulated by the increase in the value of fiber. Their use has resulted in a significant reduction in terms of pounds of both BOD and suspended solids per ton. Both black liquor recovery systems and save-alls were stimulated originally by the economic incentive to save materials useful in the production process, rather than by waste problems.

Table 2.   Production of Wood Pulp in the United States, by Process and Year
(*per cent of total production*)

Process	1940	1945	1950	1955	1960	1965*
Mechanical	18.2	18.0	14.9	13.2	13.0	11.8
Unbleached sulfite	11.1	8.0	5.0	3.1	2.1	1.5
Bleached sulfite[1]	18.0	15.2	14.2	13.9	12.6	11.4
Unbleached sulfate	35.3	35.6	38.4	37.0	34.3	35.4
Bleached sulfate[2]	6.5	8.4	12.1	17.5	23.3	26.3
Semi-chemical	[3]	[3]	4.6	6.8	7.9	8.7
Soda	5.9	4.2	3.5	2.1	1.7	0.7
All other	4.9	10.6	7.2	6.4	5.2	4.4
Total[4]	99.9	100.0	99.9	100.0	100.1	100.2

Source: American Paper and Pulp Association, *Statistics of Paper–1964*, p. 10, and American Paper Institute, *Statistics of Paper, 1966 Supplement*, 1966, p. 2.
* = Preliminary.
[1] Includes special alpha and dissolving grades.
[2] Includes semi-bleached sulfate.
[3] Reported in "all other" for 1940 and 1945.
[4] Total production increased from 8.96 million short tons in 1940 to 33.3 million short tons in 1965.

Other possibilities for process changes which will reduce wastes generated appear to be on the horizon. One of these is a "dry" paper-making process that will use considerably less water as a defibrating and distributing agent in the paper-making process.[4]

A particularly difficult waste problem in the steel industry for many years has been disposal of the "waste pickle liquor" generated when steel is pickled with sulfuric acid. Attempts to develop an economically feasible sulfuric acid recovery process have met with little success under U.S. conditions.[5] Another solution is to shift to hydrochloric acid (HCl) in the pickling process itself. A recent report indicates that the acid losses in the effluent are reduced by this process change from about 13 pounds of sulfuric acid per ton of steel pickled to about 0.2 pound of hydrochloric acid per ton of steel.[6] Hydrochloric acid offers other advantages as well—a high-quality product (in terms of brightness of surface) and faster production.

In the beet sugar industry the waste load generated in pounds of BOD per ton of beets processed has been reduced greatly in the last two decades by comparatively simple and economical changes in processes (see Table 3).

The substitution of drying of beet pulp for storage of wet beet pulp in silos and the use of Steffens waste for the production of by-products, or the complete elimination of Steffens processing can reduce BOD generation by about 60 per cent. Converting to pulp drying has another advantage if there is a market nearby, because dry pulp brings a greater return than wet pulp. The other process change, i.e., a shift from cell-type to continuous diffusers, is integrally related to recirculation of screen and press water. This change reduces the BOD generated by about 10 per cent.

Specific cases, as well as general industry examples, can be cited. For example, one chemical plant over a fifteen-year period doubled the dollar value of production and at the same time reduced the BOD and phenolic waste loads per day by over 90 per cent.[7] The waste reductions were accomplished primarily by process modification, in many cases by simple changes such as increasing the temperature at which a reaction was taking place and changing a polymerization catalyst. In

---

[4] "Danish Firm Tests Dry Process for Paper," *Chemical and Engineering News*, Vol. 45, No. 6 (1967), p. 40.

[5] Under German conditions, the recovery of sulfuric acid is economically feasible.

[6] F. E. Tucker, "Recovery and Disposal of HCl Pickling Wastes," *Water and Sewage Works* (Reference Number, 1966), p. R-273.

[7] A. J. von Frank, "Process Change in a Major Chemical Plant" (Paper presented at the National Meeting, Water Pollution Control Federation, Atlantic City, New Jersey, 1965).

Table 3.   Wastes Generated in Beet Sugar Plants, by Process[1]

(*pounds of BOD per ton of beets processed*)

Operation	Potential BOD generation	After process changes	After recirculation associated with process changes
Flume water	4.5	4.5	4.5
Screen water	2.5[2]	2.5[3]	0
Press water	2.6	2.6[3]	0
Silo drainage	12.3	0[4]	0
Lime cake slurry	6.5	6.5	6.5
Condenser water	0.7	0.7	0.7
Steffens waste	10.4	0[5]	0
Total	39.5	16.8	11.7

Source: G. O. G. Löf and A. V. Kneese, *The Economics of Water Utilization in the Beet Sugar Industry* (Resources for the Future, Inc., 1968).

[1] Based on typical 2,700 tons per plant day.

[2] Average of BOD waste generation in batch diffusers and continuous diffusers.

[3] Assuming conversion to continuous diffusers but without recirculation of screen and press water.

[4] Assuming pulp dryer installation.

[5] Assuming discontinuance of Steffens processing or the complete use of Steffens waste in by-product manufacture.

the production of potato flakes, the processing of raw potatoes by steam peeling results in a BOD waste with a population equivalent of about 200 per ton in contrast to about 420 per ton using caustic peeling.[8] Where cooling is a major component of an industrial process, changes in cooling methods are changes in production processes. The adoption of air cooling, as in some chemical plants and petroleum refineries, will reduce the thermal waste load generated in the production process.[9]

It is interesting to note that air cooling may be the rational economic choice even where water is relatively inexpensive in terms of both supply and waste disposal problems. The cost associated with circulating a large quantity of air must be compared with the costs of high head pumps, pumping energy, and pipelines required to circulate water, plus the costs associated with water intake and wastewater disposal. There is obviously no waste to be disposed of from air cooling units. In addition to the lower investment costs with air cooling, there are operating savings from less equipment maintenance and improved continuity of operation.

[8] O. O. Olson and W. Van Heuvelen, "Combined Industrial and Domestic Waste Treatment in Waste Stabilization Lagoons" (Paper presented at annual meeting, Water Pollution Control Federation, Kansas City, 1966).

[9] R. T. Mathews, "Air Cooling in Chemical Plants" (E. I. du Pont de Nemours and Co., Wilmington, no date) mimeo.

In many cases it is difficult to separate changes in production processes from changes in products. Change in consumer demand over time is one stimulus for development of new production processes. Several examples illustrate the nature of product changes, with their implications for changes in wastes generation.

In petroleum refining the product mix has shifted significantly over time toward the production of more gasoline per barrel of crude throughput. Continued changes in product mix are in prospect. For example, by 1985 the demand for jet-fuel will require about 16 per cent of all crude runs in the United States, in contrast to only about 3 per cent in 1965.[10] This will require additional use of hydro cracking with consequent changes in waste generation per barrel.

In pulp and paper manufacture, there has been a steady shift toward a wider variety of products, such as colored paper and coated products of various types. Many of the coatings and sizings which have been developed to provide particular characteristics in the final products make reuse of the waste fiber more difficult or impossible, with a consequent increase in the waste load generated per ton of product. There also has been an increase in the proportion of pulp output which is bleached, from about 25 per cent in 1940 to almost 40 per cent in 1965 (see Table 2). Bleaching increases the waste load generated in pounds of BOD per ton by about 25 per cent.[11]

An example of a significant change in waste load through product change is the shift from hard detergents to soft detergents which are readily degraded by the biota in natural watercourses and in waste treatment plants.[12] The change took place in Germany in October, 1964, and in the United States in the summer of 1965. Even so, soft detergents are still "under fire" because of their phosphate content, which contributes to algae growth in streams and lakes, and research is now oriented toward finding a substitute for phosphate.

Process and product changes have obviously had different effects on wastes generation. However, the dominant tendency has been toward a reduction in wastes generated per unit of raw or finished product. Two points are important: (1) most of the changes in production processes and product mixes have occurred independently of problems of water quality management (and of air and solid wastes management);

[10] *Chemical Week,* Vol. 100, No. 15 (1967), p. 53.

[11] E. B. Besselievre, *Industrial Waste Treatment* (McGraw-Hill, 1952), Table 11–2, p. 110. It is also interesting to note that bleaching increases gross water applied per ton by 20–30 per cent.

[12] See "Phosphates May Lose Detergent Markets," *Chemical and Engineering News,* Vol. 45, No. 19 (1967), pp. 18–20.

(2) there are usually several ways at least of producing a given product mix, so that there are possibilities for modifications of production processes to reduce the wastes generated per unit.

One other type of in-plant change that can reduce waste generation is in-plant recirculation of water. As the extent of water recirculation in a plant increases, a decrease may occur in the waste load generated per unit, e.g., pounds of BOD and/or suspended solids per ton. This has occurred in the beet sugar industry and in the canning of some fruits. In the latter, where flume water is recirculated, less sugar is dissolved from the fruit in processing, thereby decreasing the BOD load per ton.

The separation of the effect of water recirculation *per se* on waste generation from the effect of changes in production processes and from materials recovery is not clearcut. In-plant recirculation of water may require modifications of production processes. Conversely, some production processes enable recirculation of water, as noted in the previous description of process changes in the manufacture of beet sugar. It is clear, however, that water recirculation in some cases has significantly reduced waste generation per unit.

Methods for Reducing Wastes After Generation

Materials recovery and by-product production are two methods for reducing wastes after generation. They form a logical pair, because the types of processes are often very similar. We differentiate between them on the basis of the final destination of their outputs. In materials recovery the output is reused within the same production unit as an input to the production process. By-product production yields consumption goods or intermediate goods used in other production processes.

Examples of materials recovery are to be found in almost all, if not all, of the heavy water-using or water-polluting industries. Only a few will be mentioned here for illustration. The recovery of chemicals in black liquor recovery systems in the production of sulfate pulp and the utilization of save-alls in paper production have been mentioned previously. In the manufacture of synthetic phenol by the sulfonation process, liquid wastes have been essentially eliminated by process engineering, and the value of recovered materials is reported to exceed recovery costs. In steel production, sedimentation to eliminate mill scale from waste discharges has resulted in the recovery of iron that can be used in the production process.[13] Plating compounds, a potentially

---

[13] A saving of $1,925 per day from mill scale recovery has been reported for the new Inland Steel mill in East Chicago. See "The Money Industry May Be Pouring Down the Drain and How to Get It," *Mill and Factory* (November 1966).

troublesome waste load, can be recovered from rinse water by evaporation. This procedure concentrates the rinse water sufficiently for reuse in the plating bath, which not only conserves valuable plating compounds but also significantly reduces waste and thereby the outlay for neutralizing chemicals. One plant anticipates an annual net saving of about $100,000 from use of the procedure.[14] Waste liquor from citrus peel processing, normally a waste disposal headache, is concentrated to syrup and returned to the process. This procedure saves fuel as well as reducing the waste.[15]

A number of industries have achieved substantial reductions in their final waste loads through by-product production. In beet sugar production, the recovery of monosodium glutamate and potash from the Steffens waste has significantly reduced the BOD generated. In canning apples, the utilization of the "waste" segments of the apple for vinegar production has reduced the waste load per ton. Cottage cheese whey has been converted into protein food supplements, thereby eliminating a difficult waste problem.[16] Some of the by-products from waste materials in food processing are quite imaginative. For example, bran waste from milling has been used to make inexpensive sets of plates, casseroles, and trays, and coffee grounds have been used to produce discs and shelves.

As indicated, many alternatives are available for the reduction of wastes after generation by materials recovery and by-product production. In many cases these methods result in net profits to the industrial operation, even without counting the broader social costs avoided by the reduction or elimination of wastes discharged to watercourses.[17]

After economic processes of materials recovery, by-product production, and effluent reuse have been exhausted, there are often residual waste loads which may have to be reduced or otherwise handled prior to final discharge. Some common methods for treating industrial wastes, also applicable to municipal wastes, are listed below:

[14] "Plating Wastes Treatment Problem Solved," *Water and Sewage Works,* (Reference Number, 1966), pp. R-274–R-276.

[15] D. B. Vincent, "Waste Heat Evaporates Waste," *Food Engineering,* Vol. 39, No. 2 (1966), pp. 84–88.

[16] "Upgrades Cheese Whey, Solves Disposal Problems," *Food Engineering,* Vol. 37, No. 11 (1965).

[17] For a particularly interesting and explicit analysis of potential net gains from materials recovery and by-product production in one major waste discharging industry, see W. J. Fullen and K. V. Hill, "The Economics of Poor Housekeeping in the Meat-Packing Industry," *Journal Water Pollution Control Federation,* Vol. 39, No. 4 (1962), pp. 659–64. The senior author states (p. 659) that many years of study have enabled him to demonstrate that "the capital cost of conventional methods preventing salable products from becoming waste are by far cheaper than the capital cost of waste treatment facilities."

Screening	Neutralization	Incineration
Flocculation	Chemical oxidation	Biological filtration
Chemical coagulation	Chemical reduction	Activated sludge
Flotation	Wet oxidation	Anaerobic digestion
Sedimentation	Fermentation	Stabilization lagoons
Centrifuging	Emulsion breaking	Spray irrigation
Filtration	Evaporation	Disinfection
Stripping	Distillation	

In addition, the waste loads from some industrial operations may contain substances requiring special treatment, such as colors, odors, special chemicals, and toxic materials.

The waste treatment methods listed above might be characterized broadly as physical, chemical, and biological processes. They have greater or lesser applicability to the two major types of wastes, non-degradable and degradable. With respect to the former, suspended and dissolved solids are the major wastes. Suspended solids can be removed by sedimentation, with or without the aid of flocculants such as poly-electrolytes, by filtration through various kinds of screens and filters, and by centrifuging. Dissolved solids can be removed, to any desired degree, by one or more of the processes of distillation, ion exchange, electrodialysis, and reverse osmosis. It is possible to obtain completely pure water from waste discharges, but there will still be some sort of residual waste, either a concentrated brine or a semi-solid sludge. Ultimate disposal still remains a problem.

The degradable wastes of primary concern are organic wastes, bacteria, and thermal discharges. Organic wastes are removed by physical processes, such as sedimentation, to some degree, and by chemical and biological processes, such as chemical oxidation and aerobic digestion, respectively. Bacteria are at least partially removed by biological processes and by disinfection. Thermal loads are removed by one or more types of air or water cooling systems.

Conventional treatment of domestic wastes consists basically of physical and biological processes, and is a comparatively standardized process. It can greatly reduce BOD, but will not completely eliminate it, and is frequently designed to improve bacteriological quality and essentially eliminate suspended solids.[18] Ordinarily the treatment of degradable organic wastes—either domestic or industrial—begins with the removal of the larger suspended solids by screening and grit chambers and the more finely divided suspended solids by sedimentation. New practices,

[18] It is important to emphasize that there are complementarities in waste treatment, i.e., treatment to reduce one type of waste may also reduce another type. A good example is sedimentation, which reduces both suspended solids and BOD.

such as the addition of polyelectrolytes have done much to improve the efficiency of the sedimentation process. This sedimentation stage, known as primary treatment, results in a wet, difficult-to-handle sludge, which is usually digested in heated anaerobic tanks before final disposal. In some cases the sludge is burned, usually after some degree of drying, or concentrated with centrifuges, prior to disposal. When waste treatment plants are operated adequately, primary treatment of an effluent containing an organic waste, with sludge disposal, can reduce the first stage BOD by 35 to 40 per cent.

What is generally termed a secondary stage of treatment is biological in character and essentially controls and accelerates the oxidation processes which occur in natural waters. Two major techniques are presently used, with various modifications. One is the trickling filter, in which a biological film is grown on rocks or some type of plastic medium, and the waste is applied intermittently, allowing air contact with at least the surface of the film. The other technique is the activated sludge process, in which air or oxygen is forced into a tank containing a mix of waste and actively feeding biota. Part of the settled sludge containing the biota is recirculated and mixed with the entering waste in the aeration chamber.

Each of these methods has certain advantages. Trickling filters require relatively little attention during operation, and the biological growths upon which the effectiveness of the filters depends are somewhat less susceptible to toxic substances than the activated sludge process. An activated sludge plant is somewhat more flexible in operation and design; the major variables are the proportion of sludge recirculated, the length of aeration time, and the amount of air or oxygen introduced. Rapid turnover of waste and sludge generally saves space and power, but requires well-trained personnel and continuous monitoring of plant performance. Treatment in all activated sludge plants can be made more effective by increasing the quantity of air passed through the sludge tank, although there is a definite limit to this procedure. Costs in activated sludge and other types of treatment plants increase rapidly as the removal of BOD is pushed above 95 per cent (see Figure 8).

Small package plants, called extended aeration plants, have been used with considerable success for handling relatively small volumes of wastes, usually from strictly domestic sources. These plants are easy to operate, the sludge withdrawals are small enough in volume to be discharged with the final effluent, and much more of the solid matter is in mineralized form.

When secondary treatment is undertaken, the supernatant liquor from the sludge digestor, or other liquid resulting from the handling of sludge, is routed through the secondary treatment process. Secondary

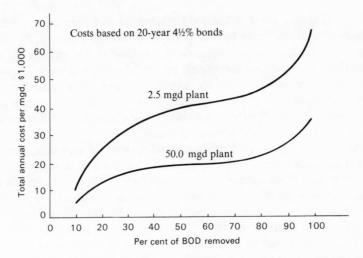

Figure 8. Relationship between degree of BOD removal and costs. *Source*: R. J. Frankel, "Cost-Quality Relationships in an Engineering-Economic Model for Municipal Waste Disposal," ASCE Water Resources Engineering Conference, Mobile, Alabama, 1965.

treatment in turn gives rise to some additional sludge which is routed into the digestors.

Primary and secondary treatment combined usually can reduce BOD by between 80 and 95 per cent. The procedures outlined above, plus disinfection of the final effluent in some instances, have been the essential elements of the primary-secondary waste treatment sequence for more than fifty years.

Although the conventional treatment processes are effective in reducing BOD, they have been much less effective in removing plant nutrients, nitrogen and phosphorus.[19]

During secondary treatment the nitrogen content of the organic waste is successively converted to nitrites and nitrates. Over-all, the volume of potential plant nutrients is reduced modestly during secondary treatment, but the content of nitrogen in nitrate form of course increases. Within limits, the extent to which nitrification occurs in the treatment process rather than in the receiving water can be controlled.

Other treatment methods that have become increasingly common and that achieve waste reduction comparable to secondary treatment are oxidation ponds (or stabilization lagoons) and spray irrigation systems.

[19] See J. B. Nesbitt, *Removal of Phosphorus from Municipal Sewage Plant Effluents*, Engineering Research Bulletin, B-93 (Pennsylvania State University, 1966).

Both methods are used in the food processing and pulp and paper industries. Ponds are used by the petroleum refining industry, by some large metropolitan areas (Melbourne, Australia, for example), and increasingly by smaller communities. Ponds, lagoons, and spray irrigation are used alone as complete treatment processes or as secondary or tertiary treatment in combination with other treatment processes. Ponds and spray irrigation systems may also be used in series, as in a number of installations in the food processing industry.

Stabilization lagoon or oxidation pond systems in industrial applications may range from a single large pond to a series of as many as eight or nine ponds. Pond capacity may be sufficient to store the entire waste effluent from a plant with a seasonal production schedule, as in some beet sugar and canning installations, or during the low streamflow period for plants with continuous production schedules. Alternatively, the pond system may be operated to produce a continuous outflow, as occurs in some installations in the canning, petroleum refining, and pulp and paper industries.[20] A series of ponds may also have aeration devices of one kind or another between ponds and/or floating or fixed aeration devices on or in one or more of the ponds themselves.

Algae play an important role in ponds and lagoons, as they furnish a substantial share of the oxygen requirements of aerobic bacteria, and they utilize the gases from the anaerobic BOD removal in the bottom sludge banks of such ponds and reduce or prevent their escape to the atmosphere. Such ponds and lagoons, when properly designed and loaded, are capable of stablizing oxygen-demanding wastes to a high degree.

In the Ruhr industrial area of West Germany, where comparatively large, shallow impoundments have been constructed in several rivers to serve essentially as large oxidation ponds in the streams themselves, the impoundments are sometimes specially designed to handle the specific types of wastes they receive. One, for example, neutralizes acids and precipitates organic materials simultaneously.

One effect of the use of ponds, lagoons, and spray irrigation systems (and underground disposal) is the increase in the consumptive use of water per unit of raw product or final product, compared with conventional treatment. Data from the petroleum refining industry show that the mean consumptive use was nearly 50 per cent greater for refineries using ponds and underground disposal than for those using

---

[20] For example, see G. Dickson, "Vegetable Cannery Liquid Waste Treatment by the 'Ever-Full' Lagoon System" (Paper presented at the 11th Ontario Industrial Waste Conference, 1964); and C. E. Fiske and W. E. Garner, "Stabilization Pond Treatment of an Oil Refinery Effluent," *Water and Sewage Works* (Reference Number, 1966), pp. R-277–R-280.

conventional treatment. Although the increase was small in absolute terms—about 14 gallons per barrel of crude throughput—it could be significant during periods of low streamflow, as in the summer months when the consumptive use in waste treatment by these methods and demands for water are both at a maximum.

It is important to note that both the oxidation pond or stabilization lagoon and the extended aeration treatment methods differ from standard waste treatment in that their effluents contain virtually all of the plant nutrients originally in the waste discharge. In the ponds, they are embodied in algae; in the latter, in mineral form. Thus the effluents from these types of treatment processes fertilize receiving waters more than effluents from conventional treatment plants do. Considerable attention is being devoted to developing methods for removal of plant nutrients from final effluents. Some recent results suggest that progress is being made on this problem. If fish or algae were harvested from oxidation ponds, the process of biological treatment would be accelerated and a major portion of the plant nutrients, as well as some other chemicals, would be extracted from the waste water.[21]

Chemical treatment includes a variety of processes ranging from chemical oxidation of substances in waste discharges to neutralization of acid or alkaline wastes. Most types of chemical treatment involve low capital costs and high operating costs; this makes them particularly useful for specialized treatment problems, for final finishing of a sequence of waste treatment, and for infrequent application during critical periods of water quality.[22] Some laboratory experiments with chemical treatment have shown a reduction of 60 to 85 per cent in BOD without biological treatment. Disinfection, by use of chlorine or ozone, can also be considered a type of chemical treatment.

One final point should be made concerning waste treatment. The increasingly stringent quality standards of final effluents make the economics of in-plant water recirculation more favorable. In some cases, water may be suitable for reuse within a plant—even as process water— and yet not meet the quality standards for effluents.[23]

The other major type of degradable wastes consists of thermal loads, which are of increasing importance. The most common method of re-

[21] At the present time fish are harvested in a few locations in Europe and Asia. Algae have been harvested only on an experimental basis. See C. Neos and M. M. Varma, "The Removal of Phosphate by Algae," Water and Sewage Works, Vol. 113, No. 12 (1966), pp. 456–59.

[22] See the discussion of chemical processes in Robert K. Davis, The Range of Choice in Water Management: A Study of Dissolved Oxygen in the Potomac Estuary (The Johns Hopkins Press, for RFF, 1968).

[23] A. J. von Frank, "Organic Chemicals and Petrochemicals" (Paper presented at Annual Meeting, American Chemical Society, New York, 1966).

ducing the heat load discharged is the installation of cooling towers. The magnitude of heat load reduction possible by this process is exemplified by the installation at the Philadelphia refinery of the Atlantic Refining Company, where the cooling tower program resulted in an 85 per cent reduction of heat load discharged to the river.[24]

Whether or not a cooling tower is installed at a particular plant is a function of both the internal economics of over-all water utilization in the plant and of the offsite costs resulting from the discharge of thermal loads. With respect to cooling towers, the economics of recirculation are such that if recirculation is adopted, it will be done essentially completely.[25] As a result, little or no heat will be discharged, but there will be an increase in the discharge of dissolved solids, stemming from chemical treatment of the recirculated water and concentration from evaporation.

Cooling towers may also aid in reducing other waste loads. For example, in the Toledo refinery of Sun Oil Company, a cooling water stream containing phenols passes through a cooling tower which functions essentially as a trickling filter. Biological oxidation reduces the phenol content in the effluent by over 99 per cent.[26] Other applications of the same procedure have been reported.[27]

A final method for handling residual wastes is the reuse of a municipal or industrial effluent by a subsequent user or users, usually after one or more types of man-made or natural treatment.[28] Sewage effluent is

---

[24] D. R. Roth, *et al.*, "Atlantic Selects Air Flotation Process for Refinery Waste Treatment" (Paper presented at 25th Midyear Meeting of the Division of Refining, American Petroleum Institute, Detroit, 1960), p. 2.

[25] For a definitive discussion of the economics of cooling towers see Cootner and Löf, *op. cit.*, pp. 60–77. See also B. Berg, R. W. Lane, and T. E. Larson, "Water Use and Related Costs with Cooling Towers," *Journal American Water Works Association*, Vol. 56, No. 3 (1964), pp. 311–29.

[26] H. F. Elkin, "Biological Oxidation and Reuse of Refinery Waste Water for Pollution Control and Water Conservation" (Paper presented at 21st Midyear Meeting of the Division of Refining, API, Montreal, 1956), p. 1. See also E. F. Mohler *et al.*, "Extended Experience With Reuse and Bioxidation of Refinery Waste Water in Cooling Tower Systems" (Paper presented at the 37th Annual Ohio Water Pollution Control Conference, Toledo, 1963).

[27] R. M. Smith, "Use of a Cooling Tower as a Trickling Filter in Pollution Control" (Paper presented at Cooling Tower Institute Meeting, January 1964).

[28] We have designated effluent reuse by the user generating the effluent as a recirculation of water. Such use is a common occurrence in industry. In municipalities, treated municipal wastewater has been recirculated for public water supply only in conditions of extreme scarcity of supply. No known disease resulted in these instances. See Bernard B. Berger, "Public Health Aspects of Water Reuse for Potable Supply," *Journal American Water Works Association*, Vol. 52, No. 5 (1960), pp. 599 ff.

To permit continuous recirculation for potable supply, current waste and water treatment processes would have to be supplemented. At present there are two major problems, the buildup of dissolved solids and the removal of viruses. With

used for various purposes in industrial operations, particularly in the southwestern United States.[29] The practice is less common in the East, although effluent from the Baltimore municipal treatment plant is used in the Sparrows Point plant of Bethlehem Steel, primarily for cooling water in steel production. Effluents from municipal waste treatment plants have long been used for irrigation. Among the many cities that use all or part of their sewage effluents for irrigation are Grand Canyon and Tucson in Arizona; Bakersfield, Fresno, San Bernardino, and San Francisco in California; and over 200 towns in Texas including Abilene, Kingsville, Lubbock, Midlands, San Angelo, and San Antonio.

Different reuse methods have varying effects on residual waste loads. Irrigation tends to remove virtually all of the residual wastes from the effluent, while industrial reuse may or may not reduce the residual waste load. Irrigation use, however, results in considerable net depletion of water, which is not necessarily unproductive.

Artificial recharge of groundwater aquifers represents another method of effluent reuse. In this case, however, generally a larger number of intermediate processes are involved than in the cases mentioned previously. Usually the effluent from a municipal waste treatment plant is inserted into a groundwater basin by means of injection wells or spreading grounds. In the latter case, the wastewater undergoes additional purification as it passes through the unsaturated zone. The purification process in the soil results from the action of soil bacteria, filtration, adsorption, and perhaps other processes.[30] In other cases the waste effluent from the sewer system is conveyed directly to a wastewater reclamation plant, as at Whittier Narrows, California,[31] where it is treated and then used for groundwater recharge. Another extensive

respect to the former, based on developments to date, combinations of treatment processes could be devised which would continuously produce potable water from waste effluents at lesser costs than would be involved in, for example, the conversion of sea water or the treatment of effluents from a watercourse highly contaminated with certain industrial wastes. (See C. F. Garland, "Waste-Water Renovation and Reuse," Infilco National Seminars, Reprint #134, 1966.) Complete certainty about methods for removing viruses has not been achieved as yet.

[29] R. Stone, and J. C. Merrell, "Significance of Minerals in Waste-Water," *Sewage and Industrial Wastes Journal*, Vol. 30, No. 7 (1958), pp. 936 ff.; and S. L. Terry, "Use of Sewage Plant Effluent as Cooling Tower Makeup," in *Selected Papers on Cooling Tower Water Treatment*, Circular 91 (Illinois State Water Survey, 1966), pp. 112–21.

[30] Groundwater aquifers have been recharged for municipal use in the Ruhr area of Germany for many years, with water obtained from heavily used rivers. For a brief description of this procedure see *Gelsenwasser—Herausgegeben anlaesslich des 75 jaehrigen Bestehens des Wasserwerk fuer das noerdliche Westfaelische Kohlenrevier, Gelsenkirchen* (Gelsenkirchen, January 1962).

[31] J. D. Parkhurst, "Progress in Waste Water Reuse in Southern California," *Journal of The Irrigation and Drainage Division, Proceedings ASCE*, Vol. 91, No. IR1 (1965), pp. 79–91.

system has been in operation for several years at Santee, California, where treated effluent is discharged into a series of ponds, the final ones having now been approved for water-contact sports. The final outflow is recharged to the groundwater basin.[32]

Caution is necessary in using wastewater from domestic and/or industrial operations for groundwater recharge. Even with treatment the minerals in the effluent before recharge remain, so that the total dissolved solids content is likely to increase (although there may be wide dispersion in the groundwater aquifer). Further, because there is likely to be some residual load even after treatment and the process of groundwater recharge, it is possible for groundwater contamination to occur. However, the well-publicized quality degradation of groundwater resources in certain areas, such as Long Island and Minneapolis-St. Paul, happened in situations where there was no centrally designed and operated wastewater treatment and recharge facility.[33] Recent analysis suggests that groundwater recharge for water renovation may have much wider applicability and be more economical than has previously been appreciated.[34]

An important point in connection with all measures of handling wastes is the existence of economies of scale. In materials recovery this is illustrated by the costs of the Blaw-Knox Ruthner sulfuric acid recovery process for handling waste pickle liquor. On the basis of 8.5 per cent free acid in the liquor, costs are about 3.5 cents per gallon when 30,000 gallons per day are processed and about 3 mills per gallon when 160,000 gallons per day are processed.[35] Similarly, significant economies of scale exist in waste treatment. For example, in a study of fruit and vegetable canneries, the costs (annual charge on capital investment plus operation and maintenance costs) for lagoons and/or spray irrigation systems were found to vary from about 2 cents per pound of BOD removed for operations removing more than 500,000

[32] R. L. Stoyer, "Special Uses for Water Reclaimed from Sewage" (Paper presented at 21st Annual Meeting, Soil Conservation Society of America, 1966). The final effluent from the five Santee lakes is to be sold to industrial and farm users for 12 cents per 1,000 gallons, in contrast to the 50 cents per 1,000 gallons currently paid for municipality-supplied fresh water. (Worthington Corporation, *Water*, 1966, p. 11.)

[33] An area-wide management system for Long Island is being contemplated. Preliminary research to obtain the requisite data for such a system is under way. See J. J. Batta and N. J. Bartilucci, "Wastewater Reclamation by Groundwater Recharge on Long Island," *Journal Water Pollution Control Federation*, Vol. 39, No. 3 (1967), pp. 431–45.

[34] R. J. Frankel, "Economics of Artificial Recharge for Water Supply," *Symposium of Haifa*, Publication No. 72 (Gentbrugge, Belgium: Association Internationale d'Hydrologie Scientifique, 1967).

[35] National Technical Task Committee on Industrial Wastes, Blaw-Knox Ruthner sulfuric acid recovery process, Process Sheet No. 3, no date.

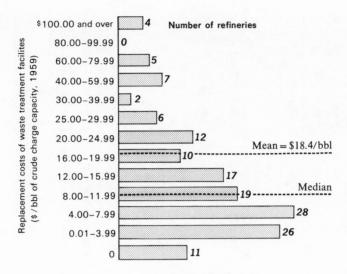

Figure 9. Frequency distribution of replacement costs of waste treatment facilities for U.S. petroleum refineries, in dollars per barrel of crude charge capacity, 1959. (Based on original data from the American Petroleum Institute.)

pounds of BOD in a canning season to 30 cents per pound for operations removing less than 100,000 pounds. Extensive analyses by the U.S. Public Health Service show similar economies of scale for municipal waste treatment plants.[36] In densely developed areas the costs of collective facilities for conveying and treating municipal and industrial wastes can often be much less than the sum of the costs of separate facilities for each municipality and industrial plant.

Concluding Comments—Reducing Waste Discharges

The foregoing discussion has focused on the wide variety of methods by which the quality of receiving waters can be improved by reducing waste loads discharged to them. The various methods can be combined in a myriad of ways to meet the needs of a single industrial operation or urban area or a complex consisting of many operations and/or areas.

Consider just waste treatment to reduce waste loads. Even in a single industry the combination of treatment processes applied in different plants varies widely, primarily as a function of the raw materials utilized, the production processes involved, the final products, and environmental constraints, including effluent controls. Consequently, there is a wide

[36] *Modern Sewage Treatment Plants—How Much Do They Cost?* (Public Health Service Publication 1229, 1964).

Table 4. Estimated Average Reduction of BOD in Beet Sugar Processing, 1949 to 1962[1]

(pounds of BOD per ton of beets processed)

Type of waste	1949					1962				
	BOD generated[2]	BOD removed			BOD discharged	BOD generated[2]	BOD removed			BOD discharged
		By process changes and recirculation[3]	By waste treatment	Total			By process changes and recirculation[3]	By waste treatment	Total	
Flume and washer water	4.5	n.a.	n.a.	0.9	3.6	4.5	n.a.	n.a.	1.7	2.8
Cooling water and condensate	0.7	n.a.	n.a.	0.1[4]	0.6[4]	0.7	n.a.	n.a.	0.2	0.5
Pulp screen and press water	4.9	0.5	0.6	1.1	3.8	5.3	4.0	0.4	4.4	0.9
Silo drainage	12.3[5]	5.8[6]	1.2	7.1	5.2	12.3[5]	12.1[6]	0.1	12.2	0.1
Lime cake slurry	6.5	0	3.1	3.1	3.4	6.5	0	6.1	6.1	0.4
Steffens filtrate	5.4	1.2[7]	0.7	2.1	3.3	4.9	3.5[7]	1.0	4.5	0.3
Total BOD	34.3	n.a.	n.a.	14.4	19.9	34.2	n.a.	n.a.	29.1	5.0

Source: Löf and Kneese, *op. cit.*

n.a. Not available.

[1] Based on 113,000 tons of beets per day processed in 1949; 158,000 in 1962.

[2] Based on BOD per ton of beets sliced in an "unimproved" plant, from "Industrial Waste Guide to the Beet Sugar Industry" (U.S. Public Health Service, Environmental Health Center, Cincinnati, December 1950), mimeo.

[3] The proportions of the BOD generated which were removed by process changes in 1949 and 1962 were at least 22 per cent and 57 per cent respectively.

[4] Based on estimated 10 per cent reuse as diffuser make-up water.

[5] BOD which would be generated if all spent pulp were handled in silos, i.e., no pulp drying.

[6] BOD not generated because of use of pulp driers.

[7] By recycle to production process and concentrated Steffens filtrate production.

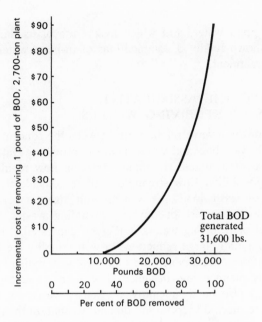

Figure 10. Incremental cost of reducing BOD content of lime, flume, and condenser water wastes from a beet sugar plant processing 2,700 tons of beets per day. *Source*: George O. G. Löf and Allen V. Kneese, *The Economics of Water Utilization in the Beet Sugar Industry* (Resources for the Future, Inc., 1968).

range in waste treatment costs in any given industry. This is illustrated for the petroleum refining industry in Figure 9.

What can be done to reduce waste loads discharged to receiving waters is clearly exemplified by the performance of the beet sugar industry. Table 4 shows the decrease in unit waste load (pounds of BOD per ton of beets processed) discharged daily during the production season by the industry between 1949 and 1962, and the measures adopted to bring about the decrease.

The types of measures to reduce waste loads used by the beet sugar industry are likely to be integral components of optimal water quality management systems. The planning of such systems requires the development of relationships between the incremental quantity of wastes removed and the incremental cost of removal.[37] Such a relationship is illustrated in Figure 10, as derived from data for the beet sugar industry. The relationship applies to a plant which has already installed pulp drying equipment and a continuous diffuser to which it recirculates pulp

[37] This will be evident in the discussion of marginal costs in subsequent chapters.

screen and press water, and which makes use of its Steffens residual. The costs shown relate to combinations of in-plant water recirculation and waste treatment.

INCREASING THE ASSIMILATIVE CAPACITY OF RECEIVING WATERS

Because of the inverse relationship between the concentration of most water quality variables and water quantity, providing water for dilution by fuller use of available streamflow through flow regulation suggests itself as a possibility. Low streamflows often coincide with heavy concentrations of waste loads, as well as with high temperatures. Where the waste loads consist of oxygen-demanding wastes, the dissolved oxygen level of receiving waters is thereby depressed.[38] Periods of low flow and potentially large reductions in water quality are the conditions for which effluent treatment plants and effluent redistribution systems are generally planned and designed. The assimilative capacity of tidal estuaries may also be significantly affected by variations in inflow; but the effects are more dispersed and difficult to analyze than in the case of flowing streams.

Dilution of wastes beyond that normally provided by natural streamflow during low-flow periods can be provided by modifying the pattern of streamflow, by modifying the time pattern and/or locations of waste discharge, or by some combination of the two. The most common practices are to increase flows during low-flow periods by controlled releases from reservoir storage, and to modify the pattern of waste discharge by temporary storage of wastes. Flow can also be increased by withdrawing water from groundwater sources and releasing it into surface watercourses. An interesting variation of low-flow augmentation is the recently inaugurated Buffalo River Improvement Project, in which water is pumped from Lake Erie, used as cooling water on a once-through basis in five industrial operations, then discharged into the Buffalo River to maintain a minimum flow.[39]

The effectiveness of augmenting flow depends on both the type of waste and the type of receiving water involved. With respect to organic wastes, for example, increasing assimilative capacity by flow augmentation is effective for streams, but not for lakes, and only to a limited

---

[38] Organic waste loads may result in water quality deterioration in downstream areas during high-flow periods, if the current is so fast that there is not enough time for decomposition. This phenomenon has been observed in the lower Meramec River and the Delaware estuary.

[39] "After Almost 30 years . . . a Dream Come True," *Water and Wastes Engineering*, Vol. 4, No. 5 (1967), pp. 96–98.

extent for estuaries. Increased flows could actually reduce water quality in lakes and estuaries by carrying greater quantities of partially assimilated wastes into them. With respect to nutrients, increased flows would likely result only in a more rapid discharge of these substances into lakes and estuaries, because less time would be available for adsorption and sedimentation in stream channels. In contrast, with respect to non-degradable wastes such as chlorides, increasing the flow into estuaries can result in a significant improvement in water quality. It appears difficult, if not impossible, to increase the assimilative capacity of groundwater bodies by augmenting inflows.

Flow augmentation may play a large role in future water resources management in the United States. Large-scale planning efforts of the U.S. Corps of Engineers in several basins in the East will include flow augmentation for water quality improvement as an important feature. The final report of the Corps on the Potomac River Basin recommended a large amount of reservoir storage for increasing low flows to improve water quality.[40]

The effects of reservoir storage itself on the quality of water later released may be favorable or unfavorable.[41] On the positive side, bacteriological quality tends to be stabilized, and summertime releases from reservoirs tend to be cooler than normal streamflows. On the other hand, some early hopes for effective dilution through releases from reservoirs were disappointed because of the failure to consider the impact of impoundment on the dissolved oxygen content of releases. Water from deeper parts of reservoirs is often virtually devoid of oxygen, because of the combined effect of BOD demand and reservoir stratification. When this condition is present—as it is especially likely to be in areas experiencing hot summer seasons—it takes larger releases from reservoirs to achieve a given effect on dissolved oxygen downstream, and the costs of achieving the desired water quality level are increased.

There are several ways of coping with the unfavorable effects of water storage in reservoirs. Multiple outlets can be installed—as at the Oroville Dam storage unit on the Feather River in California—so that water can be released from different levels in various combinations to achieve the desired water quality. If there is a power installation at a reservoir, air or oxygen can be introduced into water in the turbines. In many cases this can be done rather simply by using vacuum breakers

[40] U.S. Army Engineer District, Baltimore, Basin Studies Branch, *Potomac River Basin Report*, Vol. 1 (1963).

[41] An excellent summary is contained in J. M. Symons, S. R. Weibel, and G. G. Robeck, "Impoundment Influences on Water Quality," *Journal American Water Works Association*, Vol. 57, No. 1 (1965), pp. 51–75.

already installed in the dam. Turbine aeration involves some power loss, and therefore is not costless.[42]

Reservoirs can have significant effects on other elements of water quality such as suspended sediment, turbidity, and certain chemical constituents.[43] An in-stream reservoir acts as a settling basin, and will eliminate or reduce problems of suspended sediment or turbidity. The clearer water may mean lower treatment costs for downstream water users,[44] or it may promote increased algae growth with associated taste and odor difficulties.

Another method for modifying water quality in impoundments (and in natural lakes) is by mixing. The purpose is to destratify the impoundment or to prevent stratification from occurring. A number of installations have been made in the last ten years.[45] Results show that it is possible to destratify an impoundment by mixing and to improve the quality of the entire water mass, but they also show that stratification can reoccur after mixing ceases. Hence, prevention of stratification appears to be the better approach. The desired circulation patterns can be achieved through reservoir design—its shape and location of inlets and outlets—as well as by mechanical mixing.[46]

The degree to which the assimilative capacity downstream from an impoundment is improved is dependent not only on the reactions which take place in the impoundment but also on how the reservoir is operated. Depending on the time pattern of releases, there can be favorable or unfavorable effects on the assimilative capacity. For example, when a

[42] Turbine aeration has been used both in the United States and Europe. See A. J. Wiley, et al., "Commercial-Scale Operation of Turbine Aeration on Wisconsin Rivers," *Journal Water Pollution Control Federation*, Vol. 32, No. 2 (1960), pp. 186–94; and H. R. Amberg, et al., "Re-aeration of Streams with Molecular Oxygen," *Industrial Water Engineering*, Vol. 4, No. 2 (1967), pp. 15–20. The most definitive German source is Hubert Wagner, *Die Kuenstliche Belueftung kanalisierter Fluesse* (The Artificial Reaeration of Canalized Streams), Bundesanstalt fuer Gewaesserkunde, Koblenz, 1956.

[43] In recent years considerable attention has been directed toward needed research on these problems, e.g., J. M. Symons, S. R. Weibel, and G. G. Robeck, *Influence of Impoundments on Water Quality, a Review of Literature and Statement of Research Needs*, Public Health Service Publication No. 999-WP-18 (1964, revised 1966).

[44] G. J. Hopkins and J. K. Neel, "Water Quality in the Missouri River," *Proceedings ASCE*, Paper 1542 (1958).

[45] These are summarized in W. H. Irwin et al., "Impoundment Destratification by Mechanical Pumping," *Journal of the Sanitary Engineering Division, Proceedings ASCE*, Vol. 92, SA6 (1966), pp. 21–40. A summary of recent experience in England is contained in D. A. Okun, "Digest of Sanitary Engineering Research Reports," *Public Works*, Vol. 98, No. 5 (1967), pp. 144–48.

[46] See B. E. Nagler, "Pretreatment Storage and Monitoring Water Quality to Reduce Pollution," *Journal American Water Works Association*, Vol. 59, No. 6 (1967), pp. 680–84.

power plant at a reservoir is used for "peaking," the release pattern will vary substantially. Flows will be high during the portion of each weekday when the peaking load is being met, and low during the night and on weekends. This pattern is in contrast to the more continuous pattern of waste discharges. Reregulation of the power releases can compensate for the varying flow, but of course at increased cost.

Another way of increasing the assimilative capacity of streams and lakes is by artificial reaeration with either air or oxygen.[47] Mobile or fixed aerating devices can be installed in reaches of streams where needed to replenish the dissolved oxygen supply and prevent anaerobic conditions. Reaeration differs from methods for modifying wastes prior to discharge in that nothing is removed from the receiving water, and from methods for increasing the degree of dilution in that there is no increase in streamflow velocity to alter the length and shape of the oxygen sag. The effect is analogous to that of a lengthy oxidation pond artificially aerated.

In various coastal areas of the United States[48] the heavy use of groundwater resources has led to saltwater intrusion. One solution to this problem is to reduce the pumpage from the affected groundwater aquifers. Another is to establish barriers to the intrusion. In Southern California, the Manhattan Beach Project for reducing seawater intrusion and preventing further deterioration of the available groundwater supply created a saltwater barrier by a series of injection wells.[49] The well system provides a groundwater gradient toward the ocean which prevents further intrusion and enables the continued use of the groundwater aquifer. Impermeable physical barriers are another way of preventing saltwater intrusion.

Surface water is also subject to saltwater intrusion. Decreased outflow from upstream areas of rivers which empty into tidal estuaries has resulted in sporadic seawater intrusion, as in San Francisco Bay and the Delaware estuary. This type of intrusion can be reduced by increasing the flow into the estuary, or by constructing physical barriers to upstream saltwater movement. The first method has been utilized for many years in connection with San Francisco Bay, where the Central Valley Project has been operated to provide releases to reduce seawater intrusion. The second method has been proposed and studied for both San

[47] E. J. Cleary, "The Re-aeration of Rivers," *Industrial Water Engineering*, Vol. 3, No. 6 (1966), pp. 16–21.

[48] For example, Southern California, Dade County (Florida), Long Island (New York), and some areas in New Jersey and Delaware.

[49] See D. K. Todd, *Ground Water Hydrology* (John Wiley, 1959), pp. 287–90.

Francisco Bay[50] and the Delaware estuary.[51] The difficulty with physical barriers is that they impede navigation, affect aquatic life, and aggravate problems of managing wastes discharged upstream. Seawater encroachment in tidal estuaries will become more serious, as upstream development increases the consumptive use of water.

Effluent redistribution to make more efficient use of the available assimilative capacity can be achieved in a number of ways including regulated discharge, transfer of the effluent to a different location for discharge, and underground disposal. In general, these methods have little, if any, effect on waste loads as such, and they do not modify the receiving water.

Regulated discharge involves the temporary storage of waste effluents for discharge at times when more water is available for dilution.[52] In an estuary, this may mean storage during the ebb tide and discharge on the flood tide. Often it involves storage of wastes during low-flow periods in the summer and discharge during winter and/or spring when streamflow is higher. Some degradation of wastes takes place during seasonal storage, and this procedure is used by a number of food-processing, pulp and paper plants, and petroleum refineries. The efficient use of regulated discharge depends on sophisticated studies of the operation of such a system,[53] and on a data collection system that provides continuous information on the quantity and quality of receiving water and the quantity and quality of wastes to be discharged.

Transferring of wastes from one location of potential discharge to one or more other areas where the assimilative capacity is larger is usually practiced in areas near tidal estuaries or oceans. This system is

[50] U.S. Corps of Engineers, *Technical Report on Barriers* (1963), U.S. Army Engineer District, San Francisco, California.

[51] U.S. Corps of Engineers, *Delaware River Basin Report*, Volume I, Main Report (1960, revised 1961), pp. 159–63, and Appendix S, "Salt Water Barrier," U.S. Army Engineer District, Philadelphia, and U.S. Army Engineer Division, North Atlantic (New York).

[52] Discharge programmed in correspondence with streamflow is quite common in the German potash-producing regions. Among the streams primarily affected are the Werra, the Weser, and the Aller. In the area of the Werra River, for example, the responsible authorities have made it mandatory that (potash) waste discharges be co-ordinated with streamflow and that the discharger install equipment which automatically measures and records the amount and specific gravity of the effluent. Releases are scheduled according to a release table which indicates both the stream stage and the content of chlorides in the stream. The control houses are outfitted with instruments which indicate the quality of the stream, the quality of the effluent, and the stream stage. Friedrich Sierp, *Gewerbliche und Industrielle Abwaesser* (Berlin: Springer-Verlag, 1959), p. 613.

[53] Examples include M. M. Montgomery and W. R. Lynn, "Analysis of Sewage Treatment Systems by Simulation," *Journal of the Sanitary Engineering Division, Proceedings ASCE*, Vol. 90, No. SA1 (1964), pp. 73–97; and D. P. Loucks and W. R. Lynn, "Probabilistic Models for Predicting Stream Quality," *Water Resources Research*, Vol. 2, No. 3 (1965), pp. 593–605.

now used by the Toms River Chemical Corporation,[54] which formerly handled the wastes generated in the production of synthetic and organic dyes by equalization, neutralization, clarification, chlorination, aeration, and discharge to the adjacent Toms River. When the residual waste load from growth in production approached the assimilative capacity of the river, ocean discharge was adopted. This made possible the elimination of both chlorination and aeration. The entire waste-handling system is continuously monitored.

In underground disposal, effluents are discharged into relatively deep formations that contain so little water or water of such poor quality that they are not expected to be used for water supply. This method of disposal is used largely by the chemical, petrochemical, and paper industries for wastes that are difficult or very expensive to treat.[55] Underground disposal represents a consumptive use of water, since the effluent is not available for reuse.

CONCLUSION

The wide variety of measures for water quality management discussed above could be incorporated in plans for a water utilization system in a region (say a river basin). Planning, however, is only the first step in the management problem. The system must be implemented and—once in existence—must be operated to produce a specified time pattern of outputs of water and water-related goods and services, including water quality, at specified locations. This it must do in the face of uncertainties relating to hydrologic events and to demands on the water resource over time. Efficient and effective operation of a water utilization system involves not only day-to-day operation of individual units in the system, such as waste treatment plants and reaeration devices, but integrated operation of all units in the entire system. This is no mean task. Before concluding our comments on the technical and engineering aspects of water quality, we turn to a short discussion of system operation.

Operating a system means determining when to push buttons, turn valves, open and close gates, and so on for the various units involved in, and economic activities related to, a water utilization system.[56] Such operation requires a communications-control network consisting of data collection, data communication, data analysis and interpretation, sig-

---

[54] "Ocean Disposal of Industrial Wastes," *Industrial Water Engineering*, Vol. 4, No. 1 (1967), pp. 31, 57.

[55] E. C. Donaldson, "Subsurface Disposal of Industrial Wastes in the United States" (Bureau of Mines Information Circular 8212, 1964).

[56] Including, in the short-run, reducing or eliminating waste-generating production at industrial plants. For example, during the period of lowest water quality in the lower Willamette River in 1966, production of at least one significant waste producer was reduced substantially.

Communications-Control Network for Water Quality Management

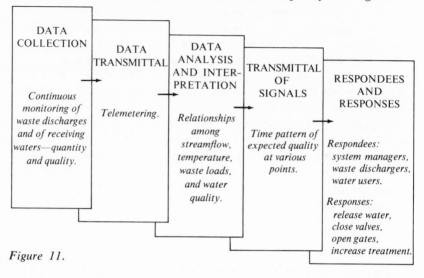

DATA COLLECTION	DATA TRANSMITTAL	DATA ANALYSIS AND INTER-PRETATION	TRANSMITTAL OF SIGNALS	RESPONDEES AND RESPONSES
Continuous monitoring of waste discharges and of receiving waters—quantity and quality.	*Telemetering.*	*Relationships among streamflow, temperature, waste loads, and water quality.*	*Time pattern of expected quality at various points.*	*Respondees: system managers, waste dischargers, water users.* *Responses: release water, close valves, open gates, increase treatment.*

Figure 11.

naling, and response, as illustrated in the generalized schematic in Figure 11. Data collection involves continuous recording of streamflow, precipitation, soil moisture, continuous monitoring of various water quality parameters in receiving waters and waste discharges, continuous recording of the volume and quality of water in storage reservoirs and in groundwater basins. In the last decade, considerable advances have been made in the development of instrumentation for continuous analysis of various water quality variables such as dissolved oxygen, temperature, turbidity, pH, total dissolved solids, conductance, and COD (chemical oxygen demand).[57] From the data collection points the information must be transmitted to a control center. Again, recent developments have improved this component of the management system through such techniques as automatic telemetering of data.

In the analysis and control center, the data are compiled and printed out or stored. Assuming basic relationships have already been developed, such as among streamflow, waste loads, and water quality, and streamflow and stream velocity, estimates can be made of water quality at various points in the system. This information is relevant to both short-run and long-run situations. Examples of the former are accidental spills of toxic materials and intense storms producing high concentrations of suspended sediment which might clog water intakes or groundwater recharge facilities. Long-run situations involve protracted periods of low flow.

[57] See G. E. McCallum and H. Stierli, "How Automation Plays a Part in Water-Quality Surveillance," *Water Works and Wastes Engineering*, Vol. 1, No. 5, (1964), pp. 68–70.

From the control center this information can be transmitted to various operators and water users in the area. The operators and water users at various locations can then respond to the "signals" received in terms of pushing buttons, turning valves, opening and closing gates. Artificial reaeration devices can be started; releases from reservoirs can be made; additional chemicals added in various treatment processes. Artificial groundwater recharge facilities may be by-passed. If necessary, generation of wastes can be reduced by curtailing production.

Despite all of the problems relating to system operation, the net gains which can be expected from the development of what we have called a communications-control network appear to be significant. Such networks were probably conceived first to preclude serious damage from accidental spills of toxic materials or substances that would disrupt waste treatment and/or water treatment facilities (e.g., phenols, cyanide, arsenic) or to monitor the performance of waste treatment plants in relation to receiving waters.[58] As demands on the water resource increase, with a concomitant increase in interactions among various water users, the need for, and the potential savings from, sophisticated system operation will increase. Savings stem from the possibility for more nearly optimal system plans, i.e., reduction in size of some system components, and from the possibility of incremental operation of water quality management systems once they are in existence. The latter refers to the use at any given time of those measures which provide the desired water quality at least cost. The benefits from this type of system operation, including computer control, are well documented in the power industry.[59]

It should be emphasized that the planning of any water management system involves assumptions about the way the system components are to be operated when they are finally in place. Accurate planning *requires* determination of the performance of proposed systems under various possible hydrologic events. Accordingly, to achieve a valid assessment of system performance requires structuring the simulation of the water utilization system in the planning phase in a manner as close as possible to the situation that will exist in the real world. Even so, the efficiency of operation of system components assumed in the planning phase can be approached, but never achieved, in actual system operation.

The degree of articulation and integration of water quality management system components implied in the above paragraphs has so far not been achieved even in system operation, much less in the planning of actual systems. The Ohio River Valley Water Sanitation Commission, however, has made substantial progress on the operation phase, especially

[58] See C. V. Gibbs, "Receiving Water Monitoring," *Water Works and Wastes Engineering*, Vol. 1, No. 9 (1964), pp. 52–55.

[59] See H. G. Stewart, "PJM Looks to Computer for Savings, Reliability in Operation and Scheduling," *Electrical World*, Vol. 165, No. 12 (1966), pp. 90–91, 158.

with respect to a communications network.[60] In most regions, water quality management is at a primitive level. At the same time, the technical and analytical means for implementing such systems are developing rapidly. Institutional means lag far behind.

Our discussion of the engineering and technological facets of water quality management has simplified many of the processes and relationships, but one central point should be clear. Technologically, there are many alternative measures available to achieve whatever levels of water quality are desired. These include various types and degrees of intake water treatment, measures for reducing the generation of wastes, measures for modifying and disposing of wastes after generation, and measures for increasing or making better use of the assimilative capacity of receiving waters.

These measures substitute for one another economically at various rates depending upon the particular waste loads and receiving water bodies involved. Decisions concerning the proper balance among the various measures cannot be made rationally on technical grounds alone, because not all of the benefits from water quality improvement can be measured in dollar terms. Accordingly, values must be introduced into the decision-making process. Further complicating the decision process are both the stochastic nature (uncertainty of occurrence) of hydrologic phenomena and the inadequate understanding (as yet) of the impacts of waste discharges on water quality of various receiving waters and of the effect of various levels and time patterns of water quality on various water uses.

Identifying alternatives for a water quality management system and devising plans which combine them optimally is a demanding task. Moreover, planning and implementation are complicated by the fractionation of decision-making responsibility for the various possible components of such systems. Some measures are within the purview of the individual water users and waste dischargers, some are the responsibility of state, regional, or federal agencies, and some do not fall within the conventional purview of any agency whatsoever.

The problem is further compounded by the fact that water quality improvement is generally only one of the desired outputs from a water management system. Both system planning and operation are affected by the complementary and competitive relationships among the various outputs—water quality improvement, energy generation, navigation, flood damage reduction, irrigation, water supply, and water-based recreation.

We now turn to the economic aspects of regional water quality management.

[60] See W. L. Klein, "Operating a Robot Monitoring System," *Proceedings, 14th Southern Water Resources and Pollution Control Conference* (1965), pp. 44–51.

ECONOMIC CONCEPTS AND POLICIES FOR
CONTROLLING INDIVIDUAL WASTE DISCHARGES

II

The limit on improving water quality in our regions is essentially an economic one. Although further technological advance may allow better quality with a smaller expenditure of resources, the controlling question will continue to be, "How much of society's resources shall we devote to maintaining and improving water quality?"

Here, in Part II, the primary aim is to develop certain basic ideas of economic theory in specific application to problems of water quality management. For the sake of simplicity it is assumed that no economies can be achieved by collective water supply and waste disposal facilities serving separate economic units such as industrial plants and municipalities. In later chapters, however, it is pointed out that certain water quality improvement measures can often be used efficiently only on a large scale and not by individual water users and waste dischargers.

The simplified situation presented in this part is one in which there are several water users along a stream. These water users are close enough together and the amount of dilution water is small enough for the costs of downstream users or the range of opportunities available to them to be affected significantly by upstream waste discharges. However, the water users are not close enough together to make treating their wastes in common treatment plants a feasible procedure. Also, technical or economic factors make it impractical to augment low streamflows or practice mechanical reaeration. The alternative ways of adjusting water quality which *are* available in the region include all forms of treatment of water or wastewater at the individual water supply intake and wastewater outfall, temporary storage of wastes, alterations of manufacturing output, modification of industrial processes, temporary shut-down of industrial plants, and longer-run measures such as adjustments of industrial locations and changes in the location of industrial or municipal outfalls.

We made an effort to be reasonably comprehensive—though not de-tailed—in our earlier discussion of the various types of wastes and their effects, but we now simplify greatly and, in general, distinguish only between degradable and nondegradable wastes in developing principles and illustrating them. This distinction permits exploration of the relevant theory without undue complexity. Later when we examine measurement problems and introduce case material, we once more speak in terms of a fuller complement of individual wastes.

In general, this study is not concerned with the costs that must be incurred in moving water from a source to a final user or in draining a metropolis or industrial premises. Consideration of the problems of efficiency in planning and operating delivery and drainage systems is limited here to the suggestion that the relocation of points of intake and discharge may sometimes be an efficient alternative to other water quality control measures. The focus of this study is upon water quality in the streams or groundwater resources of a region and the optimum measures for its management. References to "watercourses" in the following chap-ters can usually be taken to mean either groundwater or surface waters. The same economic principles apply to groundwater and surface waters, but the type of analysis needed is affected by the fact that waste assimila-tion is the only "in-stream" use of groundwater, and the fact that quality deterioration is more difficult to reverse in groundwater.

Chapter 5 briefly explains why reliance on *private* incentives and competitive markets to allocate productive resources generally produce results that have *social* merit; it then points out why and how this allo-cative process may be distorted when watercourses are used for waste disposal. This form of market failure occurs because water quality deterioration produces "technological external diseconomies." These terms, traditionally used in economic theory, are explained in some de-tail in order to set the stage for their use later in the book. The definition of property rights in water and legal adversary proceedings are briefly evaluated as ways of handling external diseconomies. The possibility of enlarging firms so as to "internalize" the undesirable external effects and thus have them directly weighed in private decisions is also assessed.

The apparent deficiencies of these procedures lead to an examination in Chapter 6 of what might be called public administrative procedures— still focusing on individual points of waste generation and discharge. These procedures include effluent charges based on imposed damages and the more traditional procedure of effluent standards. Following an outline of the underlying analysis and knowledge of costs that are needed if effluent charges or standards are to achieve optimal control at in-dividual points of waste discharge, attention is given to some of the more difficult problems encountered in making the requisite cost measurements. Chapter 7 discusses what might be done in the absence of explicit damage functions and contains a comparison of charges and standards based upon criteria of efficiency and equity. Chapter 8 presents two case studies chosen to illustrate the principles and procedures examined in this Part. The first is an evaluation of comparative programs of quality management proposed for chloride management in the Ohio River Basin. The second reports on an empirical study of effluent charges as a water quality management device in the Delaware River estuary area. Chapter 9 ends Part II with a discussion of economic policies for controlling individual waste discharges.

The additional problems involved in taking account of opportunities to reduce costs of regional water quality management programs by the use of collective facilities that provide services for more than one firm or local unit of government are addressed in Part III.

Water Quality and Resources Allocation by Private Markets

5

THE "WELFARE MAXIMIZING"
RESULTS OF MARKET PROCESSES

To deal meaningfully with policy issues presented by water quality management, it is essential to have a concept of the functioning of the economy. While the American economy is a mixed one with heavy doses of public production and regulation, the best simple model for understanding its basic functioning and for providing a benchmark against which to measure its performance is the economist's model of the competitive market.[1] This is really an abstract model of how choices concerning resources use are made in a decentralized decision-making system, one where markets are competitive and the individual decision makers (industries and individuals) act rationally to maximize their private benefits. If we accept certain ethical assumptions, i.e., that the over-all distribution of income is justifiable on ethical grounds and that individual preferences should be satisfied to the maximum extent possible given the distribution of income, a normative or standard-setting value is attributable to the outcome of the market process. Such a decentralized decision-making system will produce maximum welfare or, in other words, precisely those goods and services wanted by consumers, in just the quantities wanted, and in the cheapest possible way.

In a well-functioning competitive economy each productive resource will be used up to the point where the cost of an additional unit is just equal to its contribution to the value of production. For example, in the case of labor, a firm will hire additional workers until the wage paid to the last worker employed just equals the dollar value of the extra product he produces. Up to that point each worker will have added more to the firm's revenues than to its costs. Now if this condition pre-

---

[1] For a rigorous discussion of the economic principles with respect to the operation of a market system, see James Henderson and Richard Quandt, *Micro-Economic Theory* (McGraw-Hill, 1958).

vails in each firm and if the price of labor is uniform as between any two firms (which it would tend to be if resources are mobile), the last unit of labor used in each firm will contribute an identical value of product. Thus, if the wage for a given quality of labor is uniform in the market, the value of the product of the last unit of that type of labor hired in any one activity will be equal to that of the last unit hired in any other activity. This is important because it means that the market price paid for a resource represents the product which that resource could have generated in another line of activity. For example, if a firm hires an additional unit of labor for one dollar, production elsewhere is reduced by one dollar owing to the withdrawal of that unit of labor. As the welfare economist puts it, the market price of the resource is equal to its opportunity cost, i.e., its contribution to the value of output in all alternative uses.

Consumers attempting to achieve maximum satisfaction from a given amount of income tend to allocate their expenditures so that the last dollar spent for any particular item will yield an amount of satisfaction equal to the last dollar spent on any other item. When this condition holds, it follows that the market price of a particular commodity reflects its worth, or goodness, or power to satisfy wants. If the unit price of one commodity is twice as high as that of another commodity, the last unit of the higher priced commodity which an individual buys must yield twice as much satisfaction as the last unit of the lower priced one. Consequently, the relative market prices of goods reflect the valuation that consumers place upon the purchase of marginal units.

If, in addition, the distribution of purchasing power conforms to the ethical standards of the community and if consumer sovereignty over resource allocation is accepted as ethically correct, the prices of goods and factors of production accurately represent their contributions to social welfare.[2] Thus prices provide automatic, socially valid guidelines for investment and production. For example, assume that a dollar's worth of labor can be moved from an activity where it yields a dollar's worth of product to another activity where it yields more than a dollar's worth of product because the cost of the last unit of labor in that activity is not yet equal to the value of the product it yields. Not only does private benefit maximization indicate and induce a shift of labor under these circumstances, but, when the shift is made, both the total value of production and the total satisfaction derived by society from its use of resources are increased.

In highly idealized form these notions provide a social justification for

---

[2] "Transfers" can serve to "correct" the income distribution. Unhappiness with the income distribution generated in competitive markets does not mean that competition should be abandoned; it means that transfers should be made or resource endowments altered.

market processes and a possible justification for public intervention in instances where some obstruction prevents private market processes from equating marginal social costs and benefits.

Like all models, this is an abstraction from reality. It helps to identify the ideal functioning of a decentralized system and to isolate and forecast the effects of departures from such an ideal system. But no one who is exposed to the day-by-day operations of the economy will be surprised that things do not work out in the way specified in the model.

The aspect of market failure that is of particular concern in this book is the fact that what the consumer consumes or what a business firm uses in the way of inputs is not entirely within its control. That is, supply and demand as expressed in markets are not the only forces that govern what is consumed and what is used as inputs in business firms. Some goods and services flow to consumers or businesses whether they want them or not and without their paying for them or being able to avoid them by making a payment. The activities of one economic unit may generate "real," as contrasted with price or monetary, effects that are external to it. The economist refers to these as external effects or "externalities." They have also been called "spillover effects" or "third party effects," and like the side effects of medication they are the unintended accompaniments of an act. In most situations, external effects are not large enough to negate the over-all tendency toward optimal resource allocation resulting from free markets. In specific sectors, however, these effects are significant and may require correction via public policy. This can be the case with various types of waste discharges. A downstream water user, be he a recreationist or a manufacturer, can usually not control the quality of water he receives as return flow from upstream users.

Such external costs are not taken into consideration when the firm or other relevant decision-making unit such as a local government decides whether and how much waste to discharge. The distorting effects of such externalities have been analyzed in considerable technical detail by economists. The basic problem which results can be expressed rather simply, however.

A society which relies completely on a decentralized decision-making system and in which externalities occur, as they would in virtually any society which contains significant concentrations of population and industrial activity, will find that certain resources are not used optimally. Particularly, the natural environment has a certain capacity to assimilate residual wastes and this capacity is extremely valuable. To completely eliminate all residual wastes would be immensely costly. But on the other hand, if no price is put upon the assimilative capacity of the environment, it will be used too much. For example, the assimilative capacity of a stream may be large, but at some point significant external costs appear. Fish will die; industrial plants and municipalities will have to treat their intake water at rising incremental costs. These are real costs, but they are external to the waste discharger, be he manufacturer or municipality, and because he does not bear them he does not weigh them in his decisions. He will not design his manufacturing processes to take account of them; he will use too much of certain inputs which have particularly large external costs; he will not treat his effluents, even though doing so might involve lesser costs than are imposed on the downstream users.

If we wish to realize the great advantages of decentralized decision-making mechanisms, in other words the market, we must find ways to optimally control these external effects or direct interdependencies between decision-making units in the economy. This means that in some fashion the external costs stemming from residual wastes discharged to the environment must be weighed against, and balanced with, the costs of controlling the amount of these residuals.

The concept of externality is so important to the analysis in this book that a reasonably detailed discussion of it is desirable.

TECHNOLOGICAL EXTERNAL DISECONOMIES

Water pollution and air pollution are economists' classic illustrations of the theoretical concept they refer to as "technological external diseconomies." This term describes a situation where a particular action produces uneconomical results—higher costs, less valuable production—and the costs of the action are transferred from the economic decision unit (say, a firm) pursuing the action to a managerially independent unit by a technical or physical linkage between production processes, and not by a market transaction. The costs may take the form of an actual outlay, a reduction in income or satisfaction, or complete foreclosure of some opportunities.[3]

Technological links may produce considerably different results when they are internal to a decision unit than when they are external. To illustrate, assume that a farmer has enough water to irrigate plot A or plot B, but not both. Assume that sprinkler irrigation is the only feasible method, and that the water available is just sufficient to meet the consumptive use requirement of the crop on either plot, that is, no return flow will occur from the irrigation. If plot A is irrigated, plot B cannot be irrigated. (It is assumed that it is not feasible to irrigate parts of each.) In deciding whether to irrigate plot A, the farmer will consider

---

[3] For an extended discussion of external economies and diseconomies, see Roland N. McKean, *Efficiency in Government Through Systems Analysis* (John Wiley, 1958), Ch. 8.

the return lost on plot B, and plot A will be irrigated only if its net return is higher. Consequently, the resource will be allocated in the way that maximizes the value of production. If, however, plot B is on another farmer's land and the owner of plot A cannot sell his right to the water, the owner of plot A will not consider the return lost on plot B in determining whether to irrigate plot A. If plot B actually presents the superior productive opportunity, failure to irrigate it because the water is pre-empted is a technological external diseconomy.

Now suppose that the owner of plot A *can* sell his right to the water and that the farmer owning plot B can afford to, and has an incentive to, pay more for the water than it is worth if applied on plot A. In this case, the efficient result would once again be produced.

But suppose that a third farmer appears who has an even more productive piece of land, and that no financial or legal constraint bars him from bidding the water away from the owner of plot B. (Again assume that sprinkler irrigation is the only feasible method, and that the amount of water available is sufficient to meet only the consumptive use requirement on the new land, plot C.) The value of the output (the social product according to the economic value theory explained above) will be greater if the water is applied to plot C, but the farmer who owns plot B will suffer a loss because he is priced out of the market. The cost, or loss, in this case is a "pecuniary" diseconomy rather than a technological one, and there is no distortion of resources allocation. The price of the water rose because there was competition for its services, and the new price reflects the productivity of the water in alternative uses.

This example also illustrates the close relationship between technological diseconomies and property rights. By altering the character of the right to the water—making it salable—the technological external diseconomy was eliminated in this instance. This result emphasizes the fact that in dealing with the reduction in output caused by technological spillovers the possibility of adjusting property rights to permit the external opportunity costs to be internalized is among the possibilities which must be analyzed. For a variety of reasons, however, this method appears to be of limited use in dealing with water quality-related inefficiencies. We return to this point further on.

Where technological spillovers are significant, the type of resource misallocations that will occur can be foreseen in a general way. For example, when disposal of wastes into watercourses neglects downstream costs, the costs are understated for some economic units and overstated for others relative to social (opportunity) costs. This tends to induce overproduction and overconsumption of some items and underproduction and underconsumption of others. To illustrate, when an upstream steel mill dumps its wastes into a watercourse without consideration of the downstream costs imposed, it produces steel which is artificially "cheap" because nothing is paid for the use of a valuable resource, i.e., for the waste dilution, degradation, and carriage capacity of the watercourse. From a social point of view, the value of this resource is measured by the alternative uses which can be made of the water. *Failure of municipal and industrial waste dischargers to consider that subsequent water uses may be made more expensive or foreclosed entirely by their discharges is perhaps the basic element of the water quality problem.*[4]

When offsite costs are ignored, an excessive amount of waste tends to be deposited in receiving waters. Little effort is made to treat wastewater, to recover materials from wastewater, or to design and operate industrial processes that will reduce the generation of wastes, although studies of waste loads generated per unit of physical output by plants producing identical goods by different processes show that a sizable proportion of wastes can be "engineered away." This emphasizes the importance of providing the appropriate incentives for such procedures. *A society that allows waste dischargers to neglect the offsite costs of waste disposal will not only devote too few resources to the treatment of waste but will also produce too much waste in view of the damage it causes.* In a general way this may be considered the rationale for some form of social or political intervention in waste disposal decisions.

Neglect of external costs, however, does not mean that the amount of resources devoted to dealing with the externality—water quality improvement in general, including the treatment of water supplies—will necessarily be less than if external costs were properly weighed and acted upon. For example, assume that waste discharge reduction and water supply treatment are the only alternatives possible. If waste reduction

---

[4] To use a bit of economic jargon, externalities may affect production functions and cause distortion (failure to be able to optimize) in them, thus causing the economy to fail to produce maximum welfare. They may also affect consumers' utility functions directly. For example, a smelly river may make it impossible for a consumer to maximize his own utility by adjusting the activities which contribute to his utility. An externality is present in a consumer's utility function when,

$$\mu^A = \mu^A (x_1, x_2, \ldots, x_m, y_1)$$

This means that the utility of an individual A is dependent on activities $(x_1, x_2, \ldots, x_m)$, which are exclusively under his control, and on activity y_1 which pollutes the air. Neglecting budgetary constraints, the consumer maximizes his utility by setting the partial derivatives of the x's to zero. But he may not be able to do this in regard to the y_1 which he cannot control. Thus a marginal externality exists when $\delta\mu^a / \delta y_1 \neq 0$.

In the above example a marginal external diseconomy exists, that is, $\delta\mu^a / \delta y_1 < 0$. An analogous analysis applies to production externalities.

See the excellent article "Externality" by J. M. Buchanan and W. C. Stubblebine in *Economica* (November 1962).

were *less* costly, over the appropriate range, than water supply treatment, the neglect of external costs would result in *more* resources being devoted to water quality improvement than if the externality were "remedied" through co-operative action leading to application of the less expensive waste reduction measures.[5]

MARKETS AND EXTERNALITIES

While at first it may appear so, the market system does not inevitably result in neglect of downstream costs by waste disposers—or more generally in neglect of externalities. Under some restricted circumstances, bargaining between a waste discharger and a damaged party can achieve a result that we later term optimal—since it minimizes the over-all costs associated with the waste disposal activity. This is more likely to occur when adjustments are made by individual firms rather than by industries as a whole. Assume, for example, that a firm which produces a nondegradable waste material toxic to fish is considering location on the banks of a stream where a downstream firm is engaged in commercial fishing. The stream has no other users, and there are essentially no increments to flow between the plant site and the fishing area. Assume further that the fishing firm realizes an annual return of 10, that it has no fixed capital, and that it uses resources with a value of 100 that can be transferred at no cost to other productive uses at either the same or a different location.

The fishing firm will be willing to pay up to 10 annually to prevent the other firm from putting its waste into the stream to an extent that would kill the fish. It is, of course, assumed that the toxic waste is strictly a result of a productive process. The possibility of some enterprising individual threatening to put toxic material in the stream merely to collect the 10 is thus excluded.

In the most elementary case where the fish are simply killed or not killed, the firm with the potentially lethal waste will either accept 10 and not kill the fish (by treating its wastes or not locating on the stream), or else simply kill the fish. If the firm is calculating rationally and kills the fish, this must mean that it would cost more than 10 not to do so. Consequently, the discharging firm's cost saving plus the value of production from the transferred resources of the fishing firm is greater than the value of continuing to fish in the stream. In terms of resource allocation, the result would be precisely the same if a public agency were to impose the offsite social cost (10) of killing the fish upon the waste discharging firm. The firm would still kill the fish if it costs more than

[5] For development of an analogous point, see J. M. Buchanan and M. Z. Kafoglis, "A Note on Public Goods Supply," *American Economic Review* (June 1963).

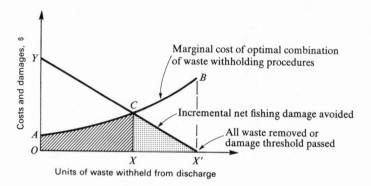

Figure 12.

10 not to kill them, and it would not kill them if it does not.[6] In either case, the net value of fishing becomes an "opportunity cost" to the firm. But the two results are the same *only* from the point of view of allocating resources in the short run. They differ in longer-term adjustments, and in income distribution. Moreover, on equity grounds it might be considered justifiable to compensate the fisherman for his loss of the opportunity to fish. This point is considered later.

An additional point to be made here is that the social cost of killing the fish is 10, not 110 (market value of the fish), as is often implied in exhortations to assess waste dischargers with the cost of damages they cause. If a charge of 110 were levied on the firm discharging wastes into the stream, the allocation of resources would be distorted because the discharging firm would be induced to spend up to 110 in treatment, net cost of waste recovery, or locational disadvantage in order to avoid killing fish with a net social value of 10. The waste discharge might indeed kill $110 worth of fish, but, by our assumption, it would release $100 worth of resources for alternative uses. Thus while the waste discharge would result in a drop of $110 in the output of fish, it would result in an increase of $100 in the output of some other things. As a result, there would be a net loss of $10 of total output.

A more realistic situation is one in which waste load reduction (waste recovery, treatment, process changes, etc.) and fish kills can be varied continuously. In this case the fishing firm would be willing to pay an amount up to the net value of fishing in that particular location for each relevant level of fish kills avoided. Similarly the firm would be willing to pay up to the net value of damage avoided for removal of phenols or other substances that impart undesirable flavors and thereby reduce the market value of the fish. This situation is shown in Figure 12.

[6] For an elaboration of this point, see R. H. Coase, "The Problem of Social Cost," *Journal of Law and Economics* (October 1960).

The line YX indicates the incremental net benefits of fishing preserved. The x-axis indicates amounts of waste withheld from discharge. At point X', all wastes are withheld or the threshold of damage is passed. The damage and withholding cost functions are related by a technical relationship which may be very complicated, involving processes of biochemical degradation and hydrologic variation (discussed in Chapter 2). For the time being, the predictability of this relationship is assumed and its stochastic or probability character neglected.

For each level of waste withheld from discharge, there is an optimum combination of waste withholding measures which in turn is associated with a certain cost. The marginal cost of optimum combinations of measures is indicated by the function AB. If a public authority were able to levy the incremental damages resulting from waste discharge upon the waste discharger, the latter would withhold waste to the point X. At this point the costs (internal and external) associated with his waste disposal (damage costs and abatement costs $OACX'$) are minimized. Alternatively, one can say that the net benefits (ACY) associated with abatement activity (treatment, process and product adjustment, etc.) are maximized. The party experiencing the external diseconomy would have an incentive to pay up to the marginal damage avoided for each unit of waste material and accordingly private negotiation would also tend to lead to the optimum solution neglecting, for the time being, longer run adjustments.

Now assume that instead of the waste discharger possessing a legal right to discharge wastes (as has been implicitly assumed), the fisherman has a legal right to use of the stream in its "natural" state. The waste discharger would then have an incentive to pay the fisherman up to the incremental cost of withholding a given unit of waste discharge. Again the same result would tend to follow. In this simple model, regardless of the system of property rights, so long as a definite and secure property right exists, free negotiation between the parties will tend to balance costs and returns at the margin, that is, the gains from trade will tend to be realized.[7] It should be noted, however, that not *all* of the externality is eliminated.[8] The equilibrium level of waste reduction activity leaves some residual damages. The mere presence of an external diseconomy, therefore, cannot be taken as prima facie

[7] One reason, although not the major one (see the following discussion), why private negotiations do not result in optimal water quality is the fact that under the "reasonable use" interpretation of the riparian rights doctrine which dominates eastern water law there is great ambiguity concerning the actual privileges which the "rights" confer.

[8] Buchanan and Stubblebine, *op. cit.*, make a significant distinction between Pareto-relevant and non-Pareto-relevant externalities. At the optimum point only Pareto-relevant externalities will have been eliminated.

evidence that net gains would accrue from its reduction. In other words, a complete prohibition of the use of the waste assimilative capacity of the environment is normally not economically optimal. This is true even when longer-run adjustments are considered.

Although it is possible for market transactions to take externalities into account under certain circumstances, transactions of this kind are rarely organized. The damaging effects of waste discharges may be widespread and diffuse, and the linkages between dischargers and damaged parties are so technically complex, especially in highly developed areas, that establishing a market which would systematically take account of external costs would be a very complex and expensive procedure.[9]

PROPERTY RIGHTS AND LEGAL PROCESSES

Efforts to use litigation to balance costs and returns from water-quality control suffer from the same disabilities as market transactions. After all, it is the structure of property rights and the potential recourse to litigation which makes orderly private exchanges possible. Like bargaining, litigation based on property rights relating to water quality will not produce optimal results when longer-term adjustment involving changes in industrial capacity are considered. But, within the short-run frame of reference, what role can, and should, litigation play in water quality management?

The point was made earlier that there is a close relation between the nature of property rights and the occurrence of external diseconomies. Is it possible to structure property rights in water in such a way that upstream waste dischargers will take appropriate account of downstream costs? In the example used above, the party benefiting from the fish had to pay. Presumably this was the case either because the law specified that the waste discharger had a right to discharge his wastes into the stream regardless of damages caused downstream or because the law specified nothing about such rights and the upstream discharger simply exploited his physically superior position. An alternative possibility, and one more generally consistent with the principles of riparian water law, is that the upstream user is liable for damage downstream.[10]

---

[9] Difficulties for the "market solution" also arise from interaction between damage and cost functions due to "non-separability" in externalities and when damage functions are non-linear and several waste dischargers affect the same water users. Some discussion of these difficulties which also afflict "administrative" solutions is presented in Chapter 6.

[10] "Reasonable use" interpretations of riparian doctrine have considerably altered earlier interpretations which viewed the downstream user as privileged to receive the flow of the stream "undiminished in quanitiy and quality." The court's definition of reasonable use has often involved a balancing of upstream and down-

To reiterate an earlier point, the definition of damages is highly important if efficient behavior is to result from actual or potential damage claims. To repeat part of the earlier example, if an award of 110 were made to the downstream fisherman for fish killed by the upstream waste discharge, costs, in terms of resources used, would be increased by more than the net value of the fish. The upstream firm would be induced to spend up to 110 in treatment, net cost of waste recovery, or in locational disadvantage in order to avoid killing fish with a net value of 10.

Even if the law of property were to be framed so that damages avoided were always "net,"[11] it is unlikely that optimal water quality management programs could emerge from legal remedies.[12] Several major deficiencies of legal remedies are listed below.

1. Adversary proceedings involving private parties are at best a cumbersome procedure, and, if the law is enforced with any degree of precision, delays in deciding cases might themselves cause substantial inefficiencies. Litigation in water cases may be long and drawn-out. To cite but one example, court action in the case of *U.S.* vs. *Fallbrook Public Utility District, et al.,* became final in 1966 after fifteen years.

2. The wide dispersion of damages often associated with waste discharges into either surface or ground waters makes it hard to bring suit for the full damages. Many hundreds or even thousands of recreationists may be damaged. Costs may be imposed on numerous users of surface and/or ground water. Although many of them may have their costs

---

stream use. The court's efforts to "balance equities" in cases of this kind have often involved considerations of upstream and downstream costs. In a general way the "reasonable use" interpretation of riparian right is consistent with the conceptual structure described in this chapter. Significant elements of "prior appropriations doctrine" have also crept into the water law of the riparian states (generally those of the humid East and Midwest). See J. H. Beuscher, "Appropriation Water Law Elements in Riparian Doctrine States," *Buffalo Law Review,* No. 10 (1961).

"Reasonable use" has become an integral component of prior appropriation law as well. For a general discussion relating to this point, see C. O. Fisher, "Waste and Other Problems in Western Law," in Haber and Bergen (ed.), *The Law of Water Allocation in the Eastern United States* (Ronald Press, 1958), pp. 95–118. Reasonableness in relation to water quality deterioration is summarized by A. Moskovitz, "Quality Control and Re-Use of Water in California," in L. O. Graham (ed.), *Conference on Legal Problems in Water Resources* (Committee on Research in Water Resources, University of California, Berkeley, 1957), pp. 18–20.

[11] If resources, including labor, are highly immobile, the net loss (gross loss minus value of resources in alternative uses) may approach the gross loss.

[12] The present discussion continues to be only about situations where no significant economies can be realized through provision of collective facilities for different economic and/or local political units. Where such economies can be realized, legal remedies alone clearly cannot lead to optimal results.

increased only slightly, the aggregate costs may still be large. For example, one study indicated that a concentration of phenols in the Ohio River greater than 0.02 ppm had an adverse effect on the quality of water obtained from wells recharged by induced infiltration from the river.[13]

The wide dispersion of damages aggravates the problems of bringing suit. Organizing action among many damaged parties is both difficult and costly, as in private bargaining. And the extremely high costs for measurements, technical data gathering, and expert testimony prevent most private parties from acting on their own.

3. Waste discharges impose costs in a highly variable fashion over time because both hydrologic events and the time pattern of waste discharges may be quite variable. This means that the most efficient result from an over-all water quality management standpoint can often be achieved by measures which are put to use, or to high levels of use, only at infrequent intervals of varying durations. It would appear to be difficult to frame laws with sufficient flexibility to permit realization of such efficiencies.

4. Damage from waste discharges may be dispersed over a wide area, and in the case of groundwater the effects may be long lasting or even permanent. Once contaminated, a groundwater aquifer can be reclaimed only with great difficulty, if at all. Classic examples are the intrusion of saline water into fresh groundwater aquifers following overpumping, and the contamination of groundwater aquifers by oil spills[14] or by detergents.[15]

5. The previous points limit the efficacy of property law and legal proceedings in moving toward optimal water quality management even where rights are clearly defined. But legal standards applied by the courts are notoriously vague. The words "reasonable" and "substantial" hold sway and the courts attempt to balance "utility of conduct" against "gravity of loss." Accurately forecasting what a court will do under specific circumstances is difficult if not impossible. High uncertainty of

---

[13] M. Noecker *et al.*, "Water Resources of the Pittsburgh Area, Pennsylvania," U.S. Geological Survey Circular 315, 1954, p. 46.

[14] Morris Deutsch cites examples of both in *Ground-Water Contamination and Legal Controls in Michigan* (U.S. Geological Survey Water-Supply Paper 1691, 1963), pp. 57–58 and p. 15, respectively. One of the authors is personally familiar with a case in Bucks County, Pennsylvania, in which a shallow aquifer used for domestic supplies was made unusable for the purpose by a spill from an oil storage facility. It appears that it will never again be possible to use the aquifer for domestic water supply. The case also illustrates the time delay that can be involved in private negotiation, the final agreement having been reached about twenty-five years after the spill occurred.

[15] *Effect of Synthetic Detergents on Ground Water of Long Island, New York* (New York State Water Pollution Control Board, Research Report No. 6, 1960).

outcome plus substantial costs act against the use of courts to control adverse effects on water quality.[16]

6. Finally, and perhaps most fundamental, even if a clear right is given to either the dischargers or the parties damaged by waste discharges and if compensations reflecting the value of the property right can be arranged, longer-term adjustments in the economy will not tend toward optimality. This is because assignment of a property right is made by virtue of participation in a particular kind of economic activity. The right cannot be held independently of the activity; it automatically accrues when the activity is undertaken. That is, the right to the services of water would not be a general one that could be exchanged among all interested parties in a market that would place a price on it and thus tend to make the services available to the most productive user. If waste dischargers must compensate for damages, a party can collect only if he engages in an activity likely to be damaged. If a reduction in waste discharge is to be induced by a damaged party, the payments are made only if a potentially waste discharging activity is undertaken.

Much of the literature concerning externalities, including an earlier book by one of the authors, has asserted that the assignment of property rights with respect to externalities is unimportant so long as they are clearly defined and enforceable. If, however, the right to the use of an asset (or resource) is made contingent upon engaging in a particular activity, and the right to the use of the asset is given free to parties engaging in the activity, excessive activity in that line will be generated.[17] Clearly, long-run efficiency requires that a price be placed on the asset reflecting its value in alternative uses. This could be achieved if a single firm controlled all such uses or if a public agency assigned the price. We return to these possibilities in the next chapter.

This discussion has enabled us to define clearly the nature of ex-

---

[16] See the discussion by P. R. Freeman, "Judicial Expression," in J. E. McKee and H. W. Wolf (ed.), *Water Quality Criteria* (California, State Water Quality Control Board, Publication No. 3-A, 1963), pp. 81–83. Freeman (p. 66) quotes from a decision in *Town of Smithfield* vs. *City of Raleigh*, as follows: "Indeed, it seems that the trial judge subjected the question to 'trial by water', because the record discloses that his Honor 'had drunk of the water, bathed in it, and suffered no ill effects'. The ancient mode of trial by water was aforetime deemed efficacious in determining the guilt or innocence of witches and by applying the practice of the ancient law the distinguished jurist has found the waters of the Neuse River not guilty. . . ."

Freeman states elsewhere in his discussion (p. 87), that there has been a decided trend toward more scientific methods for assessing damages, since the above procedure was recorded in 1935.

[17] For a fuller discussion of this point, see J. Hayden Boyd, "The Problem of External Diseconomies" (Doctoral dissertation, University of Minnesota, Economics Department, 1967). Boyd was, so far as we know, the first to make this point.

ternalities, their relationship to property concepts, and the limitations of private bargaining and litigation for dealing with externalities. The general conclusion is that efficient water quality management cannot be achieved through the courts.

POSSIBLE ROLE OF THE JUDICIAL PROCESS

Despite the above limitations, the judicial process, if properly structured, might play a useful and even essential supplementary role.[18] First, in some instances it could provide a recourse for damaged parties who feel their interests have not been appropriately taken into account by a management agency. However, this role may be quite limited, since it appears that the concept of private rights being subject to the sovereign servitude of the public applies to such cases. Under these circumstances, the suggestion for the establishment of an "ombudsman," noted below, is particularly relevant. Second, the judicial process might provide some relief from damages caused by waste discharges where there is no competent management agency. Finally, the court is a necessary means by which a water quality management agency can enforce its directives, if necessary.

A Committee on Pollution Control of the National Academy of Sciences published some useful recommendations for strengthening the role of the judicial process in connection with water quality problems.[19]

First, borrow from Swedish practice and appoint an ombudsman— a public official who would intervene with public agencies on behalf of private complainants. His authority might include bringing suit, at his discretion and at public expense, on behalf of private complainants. Presumably this authority would include situations involving federal agencies. Or action might be mandatory when a specified number of persons request intervention and show that they are adversely affected by water quality degradation or waste discharges.

Second, designate one or more courts in each state to hear all cases dealing with water, so as to develop specialized judges and thus lessen the problems of interpretation of technical data and proof. The court in the county in which the state's water quality agencies are located seems a sensible choice for this function.

Third, pass legislation to remove the requirement that "special damage" be proven in so-called public nuisance pollution cases brought by private individuals. Suppose A's waste discharge destroys the public recreational fishing in a river. It also destroys B's commercial fishing.

---

[18] To date there is very little case law involving private parties vs. public agencies in water quality management situations. See Freeman, *op. cit.*, pp. 65–87.

[19] *Waste Management and Control*, a report to the Federal Council for Science and Technology (Washington: National Academy of Sciences, National Research Council, Publication 1400, 1966). See especially App. 7.

B has sustained special damages that other members of the public have not. This special damage rule has roots deep in history. Courts are concerned lest they be flooded with claims. But the rule has been strongly criticized.

Finally, authorize the courts to appoint water quality management or over-all water resources management agencies as "masters in Chancery" to aid the court in the technical aspects of cases. An alternative is to permit the management agency to decide cases among contending parties, i.e., administrative law, as is the situation with respect to water rights (dealing with quantity) in some areas. Wolman described the operation of administrative water law in British Columbia in these terms:

> The fundamental principles upon which this system is founded are that water in the streams is a public asset and that no prescriptive or riparian right should be permitted to interfere with its beneficial use. Its law has been tested in the courts and has stood the test of time. It is interesting that no legal action over water rights has occurred in the province for nearly the last 30 years, a record which alone should call the attention of this form of legislation to the interested water practitioner.[20]

While potentially valuable, these changes in law and judicial procedure could not be expected to yield optimal water quality management. History and reason suggest that even where opportunities for influencing water quality in streams are limited to control at individual points of waste discharge—the assumption underlying this part of the book—a regional or river basin management agency must assume the central responsibility. In the next section of this chapter, we introduce a conceptual structure which may be helpful in understanding the functioning of such an agency.

"INTERNALIZING" THE EXTERNALITIES: THE BASIN-WIDE FIRM

The suggestion has sometimes been advanced that, since technological externalities permit higher aggregate profits when production processes are jointly planned and operated, mergers will take place or groups will be formed until a "natural" decision unit is established.[21] However, with

---

[20] Abel Wolman, "Utilization of Surface, Underground, and Sea Water," in *United Nations Special Conference on the Conservation and Utilization of Resources* (1951), p. 100.

[21] The problem of how the size of the firm (the basic production decision unit in a market economy) is determined has been frequently discussed in the economic literature. One line of discussion has concerned itself with diseconomies of scale for the production of a single product. Another has addressed the question of how the number of products entering into the output of a firm is established. See R. H. Coase, "The Nature of the Firm," *Economica*, Vol. IV (1937). George Stigler has stated that technically related production functions may be one motiva-

respect to water quality in a highly developed basin, the technical ties between, say, any given pair of production processes or production and consumption processes located at different points will probably be comparatively weak despite the fact that in total the external diseconomies are large. The planning and operation of spatially separate and technologically diverse production processes pose complexities for management and therefore are not costless. Consequently, externalities would tend not to be fully internalized even though aggregate profit could be increased in this way *if* integration were costless.

The term "natural decision unit" is deceptively simple, since different decision units are "natural" for different processes. Thus the term "optimum" decision unit would seem to be preferable to "natural" decision unit. The natural decision unit idea has probably gained impetus from the fact that discussion has frequently been in terms of two decision units strongly connected by technological ties but otherwise operating in an environment free of externalities. Moreover, the internalization of externalities into a private decision-making unit for an entire basin would most probably result in changes in market structure (monopolization) contrary to social policy and inconsistent with efficient production because of its market power.

Nevertheless some clarification of concepts may be gained by considering a simple, hypothetical case in which the externalities are internalized in a firm even though in actuality this cannot be considered either a feasible or a desirable solution. Assume that a single firm with two plants is the sole commercial user of a stream which is also valuable for sport fishing. Suppose also that the firm controls access to the stream and can levy charges for recreation use, and that it buys all its inputs and sells all its other outputs in competitive markets.[22]

If this firm attempts to maximize its profits, which under our assumption is the same as maximizing net social return, how will it manage its water utilization? If it operates two plants on the same stream, the firm will have an incentive to take into account the effects of upstream activities on the downstream plant. Negative downstream effects, termed damage costs, are emphasized in this book, but favorable effects are not impossible. If, for example, the upstream plant A uses large quanti-

---

tion for merger. See *Production and Distribution Theories* (Macmillan, 1946). A recent suggestion that externalities give rise to "natural" decision units which "internalize" them is found in O. A. Davis and A. Whinston, "Externalities, Welfare, and the Theory of Games," *Journal of Political Economy* (June 1962), pp. 241 ff.

[22] These restrictions will be meaningful to economists but need not detain other readers. Briefly the reason for them is to assure that marginal revenue equals price for all outputs and that the marginal cost of acquiring factors equals their price or wage.

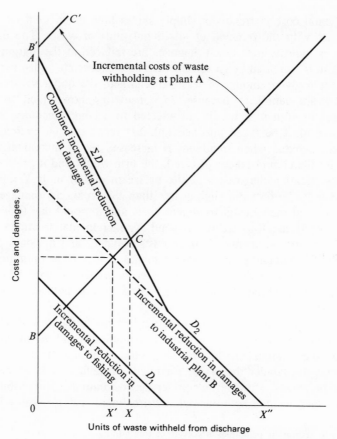

Figure 13.

ties of water for cooling and its effluent consequently warms the stream, the downstream plant may benefit if its processes require warm water.

Presume, however, that plant A produces a nondegradable waste which is toxic to fish and damaging to plant B in direct proportion to its concentration.[23] For simplicity, assume initially that the only quality control procedure available at plant A is *effluent treatment*. The considerations entering into the profit-maximizing behavior of the firm are portrayed by the curves in Figure 13. At point X the firm will be discharging the amount of waste which under the stated conditions is optimum.

A word of explanation is in order about the pictured functions. The

---

[23] For purposes of the present example it is assumed that plant B does not produce a waste discharge. Some of the complexities that might result if it did are discussed subsequently.

incremental cost of treatment simply shows how much total treatment costs rise with the removal of additional units of waste. The damage functions indicate how much damages are reduced at the margin when treatment is increased by an increment. The damages are added vertically (i.e., for a given amount of waste discharged, the dollar values of D_1 and D_2 are summed) because, in considering how much to treat, damages to both uses which are affected in a complementary way by treatment must be taken into account. ΣD represents the increment in damages avoided when treatment is increased by an increment.[24]

Under the circumstances pictured, the firm would find it profitable to continue treating the wastes at the upstream outfall until X units are removed. If the firm did slightly less than this, marginal damage costs would exceed incremental treatment costs and it would pay to increase treatment. If the firm treated beyond X, incremental treatment costs would exceed incremental damage costs avoided, and it would pay to reduce treatment and permit higher damages. X is thus the optimum level of water quality in the sense that the costs associated with waste disposal are at a minimum there. These costs include both *damage costs* and *treatment costs*.[25]

Alternatively, one can say that the net benefits to the firm of reducing its upstream waste discharge are at a maximum at this level of removal. As previously indicated, this is a fully equivalent statement if we term the damages avoided by waste treatment "benefits" and the costs of treatment "costs." However, we prefer the cost minimization terminology (where costs include both damage and treatment costs), because it calls

---

[24] A discussion of principles involved in this adding-together approach may be found in G. S. Tolley and V. S. Hastings, "Optimal Water Allocations, The North Platte River," *Quarterly Journal of Economics* (May 1960). A much earlier discussion is found in H. R. Bowen, *Toward Social Economy* (Rinehart, 1948), pp. 176–79.

[25] The results indicated above can also be stated in terms of the differential calculus. The firm confronts two damage functions D_1 and D_2 and a treatment cost function TC. The following conditions hold:

$$D_1 = f_1(R) \quad f_1^1 < 0,$$
$$D_2 = f_2(R) \quad f_2^1 < 0,$$
$$TC = f_3(R) \quad f_3^1 > 0.$$

The objective (objective function) is to minimize

$$Z = D_1 + D_2 + TC = f_1(R) + f_2(R) + f_3(R),$$

which will be the case when

$$\frac{dZ}{dR} = f_1^1(R) + f_2^1(R) + f_3^1(R) = 0,$$

if

$$\frac{d^2Z}{dR^2} > 0.$$

attention to the fact that water quality management is primarily a matter of avoiding costs. More importantly, the terminology is convenient at later points when water quality "standards" are discussed.

If the firm did not have authority to charge for fishing, it would have no incentive to consider the value of fishing in its decisions and would withhold only X' units of waste. The result would be an under-allocation of resources to waste discharge control.

One other possibility should be mentioned here. If incremental costs of waste treatment were as high as shown by the function $B'C'$, the firm would undertake no waste reduction effort because incremental costs would exceed the incremental reduction in damages. This is a case where it is simply less costly to endure water quality deterioration than to do anything about it.

If the firm had other ways of reducing its waste load, the principles would be the same. Say, for example, that plant A could, in addition to treating wastes, introduce process adjustments or reduce its output. In order to minimize costs associated with waste disposal, the firm would have to "trade off" between alternatives until their incremental or marginal costs are equated (i.e., $MC_A = MC_B = \cdots = MC_N = MC$ of pollution damages.)[26] Certain complexities occur when we introduce

---

[26] Let the output of waste reduction be a function of the level of use of a number of alternative inputs and let X_1 indicate the quantity of input of an alternative x_1. We can then write a production function

$$Q = f(X_1, X_2, \ldots, X_n).$$

Given any quantity of waste reduction Q^*, the firm will try to produce it as cheaply as it can. This means it is trying to minimize its costs M (in the sense of foregone net revenues as well as outlays) on the inputs used to produce Q^*, where the cost is given by

$$M = P_1X_1 + P_2X_2 + \ldots + P_nX_n,$$

where P_1 is the cost per unit of input 1, etc. The firm is constrained in minimizing M by the production function indicate above.
This constraint can be written in the form:

$$f(X_1, X_2, \ldots, X_n) - Q^* = 0.$$

This expression is multiplied by the artificial variable λ and added to the expression M (which is to be minimized) to obtain the Lagrangian expression:

$$M_\lambda = P_1X_1 + P_2X_2 + \ldots + P_nX_n + \lambda[f(X_1, X_2, \ldots, X_n) - Q^*].$$

This expression is minimized in the standard way by setting each of its partial derivatives to zero:

$$\frac{\delta M_\lambda}{\delta X_1} = P_1 + \lambda \frac{\delta f}{\delta X_1} = 0,$$

$$\frac{\delta M_\lambda}{\delta X_2} = P_2 + \lambda \frac{\delta f}{\delta X_2} = 0,$$

$$\cdots \cdots \cdots \cdots \cdots \cdots \cdots$$

$$\frac{\delta M_\lambda}{\delta X_n} = P_n + \lambda \frac{\delta f}{X_n} = 0,$$

$$\frac{\delta M_\lambda}{\lambda} = f(X_1, X_2, \ldots, X_n) - Q^* = 0.$$

(continued)

hydrologic variability and waste degradation in the stream, but the basic principles remain the same.

One other item should be noted here. The relevant cost of waste disposal associated with the activity producing the waste is the cost of waste reduction *plus* the total residual damage costs—i.e., it includes the area XCX'' as well as the area $OBCX$ in Figure 13. The basin-wide firm must bear this over-all cost and consider the profitability of continuing the waste-generating activity in light of this over-all cost. This will be particularly relevant to its long-range investment decisions.

SEPARABLE AND NON-SEPARABLE DAMAGE FUNCTIONS

We now introduce some different types of damage functions, and temporarily drop the assumption that the wastes are nondegradable. The assumed form of the damage function associated with the degradable waste will cause no problems for optimization to the basin-wide firm. But in the next chapter we shall see that a basin-wide agency attempting to use indirect control measures—effluent charges or standards—will find that certain types of damage functions may present it with a severe problem.

The first case is where damage functions are *linear* and therefore *separable*. Assume there are two waste discharges located along a stream and that they both discharge a degradable waste.[27] Assume further that

---

This set of $n + 1$ simultaneous equations can be solved for the optimal values of the n inputs $X_1, X_2, \ldots, X_n$ and the Lagrangian multiplier λ.

The optimization rule indicated above can be readily derived from these equations. If we write the first two equations as:

$$P_1 = -\lambda \frac{\delta f}{\delta X_1}, \quad \text{and} \quad P_2 = -\lambda \frac{\delta f}{\delta X_2},$$

and divide one equation by the other, we get

$$\frac{P_1}{P_2} = \frac{\dfrac{\delta f}{\delta X_1}}{\dfrac{\delta f}{\delta X_2}}.$$

Since $\delta f/\delta X_1$ is equal to the marginal (physical) product of X_1 and likewise $\delta f/\delta X_2$ is the marginal product of X_2, we can write

$$\frac{P_1}{P_2} = \frac{MP_1}{MP_2},$$

which is our optimizing rule. When this rule holds for all input combinations, it also follows immediately that the cost of increasing output by a small increment by means of one input is equal to the marginal cost of increasing it by the same increment by using more of any other input, or $P_1/MP_1 = P_2/MP_2$. In the text, this is the rule for minimizing costs. In order to minimize costs associated with waste disposal in a basin, the marginal cost of all relevant alternatives must be equalized.

[27] This example is developed in J. C. Liebman, *The Optimal Allocation of Stream Dissolved Oxygen Resources* (Cornell University Water Resources Center, 1965), p. 41 ff.

the damages which result from the biochemical oxygen demand of the discharges can be expressed as a simple multiple of the area under the dissolved oxygen deficit curve from the first plant to a distance T days downstream; that is:

$$C = K \int_0^T Ddt,$$

where C is the damage, K is a constant, and D is the D.O. deficit at any point.[28] Writing D as a function of $L_1 + L_2$ (the amount of BOD discharged at plant 1 and plant 2, respectively) and D_a (the initial deficit), and performing the integration gives an expression of the form

$$C = K(K_1L_1 + K_2L_2 + K_3D_a),$$

where K_1, K_2, and K_3 are functions of the parameters of the Streeter-Phelps equations (see Chapter 2). It follows that the damage due to the first discharge is KK_1L_1 and independent of the level of the second discharge or the initial deficit; and the damage due to the second discharge is KK_2L_2, which is independent of the level of the first discharge and the initial deficit.

The second case consists of damage functions in which this type of independence does not exist. If the damage functions are nonlinear, that is, if the damage from an additional part per million of deficit is larger (or smaller) than the damage from the preceding part per million of deficit, damages attributable to individual waste discharges are no longer independent.

Assume, for example, that damage is a multiple of the integral of the squared deficit:

$$C = K \int_0^T D^2dt.$$

Then, integration yields an expression of the form

$$C = K(K_1L_1^2 + K_2L_2^2 + K_3L_1L_2 + K_4L_1D_a + K_5L_2D_a + K_6D_a^2).$$

In this equation, the damages attributable to the first discharge are made up of the first, third, and fourth terms. The third term depends upon the level of the second discharge, and therefore the first firm cannot minimize its cost without knowing the decisions which have been reached by the second firm. The basin-wide firm would not be bothered by such a damage function because it would have no difficulty adding its treatment cost functions to this expression and minimizing the resulting total costs. Inseparability poses no problem because the firm

[28] Notation relating to the oxygen sag is explained in the Appendix to Chapter 2.

internalizes the externalities associated with waste discharges and is indifferent to the distribution of costs among its individual plants so long as the over-all result is profit maximization.

The agency attempting to produce the same result by means of indirect controls—the more realistic case—may, however, find itself in considerable difficulty due to inseparability in situations where more than one waste discharge is involved. This matter is explored in the next chapter.

Causing Offsite Costs to Be
Reflected in Waste Disposal Decisions

6

Under a free market economy municipalities and private firms can escape certain costs associated with waste disposal by passing the problem along to other parties, and may find it to their economic advantage to do so. The ultimate costs throughout a whole watershed are not reduced—in fact, they are increased if offsite costs exceed the costs of reducing waste discharges—but they are borne by someone other than the dischargers. As we have already seen, the incentive to neglect offsite costs would disappear if a single competitive firm managed all phases of water supply and use throughout an entire basin, and if there were no public goods involved, because the external diseconomies would then become internal. The basin-wide firm idea, though useful for illuminating the character and role of external diseconomies, is not a satisfactory solution. Public intervention, however, can cause offsite costs to be reflected in the waste disposal decisions of individual firms and of local government units, and is needed for optimal resources allocation.

Some possible means of public intervention—effluent charges, incentive payments, and enforcement of quality standards—are considered in this chapter from the economic viewpoint. Discussion of political and administrative details of just what kind of organization might do the intervening, and by what means, is reserved for Part IV.

In areas of considerable urban and industrial development the offsite costs associated with unregulated waste discharge are likely to be great enough to justify public regulation, despite the costs and distortions which may be entailed in the regulation itself.[1] Here the focus is on the economic aspects of dealing with the external costs of waste discharge, and the assumption is made that regulatory public agencies exist and

[1] As judged in terms of the criteria of economic welfare theory. See James M. Buchanan, "Politics, Policy and the Pigovian Margin," *Economica*, Vol. 29 (February 1962).

that they have sufficient geographical scope to internalize the major external costs associated with waste discharge in their areas. It is also assumed that the objective of these agencies, generally referred to as "river basin authorities," is to obtain the maximum net benefit from the water resources.

How can the basin authority induce the individual municipality or industry to consider offsite costs in its decisions involving waste generation, treatment, and discharge? This question is discussed, first, in terms of the method to be used. Emphasis is placed on a device whereby the basin authority would levy charges on effluents discharged. The alternative possibility of framing a system of payments for waste discharge reduction to achieve optimum water quality is also explored.

Attention is then directed to the variety of considerations involved in actually determining the costs associated with a given waste discharge. How can the effects of hydrologic variability be reflected in a system of effluent charges? Can the value of recreational, aesthetic, and public health uses be measured? In Chapter 7 we address the question: How can the effluent charges system be applied when a receiving water quality standard is imposed to reflect a value which cannot be measured explicitly? Also in Chapter 7 systems of effluent charges or payments are compared with the traditional regulation device—effluent standards.

ECONOMIC INCENTIVES FOR
REDUCING WASTE DISCHARGE

Charges

Economists have long held that technological spillovers can be counteracted by levying a tax on the unit responsible for the diseconomy and by paying a subsidy to the damaged party. Some have even demonstrated that under certain conditions the appropriate tax is just large enough to pay the appropriate subsidy.[2] This idea makes a good bit of sense when one views the uneconomic effects of spillovers as resulting basically from a maldistribution of costs. However, in the case of waste loads, and from the point of view of resources allocation, it is not necessary both to levy a tax and pay a subsidy if the waste discharger and the damaged party do not themselves bargain about the externality. In principle, either a charge on effluents or a payment to reduce discharge will serve to induce the combination of measures that will minimize the costs associated with waste disposal in a region. But if bargaining takes place, a unilateral fee or subsidy will not produce an efficient result. To see this, assume that a public authority is created and directed

---

[2] James E. Meade, "External Economies and Diseconomies in a Competitive Situation," *Economic Journal,* March 1952.

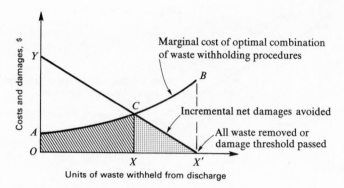

Figure 14.

to impose the cost of incremental damages upon the waste discharger. In other words, the authority endeavors to compute the relevant portion of a function like YX' in Figure 14 and to confront the waste discharger with it. The horizontal axis measures units of waste withheld from discharge by the waste discharger and the YX' function indicates the incremental effluent charge which the waste disposer must pay for every unit of residual waste discharged.

If damages are properly determined and assessed, does optimization require that the loss to the "damaged" party be compensated? If the authority were in fact to levy a charge equal to the damages associated with each increment of waste discharge, it would collect just enough in tolls to cover the residual damages (area XCX').[3]

From the viewpoint of efficiency (as contrasted with equity) compensation must be paid if the parties can and do negotiate. Otherwise, optimal resource allocation will be prevented both in the short run and the long run, because the level of waste reduction that minimizes the sum of party 1's cost for waste reduction plus party 2's residual damages does not necessarily minimize party 1's cost plus party 1's charge plus party 2's damage. Consequently, a schedule of charges equal to marginal damages imposed and not used to pay compensation will not eliminate what have been termed "Pareto-relevant" externalities at the optimum level of waste reduction, i.e., from the viewpoint of the parties further gains from trade are possible.[4] Figure 15 illustrates the reasoning involved.

---

[3] If, on the other hand, a single charge were imposed at a level which would cause incremental damage and reduction costs to be equated, the authority would collect more than the residual damages unless the total damage cost function were linear (i.e., resulting in a flat YX'). The excess is basically an economic rent. More will be said about this later.

[4] A particularly clear exposition of this point as it relates to externalities generally is found in Ralph Turvey, "On Divergencies Between Social Cost and Private Cost," *Economica*, Vol. 30 (August 1963).

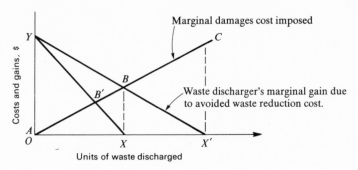

Figure 15.

Increments to waste discharge are measured along the *x*-axis rather than, as in Figure 14, reductions in waste discharge. Function *AC* indicates the incremental damage costs imposed and *YX'* indicates the marginal gain to the waste discharger due to not having to reduce his waste discharge (say by treatment). If the marginal cost of offsite damages is levied upon the waste discharger, his net gain becomes function *YX*. At the optimum point *X*, his marginal gains are cancelled by the marginal damages imposed so that his net gain is zero. This is another way of saying that *X* is the optimum point. Acting by himself, if marginal offsite damage costs are imposed upon him, the waste discharger would tend to move to this point. As noted in the previous chapter, an external effect continues to exist at the optimum point. This simply indicates that the benefit to the discharger from not reducing the waste load further is greater than the damage imposed on other parties.

Unless, however, the damaged party is compensated so that he experiences no damage costs at the rate of discharge indicated by point *X*, he will be willing to pay the waste discharger to reduce his waste discharge further to the point where the discharger's marginal net gain equals the marginal damage imposed. This is indicated by point *B'* in Figure 15. On the other hand, if he is compensated and his compensation is contingent on engaging in the pollution damaged activity, this will tend, as we saw in the previous chapter, to lead to inefficient longer-term adjustments.

If the parties can not or do not negotiate, the social optimum can be attained by taxing the waste discharger and not compensating the damaged party. We therefore conclude that achievement of an optimum by means of effluent charges would not in general involve compensation of parties adversely affected by waste discharges. In the remainder of the book we assume that the parties involved cannot negotiate with each other and that no compensation is paid.

The discussion up to this point has been conducted in terms of effluent charges representing incremental offsite or external costs imposed. It is not difficult to demonstrate that, *in principle*, the same result could be achieved by making payments for the reduction of waste discharge— even under conditions where longer-run adjustments such as plant location and process change are involved. The distribution of income would of course be different under the two arrangements.

Payments

We believe that a system of payments, or "bribes" as they have recently been termed in the literature, could in principle achieve the same result as an optimal charges scheme, despite some recent statements to the contrary.[5]

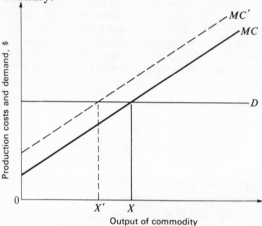

Figure 16.

Assume that a profit-maximizing firm has an incremental production cost curve as indicated by *MC* in Figure 16, that the price at which the firm can sell the commodity it produces is given, as indicated by the curve *D*, that the *only* way the firm can diminish the amount of a residual substance which it discharges into a stream is to reduce production, and that residual waste per unit of output is a constant. If a regulatory authority imposes a unit charge on the effluent of the firm, the incremental production cost function will shift upward by the amount of the charge per unit of output (i.e., charge per unit of effluent times effluent per unit of output) from *MC to MC'*.

[5] See D. F. Bramhall and E. S. Mills, "A Note on the Asymmetry Between Fees and Payments," *Water Resources Research* (Third Quarter 1966), pp. 615–16; M. J. Kamien, N. L. Schwartz, and F. T. Dolbear, Jr., "Asymmetry Between Bribes and Charges," *Water Resources Research* (First Quarter 1966), pp. 147–57; and A. Myrick Freeman III, "Bribes and Charges: Some Comments," *Water Resources Research* (First Quarter 1967), pp. 287–98. See also F. T. Dolbear, Jr. "On the Theory of Optimum Externality," *American Economic Review* (March 1967).

On the other hand, if the regulatory authority offers to pay the same amount per unit for reducing waste discharge, the incremental cost function will still be *MC'*. A firm rationally trying to maximize its profits will view the payment as an opportunity cost of production because waste discharge is, by assumption, a straightforward function of production. This proposition can perhaps be clarified by the numerical example below:

Output of product	Total cost of production	Incremental cost of production	Effluent charge on waste discharge per unit of production	Payment for reduction of waste discharge per unit of production	Minimum product price necessary to induce indicated no. of units of production with charge or payment
0	10	. . .	. . .	. . .	$. . .
1	11	1	1	1	2
2	13	2	1	1	3
3	16	3	1	1	4
4	20	4	1	1	5
5	25	5	1	1	6

If, for example, the incremental cost of producing the fifth unit (neglecting the cost of waste discharge) is $5.00, and a public authority stands ready to pay $1.00 if the manufacturer does not discharge the waste associated with that unit, he will produce that unit only if the price is at least $6.00. If the price were less than $6.00, his *net* income would be higher if he simply accepted the $1.00 payment. The $1.00 payment thus becomes an *opportunity cost* even though it is not a direct outlay. The point is that in the sense of *opportunity* cost, which is the relevant concept of cost for decision purposes, the two procedures have entirely the same effect on incremental costs.[6]

The question may well be raised whether in terms of longer-term adjustments, i.e., a firm's decision to enter or leave an industry or to expand or contract production capacity, the effect may not be different. The answer is in principle "no," but great informational and administrative difficulties emerge if the payments route is adopted. These are discussed later.

In Figure 17, *AC* indicates the long-run average cost curve of a plant. This curve indicates the average costs of producing various levels of output (including an average return on investment) under conditions where a plant can be designed to produce a given output at least over-all

---

[6] For a mathematical development of this point, see Kamien *et al.*, *op. cit.*

cost. If the price is as indicated by D, the firm would construct a plant for which costs were lowest at output level X. This is the relationship which would tend to prevail in equilibrium in a competitive industry. A charge on effluent per unit would raise the average cost function by the same amount for each unit of output. Consequently, the new average cost curve would be a simple vertical displacement of the old, as shown by AC'. A payment would have the same effect because it is an opportunity cost. The price of output must be high enough to cover the amount of the available payment as well as costs of production (including a normal return on investment), if it is to be worthwhile for the firm to produce an additional unit. In effect, the plant's cost curve (reflecting the value of all foregone opportunities if production is carried on) is raised by the amount of the payment if the payment is available to it whether it is producing or not.

Assume that all plants in the industry are initially earning no "excess" return (i.e., they are earning only the minimum necessary to keep their resources employed in the industry). Assume further that they have their cost curves raised by a charge or payment by the amount indicated in Figure 17. The new long-term equilibrium adjustment would then find the industry price higher by the amount of the subsidy or the payment, fewer firms in the industry, and fewer resources devoted to producing the output of the industry. All this would reflect the fact that costs imposed elsewhere in the system, and previously neglected by management, have been internalized to individual firms.

A system of charges or payments reflecting downstream costs would, however, probably not raise the opportunity costs of all firms by the same amount. Under these circumstances—and assuming costs were otherwise the same—the plants inducing the highest offsite costs would be selectively shut down. Plants making an "excess" return, would not be shut down, but their output would be reduced, and prices would tend to rise to reflect the opportunity cost of production.

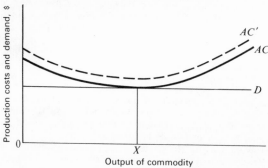

Figure 17.

The effects of waste disposal costs on prices, location, and decisions to enter or leave an industry will usually be small, because these costs are generally quite low relative to other costs of production and because the firm has the option of treating or otherwise modifying final waste output.

Decisions on location and/or industry entry or exit, however, have a major effect on the administration of a system of payments. Payment must be continued after shutdown of a plant, if the procedure is to have the desired results. While this might be manageable, serious problems would occur if a shift in demand for the product should increase the potential profitability of the plant, or if other dynamic adjustments should take place.[7] Moreover, plants might introduce processes that produce a greater quantity of waste in order to obtain payment for reducing waste.

Even more perplexing would be the handling of proposals for new industrial locations. The administrative authority would have to stand ready to make payments to industrial plants which never do locate in the area but which would do so if a payment reflecting the costs their effluents would impose were not made.[8] Payments on this basis would of course be an open invitation to extortion. If charges were levied, however, the authority would only have to provide the prospective firm with an estimate of the unit charge to be placed on its effluent.[9]

To recapitulate, the basic point about the payments-charges contro-

---

[7] Major administrative and informational problems arise in both the short and long run if cost and revenue functions of the waste discharging firm shift. In general, the reason is that there is no "natural origin" for the bribe payment. In the charges case the basin agency simply collects for every unit of waste discharge which causes external cost. The authority need not and does not concern itself with how much would have been discharged by an industrial firm in the absence of the charge. In the case of a bribe, however, a total amount of payment to the firm is involved which is contingent upon the amount the firm would have discharged in the absence of the bribe—the dotted area in Figure 14. In order to determine this quantity when cost or revenue functions shift, thus altering the privately optimum level of production of the firm and associated waste discharge, the authority must have full knowledge of the firm's altered cost and revenue functions. For a rigorous development of this point, see the excellent article by Kamien et al., op. cit. See also the following discussion, "Asymmetry Between Bribes and Charges: A Comment," by Gordon Tullock and "Asymmetry Between Bribes and Charges: Reply," by Kamien et al., Water Resources Research (Fourth Quarter 1966), pp. 854–57.

For a municipality, this problem is not so severe because the amount of waste discharge without treatment would be closely related to the sewered population, although it must be remembered that sizable amounts of industrial wastes are discharged to many municipal waste handling systems.

[8] This is to avoid making the payment contingent on actually engaging in the activity—an arrangement which, we have already seen, would lead to inefficiency.

[9] This procedure is followed by many municipalities that levy charges on industrial wastes discharged to their waste-handling systems.

versy is that only the payments scheme requires information about a "status quo" point or rate of discharge. Obtaining such information would be difficult; if industries enter or leave, it might be impossible. Moreover, the payments technique would make it easy for the unscrupulous operator to benefit by exaggerating his potential waste load.

Thus far, it has been assumed, for the sake of simplicity, that the only way in which waste loads can be reduced is by decreasing production. Waste loads can, of course, be reduced by other means including industrial process changes, materials recovery, by-product production, and treatment. That a payment per unit reduction of waste load will produce the same balance between production cutback and treatment (or other methods) as a charge of equivalent amount can be conveniently shown by means of an isoquant diagram (Figure 18). The isoquants CC' and KK' indicate along their lengths a constant amount of waste reduction (say, pounds of BOD) which can be achieved by alternative combinations of treatment or production decrease.

The lines AA' and BB' indicate the number of units of treatment capacity and reduction in output that can be purchased at equal cost. In principal they could relate to any combinations of alternatives. In many industries, internal process adjustments will be economical substitutes for external treatment. If more than two alternatives are involved, diagrammatic presentation becomes cumbersome if not impossible, and mathematics must be used. Such an exposition is contained in footnote 26, Chapter 5.

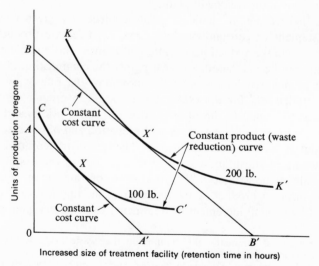

Figure 18.

Point A' in Figure 18 is established by spending all of a given amount of funds on increasing waste treatment. Point A shows the number of units of production which can be foregone at the expense of an amount of net revenue equivalent to the outlay necessary to reach A' (disregarding waste disposal costs). The line AA' represents all the alternative combinations of production foregone and outlay for increased treatment which can be obtained at the same cost. The line BB' represents a similar set of alternatives for a higher cost level. For simplicity these functions are pictured as straight lines although this is not essential to derive the optimization criteria outlined below. An infinite number of curves like AA' and BB' corresponding to all possible levels of cost could be drawn.

Expenditure on treatment and loss of revenue on foregone production of incremental units may be in the interest of the firm either to avoid a charge on effluent or to obtain a payment for reducing discharge. A central point is that for any level of cost (outlay or foregone revenue) the firm will seek that combination of measures which will achieve the greatest reduction in waste discharge. That combination is attained for the cost level BB' at point X' where the constant cost curve is tangent to the constant product curve KK'.

An infinite number of curves like KK' and CC' could also be drawn corresponding to each level of waste reduction. The convex-to-the-origin slope of these curves indicates a diminishing marginal rate of substitution between the two alternatives. As treatment capacity is expanded, it substitutes less well for output reduction. Another way of saying this is that there are diminishing physical returns to increased retention time in the treatment plant.[10]

Points like X and X' indicate greatest effect at a given cost as no higher isoquant or constant product curve (in this case product refers to waste discharge reduction) is attainable given the combinations of input that can be purchased. At such points the combination of the two alternatives pictured is economically optimum—the rate at which one can be "traded off" for the other at the margin in order to produce a given output is equal to the ratio of their respective prices, and we can conveniently refer to the cost of output reduction and of increased treatment input as their respective "prices." The rate of tradeoff or marginal technical rate of substitution is equal to the slope of the isoquant. It is also readily demonstrable[11] that the slope of this curve equals the marginal physical product of treatment (i.e., the physical output result produced by a small increment of treatment) over the marginal physical

---

[10] For reasons of symmetry, the assumption that waste loads decline linearly with reduction in output is retained.

[11] See William Baumol, *Economic Theory and Operations Analysis* (Prentice Hall, 1965).

output reduction. Since the slope of the price line (like AA') equals the ratio of the prices of the two alternatives we can write the following optimizing rule:

$$\frac{P_T}{MPP_T} = \frac{P_O}{MPP_O}.$$

A marginal cost function analogous to the one pictured in Figure 16 but relating the marginal cost of an optimum combination of waste reduction measures to the degree of waste reduction achieved can readily be constructed from the information contained in an isoquant diagram by establishing numerous points such as X and reading off corresponding costs and outputs. The optimal waste reduction level can then be established by equating the marginal cost of the optimum combination of output reduction and treatment (or other methods) with the charge or payment representing the downstream incremental cost. When this condition exists the marginal costs of all relevant alternatives (including treatment, process change, output reduction, and pollution damages) are equated and the level of waste production and treatment is optimized. The major point here is that since the costs of alternatives are evaluated equivalently under the charges and payments procedures, both the combination and level of use of alternatives will be the same.

In actuality, lines like AA' and BB' would frequently be curved. They would probably be convex to the origin, since with rising marginal costs the cost per unit of reducing output would tend to rise. (There is an important distinction here between a rising price and rising incremental costs.) Straight lines (given P's) were assumed in order to simplify the derivation of the optimizing rules, and the demonstration that effluent charges and payments for waste reduction lead to the same optimizing rules. Conclusions with respect to charges and payments remain the same even if equal cost lines like AA' curve, provided certain constraints on their curvature are met.[12]

The basic and quite reasonable rule remains that in order to minimize costs the marginal costs of all relevant ways of achieving a given result must be equalized. Moreover, the result will be the same whether the cost is an actual outlay or the foregone opportunity to receive a payment.

This section has illustrated that, under idealized conditions, payments and charges serve equally well to achieve optimal amounts of waste discharge reduction for both the short-run or the long-run situation and for multiple alternatives to reduce waste as well as for output reduction.

---

[12] For an example of the application of isoquant analysis to a design problem where the equal cost lines curve, see Maynard M. Hufschmidt, "Application of Basic Concepts: Graphic Techniques," in Maass *et al.*, *Design of Water Resource Systems* (Harvard University Press, 1962).

Table 5. Simple Illustration of Damage Distribution

Plant no. (serially located along stream)	Chloride load discharged (1,000 lb. per day)	Chloride load at plant intake (1,000 lb. per day)	Flow Condition I				Flow Condition II			
			Streamflow (mill. gpd)	Chloride concentration (1,000 lb. per mill. gpd)	Damage per day ($1,000)	Total damage per day ($1,000)	Streamflow (mill. gpd)	Chloride concentration (1,000 lb. per mill. gpd)	Damage per day ($1,000)	Total damage per day ($1,000)
1	1.0									
2	0.5	1.0	1.0	1.0	1.00	1.00	0.5	2.0	2.00	2.00
3	1.5	1.5	1.0	1.5	3.00	4.00	0.5	3.0	6.00	8.00
4	1.0	3.0	2.0	1.5	3.00	7.00	1.0	3.0	6.00	14.00
5	0.5	4.0	2.0	2.0	1.00	8.00	1.0	4.0	2.00	16.00

Flow Condition I

Damages caused at	Damage caused by:				Sum of damages caused to
	Plant 1	Plant 2	Plant 3	Plant 4	
	(——————————————— $1,000 ———————————————)				
Plant 1	0.00	0.00	0.00	0.00	0.00
Plant 2	1.00	0.00	0.00	0.00	1.00
Plant 3	2.00	1.00	0.00	0.00	3.00
Plant 4	1.00	0.50	1.50	0.00	3.00
Plant 5	0.25	0.125	0.375	0.25	1.00
Sum of damages caused by:	4.25	1.625	1.875	0.25	8.00

Flow Condition II

Damages caused at	Damage caused by:				Sum of damages caused to
	Plant 1	Plant 2	Plant 3	Plant 4	
	(——————————————————————————————)				
Plant 1	0.00	0.00	0.00	0.00	0.00
Plant 2	2.00	0.00	0.00	0.00	2.00
Plant 3	4.00	2.00	0.00	0.00	6.00
Plant 4	2.00	1.00	3.00	0.00	6.00
Plant 5	0.50	0.25	0.75	0.50	2.00
Sum of damages caused by:	8.50	3.25	3.75	0.50	16.00

But it has also illustrated the extensive informational and administrative requirements of the payments scheme. Accordingly, the discussion in the remainder of the book is almost entirely in terms of "putting the costs on the waste discharger." If costs are properly defined, this procedure tends to produce an optimal allocation of resources and optimal residual or final waste loads. However, water quality management is such a complex matter that any procedure is bound to be accompanied by problems of adjustment, equity, or inefficiency, or perhaps all three. The effluent charge procedure is no exception. It presents problems of adjustment and equity—especially when locations have been made on the assumption that a certain amount of waste can be discharged freely.

PROBLEMS IN DETERMINING CHARGES

The Nature of Damage Functions

Basic to an optimum system of effluent charges, or for that matter any procedure aimed at achieving an economically optimal level of water quality, is delineation of the "damage cost function," which is the functional relationship between the amount of a waste discharged and damages.

In this early discussion we do not distinguish between short-run and long-run damage functions. This important distinction is introduced later. Also we initially ignore the stochastic character of the function resulting from environmental variability—primarily temperature and streamflow. This permits us to first discuss basic principles without introducing duration and frequency as affecting the magnitude of damages.

The simplest situation occurs when this function is linear, i.e., each additional unit of waste discharge results in an equal increment of damage. In general, the present exposition will assume linear damage functions. Such a situation is illustrated in Table 5 where it is assumed that five plants are arrayed along a stream, that streamflow increases along the course of the stream (say, because a tributary enters), and that the waste it contains is nondegradable (say, chloride). The non-degradability assumption does not change the analysis in any way, but it simplifies the example.

Since damage per day is assumed to be in direct proportion to concentration, a level of charges equal to incremental damage costs can be worked out for each level of flow and for each plant. For example, at flow level one, the charge for plant 1 is $4.25 per pound of waste discharged which is the sum of the damages caused by plant 1 to plants 2, 3, 4, and 5. (At flow level two, the charge for plant 1 is $8.50 per pound, because the same waste discharge results in a doubling of the concentration.) The charge for plant 1 is the same regardless of the level of discharge of the other plants. If plant 1 reduced its discharge by half in response to the charge levied on it, its assessment would drop by half to $2.125—the amount by which downstream damages are reduced. This "separability" characteristic of linear damage functions is very important since it greatly reduces the amount of information which a regulatory authority must have to implement an efficient effluent charge system.

The manner in which a plant maximizing its profits (or minimizing its losses) will respond to an effluent charge levied on it at a given level of streamflow and the effect of this response on costs associated with its waste disposal are shown in Figure 19. Under the circumstances pictured, the plant will reduce its waste discharge from point D to point E, thus minimizing the costs associated with its waste disposal.

The marginal cost of withholding wastes in an optimal manner includes, in the case of chlorides, such alternatives as temporary storage, process adjustments, and reducing production. The marginal cost function rises after some point because it becomes progressively more

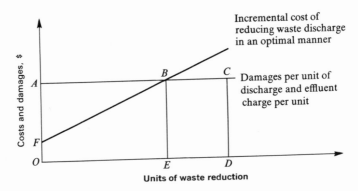

Figure 19.

OD	= Units of waste discharge if no charge levied on effluent.
OA	= Damages per unit of waste discharge and effluent charge per unit.
$OACD$	= Total damages associated with unrestricted waste discharge, i.e., no effluent charge levied.
OE	= Reduction of waste discharge with effluent charge OA.
$OFBE$	= Total cost of reducing effluent discharge to ED.
$OFBDC$	= Total cost associated with waste disposal with ED waste discharge, i.e., residual damage costs plus cost of reducing discharge.
$OABE$	= Total damages avoided.
ABF	= Net reduction in waste disposal associated costs by reducing waste discharge by OE, i.e., $OABE$ minus $OFBE$. This also equals the total cost of *not* reducing the effluent discharge.

expensive to withhold production (say, as inventory is run down), or to adjust production processes.[13]

The costs of increments of effluent storage capacity may rise if it is necessary to purchase higher-priced land for storage or if the land providing gravity flow to the stream is exhausted and some pumping costs are incurred. The firm acting to minimize its costs (charges plus costs of avoiding them) would continue to use each alternative until $MC_A = MC_B = MC_C = \ldots = MC_N =$ unit charge; in other words, until no further marginal "tradeoffs" are possible which will reduce costs. (In Part III problems of long-run planning are contrasted with short-run problems of adaption with existing capacity.)[14]

The relative simplicity of a system of effluent charges based upon linear damage functions arises from the fact that each waste discharger's damage costs can be determined separately. In contrast, non-linearities are associated with interaction between waste discharges in the sense

[13] If the costs of an optimal combination of waste reduction procedures have the shapes conventionally attributed to cost functions (text illustrations show only the relevant range of such functions), marginal costs and the effluent charge will be equal at more than one point. This is illustrated in the figure below.

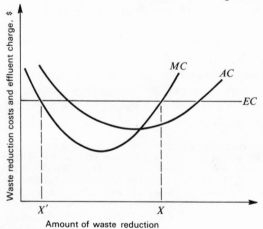

Amount of waste reduction

Marginal cost for function EC equals the effluent charge at levels of waste reduction X' as well as at X. However, at X' over-all costs associated with its waste disposal are at a *maximum* rather than a *minimum* for the firm. Fortunately, if the firm reduces wastes at all, it will have no incentive to stop at X', for if it continues, over-all costs will fall until waste reduction level X. Under certain circumstances when charges are used to implement a stream standards system, this cost minimizing result will not follow. This point is discussed in Chapter 7.

The same principles will apply to a municipal treatment plant having similar cost curves.

[14] The principles indicated for the short-run in the preceding footnote hold equally for the long-run where all inputs are variable, i.e., no fixed plants. It is only necessary to substitute long-run for short-run in the cost curve labels.

that the incremental external cost associated with one cannot be determined unless the level of discharge of the other is known. To put this in another way, there are cross product terms in the damage function. We refer back to the damage functions indicated on pages 94–96, where the "separability" case yielded a damage function of the form $C = K (K_1 L_1 + K_2 L_2 + K_3 D_a)$ whereas the nonseparable function was $C = K (K_1 L_1{}^2 + K_2 L_2{}^2 + K_3 L_1 L_2 + K_4 L_1 D_a + K_5 L_2 D_a + K_6 D_a{}^2)$.   In this equation, the damages from the first discharge are made up of the first, third, and fourth terms. The third term depends upon the level of the second discharge and, therefore, the damages attributable to the first discharge cannot be determined without knowing the second discharge. The problem this presents is that instead of merely needing to know damage functions and being able to achieve an optimal solution by imposing damage costs on the waste dischargers and letting them respond, the agency must now know the cost functions for waste reduction at each interdependent point of waste discharge. It must determine the optimum level of waste reduction for each point *before* charges are assessed on effluents in order to obtain an optimal solution. This means that the effluent charges system loses perhaps its major advantage over other systems of control such as payments or effluent standards. This point is explored further below.

In some cases it might be preferable to assume linearity even when it is known that the discharge-damage relation is actually somewhat more complex because taking account of greater complexity may rapidly increase costs and yield strongly diminishing returns. In other words, among the incremental costs that should not be neglected are the costs of refining the system of charges.[15]

[15] The use of linear separable functions may not be a good approximation of the actual conditions should any of the following situations hold to a significant degree: (1) Damage costs definitely do not increase in direct proportion to the increase in waste concentration; (2) The relationship between different types of wastes is either synergistic or cancelling rather than additive; (3) A downstream treatment process simultaneously removes two or more types of wastes coming from different sources. In the third case, an inevitable element of arbitrariness is introduced into allocating the costs to individual waste-discharging firms which emit different wastes or the same wastes in different proportions. When the costs of removing residual materials from intake water are strictly "joint," there is literally no non-arbitrary way of determining who is responsible for what. In some or many cases, however, the costs are probably not truly joint. In these cases, for any given level of concentration the cost of dealing with an increment of the waste can be estimated.

In the first two cases, the complexity occurs because the cost for which plant 2's discharge can be held responsible becomes in part a function of how much plant 1 discharges.

There is currently much uncertainty concerning the character of damage functions but there is evidence that some of them are non-linear. Research is needed to define how pervasive this situation is and whether the additional data and analytical requirements of taking non-linearities into account could be justified in devising actual management programs.

Some Additional Theoretical Problems in Determining Optimal Charges

Even when damage functions are linear, "separability" problems may arise if waste disposers impose damages on a series of downstream units and the waste discharge of one firm affects the marginal production cost of another. A separable externality is defined as one that occurs when the total cost of a productive process is affected by the level of output in another process (and hence the level of upstream waste discharge), but marginal cost is not.[16] The separability case requires that the marginal production cost of each firm linked to another by a technological externality be given entirely in terms of its own output. This would follow, for example, if factory A discharged a waste which caused factory B to put in a water supply treatment plant which thereafter would be operated in an invariant fashion. The new total cost function becomes a vertical displacement of the old and marginal costs are not changed, as is shown in the following example.

Plant B output	Total cost before factory A	Marginal cost	Total cost after factory A	Marginal cost
1	1.0		2.0	
		1.5		1.5
2	2.5		3.5	
		2.0		2.0
3	4.5		5.5	

Since marginal costs of one firm are not changed by the output decisions of the other firm, the externality does not cause output to be different from what it would have been in the absence of the externality presuming it continues to be in the affected firm's interest to produce at all. The effect of the externality is intra-marginal and thus merely affects the firm's profit position and the decision whether to continue production or to stop. In this instance, the appropriate effluent fee is simply a lump sum equal to the increase in total cost.[17] This is a fee

---

[16] Otto A. Davis and Andrew H. Whinston, "Externalities, Welfare, and the Theory of Games," *Journal of Political Economy* (June 1962), pp. 241 ff. For an excellent brief article relating Davis and Whinston to the previously cited articles by Coase and Buchanan and Stubblebine, see Ralph Turvey, "On Divergences between Social Cost and Private Cost," *Economica*, Vol. 30 (August 1963), p. 309.

[17] Except where the externalities are mutually or reciprocally imposed on each other by plants. Such a case could arise for example if two thermal power plants both used a lake for cooling water and by raising the temperature of the lake reduced each other's cooling efficiency. In this case the cost functions of the two would be related in the following manner:

$$C_1 = C_1(q_1, q_2) = f_1(q_1) + g_1(q_2)$$
$$C_2 = C_2(q_1, q_2) = f_2(q_2) + g_2(q_1)$$

where subscripts refer to the respective plants, C indicates costs, and q the output level. These externalities are non-separable because each cost function can be

levied for the privilege of discharging at all. The only question involved is whether to discharge or not.

A non-separable externality is defined to occur when the marginal cost in a productive process is affected by the level of output in another process. For example, assume that a petroleum refinery A, which expels a hot effluent, locates upstream from a petroleum refinery B, which is operated by a different firm and which uses the stream for cooling water. Cooling efficiency for plant B will drop, and for the purposes of our example we assume it will have to pump more water for cooling per unit of output. The marginal costs of plant B *for a given level of output* will be affected by the externality, shown below.

Plant A discharge	Total pumping costs before plant A	Marginal cost	Total pumping costs after plant A	Marginal cost	Total external cost of plant A discharge	Marginal external cost
1	1.0		2.0		1	
		1.5		2.5		1
2	2.5		4.5		2	
		2.0		3.0		1
3	4.5		7.5		3	

The reader will note that, so far as we have gone, the damage function is linear in the illustrated case. But the response of plant B would be to adjust output (assuming other less costly alternatives such as pre-cooling of influent are unavailable).

A particular marginal cost function for plant B corresponds to each level of discharge of plant A. (A set of such cost functions is shown in Figure 20.) Plant A can determine its own profit-maximizing level of output, and at this rate of production a specific level of output (say, x_1 corresponding to MC_1) will also maximize profits for plant B (although this will in general not be the level of output which will maximize joint profits for both plants taken together). However, it is possible to compute the amount of a levy on the output of plant A which will maximize joint profits. The appropriate level of charge will be the one which causes the marginal net loss imposed on firm B to be considered an opportunity cost in firm A. The net losses corresponding to different levels of waste discharge are shown in the shaded areas of Figure 20. The net damage

---

written as the sum of two functions, both of which involve only one variable as its argument. To obtain an optimal solution in this instance the basin agency would need to know the cost functions of both plants and their interrelationships. In this as in other cases of non-separability the use of charges loses its information requirements advantage over direct controls. For an elaboration of this point see Otto A. Davis and Andrew B. Whinston, "On Externalities, Information and the Government-Assisted Invisible Hand," *Economica*, Vol. 33 (August 1966).

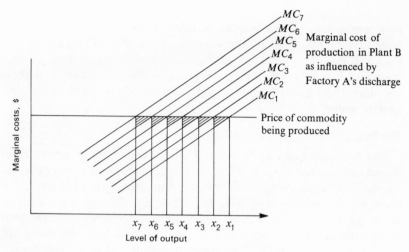

Figure 20.

or net loss function may also turn out to be linear as indeed in Figure 20 it is. But even so we are not out of the woods if different waste discharges and water users impose external costs on multiple production units.

Assume an initial equilibrium along a stream where a number of water users and waste dischargers impose external diseconomies on one another seriatim. Assume the regulatory authority starts by imposing the incremental costs of the last one of these (Z) upon the previous one (Y) and so on back up the line. When the charge is levied upon Y the outputs of both Y and Z change. As the cost imposed by X on Y is levied on X the output of Y changes again; accordingly so does that of Z. We have an interdependent system, and a simultaneous solution is necessary for the entire system. Not only is the problem analytically complex, but it would require detailed information on the costs of reducing waste discharges as well as damages imposed, and once again we lose the two major advantages of the effluent charges system as a means of water quality management. Decentralized decision making is no longer possible, and the information needed by the basin agency is no longer limited to damage functions.

Things may not be so dark, however. For one thing, municipal waste loads are not sensitive to damage costs imposed upon the municipality, and thus do not give rise to serial effects. Recreation, one of the major uses affected by quality deterioration, ordinarily does not itself produce a significant waste load.[18] Moreover, some industrial damages such as

---

[18] Although there certainly are exceptions especially where large power boats operate. Water quality deterioration can occur both from waste discharge from the sanitary facilities of the boats and from residuals from the oil and other fuel used for power.

corrosion appear to be separable. In other instances, effects on marginal costs may be too small to affect output appreciably. The basin agency may well find it a useful rule-of-thumb to assume linear damage functions and neglect serial effects. However, it must be aware that these are simplifications, the benefits and costs of which must be weighed against reality.

The Probabilistic Character of Damages

The Expected Value of Damages. One aspect of damage measurement importantly related to the problem of levying appropriate effluent charges (as well as establishing standards) is the probabilistic character of damages. As already explained, the damaging effect of a given waste discharge is heavily dependent upon the natural environmental conditions which prevail when the discharge is made. Most important are conditions of water availability and temperature. Although records are often short, methods have been devised which permit analysis of the characteristics of frequency distributions of streamflow and temperature. In general, they rely on chain-like statistical sequences known as Markov processes.[19] We take for granted that the statistical problems can be handled and proceed to discuss the effects of probability or risk elements on damage functions.

Let us direct our attention in the first instance to an individual outfall, at which a nondegradable waste is discharged.[20] Assume that there are two water users downstream from the given outfall and that the damages they incur are directly proportional to the concentration of the waste in the raw water, as shown in Figure 21. For example, these users might have damage functions, D_1 and D_2, each of which represents the costs of the optimum combination of water supply treatment measures and residual physical damages, for each level of concentration. For each quality of raw water, the downstream users would, as we have seen previously, have an incentive to combine the alternatives open to them in this way. Because the functions are linear and separable, the total damage corresponding to any level of concentration is the sum of the damages to each user, i.e., $D_1 + D_2$.

Since, for a nondegradable waste, dilution is the only factor affecting concentration, at any given point of use the damages will vary with the streamflow, as shown in Figure 22. Since streamflow is a stochastic phenomenon, downstream damages are necessarily probabilistic vari-

[19] See Maynard M. Hufschmidt and Myron B Fiering, *Simulation Techniques for Design of Water Resource Systems* (Harvard University Press, 1966), particularly Chap. 2; and N. C. Matalas, "Mathematical Assessment of Synthetic Hydrology," *Water Resources Research*, Vol. 3, No. 4 (Fourth Quarter 1967).

[20] The procedure and principle are the same for degradable wastes and non-linear damage functions but the exposition is more complicated.

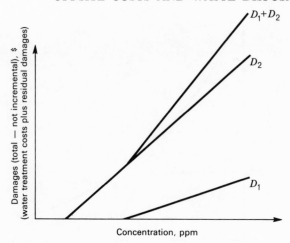

Figure 21.

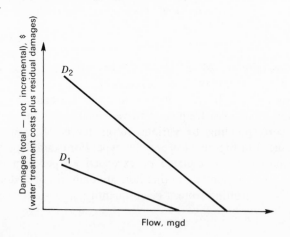

Figure 22.

ables. Figure 23 indicates the per cent of time any given level of flow is expected to occur.[21] Based on the flow-damage and flow-probability

[21] Because it is not directly germane to the discussion, we ignore the problem of the basic hydrologic data used to define the flow-duration curve. It should be noted that the use of daily, monthly, and annual flows will result in different curves, and that the hydrologic data for analysis of low-flow periods are usually organized in terms of recurrence intervals for flows for different periods of time, i.e., 1-day, 7-day, 30-day, and 50-day. (See, for example, R. K. Linsley and J. B. Franzini, *Water-Resources Engineering* [McGraw-Hill, 1964], pp. 127–132.)

The time period used in the analysis of hydrologic events for water quality management systems is of crucial importance in assessing losses—damages plus treatment costs, and costs of waste reduction at outfalls, particularly as the systems become more complex with closely articulated components. As complexity increases, the importance of analyzing daily flows increases. For an analysis of the stochastic nature of such flows see R. G. Quimpo, *Stochastic Model of Daily River Flow Sequences,* Hydrology Paper 18 (Colorado State University, 1967).

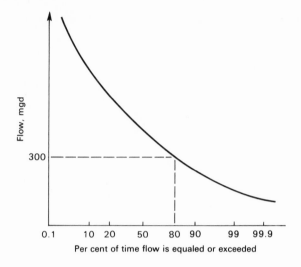

Figure 23.

relationships, Figure 24 relates the costs at a point of use to the corresponding probability of occurrence.

Damages avoided by reducing waste discharge can be estimated by constructing a new cost-frequency curve which shows the probability of damages corresponding to various lower levels of waste discharge. Curves 2 and 3 in Figure 24 are of this type. For example, a flow of 300 mgd is expected to be equaled or exceeded 80 per cent of the time (Figure 23). Corresponding to that flow are damages of X dollars (curve 1, Figure 24), resulting from a given quantity of waste discharge. If the

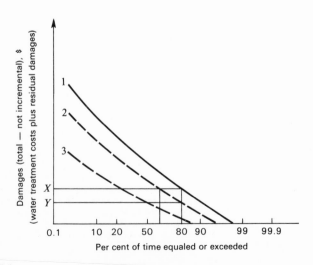

Figure 24.

quantity of waste discharge is reduced, but the flow regime remains unchanged, the damages associated with the *same* level of discharge are decreased, i.e., to Y dollars (curve 2, Figure 24). To put it another way, the same level of damages, i.e., X, now corresponds to a flow which is equaled or exceeded only about 60 per cent of the time. Thus, the probability distribution of damages has been changed.

Taking the integrals of these functions (roughly, multiplying probabilities times costs) gives the expected value of damages. Then, taking successive differences between the integrals corresponding to different levels of waste discharge yields a series of expected values which can be used to construct a curve showing the relationships between diminished residual waste discharges and the reduction in the expected value of damages. Such a relationship is shown in Figure 25. (For illustration, the relationship is shown as linear in form, although it is not likely to be linear in reality.)

Relationships showing the incremental or marginal reduction in cost can be derived by taking the first derivative of the function representing the expected value of damages avoided shown in Figure 25. Since this is linear, the value of marginal damages avoided will of course be a constant.

An effluent charge that does not vary over time should ideally reflect the *expected* value of damages avoided when waste discharge is reduced incrementally. The waste discharger would then have an economic incentive to plan and design his waste reduction facilities in a way that should minimize the over-all costs associated with his waste discharge, given that his waste reduction facilities are to operate at a constant level regardless of the variation in flow and changes in the concentration of waste at the points of downstream use.

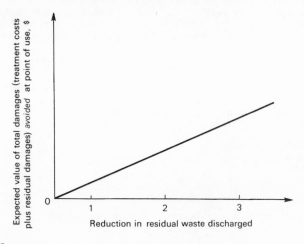

Figure 25.

However, neglecting for the moment the added costs of administering a more complex system of charges, this is not the minimum cost which could be obtained if the effluent charge reflected changing external (downstream) costs over time. If the charge did do this, the waste discharger would be induced to consider the expected value of the charge (damages) as he or the management agency calculate it in determining the capacity of his facility (a treatment plant, for example), and would *operate* the plant to reflect short-run changes in external costs. He would also consider the percentage of the time the plant would operate at various levels of waste reduction in designing it (i.e., in trading off capital costs against operation costs). Reason suggests—and empirical research demonstrates—that this approach can reduce over-all social costs below the level entailed in constant rate operation.[22] This is the rationale for searching for ways of devising an effluent charge system which will reflect shorter-term variations in external cost.[23]

Treatment Plant Design. To be a bit more concrete about the last point, we focus briefly on the matter of designing and operating a waste treatment plant in such a manner as to minimize cost.[24] For simplicity we contemplate a situation where the objective is to maintain a given standard in the stream. This yields results that are somewhat different from those produced by a true equating of internal and external marginal costs (see Chapter 7). However, the simpler situation can serve to illustrate the point.

[22] Not all waste reduction facilities are amenable to varying levels of operation. Waste treatment plants and temporary storage facilities are probably most flexible and process changes least flexible. Once a process is changed to reduce the amount of waste generated, it is operated at the fixed design capacity. Materials recovery and by-product production are probably intermediate in flexibility.

[23] It would also be helpful in the design of a waste reduction facility to know the duration of various levels of charges as well as the per cent of the time they are expected to be in effect. Some processes, for example, have significant start-up and shut-down costs. The following method of presenting damages would be helpful in this connection:

Hypothetical Damage Table: Damages vs. Chloride Concentration and Duration

Chloride concentration	Damages when duration of chloride concentration is:				
	1 day	7 days	14 days	30 days	60 days
	(— — — — — — — — — — — — $1,000 — — — — — — — — — — — — —)				
50 ppm	0	0	0	0	2
100 ppm	1	2	4	7	11
150 ppm	3	6	11	17	25
200 ppm	6	12	19	28	42
250 ppm	11	20	32	45	60

[24] The same approach is applicable to water treatment plants.

Plants are usually designed to achieve lowest cost at a particular level of waste removal predicated on a particular low streamflow of relatively infrequent occurrence, say 10 per cent of the time. More often than not, the plant is then operated at about that level regardless of changes in the stream's assimilative capacity. Long-term costs would tend to be lower if the plant were designed to operate most efficiently at a higher, more frequent flow.[25] The added treatment required at low flows might be provided by adding chemicals, by increasing the degree of aeration or the amount of recycling, or by other means that entail high operating costs. Operating costs can be quite high during the rare periods of extremely low flow and still yield a comparative advantage over additional capital investment.

For example, let us assume that a plant is designed to deal with a low-flow condition that is likely to occur once in ten years. Let us further suppose that the probability of this event occurring in any given year is equal to that for any other year. The expected value of the extra cost of dealing with such an extreme low flow can then be treated as an annual average. It is possible to establish how high this annual average can be without its present worth exceeding a dollar of current investment by determining the present worth of a constant expenditure stream of $1.00 per year. The present value of such a perpetuity discounted at 5 per cent annual interest is $20.00.[26] This means that 5 cents could be spent annually, or 50 cents during the once-in-ten-year-probability low flow, and the expected present value of such an expenditure stream would not exceed $1.00. In other words, 50 cents could be spent every 10 years in perpetuity, and the cost would probably be no greater than spending $1.00 for capital equipment now. This means, for example, that if $2 million of the capital value of a large plant is for the purpose of dealing with the once-in-ten-year condition, $1 million could instead be spent on operating costs every ten years in perpetuity at no greater expected cost.

[25] For a theoretical discussion of the concept of "flexibility" in plant design, see George Stigler, "Production and Distribution in the Short Run," *Journal of Political Economy*, Vol. 47 (1939), reprinted in American Economic Association, *Readings in the Theory of Income Distribution* (Blackiston Company, 1949). The virtue of flexibility is recognized, at least to some extent, in turbine design. The turbine is designed to operate most efficiently at the expected "normal operating level." There is a maximum range of heads for which the turbine is designed in the ratio generally of 2:1. An early paper pointing to the possible economies to be achieved by flexibility in river basin planning was Blair T. Bower and Harold A. Thomas, Jr., "Flexibility in River Basin System Design," Harvard Water Resources Program, 1957, mimeo.

[26] The formula for the present value of an annuity of unit value per period for a term of n periods at rate of interest i is:

$$\frac{[1 - (1 + i)^{-n}]}{i}.$$

Some empirical information is now available concerning the possible cost savings for variable rate operation. One study by Frankel explored the hypothesis that significant cost savings might be achieved in connection with a waste management system based upon streamflow conditions in the Eel River in California. Frankel first estimated the costs of achieving stream standards based upon continuous rate operation of conventional waste treatment plants. Next, by varying the degree of treatment to just maintain the standard, he found that operating costs could be reduced by about 15 per cent per year. He also explored the possibility of storing wastes during low flows and discharging at higher flows, and found that this produced a saving in costs of about 30 per cent over continuous rate operation of treatment plants to maintain the minimum standard.[27]

The importance of tailoring waste removal operations to external costs, or to the requirements of a stream standard, will become greater when a high degree of treatment is required. In a study of high-level treatment alternatives to meet projected waste levels and desired water quality standards in the Potomac estuary,[28] Robert K. Davis found that varying the level of operation of advanced treatment facilities could not only reduce cost greatly but might alter the cost relationships between methods. This result is illustrated for two types of advanced treatment techniques in Table 6. Both techniques are able to meet the specified standard either by continuous operation or by an average of 3.5 months of intermittent operation per year.

A system in which effluent charges would be varied to reflect changing

Table 6.   Present Value of Treatment Costs

Process	Continuous operation	3.5 months per year operation
Step aeration plus microstraining	$ 49,000,000	$39,000,000
Chemical precipitation	110,000,000	32,000,000

Note: Adjustments made in capital costs to account for replacement necessary to achieve fifty-year life of project. Interest is 4 per cent.

[27] These results are reported in Richard J. Frankel, "Water Quality Management: Engineering-Economic Factors in Municipal Waste Disposal," *Water Resources Research*, Vol. 1, No. 2 (Second Quarter 1965), p. 184. D. P. Loucks came to somewhat similar conclusions in "Risk Evaluation in Sewage Treatment Plant Design," *Proceedings ASCE, Journal of the Sanitary Engineering Division*, Vol. 93, No. SA1 (February 1967), pp. 25–39.

[28] Robert K. Davis, "Some Economic Aspects of Advanced Waste Treatment," *Journal of the Water Pollution Control Federation* (December 1965).

environmental conditions, i.e., taking into account that given waste loads[29] impose different external costs over time, could be a powerful stimulant for the design of processes that can respond flexibly to changed conditions and for the optimal operation of such facilities. The probabilistic considerations with which we have dealt in this section will be of concern to us again, in Part III, when we consider regional systems incorporating large-scale measures.

Long-Run and Short-Run Damage Functions

So long as improved water quality does not itself induce water-based activities, an effluent charge based upon short-run variations in external costs and provision to the waste discharger of information concerning the expected value of future charges and their duration at various levels for planning and design purposes would tend to produce optimum results. The latter would of course reflect any expected growth of water use in the region and the general level of charges would be increased over time as the external costs of a given level of waste discharge rose. However, if improved water quality itself *induces* adjustments which affect external costs, the problem of levying an appropriate short-run effluent charge becomes more complex. For example, if downstream users, say municipalities, have already installed equipment for special treatment, the short-run benefit from improved intake water quality may be appreciably less than in the longer-run because it will not be necessary to replace equipment. Or a body of water may have very little value for recreation because the water is so poor that very few persons use it. If the quality were improved and maintained at the higher level, this would induce the development of such skills as water skiing, along with the associated investments in equipment. In these instances a certain promotional element must enter into the level of the effluent charges set, at least in the early stages of the program. As our subsequent discussion of recreation demand will show, econometric techniques promise to be able to provide us with estimates of such induced effects. But how do we take them into account in the charges approach? In these instances —presuming the adjustment periods are not excessively long—it is

---

[29] Perhaps implicit in the above discussion is the assumption that the generation of wastes, i.e., prior to waste reduction, is time invariant. In reality this is not likely to be the case. Variations in raw product inputs, rate of operation, and product mix can occur from day to day, as in a fruit cannery or in a paper plant producing a wide range of grades of paper. Thus the waste treatment plant, for example, faces a variable input as well as a varying external environment. While this fact does not change the approach or the conclusions, it does make the analysis for the waste discharger considerably more difficult in the real case.

desirable to estimate a damage function incorporating longer-run adjustments and use it as the basis for charges.[30]

If long periods of adjustment are involved the agency will then have to decide whether the present worth (see the discussion of treatment plant design above) of the future benefits at various levels of control exceeds the present worth of the costs which would be needed to achieve it. Once again the agency would need at least approximate information on the costs of various levels of waste control and the effluent charges system would lose at least some of its information cost advantage.

Special Problems in Damage Measurement

Up to this point the costs associated with waste disposal have been broadly classified as damage costs and waste reduction costs and discussed in general terms. In this section, attention is centered on some problems of measuring damage costs. Those relating to aesthetics and recreation present particularly difficult problems of measurement. Many other costs, though they offer difficulties, are, in principle, rather straight-

[30] The situation described above is depicted in the following diagram:

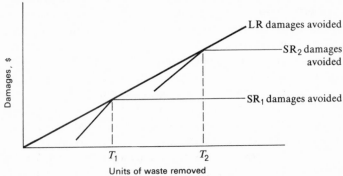

Assume that the system is initially in a long-run equilibrium in which T_1 units of waste are removed. The damages prevented equal the value of the *LR* function at T_1 which is equal to $SR_1(T_1)$. Suppose now that the amount of waste removed increases to T_2. In the short-run the benefits or damages prevented will equal $SR_1(T_2)$. In the long-run, if this higher level of waste removal is maintained, adjustments will occur (e.g., people will discover additional recreational uses of the stream, municipalities will not replace some expensive water supply treatment equipment, etc.). The *LR* function measures the gains from the increased waste reduction after all of these induced adjustments have occurred. Note that these gains are reflected in a movement along, but not a shift in, the *LR* function. On the other hand, when the target waste reduction increases to T_2 the *SR* damage function shifts along the *LR* function and when people have fully adjusted to the new expected level of water quality the relevant *SR* damage function is SR_2.

For further discussion of this kind of formulation of long-run, short-run relationships see Maynard M. Hufschmidt and Myron B Fiering, *Simulation Techniques for Design of Water Resource Systems* (Harvard University Press, 1966).

forwardly measurable and efforts to quantify some of them are well under way.

With respect to industrial damages, attempts have been made to assess the net damages that industries suffer when they have to use low quality water. Since a variety of adjustments is possible, the problem becomes complex. Several studies have been models of ingenuity in using limited data and modelling or simulating effects on industrial operations. Some results are available for the petroleum refining, fruit and vegetable canning, thermal power, and beet sugar industries. In all these instances, industrial costs turn out to be surprisingly insensitive to intake water quality within comparatively wide ranges—especially in regard to aspects of quality that are usually influenced by prior uses and discharge of effluents. Sensitivity is greater to wastes which in most cases are of natural origin, such as chlorides and magnesium. One important reason for the comparative insensitivity is that a large proportion of water use in the heavy water-using industries is for purposes that can readily accommodate low-quality water—cooling for instance. A second reason is that processes which are really sensitive to water quality—high-pressure boilers and water to go in cans and bottles, for example—need water of such high quality that extensive treatment is necessary for *any* kind of raw water used; water of distinctly low quality can be used with only minor incremental costs. High-pressure boiler feed water must be demineralized and the cost is fairly insensitive to the quality of intake water over a wide range. Thus, not much control of waste discharges can be justified by benefits to industrial users.

The situation is surprisingly similar for municipal water supplies. Much of what has been said about the need for high quality water supplies as a basis for preparation of potable water is more the product of emotion than of logic. The water of the much discussed Hudson River, which allegedly should not be used for municipal supply because of its poor quality, is actually of comparable quality to that at the Torresdale intake of the City of Philadelphia and better than the quality at the intakes of the City of St. Louis. For many years acceptable drinking water has been produced from water of such quality—albeit at the expense of some extra chemical and physical treatment. Moreover, a plant at Düsseldorf, Germany, withdraws water from the Rhine River, which is of far lower quality than the Delaware, the Hudson, or the Missouri, treats it with activated carbon and ozone, and produces quite suitable drinking water. Poor quality water does impose extra costs on municipal water systems but—except in cases of toxic or evil-tasting substances—use by municipalities ordinarily cannot justify very high levels of waste effluent control. Usually the toxic elements comprise very small and separable portions of waste effluents.

The general point of the above paragraph is brought out in a recent study of a stream system along whose shores are municipal waste dischargers and municipal water users. It involved a very careful gathering of cost data and the generation of new cost information. The study also developed a sophisticated technique for estimating by means of computer simulation the interrelationship between water quality at waste outfalls and at water intakes. It was found that vast amounts of reuse are required to justify the additional costs of advanced treatment for municipal waste disposal.[31] For example, it turned out that the magnitude of water withdrawal for municipal water treatment and reuse downstream required to justify additional upstream waste treatment costs solely on savings to downstream water treatment plants is on the order of 16–250 to 1 for small waste treatment plants and 10–30 to 1 for large waste treatment plants. Again it appears that the need to prepare potable water cannot justify particularly high standards of quality in watercourses.

The limited evidence from the studies and analysis discussed above leads to the virtually inescapable conclusion that higher water quality must be justified primarily on aesthetic and recreational grounds, if it is to be justified at all. This conclusion is reinforced by the results of the Delaware estuary study.[32] This effort, which provides the basis for one of the cases we discuss in Part III, is the only full-scale regional study which has attempted to quantify the costs and gains associated with water quality improvement. The benefits of raw water quality improvement which could be identified as accruing to municipal and industrial water users were very small compared with the costs of improvement. In fact the benefits of improved water quality with respect to some parameters for some industrial purposes turned out to be negative, i.e., higher dissolved oxygen tended to increase corrosion in these uses.

Let us turn then to a consideration of the aesthetic and recreational gains resulting from water quality improvement.

Aesthetics and Recreation. The adverse effects of water quality deterioration on the general environment are unfortunately obvious. Obnoxious odors of septic sewage may carry for miles; untreated municipal sewage contains floating and suspended materials that destroy the beauty of the water; and industrial effluents may render the water unattractive by coloring it. Fortunately, extreme nuisance is unlikely to occur in a stream which is used for multiple purposes and where a system of charges or other controls causes the costs of various other users to be

[31] Frankel, *op. cit.*
[32] See Chapter 11.

considered in waste discharge decisions. Where it is necessary to evaluate aesthetic nuisance, however, the problem is very great.

People benefit from the aesthetic qualities of nearby bodies of water whether or not they help meet the costs of providing and maintaining water quality. There is, therefore, no incentive for an individual to express his true preferences by offering to pay for the control of the general environmental effects of waste discharges, and a market cannot develop. Not only is it impossible for the market to represent preferences for water quality control or improvement, but there is no way of parceling out and selling "goods" of this kind. For the same reasons, litigation by private parties will not adequately represent such preferences either. In the absence of usable evaluations, a judgment that extreme aesthetic nuisance is to be avoided, at least in heavily developed areas, must find almost universal consensus. Minimum standards imposed, for example, to prevent the discharge of obnoxious floating materials, may be a simple and satisfactory method of handling one aspect of this problem.

There are possibilities for evaluation, however. The aesthetic damages occurring in a river or lake in which quality deterioration does not result in extreme nuisance, are pretty well limited to those who own nearby property and those who would come from some distance to enjoy the river. Methods have been proposed and are under development to assess the value of advantages resulting to these classes of users when they are beneficiaries of recreation development. The procedure is to impute a demand curve from the enhancement of property values and the access costs of users who do not own or rent riparian lands. Such a procedure may have promise as a means of gauging recreation effects where beneficiaries can be reasonably well identified. Where a waste discharge affects both recreation and aesthetics (which except in cases of extreme nuisance may be viewed as almost joint products), a measure of this kind might yield a package value for both. Methods of estimating willingness to pay using questionnaires are also being explored. Econometric methods may be applied to these evaluation procedures to project the recreation and aesthetic values which would result from the alleviation of extremely adverse water quality conditions.

One useful study of the recreational value of water quality was under way in the Delaware estuary area at the time of this writing. Parts of the estuary experience low—even zero—dissolved oxygen almost every year during low-flow periods. To raise the D.O. is an extremely expensive proposition. To achieve a target of 2 ppm, the cheapest program would cost about $100 million and a similar program for 4 ppm would cost around $300 million. Imposing as these costs are, an econometric study of potential increases in participation rates shows that these higher oxygen levels might be justified on recreational grounds alone. Preliminary results suggest that placing a value on boating of about $2.50 a day, might justify maintaining 3 ppm of D.O. even if no other benefits were considered. This level serves as a surrogate for the general quality of the water. At today's levels of discretionary income, $2.50 a day does not seem a ridiculously high figure to attach to a day of boating. As already mentioned, the analysis of non-recreation benefits from water quality improvement in the Delaware estuary suggests that they are modest when compared with the costs of improvement. The decision whether or not to achieve high levels of quality probably will turn almost entirely on recreational values.[33] Another study of the Delaware estuary, which used quite different methods, also concluded that recreation benefits can economically justify greatly improved levels of quality in the Delaware estuary. These results are reported in Chapter 11.

Another systematic study of recreational values associated with water quality was conducted by researchers at Oregon State University.[34] This study, sponsored by the U.S. Public Health Service, focused on the Yaquina Bay, which lies on a beautiful, but comparatively undeveloped, part of the Oregon coastline. Population is small and many alternative recreational opportunities are available. Water quality in the bay was threatened by paper mill waste which might reduce its biological productivity. A relationship was envisaged between the input of angling effort and the output or yield of fish taken. Angling success per unit of effort was taken to represent the quality of the recreational experience. Demand equations based on the so-called Clawson method (which imputes benefit or willingness to pay for the recreation opportunity from travel costs) were estimated for three estuarial fisheries. Among the statistical explanations of demand was a variable representing success per unit of effort. Shifts in the demand for angling in Yaquina Bay were then obtained by applying the model to assumed reductions in the quality of the fishing resource, thus shifting the calculated demand function down. Examples of the results are as follows. If waste disposal resulted in a total loss of the sports fisheries, the annual value of this loss would be about $63,000 (consumers surplus foregone).[35] Another way of

[33] Paul Davidson, F. Gerard Adams, and Joseph Seneca, "The Social Value of Water Recreational Facilities Resulting from an Improvement in Water Quality: The Delaware Estuary," in Allen V. Kneese and Stephen C. Smith (ed.), *Water Research* (The Johns Hopkins Press, for RFF, 1966).

[34] This research is reported in a paper by Joe B. Stevens, "Recreation Benefits From Water Pollution Control," *Water Resources Research*, Vol. 2 (Second Quarter 1966).

[35] This is not the figure reported in the Stevens article, *op cit.* It is based on a recalculation and was furnished the authors by letter.

putting the loss involved is that it would be about one million dollars if discounted at 6 per cent. This is less than the capital cost of a basic sewage treatment plant for a comparatively small city. A more realistic occurrence might be one which resulted in less than total destruction of the fishery. It would be much more common if waste disposal resulted in incremental reductions in water quality, fish life, and recreational values. Accordingly, the direct benefits of avoiding the losses associated with more normal waste disposal conditions would be even less. With a 50 per cent destruction of the fishery the consumers surplus loss would be about half as great. The authors of the Oregon State study were very careful to point out that many assumptions were involved in their analysis and that it did not incorporate the whole complex of goals and criteria appropriate for natural resources decision making.

While early results of recreation evaluation studies suggest that such analyses can be successfully done in certain instances and we can expect that in the future they will provide us with usable damage functions, routine detailed measurement of recreation damages is not now possible.

For the time being, at least, we will have to rely on less precise evaluation techniques in our water quality management programs. We turn to a discussion of some of these in the next chapter.

Standards, Charges, and Equity

EFFICIENT QUALITY CONTROL
AND STREAM STANDARDS

Since the level of water quality to be achieved in each of the nation's watercourses cannot be directly established on economic grounds—because all of the relevant benefits from water quality improvement cannot be computed—and since the Congress, the executive, and various state officials have expressed an urgent desire to improve water quality, it appears that some form of watercourse standards will be the mechanism used to establish water quality levels, at least for the time being. These standards will be based on some, usually vague, consideration of damage costs vs. costs of quality improvement. In the following discussion we use the term "stream standards" even though the standards might relate to any type of watercourse: stream, lake, estuary, or underground.

One form such a standard could take for a river is to set an upper limit on the concentration of a given waste, say, a material toxic to fish in the stream. Given the assumptions we have made concerning the character of the watercourse, and the opportunities available for handling water quality problems, a system of charges can be established which provides incentives for achieving this standard at lowest cost. This proposition is discussed in connection with actual cases in the following chapter. The following general statements are of significance here:

1. The symmetry of the *stream standards* situation with the earlier discussion can perhaps be most readily seen if the standard is viewed as representing a highly inelastic damage function. Everything said earlier about those cases in which the charges are to be adjusted to damage functions then becomes relevant.

To see this, consider Figure 26 where MC_1 indicates the marginal cost of waste reduction at outfall 1 and MC_2 is the marginal cost of waste reduction at outfall 2. The waste involved is assumed to be nondegrad-

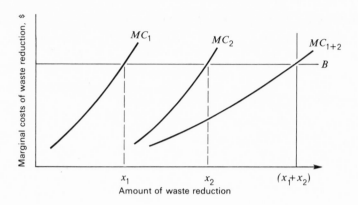

Figure 26.

able. Assume that waste reduction level $(x_1 + x_2)$ corresponds to the amount of removal needed to achieve the standard in the watercourse. The vertical damage function at $(x_1 + x_2)$, representing the watercourse standard, implies that up to that point the benefits accruing from waste reduction are infinitely large, while thereafter they are zero. This is one of the implications of stream standards that is almost always false in reality.

A charge, set at level B (which the authority finds by calculating the incremental costs of waste reduction at all relevant points of discharge or by experimentation), will be viewed as a perfectly elastic damage function by each of the two waste dischargers individually; accordingly, the separate adjustments of the waste dischargers will lead to equalization of marginal waste reduction costs at both points. This means, by reasoning described earlier, that the standard is achieved at minimum cost. A charge higher or lower than B would exceed or fail to meet the standard, but would tend to achieve whatever level is reached at least cost.

2. If a standard is set for a critical point on a stream and discharge of a given waste must be cut back to achieve the standard, a charge per unit of nondegradable waste discharge can be worked out which will achieve the standard. The same is true of degradable wastes, but in this case the charge will depend upon the degree to which the wastes are degraded in the stream between the outfalls and the critical point. From the viewpoint of this study, credit must be given for degradation in the stream, not because it is equitable, for no criteria of equity have yet been offered, but because it is necessary for the minimization of costs. To see this, imagine the extreme case where a waste is fully degraded before it reaches the critical point in the stream. If a charge were imposed on the waste discharged at the outfalls, waste reduction outlays

would be induced unnecessarily. The methods of estimating concentrations in long sections of a stream, described in Chapter 2, are essential here.

3. A level of effluent charges that would achieve the stated water quality standard could be arrived at by experimentation but the initial charge would have to be substantially correct to induce the least-cost system. Any substantial error in the initial charge[1] would be built into subsequent investment decisions involving durable plant and equipment, as well as into any further adjustments. Under these circumstances the effluent charge needed to achieve the standard might be quite different from what would have emerged had the initial charge level been the correct one, i.e., the one that achieves the quality standard at least cost.[2]

A strategy for taking advantage of the decentralized decision making inherent in effluent charges without inducing serious non-optimal adjustments must be devised. A suitable approach would appear to be to do a cost study in sufficient detail to insure that the charge initially set is not far from the minimum required to meet the standard. Changes in waste load reduction within a limited range can often be achieved by adjusting operation of treatment plants or production processes without substantial losses in efficiency. Changes in the necessary charge, as demand for assimilative capacity shifts, will probably be gradual, reflecting economic growth and changing technology. A study of the type needed to set an initial charge is reported in the next chapter.

4. The effluent charges procedure would have the advantage over other possible techniques of permitting each waste discharger to adjust in the most efficient way for his particular circumstances. Individual dischargers could withhold wastes in temporary storage, adjust production processes, change raw materials, treat wastes, cut back on production, change the character of their output, pay the charge, or use a combination of these procedures.

The charge required to achieve the standard indicates the incremental cost of achieving the standard. This means that without specific knowledge of the costs of waste reduction to upstream dischargers, the responsible authority can estimate the marginal social cost of the standard. This is important for judging its appropriateness. Presume, for example, that the standard relates to the killing of fish by, say, a toxic substance, and that it is not possible to establish the value of the "damage costs" of varying concentrations of the waste. The charges

---

[1] Or in the estimates of the expected value and duration of the charges if charges are to be varied to reflect time variation in the assimilative capacity of the watercourses.

[2] The MC curves in Figure 26 were drawn on the assumption that the effluent charge was correctly specified in the initial instance.

necessary to achieve the standard give an indication of what a small change in the standard and the accompanying physical effects *must at least be worth*. For example, if the charge is $1.00 per unit of waste, a unit reduction in the standard must reduce damage costs by at least $1.00 if the standard is worth maintaining. This type of information facilitates a decision on whether to raise or lower standards.

COMPLEMENTARITIES IN TREATMENT OR OTHER MEASURES FOR REDUCTION OF WASTE DISCHARGES

A thoroughgoing water quality control system in a river basin with reasonably complex development would probably result in a whole array of charges relating to different types of wastes. But measures to reduce one waste may simultaneously reduce others at a given point of discharge. Examples can be cited both with regard to municipal and industrial waste reduction processes. Standard physical, or primary, treatment (principally sedimentation) removes suspended solids but also some portion of the degradable organics. Standard biological treatment removes the bulk of the degradable organics, and has some effect on persistent organics, plant nutrients, bacteria, and other substances as well. Cooling towers may reduce BOD and phenols, as well as the waste heat discharged to watercourses.

Since joint costs cannot be allocated in a way that assists rational decisions, the discharger endeavoring to minimize his waste disposal costs would have to calculate the amount by which the joint effect of his action would reduce his charges, and weigh it against his specific cost of introducing and operating waste reduction measures. In a system of charges designed both to reflect downstream costs and meet the established "standards," the level of charges needed to accomplish the "standards" could still be established in the experimental manner outlined above. For example, if it is found that a charge can be reduced without having water quality drop below the level specified in the standard, this means that: (1) the charge is too high in terms of those dischargers responding directly to it; and/or (2) one waste is jointly treated with another by at least some dischargers and the charge levied on the first is high enough to induce higher than necessary joint removal of the second. The charge levied on the first would then be reduced until the standard is just met. If the influence of joint treatment is strong, the charge might be dropped to zero.

In either case, the charge which just meets the standard reflects the cost of an incremental change in the standard. An "ideal" system of charges would reflect the costs imposed downstream, and all charges levied to meet the standard would be at the lowest level consistent with the standard.

EFFLUENT STANDARDS

Consideration of *effluent* standards (as distinct from stream standards)—perhaps the most discussed method of achieving some coordination between the water quality desired in watercourses and individual waste discharges—has been purposely postponed until now so that the problem of external economies could be examined first in terms of charges and payments. These measures are the ones that have been traditionally advocated by economists for dealing with externalities; they are also consistent with the operation of the price mechanism in private markets.

Before pursuing this discussion further it should be noted that many professionals in water quality management who have advocated the standards approach have appreciated that stream and effluent standards must be viewed as potential complements in a rational program of management. Nevertheless, confused and confusing debate has been going on over the years about stream *vs.* effluent standards, as though the two were always alternatives. This is a relevant issue if a single waste discharge affecting quality in a water body is involved. Then the waste discharger can monitor the stream and adjust his discharge so as to maintain a specified standard in it. This would provide improved flexibility over a simple effluent standard which would presumably be based on some critical condition in the stream. There are a number of cases where industrial operations do precisely this in rural and small town areas. But, if there are multiple waste dischargers, achieving the standard by independent decisions based on a *stream* standard will be impossible. The problem here is another illustration of "inseparability," because what one waste discharger can do is contingent on what another does. A central agency must therefore provide information and incentives (via charges or effluent standards) which will produce co-ordinated behavior. Under these conditions, stream and effluent standards must be viewed as potential complements and not alternatives, i.e., effluent standards are meaningful only in the context of water quality goals or standards in the watercourse.

In this section, effluent standards are compared with a system of charges and payments as a tool for water quality management. A first and basic point is that *if a regional authority had full information concerning all the costs associated with existing and potential waste generation and disposal, it could establish a set of effluent standards that would have the same effect on resource allocation as an ideal system of charges.* A charge on each individual outfall tends to produce a certain quality of effluent. Standards could be set to obtain the same effluent quality at each outfall and prevent potential discharges which would come into

existence only if the full cost associated with them, including all external costs, did not have to be paid. It is important to note, however,
that the standard would have to be stated in terms of amount of wastes
discharged (pounds, tons, etc.) rather than in terms of concentrations,
which are sometimes used. In order to impose such effluent standards,
it would be necessary to forecast the response of each actual and
potential discharger at each level of flow to a system of charges which
reflected the damage costs and/or point-of-use standards in the area.
This would mean a whole system of individually tailored effluent standards. Minimization of the sum of waste reduction and damage costs
could be achieved by this system as well as by an ideal system of charges
or subsidies. Neither can claim an advantage on the basis of superior
performance under *ideal* conditions of information and authority on
the part of a responsible regional agency. The differences relate to ease
of administration and to income distribution, or equity.

A system of charges has the advantage of requiring less information
than other approaches when the objective is the minimization of the
costs associated with water quality management. This is true where a
stream standard is set, or where charges reflect damage costs and the
costs are approximately linear functions of concentrations for individual
wastes and approximately additive for different wastes.

In this case, charges based upon damage costs will tend toward a
minimization of damage and waste reduction costs, as explained in some
detail earlier, even though reduction costs are not explicitly known.
The charges technique also requires less information than effluent standards when it is used to obtain the least-cost system for achieving a
stream standard.

By a series of approximations, a charge can be set that will achieve
a specified stream standard and that will tend to produce the equi-
marginal costs for alternatives that are necessary for cost minimization.
Sample studies could produce a forecast of the appropriate level of
charges suitable for planning purposes.

Because land values, production processes, and other significant
variables differ from case to case, precise information concerning
"marginal tradeoffs" between alternative reduction procedures at different outfalls would be necessary to establish cost-minimizing combinations by the use of effluent standards. But, to set a charge, the water
quality management agency does not need to know the cost of waste
reduction for each individual waste discharger; the agency only has to
be able to estimate the average of the discharger's marginal costs. Suppose that three dischargers have marginal cost curves for waste reduction as shown in Figure 27.

These curves have been drawn so that MC_2 is an average of MC_1

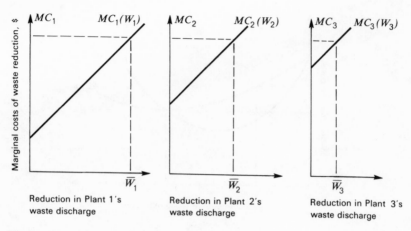

Figure 27.

and MC_3, i.e., for any level of waste reduction W by each individual firm,

$$MC_2(W) = \tfrac{1}{2}\{MC_1(W) + MC_3(W)\}.$$

Being linear, the curves also have the property that W_2 associated with any level of MC is equal to the average of W_1 and W_3 associated with that MC. Suppose now that a stream standard is established which requires that the total combined waste reduction by the three firms equals $3\overline{W}_2$. The least cost allocation to achieve this level of waste reduction is $W_1 = \overline{W}_1$, $W_2 = \overline{W}_2$, and $W_3 = \overline{W}_3$. For the water quality agency to achieve this least-cost solution through a system of effluent standards it would have to know the cost curve for each discharger. However, with a system of effluent charges all it needs to know is the cost curve for an average or typical firm such as the second plant in Figure 27.[3]

There is one circumstance where effluent standards could in principle achieve minimum cost in meeting a stream standard while charges could not. This is where a stream standard affects only one or a few dischargers and requires only low level treatment for its attainment. To see this consider the long-run average and marginal waste reduction costs for a waste treatment plant indicated in Figure 28. Say that the pictured plant is the only one affected by a stream standard, and that the plant must have reduction capacity x_1 to meet the standard. No single effluent charge would induce waste reduction to that level. The lowest effluent charge which would induce any waste reduction is B. A lower charge would induce no waste reduction because investment

[3] This formulation was suggested by Louis M. Falkson.

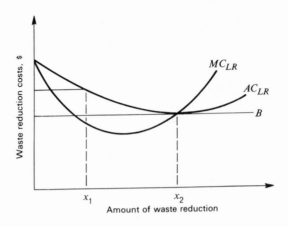

Figure 28.

costs could not be recovered. But a charge at level *B* induces treatment to point x_2, which is higher than needed and therefore excessively costly. This may be a problem in the case of a large stream with great assimilative capacity, comparatively few points of waste discharge, and a relatively large number of points where specified standards must be met. This could turn out to be a *significant* problem in using effluent charges to obtain efficient results where stream standards apply to all points along the stream as they frequently do. Empirical study of this matter is needed.[4]

SOME FURTHER COMMENTS ON CHARGES

Where actual conditions are more complicated than those outlined above, detailed information is needed on specific alternatives and their related marginal costs at each outfall for forecasting, and later establishing, either appropriate effluent charges or appropriate effluent standards. In fact, if there is substantial direct interaction among waste discharges, implementing either system becomes very complex, and reasonable rules of thumb will have to be developed for the regulation of individual waste discharges.

The charges alternative still seems to have certain advantages although these are harder to specify than in the previous cases. For example, a charge offers some incentive to take action even to the lowest level of waste discharge, while a standard (even though stated in terms of quantity rather than concentration) provides no incentive to curb waste discharge beyond the required level even though it might be

[4] See J. C. Liebman's case study of the Willamette in *The Optimal Allocation of Stream Dissolved Oxygen Resources* (Cornell University Water Resources Center, 1965).

possible to do so quite inexpensively. To put it another way, for any given level of information, the charges alternative would cost less in terms of resources because charges automatically tend toward an equalization of marginal costs.

If the complexities in an actual situation result in the specification of a stream standard rather than an actual effort to assess and distribute damage costs, the advantages of the charges procedure are those already described. And for any given degree of approximation of optimum results, the information or administrative requirements for charges are no greater than for effluent standards. If the burden of proof concerning the quality of effluents can be put on the discharger for one method, it can be for the other as well.

In a dynamic context, charges have the advantage of exerting a continuous pressure on the waste discharger to improve his waste-handling technology. Under an effluent standards system, the waste discharger has no incentive to do more than meet the standard. In the case of an effluent charge it is always in the interest of the waste discharger to develop and employ cost-reducing technology to diminish his discharge by keeping his (falling) incremental costs of waste reduction in balance with the charge.

A final point—and one that may be extremely important in implementing large-scale regional measures—is that the effluent charge yields revenue, whereas effluent standards and subsidies do not. Even if the revenues are not used for water quality management—and whether they should be is a matter for economic analysis—the revenue yielding aspect is desirable because the effluent charge does not have the resource misallocation effects of most other taxes. We expand on this point later.

SOME EQUITY QUESTIONS

This study is built largely upon the concept of economic efficiency, but obtaining the maximum net value from the use of a resource is not the only objective relevant to decision making. Equity may be a significant consideration in water quality management policy. Any change in the rules on which decisions are based will result in some rather arbitrary gains and losses. For example, if an industrial plant is built on the banks of a stream with the expectation that no effective limitation on waste discharge would ever be required, and then such limitation is imposed, the result will be a severe decline of capital values—perhaps even shutdown of the plant. Any effective control program faces this problem and we shall suggest an approach to it in Chapter 9.

Another context in which questions of equity arise is the distribution of costs of a program even where no actual cases of hardship occur. We offer no criterion of equity in this study because we can find no analytical basis for doing so. We can only record what we hope will be reasonable impressions. The idea that the waste discharger should bear the external costs of his discharge will strike most persons as equitable. This is analogous to requiring a firm or municipality to pay the full cost of the materials, labor, and energy it uses, which does not seem to offend most people's sense of equity.[5]

If effluent standards or charges are used to implement a stream water quality standard, the equity issues are considerably more complicated. At first glance it may seem equitable to require all waste dischargers in the relevant area to meet the same effluent standard or to cut back proportionally when a stream standard is being violated. However, our theory tells us that the result will be inefficient because marginal costs of reducing waste discharge will not be equated except by accident. Moreover, empirical research has shown that the inefficiency of such approaches may be substantial.[6] This result, of course, suggests that there must be some distribution of costs of an efficient program which will leave everybody better off than the equal reduction alternative. It is possibly the most important characteristic of the economist's efficiency concept that gains in efficiency produce net benefits which can be distributed in such a way that everyone is made better off. When rearrangements can no longer be made which make this possible, an efficient point has been reached. Is it really equitable to make all waste dischargers adhere to the same effluent standard when there can be large differences in the costs of achieving it?

Perhaps the scheme that would strike one as most inequitable is the efficiently programmed effluent standards approach because it emphasizes waste reduction by dischargers with low marginal waste reduction costs.[7] In effect, it could penalize those with low costs and present the high-cost waste discharger with a free property right to continue his waste discharge unmodified. It would put a premium on costly waste disposal methods.[8]

The preceding discussion of equity has focused on the distribution of costs of water quality management. Equally relevant are equity considerations with respect to who gains from water quality improvement.

[5] Compare the statement by a Dow Chemical Company official: "We are convinced that pollution control is part of the cost of doing business and we have always treated it that way. We firmly believe that industry can be clean and profitable at the same time, and we have amply proven this to our satisfaction." C. Gerstacker, "Management's Role in Pollution Control," *Industrial Water Engineering*, Vol. 3, No. 4 (1966), p. 39.

[6] See the case study of the Delaware estuary in the next chapter. See also J. C. Liebman, *op. cit.*, pp. 29ff.

[7] See the Delaware case study in the next chapter.

[8] In accordance with the reasoning in Chapter 5, it might also induce some longer-term adjustments that are unfavorable from an efficiency point of view.

If, in fact, much of the allocation of resources to water quality improvement has to be "justified" in terms of recreation and aesthetic benefits, whether or not the resulting distribution of benefits is in accord with social policy regarding income distribution must also be considered.

CONCLUSION

The effluent charge can be used to achieve stream water quality standards efficiently, i.e., at lowest economic or resource cost. It tends to induce the least costly combination of measures for waste reduction at each outfall, and the least-cost distribution of waste reduction among outfalls, thereby minimizing the real resources cost of attaining a stream water quality standard. In the process, it will normally yield a net revenue as well.

What happens is that each waste discharger is charged in proportion to the use he makes of a resource—the waste assimilative and transport capacity of the watercourse. The waste discharger can compare his marginal costs and marginal charges and decide whether it pays him to reduce his waste, and to what degree. The revenue that accrues to the agency from the charges can be viewed as a rental return on a *natural resource*. How much this will be depends on the scarcity of the resource, i.e., how small the natural flow is, how high the standard is, how highly developed the basin is.[9] It is as though parties wishing to use other parts of the public domain—public land, for instance—were competing for its use and thereby establishing its rental value, and the rental return was accruing to the public. This strikes us as equitable.

We have focused in our theoretical development on charges on actual waste discharge. In principle, of course, charges should be levied on all activities which reduce water quality sufficiently to impose external costs. This may not be administratively feasible in some instances, but it should be possible to assess a hydropower plant which draws water from the oxygen-depleted strata of reservoirs in the summer months, discharges it into a stream, and causes a reduction in the dissolved oxygen content of the stream. Similarly, other activities which divert or deplete water in such a way as to reduce assimilative capacity should be subject to charges.

Our analysis so far leads us to the conclusion that systems of charges may properly be viewed as a central tool of water quality management. We feel that regional water quality management agencies should be provided with this tool. We feel also, however, that other devices such as litigation between waste dischargers and affected parties and between individual parties and the regional agency and the selective

[9] This point is demonstrated rigorously in the Appendix to Chapter 10.

enforcement of effluent standards can be useful complements. We expand on these points in the concluding chapter of this part. But first we relate the points made so far to two actual situations where the focus is still on actions at individual outfalls or discharge points.

Cases Comparing Effluent Charges and Effluent Standards

8

In this chapter we illustrate the ideas of the previous chapters by describing how they might be applied to water quality management problems in two of the great industrial river valleys of the United States —the Ohio and the Delaware. The Ohio case is largely hypothetical, but in regard to the Delaware there are empirical results to report. The study of the Delaware illustrates the kind of information which it would be useful to have before an effluent charges system is implemented to achieve a stream standard, i.e., a specified level of water quality. In a final section we describe some experiences where charges have been levied on effluents on a smaller scale—by municipalities on industries discharging to municipal sewer systems and by industries on internal units to control the magnitude and nature of effluents.

CHLORIDE CONTROL IN THE OHIO

Three approaches are discussed in this section. The first of these is "Chloride Control Considerations for the Ohio River," a staff report prepared in 1957 for the deliberation of the Ohio River Valley Water Sanitation Commission (ORSANCO).[1] This report, subsequently cited as "Chloride Control," represents the first effort in the United States to view a waste disposal problem on a fully basin-wide basis and to articulate waste discharge at all points with a regional water quality objective. The ORSANCO proposal, which uses a stream standards-effluent standards approach, is compared with two alternatives. The first alternative bases effluent charges on damage costs and aims at minimizing the costs associated with disposal of chlorides, i.e., damages plus reduction costs. The ORSANCO proposal and this alternative are shown in Table 7.

The second alternative is limited to the stream standards approach that underlies the ORSANCO proposal but it incorporates effluent charges. It is discussed separately later.

[1] The report was made to the Commission by the ORSANCO staff and does not necessarily reflect the Commission's views.

Salinity (used synonymously with chlorides in this section), at least in the comparatively low concentrations foreseen in the Ohio, does not affect some of the uses which present the most difficult problems of evaluation and quantification. Nor is the problem of tracing and forecasting salinity levels complicated by the degradation processes characteristic of many other waste materials. However, by being comparatively amenable to systematic regional management, salinity presents an opportunity to illustrate the ideas of the previous chapter in a relatively uncomplicated form.

Before describing and assessing the ORSANCO proposal for controlling salinity, it is useful to consider some of the more significant characteristics of salinity as a waste.

The relationship of salinity to other waste discharges is basically additive. Within rather wide limits, salinity has little effect upon organic waste degradation processes or the virulence of toxic substances.[2] This means that the synergistic and/or cancelling effects that may occur with toxic and degradable wastes, for example, are ordinarily not present. Saline wastes can in large measure be analyzed separately from other residual materials in a watercourse.

Within a comparatively wide range, saline wastes have little or no effect on recreational, environmental, and health conditions. Salinity cannot be seen; within the limits ordinarily encountered it is not destructive of fish life;[3] and it is generally not dangerous to health unless concentrations become very high.[4]

Since salinity is not subject to reduction by treatment except at very high cost, generally the only economically feasible ways of reducing concentrations in watercourses are to cut back the level of salinity-producing activities and to make fuller use of stream dilution capacity. In a few instances process changes can be instituted to reduce saline discharge.

There are a number of ways in which the dilution capacity of a stream can be used more effectively: (1) wastes can be temporarily stored and discharged in a programmed manner corresponding to streamflow; (2) the streamflow pattern can be altered; and (3) the salinity-discharging industries can reschedule production so as to curtail output or even temporarily shut down during periods of low streamflow.

---

[2] See the discussion in F. Sierp, *Gewerbliche und Industrielle Abwaesser* (Berlin: Springer-Verlag, 1959), pp. 606 ff.; and F. J. Ludzak and D. K. Nornn, "Tolerance of High Salinity by Conventional Sewerage Treatment Processes" (Paper presented to the 37th Annual Conference Water Pollution Control Federation, Bal Harbour, Florida, 1964).

[3] Sierp, *op. cit.*

[4] See J. E. McKee and H. W. Wolf, *Water Quality Criteria* (2nd ed.; The Resources Agency of California, Publication No. 3-A, 1963), p. 160.

From an economic efficiency point of view, consideration must be given to the adjustments that can be made by the industries and municipalities that use the water. These include, but are not limited to: incurring corrosion costs, incurring lesser product quality, and temporarily shutting down salinity-sensitive activities during periods of low streamflow. Longer-run adjustments would include the installation of demineralizers or other desalting equipment, and the utilization of corrosion-resistant materials. The costs of these alternatives are what were referred to as damage costs in the preceding chapters.

Except for irrigated areas where the salt load is both increased and concentrated in the return flows from irrigated lands, high levels of salinity (not of natural origin) ordinarily stem from comparatively few outfalls, even in large, highly developed basins. Since household water use causes only a small increase in salinity, municipalities make a relatively minor contribution to the salinity load unless their discharges include saline industrial wastes. The main source is industrial waste discharge, principally from salt, potash, steel, chemical, crude petroleum and petroleum refining industries. "Chloride Control" indicates that during periods of low flow at least *three-quarters* of the chloride found in the Ohio originates from industrial waste discharges, and the major part of this comes from one tributary—the Muskingum.

Quality Criteria and the Stream Standard

The quality criteria—related to uses of water—upon which the "Chloride Control" recommendations for a control program are based are as follows:

	Chloride-ion concentration
Public supplies:	
Acceptable	Less than 125 ppm
Doubtful	125–250 ppm
Unsatisfactory	More than 250 ppm
Industrial supplies:	
Acceptable	Less than 50 ppm
Doubtful	50–175 ppm
Unsatisfactory	More than 175 ppm

When the report matched findings with respect to chloride in the Ohio River against its quality criteria, it was revealed that "unsatisfactory" concentrations were being approached in one stretch of the river. Periods of quality impairment violating the criteria could therefore be expected to result from industrial expansion. The report suggests, however, that by timely institution of a control program based on "proportionate discharge," the river could accommodate chloride-bearing wastes and still meet acceptable quality conditions.

"Chloride Control" proposed that the Commission "adopt a control program which would limit chloride concentrations in the Ohio River at points of use for public and industrial supplies from exceeding (1) a monthly average concentration of 125 ppm at all flows above and including the minimum monthly average flow (called the design flow) that has a probability of occurrence once in ten years; and (2) a maximum concentration of 250 ppm at any time."

The monthly average limiting value of 125 ppm was recommended because ". . . water of this quality is within the acceptable range for public supplies and would not be unsatisfactory for cooling purposes, which is the major industrial use." (p. 6.)

With respect to the design flow, "Chloride Control" stated, "Once-in-10-year drought severity or minimum flow provides a reasonable factor of safety in the design of a chloride control program for the maintenance of satisfactory quality of water for public supplies and for major industrial uses. If, in the opinion of the Commission a greater degree of protection is desired, the fifteen or twenty year minimum flow could be substituted; if a lesser degree of assurance is considered adequate, then the five-year flow might be chosen." (p. 34.)

Only the most fragmentary evidence was available concerning the costs of salinity to industrial water users. The evidence that could be marshalled related to isolated instances of damages experienced as a result of a given time of exposure to a given concentration. It provided little basis for determining a functional relationship between different levels and durations of salinity and damage costs to water users. Without better information from industry, it would be difficult to avoid rather arbitrary, ill-informed, and inefficient regulation procedures.

A Comparison of Two Approaches to Chloride Control:
ORSANCO Proposal "A" and an Effluent Charges Proposal

The general idea of the control program suggested by the ORSANCO staff is that waste discharges upstream are to be cut back in a pre-arranged, proportional manner during periods of low flow in order to avoid violating the stated quality conditions at some downstream point of use. The point of use selected was Huntington, West Virginia, which was the point on the main stem presently experiencing the highest concentration.

The report stated that during low-flow periods the chloride load in the Ohio River at Huntington was just about in balance with the as-similative capacity. Therefore, if there were further expansion of industry upstream in the basin, the quality standards could be met only by reducing chloride discharges during critical periods.

Two programs for cutting back saline discharges during periods of low flow—presumably by temporary storage of wastes—were recommended as possibilities. Proposal "A," the one preferred by the ORSANCO staff, is summarized in Table 7, and compared with an alternative possibility based on the use of damage functions and effluent charges. The table concludes with the ORSANCO staff's evaluation of their proposal and our evaluation of the alternative approach.

An additional, but important, point in the comparison of the two approaches is the amount of information required. The amount differs because the proposals are not symmetrical as to objective or effect. The objective of the system of charges is to approximate an economically optimum level of water quality in relation to chloride concentration at lowest costs; it takes into consideration both the damage costs imposed on the water users and the chloride reduction costs incurred by the waste dischargers. Other things being equal, the discharger whose wastes enter far upstream and consequently affect water reused a large number of times will bear a higher charge and therefore have a greater incentive to introduce more far-reaching control measures than a waste discharger farther downstream. For each waste discharger, the incremental reduction costs will tend to be equated with the charges (damage costs). Framing such a system of charges requires reasonable approximations of the incremental downstream costs imposed by individual effluent discharges.

In preparing "Chloride Control," the ORSANCO staff made some evaluation of salinity damages as a basis for setting the chloride tolerance limits. The staff decided that damage to the environment, to recreation, to degradation of organic wastes, and to public health would be negligible over the anticipated range of chloride concentrations on the main stem of the Ohio River. Effects on navigation equipment were disregarded because the staff had no information that would suggest a quantitative relationship between chloride concentration in freshwater streams and corrosion of boathulls, dams, locks, bridges, and dock structures.

Consequently, the only damages that would require evaluation in order to institute a system of charges are those relating to some aspects of public water supply and to industrial water uses.

The two relevant aspects of public water supply are palatability and corrosiveness. Within the range of salinity expected in the Ohio, palatability would be affected very little, if at all, and corrosive effects would

Table 7.   Comparison of ORSANCO Proposal "A" and the Effluent Charges Proposal

---

ORSANCO PROPOSAL "A"

This proposal calls for a uniform percentage cutback of both main-stem and combined tributary chloride waste loads above a main-stem point of use at times when desired quality limits might be exceeded; this action to be coupled with an adjustment of cutbacks in each tributary dependent upon the relative amount of dilution water furnished by the tributary. The following procedures are quoted from the ORSANCO proposal.

Chloride from Industries

Basis for Controlling Discharge

1. Quality conditions desired at a main-stem point of use would serve as a basis for regulating upstream discharges of chloride waste. This means that the interstate point of use where the highest concentration of chloride occurs would be the control point.

Adjusting Discharge to Flow

2. Quality control at a point of use would be achieved by scheduling the discharge of chloride wastes above that point. This means that the amount discharged from a source must be proportioned to the availability of streamflow. Variation in flow, therefore, is the determining factor in establishing schedules of permitted discharge.

Control of Tributary Loads

3. Chloride affecting a point of use on the Ohio River emanates from wastes discharged into: (a) tributaries; and (b) directly into the main stem. Because Commission concern with intrastate streams is limited to the quality of the tributary only as it enters the main stem, each tributary load would be recognized as a single source of chloride. Thus, the total chloride load at a point of use on the main stem is the sum of the tributary loads and the individual discharges to the main stem from industries and municipalities.

---

* This procedure suggests how charges can serve to co-ordinate the activities of an authority on a main stem which has large amounts of dilution capacity and scattered sources of waste discharges with the activities of an authority on an intensely developed tributary like the Muskingum or the Mahoning. (These activities might include system planning, construction, and operation.) The authority on the main stem would view the residual amount of waste delivered by a tributary as a waste outfall, and it would levy upon the tributary authority the costs which these wastes impose downstream. Costs on the main stem would vary with the over-all amount of dilution available. However, costs at points of use on the main stem would in no way depend upon the origin of the dilution water. The tributary authority on which downstream costs are assessed would then be induced to view them as opportunity costs in its own quality management activities and plan and operate its system accordingly.

Table 7.   (Continued)

EFFLUENT CHARGES PROPOSAL

In this column a system of charges for effluent discharge based on damage costs is contrasted point-by-point with the ORSANCO proposal. This procedure would tend toward a minimization of costs for any given waste load and would tend to lead to an economically optimum amount of waste discharge.

Chloride from Industries

Basis for Controlling Discharge

1. Downstream damages would serve as the basis for effluent charges and would provide the incentive for regulating upstream discharges of chloride waste. This means that there would be no single control point downstream. Control at any outfall would be a function of downstream damages.

Adjusting Discharge to Flow

2. Quality control at points of use would be achieved by causing upstream waste dischargers to view an estimate of incremental downstream damages as an opportunity cost in making their own production, plant design, and location decisions.

Unless there is a fully compensating variation in discharge, the level of salinity will rise during low-flow periods, and consequently downstream damages and effluent charges will also increase. The increased charges provide an incentive for industry to institute temporary storage combined with programmed discharge of wastes, output adjustments, and perhaps other measures. The waste discharger will have an incentive to engage in each of these alternatives until their individual incremental costs equal the effluent charges (downstream damages) which they avoid. An individual discharger will find it worthwhile to discharge in an unchanged fashion only if the charges levied for downstream damages are less than the costs of avoiding them.

Control of Tributary Loads

3. Because Commission concern with intrastate streams is limited to the quality of the tributary only as it enters the main stem, each tributary load would be recognized as a single source of chlorides.

Charges will be applied to tributaries and main-stem waste discharges in an identical fashion, i.e., each tributary will be taken as an individual outfall. The amount of each outfall's contribution to salinity at various downstream points will be computed and the resulting damages evaluated. In assessing downstream costs, the dilution contributed by a tributary is essentially irrelevant. For example, in the situation illustrated in Figure 29, all the plants could move to a single tributary or the main stem above the point of confluence without altering downstream main-stem costs. On the other hand, such moves would alter the costs occurring on the tributaries themselves or on the upper main stem.*

If the tributary authority augments flow during low-flow periods, an amendment of the above line of reasoning is in order. To *provide an appropriate incentive* to the tributary authority to use this device, it should be credited with the incremental reduction in main-stem costs which results from enhanced dilution on the main stem.

If the tributary authority did not build and operate facilities for chloride control, but did adhere to the principles indicated in this study, it would assess the costs arising within the tributary and an appropriate portion of main-stem user charges to the individual dischargers. The latter would be based upon the individual discharger's contribution to the chloride load discharging into the main stem.

* For note, see facing page.

Table 7. (Continued)

ORSANCO PROPOSAL "A"

Dilution Water

4. Dilution water available at the control point on the Ohio River would be considered as the sum total of the flow contributed from each of the upstream tributary drainage basins.

Chloride Quotas for Drainage Basins

5. Because chloride capacity of a stream is a direct function of flow, it is possible under any given set of circumstances to establish for each drainage basin a chloride allotment based on the load conditions existing at the control point. Establishment of a chloride allotment in proportion to contributed flow, and related to the loads on the main stem and the tributaries, is an equitable method for the allocation of total available capacity. It recognizes that each drainage basin in the Compact district should be entitled to that share of chloride capacity as determined by load conditions at an interstate point-of-use and for which it can provide the proportionate amount of dilution water.

Adjusting Quotas

6. The quota for any drainage basin, it should be noted, represents a proportionate share of capacity; it is not a quantity fixed for all time. As new or expanded industries in the district seek accommodation for their waste loads (either on a tributary or on the main stem of the Ohio River) the allotment previously assigned to various drainage basins would be uniformly adjusted, along with the permitted discharge from mainstem sources of chloride. How often such revisions might be required is wholly dependent on the location and size of new loads. Presumably, adjustments would be made only at periodic intervals.

Basins Contributing Heavy Salinity Loads

7. Application of the uniform percentage-reduction rule to chloride discharges from upstream drainage basins would be made with regard to establishing a balance between contributed load and allotment. At present there is at least one tributary drainage basin in the district that contributes a chloride load far in excess of its proportionate allotment as determined by dilution water. There are other drainage basins whose contribution of chloride is less than their calculated allotments based on the dilution water they supply. The interests of equity would not be served, therefore, without first imposing cutbacks on all those basins that exceed their allotments and until all of the drainage basins are in approximate balance.

Information Provided to and by Industry

8. Once the proportionate allotment for a drainage basin has been established, a load-discharge schedule based on flow variations would be computed for main-stem industries and for each tributary. These schedules would be prepared by the Commission staff in consultation with the state agencies and then submitted to the Commission for consideration; after adoption by the Commission the schedules would be referred to the states for appropriate action with their industries. Discharge schedules for individual industries would be referenced to flow as recorded at a stream-gauging station from which the industrial plant can obtain readings. Effective conduct of the program necessitates some form of record on discharges be maintained by each industrial plant for transmittal to the state agency with copies to the Commission.

Table 7.   (Continued)

EFFLUENT CHARGES PROPOSAL

Dilution Water

4. No separate attention would need to be given to, or allowance made for, dilution capacity contributed by the individual upstream tributary drainage basins, except for low-flow augmentation as noted above.

Chloride Quotas for Drainage Basins

5. See 4.

Adjusting Quotas

6. See 4.

Basins Contributing Heavy Salinity Loads

7. Application of charges to wastes discharged from tributaries would result in a heavy charge upon tributaries like the Muskingum which contribute absolutely large waste loads. Other things equal, this would result in large absolute reductions of waste loads from these tributaries. However, all other dischargers would have an incentive, proportionate to downstream costs imposed, to cut back on waste discharges.

Information Provided to and by Industry

8. Once a schedule of charges has been established for each level of flow and each major outfall, the individual plants are left to make their own flow-waste discharge schedules. Charges to the individual industrial plant or tributary will be based on the flow recorded at a stream-gauging station from which the industrial plant or authority responsible for the tributary can obtain readings. For planning purposes each plant should be provided with an estimate of the "expected value" of damages per unit of its waste discharge.

Each plant should maintain a record of its discharges, preferably by an automatic recording device, for transmittal to the state agency with copies to the Commission. Since the appropriate basis for the charge is chloride load rather than effluent volume, the salinity of the discharged water should also be recorded. The system of charges will not have a "design flow" but will view damages and user charges as continuously variable. At streamflows above certain levels, damages will probably be so small that it will not pay to administer the system. It may be found, for example, that flow conditions on the Ohio during the next decade or so are not low enough each season or even year to merit putting the program into operation.

Table 7.   (Continued)

ORSANCO PROPOSAL "A"

Chloride from Municipalities

Control of chloride from municipalities presents a special problem. The chloride content of sewage cannot be lagooned or otherwise handled on a proportionate-discharge basis such as industrial wastes. Yet some form of control should be exercised because municipal sewage could be abnormally loaded with chloride as the result of certain types of industrial activity within the community.

It is recommended, therefore, that after a control program has been inaugurated the Commission authorize an investigation of chloride content from municipal sewage-treatment works. Where it is determined that the sewage contains abnormal concentrations of chloride, then the municipality should be placed under compulsion by the state agency to which it is responsible for determining the origin of the chloride within its system and institute necessary controls.

Merits of Proposal "A"

Here are the salient reasons why Proposal A recommends itself for consideration:

From the viewpoint of rationality, the proposal rests on the sound practice of relating control to quality conditions as revealed at a point of use. Further, the control is exercised in accordance with the ability of a stream to assimilate the wastes.

In addition, a method is provided for an equitable allocation of stream capacity among the states and their industries.

The permitted discharge of waste is regulated in accordance with a flow variation—as, when and where that flow occurs.

It places responsibility directly on the producer of the waste for regulating his discharge in accordance with a regional pattern of control.

Within limitations imposed by conditions in the main stem, control of industrial loads discharged to tributaries is solely within jurisdiction of the states involved.

Table 7.   (Continued)

EFFLUENT CHARGES PROPOSAL

Chloride from Municipalities

Control of chloride from municipalities presents a special problem since it is ordinarily not feasible to segregate chlorides from the municipal sewage or to treat them and, in the case of large cities, temporary storage of total waste effluent is usually very costly.

It is recommended, however, that chloride stemming from municipal outfalls be assessed on the same basis as that from industrial outfalls. This would prompt municipalities to determine the origin of the chloride concentrations and to assess charges on the originators, who would then have an incentive for reducing such discharges.

Merits of the Charges Alternative

The proposal rests on the principle of economic efficiency that the design and management of production processes and product outputs, and waste disposal decisions should be made in light of all opportunity costs. The proposed system of charges would impose a social opportunity cost, which an enterprise escapes when discharge is not regulated. By the same token, the system charges would induce upstream waste reduction activity only to the extent that incremental downstream damage costs exceed incremental upstream reduction costs. The quality of water in the stream would be a *dependent variable* rather than a *prescribed standard*.

This procedure would tend to induce optimum use of the stream's capacity to dilute wastes, as it would tend to minimize the costs associated with a given level of waste to be disposed of and provide an incentive to produce an optimum amount of waste.

The varying of charges with streamflow provides an incentive for regulating discharge in correspondence with streamflow. However, such regulation of discharge is not mandatory. If a waste discharger finds it expensive to provide temporary storage of wastes, he may simply pay the charge. On the other hand, in instances where effluent storage can be provided inexpensively, or where product output can be economically stored and diverted to other time periods, the charges will be avoided to varying degrees.

The suggested procedure places responsibility directly on the producer of the waste for taking action which is efficient from the social as well as the private point of view. It does not impose any arbitrarily determined course of action on him.

The appropriate handling of industrial waste loads discharged into tributaries is a function of the authorities responsible for the tributaries upon which the charge is levied. Whatever action the authorities take will have to be taken in light of downstream costs, i.e., damages.

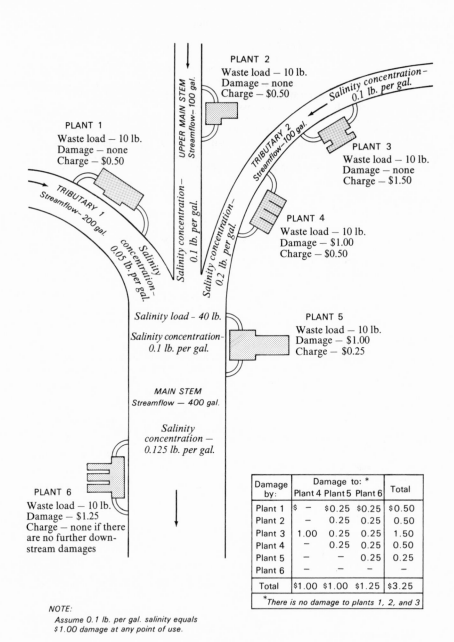

PLANT 2
Waste load — 10 lb.
Damage — none
Charge — $0.50

Salinity concentration—
0.1 lb. per gal.

PLANT 1
Waste load — 10 lb.
Damage — none
Charge — $0.50

TRIBUTARY 1
Streamflow— 200 gal.

UPPER MAIN STEM
Streamflow— 100 gal.

Salinity concentration—
0.1 lb. per gal.

TRIBUTARY 2
Streamflow— 100 gal.

PLANT 3
Waste load — 10 lb.
Damage — none
Charge — $1.50

Salinity
concentration—
0.05 lb. per gal.

Salinity concentration—
0.2 lb. per gal.

PLANT 4
Waste load — 10 lb.
Damage — $1.00
Charge — $0.50

Salinity load - 40 lb.

Salinity concentration—
0.1 lb. per gal.

PLANT 5
Waste load — 10 lb.
Damage — $1.00
Charge — $0.25

MAIN STEM
Streamflow — 400 gal.

Salinity
concentration —
0.125 lb. per gal.

PLANT 6
Waste load — 10 lb.
Damage — $1.25
Charge — none if there
are no further down-
stream damages

Damage by:	Damage to: *			Total
	Plant 4	Plant 5	Plant 6	
Plant 1	$ —	$0.25	$0.25	$0.50
Plant 2	—	0.25	0.25	0.50
Plant 3	1.00	0.25	0.25	1.50
Plant 4	—	0.25	0.25	0.50
Plant 5	—	—	0.25	0.25
Plant 6	—	—	—	—
Total	$1.00	$1.00	$1.25	$3.25

*There is no damage to plants 1, 2, and 3

NOTE:
Assume 0.1 lb. per gal. salinity equals
$1.00 damage at any point of use.

Streamflow is given at levels indicated.

Figure 29. Schematic illustration of salinity discharges and damages on the tributaries and main stem of a river system. (Quantities are per unit of time.)

likely be limited to hot water systems.[5] With regard to evaluation of the cost of corrosion, one study has reported that the "final determination of the corrosion effects of a new increment of supply or a change in treatment must usually be determined for each specific case by means of a series of empirical tests. As a result of these tests and a knowledge of the techniques and costs of corrosion inhibition, estimates can be made of the cost of corrosion and the cost of possible inhibition treatments."[6] Studies of this kind could yield cost functions in terms of chloride concentration and period of exposure, and the cost of the studies should not be a major obstacle to implementing a program of charges.

Without doubt the most important damaging effect of increasing salinity levels on the Ohio will be to industries using water for cooling, for processing, and for boiler feed. Cooling water is by far the largest use, accounting for about 75 per cent of total intake in the Ohio River Basin in 1964.

With respect to cooling water, the estimates of industrial damage reported in "Chloride Control" were obtained from a few examples from steel mills in which chloride concentrations are stated as "threshold" values. For example, the Sparrows Point plant of Bethlehem Steel Corporation utilizes the effluent from the City of Baltimore sewage treatment plant for cooling water, and the agreement between the Corporation and the City of Baltimore is quoted as stipulating that the chloride content shall not exceed 175 ppm calculated on the basis of monthly averages. For cooling rollers in steel rolling mills, a representative of a steel corporation is quoted in the report as saying that chloride concentrations above 175 ppm would cause pitting of rollers. The evidence cited on corrosion of condenser tubes related only to very high levels of chloride concentration. In sum, there was no indication that *costs* (damages) had been determined and related in any systematic way to a range of chloride concentrations.

With respect to process water, there was again no systematic attempt to relate chloride concentration to damages. The report quoted a consulting engineer as saying that a chloride concentration of more than 50 ppm would be unsatisfactory for the production of stainless steel. Certain types of production processes are so sensitive to chlorides that water with almost any chloride concentration requires some degree of treatment. Thus, a slight increase in chloride concentration at the

---

[5] Palatability presents difficulties in evaluation which corrosion and other physical destruction do not. Some evidence of its economic value might, however, be found by investigating bottled water sales for areas with differing levels of salinity in their public supplies. See also McKee and Wolf, *op. cit.*

[6] J. Hirshleifer, J. C. DeHaven, and J. W. Milliman, *Water Supply: Economics, Technology, and Policy* (University of Chicago Press, 1960), p. 198.

intake has relatively little effect on incremental costs. According to the ORSANCO report, information provided by the Interstate Commission on the Delaware River Basin to the ORSANCO staff indicates that in a number of process water applications the losses may be approximated by linear functions. However, no details are available; consequently, this presumption must be subjected to systematic, empirical investigation.

Water quality is most critical with respect to boiler feedwater, and especially for high-pressure boilers, operating at more than 1,000 pounds per square inch. The concentration of total dissolved solids in feedwater for high-pressure boilers is measured in terms of parts per billion rather than parts per million. Consequently, even with chloride concentrations in the Ohio River of less than 125 ppm, treatment of intake water is necessary to achieve the quality necessary for boiler feedwater. However, this is a very small portion of total water use.

Not only is there not enough information concerning industrial damages for introducing a system of charges, but the cutback suggested in "Chloride Control" does not seem to be related to any systematic study of costs and gains, probably in large measure because information was difficult to obtain from industry. Research to identify the costs to industrial users associated with various levels of water quality is urgently needed, but efforts of this kind can be successful only if industry cooperates.

"Chloride Control" (p. 15) quotes a statement by Harold A. Thomas, Jr., Professor of Civil and Sanitary Engineering at Harvard, in which he says in part, "There is some evidence for believing the threshold concentration for corrosion damage is lower than the 50 ppm figure sometimes quoted. This is based in part upon the fact that chloride increases corrosion by increasing the conductivity, and conductivity increases about in direct proportion to chloride increases."

This suggests that the notion of a threshold value which is embodied in the proportional cutback approach may not be entirely appropriate. The charges approach does not imply a threshold value, but views costs as being a continuous function of chloride concentrations. Moreover, Professor Thomas' statement suggests that damage may be approximately a linear function of concentration and duration.[7] If this is the case, it will ease the problem of determining and assessing the costs.

All of the major damages which salinity may cause in the Ohio appear to be amenable to reasonable quantification. Moreover, there is some presumption that damages will in some circumstances turn out to be

---

[7] This assumption also underlies the study by R. Eliassen and W. F. Rowland, *Industrial Benefits Derived from Improved Raw Water in the Contra Costa Canal* (Stanford University, Project on Engineering-Economic Planning, 1962).

a comparatively simple function of concentration and duration of chloride concentration.

A Program of Charges to Approximate a Limited Objective

A system of effluent charges could also be used to achieve the objective indicated in ORSANCO Proposal "A" of meeting specified levels of salinity at a selected downstream control point. The procedure in this case would be to set a uniform charge per unit of chloride discharged. This would have certain advantages over the ORSANCO required proportionate cutback upstream. First, the level at which the user charge must be set to be effective would provide an estimate of the marginal cost of meeting the standard, which is a vital piece of information for evaluating the policy. Second, the standard would tend to be met at lower real resources cost. Cutbacks, either by means of temporary storage or production adjustments, would tend to be made where it is most economical to do so rather than in an arbitrary across-the-board fashion. To achieve the required degree of withholding at minimum cost, the incremental costs of withholding must be equalized. This will tend to occur if all dischargers are subject to a uniform effluent charge but not if all dischargers are required to cut back proportionally. Dischargers who find it less expensive to pay the charges than to control discharge would of course do so. The funds paid to the control authority do not represent a use of resources and are available for other purposes.

To achieve even the circumscribed objective of meeting certain set standards at a control point by the use of charges, the control authority would need more information than if it simply ordered a proportionate cutback of all discharges. If the cutback were arbitrary, no information would be needed at all. However, a responsible authority would probably make at least a rough calculation of the cost of withholding discharge under representative conditions before ordering a proportionate cutback. This information could be made to yield an estimate of the response to various levels of charges which could serve as a basis for an initial system of charges. (A study of the sort we mean is reported below in the discussion of the Delaware.) Since some investment is usually needed to respond efficiently to effluent charges, the authority should make known its initial schedule of charges and indicate the charges per unit of chloride discharge for each level of streamflow, or the "expected value" of the probability distribution of charges, together with some information on the duration of various charge levels. The schedule of charges could then be adjusted to accord with the degree to which the initial schedule missed its goal and to reflect changing conditions such as the location of new industries. In short, the central merit of the charges approach is that it would tend toward an equalization of incremental costs of reduction at each discharge point. This means that the standard would be achieved with the least possible use of resources.

DISSOLVED OXYGEN IN THE DELAWARE ESTUARY

The computer model for forecasting dissolved oxygen conditions in the Delaware estuary, briefly described in Chapter 2, provided a basic tool for a study of effluent charges as a means of achieving a water quality standard in the estuary.[8] The study was made in connection with the work of a special interdepartmental committee on water quality control headed by Gardner Ackley, then Chairman of the President's Council of Economic Advisers.

The analytical model for the Delaware estuary segmented the watercourse into 30 sections, each 10,000 ft. to 20,000 ft. in length. The model permitted predicting the effects of a change in waste loads in one section upon all other affected sections. Superimposed on this model of the physical and biological behavior of the estuary is a cost optimizing model. This is in the form of a linear programming procedure. The programming model considers such items as: (1) location of a waste source with respect to the lowest part of the dissolved oxygen profile; (2) the relative cost to remove additional amounts of waste at each source; (3) the maximum quantity of waste it is deemed possible to remove; and (4) the proximity of one waste discharge to other waste discharges where removal may be less costly or the effect on the oxygen deficit more pronounced. (Thus the solutions show a number of trade-offs among individual waste sources.)

Data for the physical-biological and the economic programming models were obtained by sampling and survey methods. While data collection was conducted with as much accuracy as possible there are inevitably deficiencies in the information obtained. One that should be noted at the outset is that the waste removal cost information relates only to waste treatment and does not take account of the possibility of internal process adjustments and related measures by industrial waste dischargers. As we explained at some length in Chapter 4, over considerable ranges, internal adjustments are often more economical means for waste reduction than treatment. Thus the estimates of costs which

---

[8] See Federal Water Pollution Control Administration, *Report on the Effluent Charge Study* (1966), mimeo; and Edwin Johnson, "A Study in the Economics of Water Quality Management," *Water Resources Research*, Vol. 3, No. 2 (Second Quarter 1967). An excellent discussion of the effluent charges study is also found in Grant W. Schaumberg, Jr., *Water Pollution Control in the Delaware Estuary* (Harvard Water Program, May 1967), mimeo.

are cited later should be viewed as the maximum costs that might be associated with the various alternative waste reduction programs. None of them represent the true least cost solution.[9]

Using the data and analytical techniques sketched above and making the assumptions that direct controls would be effective and that waste dischargers would respond rationally to economic incentives, the study analyzed four programs for achieving alternative dissolved oxygen objectives in the estuary, i.e., different levels of water quality.

The first, and in a sense a standard of comparison for the others, is the least-cost linear programming solution (LC). This solution uses mathematical programming techniques to obtain the minimum cost distribution of waste removals. To implement this program as a control policy would require precise information on waste treatment costs at all outfalls and direct controls on all waste discharges. It would result in radically different levels of treatment and treatment costs at different outfalls. The reason is simply that it would concentrate treatment at those points where the critical oxygen sag can be reduced most inexpensively.

The second program is the Uniform Treatment Solution (UT), which requires all waste dischargers to reduce their waste loads by the same percentage. The percentage specified is the minimum needed to achieve the D.O. standard in the stream. This solution may be considered typical of the conventional administrative effluent standards approach to the problem of achieving a stream quality standard.

The third is the Single Effluent Charge Solution (SECH), under which each waste discharger in the estuary is charged the same price per unit of waste discharge, i.e., per pound of oxygen-demanding material. The solution examines responses of individual waste dischargers and identifies the minimum single charge which will induce sufficient reduction in waste discharge to achieve the standard.

The fourth is the Zone Effluent Charge Solution (ZECH), which uses a uniform effluent charge in each of three zones, instead of a uniform charge over all reaches of the estuary. Figure 30 shows the zones.

In none of these cases is there an explicit measurement of damages resulting from water quality degradation. Rather, the stream standard is used as a surrogate which may be viewed as a perfectly inelastic damage function. The problem then becomes one of meeting efficiency (least-cost) and equity (cost-distribution) criteria.

[9] The effluent charge study used early cost estimates based on waste treatment costs. The report of the Delaware Estuary Comprehensive Study described in Chapter 11 used more up-to-date information and considered a wider range of waste reduction alternatives, such as process changes, but did not reanalyze the effluent charges approach.

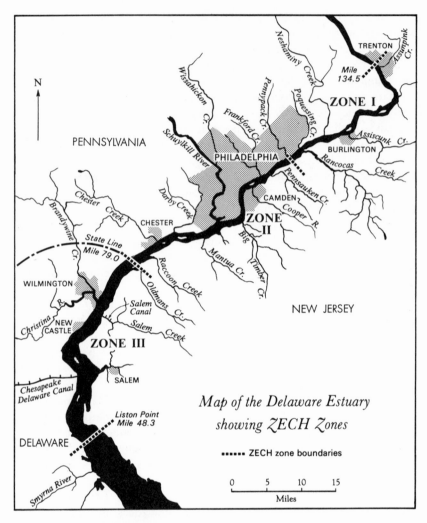

Figure 30. Source: FWPCA, *Delaware Estuary Comprehensive Study.*

The general conclusions which the Federal Water Pollution Control Administration (FWPCA) staff drew from this study were as follows:

1. Effluent charges should be seriously considered as a method for attaining water quality improvement;

2. Cost of waste treatment induced by a charge level will approach the least-cost treatment plan;

3. A charge level of 8 to 10 cents per pound of oxygen-demanding material discharged appears to produce relatively large increases in critical dissolved oxygen levels;

4. A charge of that level is not expected to cause major regional economic readjustments (such as the closing of industrial plants) in the study area;[10]

5. An effluent charge method entails greater administrative costs and management difficulties than conventional methods of water quality improvement, but the problems are not insurmountable and are not sufficiently great to negate the advantages of the charge method;

6. The charge method attains the same goal as a conventional method of improving water quality, but treatment costs are lower, and the effect on waste dischargers is more equitable. Also the charge provides a continuing incentive for the discharger to reduce his wastes discharge and serves as a guide to public investment decisions.[11]

In assessing the effects and costs of effluent charges, it was assumed that industries and municipalities would act rationally to minimize the cost associated with their waste discharges. Since internal process changes were not considered, this would mean equating marginal costs of treatment with the effluent charge. The costs reported in the text and tables below are in all instances actual economic or opportunity costs. They include only those cost items which reflect inputs of goods and services into the program and exclude cost items which represent transfer payments. It was recognized, however, that industrial plants make their decisions based upon monetary costs whether they represent actual resource inputs or transfers. For example, the corporate income tax will affect the net monetary cost of buying and operating equipment and will therefore influence decisions. For industrial discharges, therefore, the monetary costs are defined by the following functions:

$$C_I = K + (1 - r_F - r_s + r_F r_s)(OM + PT) - (r_F + r_s - r_F r_s)D,$$

where

C_I = annual cost of treatment for industrial discharges,
K = amortized capital cost, twenty-five-year economic life, 5 per cent interest,
r_F = Federal corporate income tax rate = 0.48,
r_s = applicable state corporate income tax rate for Pennsylvania, New Jersey, or Delaware,
OM = annual operation and maintenance charges,
PT = property taxes on capital investment,
D = annual depreciation based on twenty-five-year life, straight line method.

[10] In all but a few cases the total cost (cost of treatment plus effluent charge) was less than 1 per cent of the value of output. In most cases it was considerably less. See Johnson, *op. cit.*, Table 8. Another study shows roughly similar results with costs of waste treatment averaging approximately 1 per cent of *value added* in several industries. D. F. Bramhall and E. S. Mills, *Future Water Supply and Demand* (Maryland State Planning Department, April 1965).

[11] Federal Water Pollution Control Administration, *op. cit.*, p. 1.

For municipal plants, annual monetary costs are defined as:

$$C_M = K + OM ,$$

where

C_M = annual cost of municipal waste treatment,
K = amortized capital cost adjusted for federal grant available under the Water Quality Act of 1965, twenty-five-year life, 5 per cent interest, and
OM = annual operation and maintenance cost.

Since linear approximations to the true cost functions were required by the computer programs, marginal costs were assumed constant over a range of removal rates.

Efficiency Considerations

The economic costs associated with the four programs are shown below for two levels of water quality. The 3–4 ppm standard is the one that the FWPCA staff considered the practical maximum attainable in the estuary.

D.O. objective	Least-cost (LC)	Uniform treatment (UT)	Single effluent charge (SECH)	Zone effluent charge (ZECH)
		Million dollars per year		
2 ppm	1.6	5.0	2.4	2.4
3–4 ppm	7.0	20.0	12.0	8.6

The analysis indicates that the single effluent charge system would produce the specified quality levels at about one-half the cost of the uniform treatment method. At the higher quality level, the saving is especially significant. The present value of the cost stream saved is on the order of $150 million.[12]

The least-cost system is capable of reducing costs somewhat further since it programs waste discharges at each point specifically in relation to the cost of improving quality in the critical reach, but this comes at the cost of detailed information on treatment costs at each point and an

[12] A large cost difference between a uniform treatment program and a program which distributed treatment in accordance with a least-cost criterion was reported for the Willamette River by K. D. Kerri, "An Economic Approach to Water Quality Control," *Journal of the Water Pollution Control Federation* (December 1966), p. 1894. Similar results were reported for the Miami Basin in Ohio by M. W. Anderson, "Regional Water Quality Management in the Miami Basin" (Ph.D. Thesis, Carnegie Institute of Technology, Dept. of Civil Engineering), and for the Merrimack Valley in Massachusetts by A. S. Goodman and W. Dobbins, "Mathematical Model for Water Pollution Control Studies," *Journal of the Sanitary Engineering Division, Proceedings ASCE*, Vol. 92, No. SA6 (December 1966).

extremely inequitable distribution of costs.[13] The least-cost system is closely approached by ZECH at the higher quality level. In effect, ZECH "credits" upstream dischargers with the waste degradation that takes place in the stream—a necessary condition for full efficiency when effluent charges are used to achieve a standard at a critical reach in a stream. The ZECH program does not achieve full efficiency, however, because the basis for the "credit" is too broad.

At an effluent charge of 10 cents per pound of BOD, which the staff estimated would be needed for the zoned effluent charge program,[14] the administrative agency would collect about $7 million per year (rent on the assimilative capacity of the stream). As we shall explain in the next chapter, this revenue yielding capacity of the effluent charge system is a highly desirable attribute. Nevertheless, for the objective of 3–4 ppm of dissolved oxygen, the total cost to industry and municipalities— effluent charge plus cost of treatment—is about the same as the cost of treatment only under the uniform treatment program. About half of this outlay does not represent an actual resources cost but, if deemed desirable, could be redistributed among waste dischargers on the basis of equity criteria, used for general governmental purposes, or devoted to collective measures for improving water quality.

Before turning to a discussion of questions of equity, it should again be noted that an important efficiency advantage of the effluent charges programs as contrasted with the LC program is that they require less in the way of information and analytical refinement. A study of the type already performed for the Delaware estuary could serve as the basis for an effluent charge scheme. It would provide an estimate of the required charge, and changes could be made if responses to the charge indicate the need for adjustment. Actually, since the costs do not take account of the possibility of process change, the charge is probably too high and could be adjusted downward at a later point. Also, the charge provides a continuing incentive for the discharger to reduce his waste load by placing him under the continuing pressure of monetary penalties. He is induced to develop and use new technology. As new technology develops, the effluent charge could be gradually reduced while the stream standard is maintained or the standard could be

---

[13] The inequity could be reduced by having a central agency construct and operate all of the treatment plants in the area in accordance with a least-cost program and then distribute costs in relation to the amount of waste produced. This system resembles that used in the Ruhr area of Germany which is described in Chapter 12. The same effect could also be achieved by charging all waste dischargers and then making payments for extra treatment to those where treatment can be undertaken least expensively. An example of this approach is developed by Kerri, *op. cit.*

[14] See Federal Water Pollution Control Administration, *op. cit.*, Table 6.

allowed to rise if this is deemed desirable. The direct control measures implicit in the LC program on the other hand, as well as the effluent standard of the uniform treatment program, provide only a limited incentive to improved technology. Moreover, the minimum cost program would require not only detailed information about current cost levels at each individual outfall but also about changes in cost with changing technology in regard to industrial processes, product mix, treatment cost, etc.

Equity Considerations

Comparison of equity aspects of the direct control programs (LC and UT) with the effluent charges programs can be brief, since equity is very much a matter of opinion, and since our opinions on the matter have been expressed in the preceding chapter. Arguments made by the FWPCA staff are analogous to those made earlier by us. While the UT program has a superficial equity since it requires a uniform cutback of waste *loads*, it—and even more so the LC program—is highly inequitable in the distribution of *costs*. It is intuitively clear that those waste disposers having a higher cost of treatment would treat less than those with a lower cost of treatment if allowed to bid for the available assimilative capacity and this is what the effluent charge in fact accomplishes. This results in an evening out of over-all costs associated with waste disposal while still concentrating waste reduction where it is least costly.

SOME EXPERIENCES WITH SEWER
AND IN-PLANT CHARGES

Previous discussion has assumed that waste dischargers will respond to effluent charges in an economically rational manner. Since charges (prices) are the normal means of transmitting information on relative values and providing incentives to take them into account in decision making, this does not seem unreasonable. However, questions are sometimes raised as to the efficacy of effluent charges in the control of waste discharges, so a review of actual experience is useful. Sewer and in-plant charges that are contingent on the quantity and quality of waste discharged to a municipal sewer or industrial wastewater collection system provide some relevant experiences even though they are not effluent charges in our sense of the term.

Responses of industrial operations to charges can best be assessed in relation to particular situations where charges have been applied at a specific point in time, and where records are available to indicate the water utilization patterns and waste loads prior to and after the imposition of charges. Unfortunately, only a few such cases are described in the literature. They are sufficient, however, to indicate the nature of the responses which are engendered by such charges.

This section will: first, describe the nature of sewer charges levied by municipalities or sanitary districts or other governmental agencies handling wastes; second, cite specific examples of sewer charges, in terms of the formulae used; third, describe several specific examples where responses to such charges have been recorded; and last, discuss the application of in-plant charges and their impacts on industrial water utilization patterns and waste loads.

Sewer Charges—General

Sewer charges have been applied to industrial waste discharges for about half a century, but it was not until the 1930's that the practice became relatively common. Since then, the use of industrial waste charges or surcharges has increased, stimulated by expanding industrial production and/or growing urban population in areas with a fixed wastewater treatment plant capacity.

There are two basic methods for assessing sewer charges. The first is the flat-rate method, which allocates total waste treatment costs among all users on the basis of some convenient unit, such as a percentage of the water bill, number of employees, a block-rate schedule related to water intake, or some combination of these. This system is simple to administer and provides some incentive for reducing the quantity of wastewater discharged, but it completely ignores the quality of the wastewater.

The second method is the quantity-quality approach. A basic sewer charge related to volume is levied on all users of the waste treatment system. In addition, a surcharge is imposed on industrial waste dischargers to cover the *additional* costs of handling wastes that are stronger than "normal" sewage.[15] Under this method, an industry has no incentive

---

[15] Ideally, sewer charges should also reflect the additional costs resulting from time variations in waste discharges, both quantity and quality. [See R. E. Roderick, "Rate Structures for Industry," *Journal Water Pollution Control Federation,* Vol. 34, No. 4 (1962), p. 311.] If the rate structure can encourage the adoption of operations which will reduce peak discharges and slugs of pollutants, the capacity of the waste handling system can be reduced. The devising of rate formulae to induce such responses is difficult, and apparently has rarely if ever been done. Instead, stipulations regarding the time pattern of waste discharges may be included in the regulations, i.e., temporary storage of effluents may be required by the waste handling authority in order to equalize the rate of waste discharge from the individual user. Charlotte, North Carolina, has a provision requiring "equalization in all cases where the daily discharge exceeds 40,000 gallons. The storage facility must have a capacity of at least 80 per cent of the total normal flow during a 24-hour period, and it must be equipped with an approved rate-discharge controller." [See E. J. Cleary, *Guide Lines for Drafting a Municipal Ordinance on Industrial-Waste Regulations and Surcharges,* Special Report, No. 23 (American Public Works Association, 1959), p. 12.]

to reduce its waste load beyond what is considered normal for municipal sewage.

Specific Sewer Surcharge Formulae

Industrial sewer surcharges are normally levied on the basis of the strength of the waste discharge in relation to "normal" sewage. The customary measures are BOD (5-day, 20°C.) and suspended solids, but strength is also measured in terms of "chlorine demand" in cases where the waste requires extra chlorine for disinfection, odor control, and/or slime control at the waste treatment plant. "Normal" sewage is defined by ordinance, and varies from area to area depending on local characteristics. For example, the mean concentration in parts per million (ppm) defined for normal sewage with respect to BOD and suspended solids, respectively, are 180 and 225 for Youngstown, Ohio; 240 and 300 for Cincinnati, Ohio; and 300 and 350 for Clarksburg, West Virginia.[16]

The formulas shown below illustrate how surcharges are arrived at in two areas—greater Winnipeg and Allegheny County.

1. *Greater Winnipeg Sanitary District*[17]

$$R_i = \left[f_s \frac{(S_i - S_n)}{S_n} + f_p \frac{(P_i - P_n)}{P_n} \right] R_n + \frac{(C_i - C_n)}{C_n} R_c + \frac{(X_i - X_n)}{X_n} R_x,$$

where:

R_i = surcharge per 1,000 gal.,
f_s = factor derived from costs of reducing solids,
f_p = factor derived from costs of reducing BOD,
S_i = suspended solids in ppm in the industrial wastes,
P_i = BOD in ppm in the industrial wastes,
C_i = chlorine demand in ppm in the industrial wastes,
X_i = substance requiring additional treatment in ppm in the industrial wastes,
S_n = suspended solids in ppm in the sewage serving as base or normal,
P_n = BOD in ppm in the sewage serving as base or normal,
C_n = chlorine demand in ppm in the sewage serving as base or normal,
X_n = substance requiring additional treatment in ppm in the sewage serving as base or normal,
R_n = unit charge based on cost of treating normal sewage,
R_c = unit charge based on cost of required chlorine,
R_x = unit charge based on cost of treating any substance requiring additional treatment.

[16] Cleary, *op. cit.*, p. 11.
[17] N. S. Bubbis, "Industrial Waste Control in Metropolitan Winnipeg," *Journal Water Pollution Control Federation*, Vol. 35, No. 11 (1963), p. 1413.

2. *Allegheny County Sanitary Authority*[18]

$$F = 1 + 0.15\left[\frac{0.75(SS - 275)}{275} + \frac{0.25(BOD - 300)}{300}\right],$$

where:

F = Factor to be applied to basic rate,
SS = Suspended solids of particular wastes in mg/l, and
BOD = BOD of particular wastes in mg/l.

$$R_c = 0.00835P_c(C - 5),$$

where:

R_c = Surcharge rate for chlorine demand in cents per 1,000 gal. of wastes,
P_c = Contract price of chlorine in cents per pound, and
C = Chlorine demand of particular wastes in mg/l.

The surcharges computed on the basis of the above formulae are added to the volumetric sewer charges based on the following rate schedule (with a minimum charge of $2.50 per quarter year):

	Water used per quarter year (gal.)	Sewer charges (¢/1,000 gal.)
First	100,000	30
Next	1,000,000	25
Next	2,500,000	20
Excess over	3,600,000	15

Response to Sewer Charges

Industries generally respond to sewer charges by reducing the quantity and/or the strength of waste discharges, and they do this by modifying production processes, changing raw materials, tightening housekeeping procedures, or treating waste. The particular combination of measures adopted varies from plant to plant and industry to industry in accordance with the nature of the production process, the product mix, and the character of the raw materials used. The specific response of a particular plant is determined by the flexibility of its production process and the range of internal options available to it. In general, new plants have more flexibility than older ones designed to operate under different conditions of water availability and water quality controls.

A typical response to the imposition of sewer charges is to increase the recirculation of water and thereby reduce the volume of waste

[18] J. J. Olliffe, "Sewer Service Charges and Surcharges," *Journal Water Pollution Control Federation*, Vol. 35, No. 5 (1963), p. 613.

discharged per unit of raw product processed or per unit of output. In some cases, in-plant recirculation will also reduce the waste load per unit of output, as in beet sugar processing and to a small extent in the canning of certain fruits. Recirculation may also have an indirect effect on the waste load because the recovery of raw materials or by-product production is often more feasible when the final effluent is highly concentrated.

Several examples will illustrate the responses of industrial operations to sewer charges. The first is a major industrial operation in Otsego, Michigan.[19] The town's waste treatment plant had been designed under the assumption that it would have to handle about 500 pounds of BOD per day in 1983. However, by 1965 the actual BOD load from the major industrial operation alone was about 1,500 pounds per day. The City Commission decided to charge the company for all operating expenses caused by its waste discharge to the municipal system, and to impose a penalty whenever its BOD load exceeded 500 pounds per day.

The first monthly billing of the firm after the initiation of the surcharge was based on an estimated BOD load of 27,000 pounds. For the second billing period (30 days) the firm's BOD load was about 22,000 pounds. For the third billing period after the charge had been initiated, the BOD load was down to about 15,000 pounds, or approximately the limit projected for 1983. The response to the charge was obvious, and rapid.

The second example relates to the Greater Winnipeg Sanitary District. Since a surcharge was imposed on January 1, 1958, the strength of the waste discharges has been reduced substantially,[20] partly because various industries began to salvage materials and sell them for useful purposes instead of discharging them into the waste treatment system. The quantity of waste discharges has also decreased because the sewer charge is based on quantity as well as quality, and management has an incentive to reduce the quantity discharged to the system. In the third and fourth years after the surcharge was initiated the payments to the system totaled about $80,000 in each year—about $20,000 less than in the first two years despite a doubling of the number of industries paying the surcharge and despite an increase in the unit cost of treatment (R_n) in the District's facilities. Table 8 shows the changes in the characteristics of wastes from three packing plants.

The larger industrial operations tend to invest in measures to reduce their waste loads, whereas most of the smaller ones pay the surcharge, presumably because they find this more economical. Thus the tendency

[19] See R. D. Smalla, "One Way to Control Industrial Wastes," *Water and Wastes Engineering*, Vol. 4, No. 3 (1967), p. 75.

[20] See Bubbis, *op. cit.*

for charges to produce least-cost reductions in waste loads over the spectrum of waste discharges is again illustrated.

The third example is the development and initiation of a sewer surcharge in Springfield, Missouri.[21] Faced with rising waste loads in 1962, Springfield decided to apply a surcharge on industrial waste discharges above the normal strength of sewage. The rationale was that the surcharge would provide an incentive for industrial operations to reduce waste discharges and/or would provide funds for expansion of the city's treatment plant facilities.

As a first step, the city conducted an extensive sampling program to determine the volume and characteristics of the various waste discharges. Industrial plants with discharges below the specified strength limits were exempted from the surcharge. Each of the other plants was notified of the amount of the prospective surcharge, and of the fact that the city would review the assessment whenever a plant made operational changes.

Even before the first official billing, some plants began to take action. A packing plant that faced an assessment of about $1,400 per month modified its production processes and ended up with a sewer bill of only $225 per month. A commercial laundry, faced with a large monthly surcharge because its waste discharge was warm and had a relatively high concentration of suspended solids, made changes that resulted in a

Table 8.   Average Characteristics of Wastes from Three Packing Plants, Before and After Imposition of Sewer Surcharge

(milligrams per liter)

Packing plant and year	Suspended solids	BOD	Grease
Plant A:			
1957	420	470	150
1960	260	540	120
1961	160	360	110
Plant B:			
1957	1,320	920	340
1960	240	470	80
1961	310	530	120
Plant C:			
1957	840	1,270	580
1960	320	660	260
1961	400	680	300

Source: Bubbis, *op. cit.*

[21] See P. T. Hickman, "The Introduction of an Industrial Waste Surcharge Program" (Paper presented at the Annual Meeting of the Missouri Water Pollution Control Association, St. Louis, March 2, 1964).

significant *net* savings in its production costs even with the sewer surcharge. The principal savings came from the installation of a concrete
sump, which functioned as a settling basin to remove suspended solids
and BOD in the waste discharge, and as a heat exchanger, thereby reducing the cost of heating incoming water. Two potato chip manufacturers were stimulated by the imposition of a sewer surcharge to analyze
their production processes to discover why the plant effluents were so
high in BOD and suspended solids. When they found the answer to be
the large quantities of cooking oils and potato peelings that were lost
during processing, new processing equipment was installed in both
plants. The losses of oil and product were reduced, and with the decrease
in the strength of the waste discharge came a substantial reduction in
the sewer charge.

The responses of industrial operations to the imposition of sewer
charges can be generalized as follows: First, the imposition of a charge
or surcharge tends to encourage plants to make changes that in many
cases reduce not only the volume of effluents and the wastes in the
effluents but also the water intake. Second, sewer charges tend to induce
an examination of production processes that often uncovers relatively
simple modifications which may result in net reductions in total production costs.

In-plant Charges

In-plant charges are similar to sewer charges both in nature and in
the responses they engender. The extent to which in-plant charges
have been adopted in the United States (and elsewhere) is not known.
Obviously such charges are relevant only in situations where the single
plant encompasses a number of separable divisions or processes.

The imposition of in-plant charges follows logically from the industrial
rationale that efficient use should be made of all factor inputs involved
in producing a final product. The application of water and waste charges
is one effective means for inducing plant managers to focus on water
in the same cost-reduction and profit-motive context as they focus on
other factor inputs.[22] Of course the in-plant charges are based on only
those costs which are internal to the plant and not on the external costs
imposed by the plant's water activities. Optimal effluent charges, e.g.,
assessed by a basin agency, would reflect such costs.

Imposing in-plant charges is apparently an accepted practice in some
major U.S. companies. In a discussion of water management in General
Electric, Watson states, "each major operation in a multi-department

[22] This approach is expressed in K. S. Watson, "Elements of Water Management," in *Industrial Water Conservation*, Continued Education Series No. 83,
University of Michigan, School of Public Health (1959), especially p. 23.

plant will be particularly concerned that its [water] consumption is proper, if it is billed for the quantity of water consumed."[23] Dupont follows the same procedure in some of its plants. Each production area of a plant pays the costs of the plant wastewater handling and disposal system in proportion to the quantity of wastes discharged. These charges are considered to be operating costs and are added to each unit's production costs.[24] This procedure makes the individuals on the production line aware of how wastewater control—and water utilization costs in general—can add to total production costs. This in turn induces attempts to reduce such costs by various methods.

Probably the principal reason why internal charges have been successful in reducing water costs, including waste disposal costs, is the effectiveness by which this method puts across the relevant point to production personnel. On the production line the concern is with production of the final product. Small losses in efficiency very often can be accepted because they accompany increasing rates of production. In fruit and vegetable canning for example, increasing the speed of the filling operation will increase the total output and reduce labor costs per unit of product. At the same time, however, the increased filling speed is likely to lead to increased spills, which in turn increase the waste load per unit of product. This side effect would ordinarily not concern production personnel. A difference between process efficiencies of 99.8 and 99.9 in a chemical plant would be equivalent to constant conditions as far as production personnel are concerned. To the wastewater control engineer, it would represent a very significant difference in the quantity of waste produced.

The effectiveness of in-plant charges is illustrated by the experience of the Midland, Michigan, plant of the Dow Chemical Company.[25] The plant, which is located on a relatively small stream, manufactures about 800 chemicals in more than 350 processes. Both cooling water "requirements" and assimilative capacity requirements for waste disposal would be much greater than the stream could supply if stringent control measures were not taken. Several years ago, faced with a fixed water supply and with plans to increase output, the plant adopted the practice of imposing in-plant charges. Over a five-year period after the initiation of in-plant charges, production increased by about 25 per cent with less water intake and probably somewhat less waste load being discharged to the river.

[23] *Ibid.*, p. 25.
[24] R. F. Rocheleau and E. F. Taylor, "An Industry Approach to Pollution Abatement," *Journal Water Pollution Control Federation*, Vol. 36, No. 10 (1964), p. 1189.
[25] C. L. Sercu, "How a Chemical Company Solved a Water Crisis," *Effluent and Water Treatment Magazine*, Vol. 2, No. 10 (1962).

Each production unit is charged for the quantity and quality of intake water that is used, and for the quantity and quality of the wastewater discharged. The quantity of wastewater discharged is determined from meter readings or by measurement. The quality is measured in terms of organic loading defined by the chemical oxygen demand. All waste treatment costs are charged back to the production unit, as are the costs of handling and burning liquid waste tars. The water utilization costs include pumping, distribution, disposal, and whatever treatment costs are necessary to provide the quality of water needed in the particular production processes.

One of the interesting responses by the production units in the plant has been the development of cascade water utilization, i.e., the outflow from one production unit being used as the intake to other production units. The arrangements are made by the departments themselves. The Utilities Department of the plant simply charges the first (and last) user of water; each department in turn makes whatever arrangements it can with subsequent water users.

In sum, at Dow, Midland, and elsewhere, the imposition of water and waste charges on production units within a plant has stimulated the same kind of responses as the application of sewer charges by municipalities. The responses have been with respect to both process modification and changed water utilization systems.

Once more we should mention that up to now we have been concentrating on control of effluents at specific points of waste discharge. In Part III we enter into an extended discussion of the economics of incorporating larger-scale regional measures in the water quality management system. Institution of such measures, however, in no way detracts from the necessity of finding efficient means for controlling individual municipal and industrial waste discharges. Moreover, once we consider large, collectively instituted measures, it is also necessary to address the question of how they are to be financed. This will add a new dimension to our discussion of alternative means for water quality management.

First, however, in the next chapter, we reflect on the policy implications of what we have covered thus far and comment on some recent proposals for public policies in regard to control of individual waste discharges.

Policy Alternatives for Influencing
Individual Waste Discharges

9

Before broadening our discussion of managing water quality to include collective measures of various types, we review the merits of alternative policies for influencing decisions at individual discharge points.

The conclusion from our analysis is that, despite some shortcomings and problems, the effluent charges approach is the one most likely to result in efficient and equitable arrangements. In addition, the proceeds from effluent charges constitute a source of net revenue to the agency levying them, and this revenue could be used to develop and improve the water resource or for other public purposes. If a certain amount of waste can be put into a watercourse without producing damage, part of the return from a properly levied effluent charge, i.e., one that reflects marginal damage, will be a pure rental return on the naturally occurring assimilative capacity of the watercourse.

The revenue yield of the effluent charge may itself achieve a wider efficiency benefit. Economists have long argued that excise taxes are generally undesirable because they impose an excess burden by distorting the allocation of resources. By placing a wedge between marginal cost and price for certain commodities, the excise tax tends to have an effect analogous to that of monopoly, that is, it restricts production even though consumers would be willing to pay more than the cost of producing additional units of the good. When taxes affect the production of some goods and services but not others, there is a distortion or misallocation in resources use. Even the income tax, generally favored as the best of the major taxes, may impose an excess burden by distorting choices between work and leisure.[1]

[1] For an excellent discussion of these matters and extensive citations to a rather copious literature, see R. E. Musgrave, *The Theory of Public Finance* (McGraw-Hill, 1959), Chapter 7.

This line of reasoning suggests that taxation systems such as effluent charges, which bear upon activities producing an external cost, can yield an excess benefit. They improve the allocation of resources in two ways: directly, by providing an incentive to waste dischargers to control their waste discharges; and, indirectly, by providing revenues, and so reducing the need to impose taxes to finance the public provision of goods and services. Since most taxes levied by governments are deemed to be more or less undesirable on efficiency grounds, improvements in efficiency resulting from the revenue aspects of an effluent charge or tax system are likely.[2] As we have said, the revenue-yielding aspects of effluent charges will command more of our attention in the next part where we consider further opportunities to improve water quality through collective action. At this point we simply note that the revenue-yielding capability of effluent charges as compared with other means of reducing waste discharges is a desirable characteristic.

In the past few years effluent charges or effluent taxes have received a good deal of attention in the political arena. One of the main recommendations of the Environmental Pollution Panel of the President's Science Advisory Committee in November 1965 was,

> . . . that careful study be given to tax-like systems in which all polluters would be subject to "effluent charges" in proportion to their contribution to pollution. Federal and local efforts to reduce pollution of air, soil, and water have traditionally rested upon a mixture of prohibitory regulation and persuasion. The public interest can often be served by reducing pollution below the levels where these means are appropriate and effective. Effluent charges have enhanced effects because individual polluters always have a prospect of financial gain from further reductions in their contribution to pollution.[3]

The annual report of the Council of Economic Advisers, issued in January 1966, contained the following statement:

> Although it must assist in eliminating the large backlog of capital requirements, the federal government cannot and should not finance local waste treatment indefinitely. In the long run, localities should collect revenues from the polluters adequate to sustain the system and to expand it in line with normal growth. Charges based on use of treatment facilities provide long-run incentives for the abatement of pollution. *Effluent charges* on polluters in sections of the river where there is no municipal treatment could

---

[2] As far as we know, the first person to make this point was Gordon Tullock. In an unpublished paper on excess benefit, Tullock suggests that a systematic effort should be made to find instances where activities creating external costs could be taxed in order to realize both the direct and excess benefits of such taxation.

[3] *Restoring the Quality of Our Environment*, Report of the Environmental Pollution Panel, President's Science Advisory Committee (1965), p. 17.

have a similar effect; when waste discharge is costing industrial firms a certain amount for every pound discharged, the volume of waste will be reduced and the revenue collected will help to pay for collective treatment.[4]

During 1966, the House Committee on Government Operations polled the state governors on various incentive devices including effluent charges. Eight of the governors expressed qualified approval of a federal policy requiring effluent charges, five suggested that the idea needed more study, and three were opposed to federal effluent charges but felt that charges established by the state might be more desirable. The attitude toward effluent charges seems remarkably favorable considering that the idea is highly unconventional, that it hit most governors "cold," and that the alternatives involved reduction in federal taxes.[5]

Finally, over the last few years a working group of the President's Task Force on Pollution Abatement consisting of representatives from the Bureau of the Budget, the Council of Economic Advisers, the Department of Commerce, the Department of the Interior, and the Treasury Department evaluated economic incentives for industrial pollution control and came forward with a strong recommendation favoring effluent charges. There has also been considerable interest in this technique at regional and state levels. During 1966, for example, Wisconsin passed a far-reaching new water quality control law which specifies that an inquiry should be made into the feasibility of effluent charges as an aid in the implementation of water quality control programs.

Despite the interest in effluent charges, political attention and support have centered on techniques that involve subsidies such as rapid tax write-offs and tax credits. Numerous bills have been introduced into the Congress over the past several years proposing such devices.[6] A number of states have passed such legislation and many more are currently considering it. In addition, the federal government and some state governments have programs of direct grants to municipalities for either or both capital and operation and maintenance expenses relating to

[4] *Economic Report of the President*, H. Doc. 348, 89 Cong. 2 sess. (1966), p. 124, emphasis added.

[5] *Views of the Governors on Tax Incentives and Effluent Charges*, House Committee on Government Operations, 89 Cong. 2 sess. (1966).

[6] For a detailed description of these devices see H. W. Mantel, *Industrial Incentives for Water Pollution Abatement* (New York: Institute of Public Administration, 1965).

During the twenty years since 1945, on an average, three bills a year were introduced into Congress proposing various forms of tax incentives for industrial waste treatment. During the first session of the 89th Congress (1965), there were 19 such bills; in the first six months of the second session (1966), there were 24 bills. League of Women Voters of the U.S., *Current Review of Water Resources*, No. 3 (August 1966).

municipal waste treatment plants. When these plants serve industrial users—as they often do—the grants provide an indirect subsidy for industrial waste treatment.

Support for these techniques continues despite what seem to us to be compelling arguments against them from the point of view of the broader social interest. Some of the most important deficiencies of these devices are reviewed below.

First, each of these devices involves a reduction in federal revenues or an additional expenditure from the federal treasury. This means that an already overburdened tax base must be hit even harder to finance these outlays. Further use must be made of taxes which already involve "excess burdens" in order to provide replacement revenue. Should the tax credit or accelerated depreciation devices turn out to be succesful in inducing substantial outlays for industrial waste treatment facilities, their cost to the federal treasury could be large (approximate costs as calculated by the working group of the President's Task Force on Pollution Abatement are shown in Table 9). Accelerated depreciation is equivalent to an interest-free loan, and the cost to the government takes the form of waiting a longer period of time for tax payments.

Table 9. Comparative Gains by Industry Through Alternative Forms of Federal Assistance for Waste Treatment Plant Construction

Type of assistance	Percentage	Per $1 billion of capital investment
		($ million)
Accelerated depreciation:		
5 years	8.5	85
3 years	14.7	147
1 year	18.3	183
Tax credits:[1]		
Existing 7%	7	70
14%	14	140
20%	20	200
Accelerated Depreciation and Tax Credit Combined:		
14% tax credit and 3-year accelerated depreciation	28.7	287
20% tax credit and 1-year accelerated depreciation	38.3	383
Reduced interest loans:[2]		
6%	6	60
3%	12	120

Source: Jack W. Carlson, Council of Economic Advisers.

[1] Assume 48 per cent effective tax rate, fifteen-year functional life (straight line) for waste treatment facilities and 9 per cent discount rate; accelerated depreciation now available in existing tax laws, e.g., sum of digits, excluded.

[2] Fifteen years, straight reduction loan.

This proposal would allow capital expenditures to be depreciated more rapidly than is permitted under existing laws and the rate would not be consistent with the functional life of the waste treatment facilities. An investment credit might operate like the investment credit for machinery and equipment which exists under present tax laws. Credits reduce the net cost to the taxpayer for such investments, but they do not alter the basis for depreciation.

The second point is one that is often overlooked. Devices like accelerated depreciation and tax credits, or even grants to meet part of the construction cost of facilities, do not provide a net incentive to waste load reduction. They merely reduce losses on waste treatment equipment but by no means make the equipment profitable. In other words, no firm acting rationally would provide any treatment solely on the basis of this kind of incentive. This means that these devices might be effective only if they were combined with a program of enforcement. The result of laws providing tax breaks for industry, if not combined with a systematic enforcement effort, would be most unpredictable.[7]

Third, all proposals for tax breaks that have come to our attention specify that the incentive is for the installation of *treatment* equipment, although many industries can reduce their waste loads most efficiently— at least over a considerable range—by altering production processes and/or recovering materials and producing by-products. By providing no incentive for process and related changes, these proposals would tend to distort the investment decision toward treatment of wastes after generation, i.e., at the "end of the pipe." Even when compared with the narrow efficiency standard of minimizing the cost of producing a given reduction in waste loads at specific outfalls, these proposals do not pass muster. If efforts were made to widen the scope of these incentives, administration would become extremely complex, and because of the intimate relationship between over-all production processes and wastes

[7] An account of experience in North Carolina is interesting in this regard:

"A North Carolina statute exempts industrial waste treatment and water pollution abatement plants and equipment from ad valorem property taxations and provides a free five-year amortization allowance for income tax purposes in lieu of depreciation. . . .

"Approximately 12 firms have applied for and received certificates permitting them to amortize their anti-pollution facilities over a 60 month period. This is a small per cent of those firms eligible to receive certificates by making application. . . .

"It appears questionable whether the statute confers a significant benefit on the companies eligible to receive certificates as evidenced by the very small number making application and of the action by some to amortize over a longer period even with the certificate. The conclusion must be that the statute as related to rapid amortization has had little significance in the attainment of pollution control objectives."

W. R. Walker, *Industrial Water Use in North Carolina*, University of North Carolina Water Resource Papers, Number 13 (September 1964).

produced the incentives might amount to a general subsidy for technological improvement. Without careful policing of individual plants, it would be virtually impossible to distinguish costs incurred to reduce waste loads from costs incurred to increase profitability of industrial processes. In numerous instances, process changes (use of savealls in paper production, black liquor recovery in pulp production, syrup recovery in canning, etc.) result in both waste load reduction and recovery of valuable materials.[8]

Finally, tax write-offs and credits would be of little or no benefit to firms that are on the margin of profitability and that might have to close down if effective effluent controls were imposed. Research suggests that few firms are likely to be threatened in this way, but society may have a real interest in protecting some of those that are, especially if they constitute the primary local employment base—a cannery or beet sugar factory in a small midwestern town, or a pulp mill in a small New England town, for example. Special policies are required to deal with situations of this kind, and we suggest some in the final chapter.

In summary: tax breaks are blunt instruments for water quality management; they are potentially costly to the taxpayer; and they are very likely to induce inefficient means of control.[9]

Our study leads us to the conclusion that the nation should give serious consideration to reorienting its policies towards effluent charges as a component of broader systems of regional water quality management and in turn as a component of over-all water resources management. We feel that the empirical evidence presented in the previous chapter, as well as the knowledge of the way in which managerial decisions are made, demonstrates the validity of the predicted response to effluent charges. The evidence does not bear out the idea held by some that effluent charges would not reduce the wastes discharged into the nation's watercourses. We do not propose that other approaches be abandoned immediately, or even completely in the future. There is a continuing role for effluent standards as a supplement to the charges system. In the final chapter, after we have developed a good deal of background on the potential benefits from regional systems incorporating large-scale measures and reviewed some institutional arrangements which might be used to implement them, we suggest a new initiative

[8] The bills introduced into Congress normally specify that tax credits and accelerated depreciation are not to be allowed on any equipment that contributes or adds to a company's profits. This provision virtually forecloses in-plant changes.

[9] D. F. Bramhall and E. S. Mills made much the same points in their recommendations to the State of Maryland in a study sponsored by the Maryland State Planning Department. See, "Alternative Methods of Improving Stream Quality: An Economic and Policy Analysis," *Water Resources Research*, Vol. II (3rd Quarter 1966), p. 355.

in federal and state policies which we believe can lead toward an effective and efficient program for dealing with the increasingly difficult water quality problems we face. Among the instruments we feel will be important in this effort is the effluent charge. But now let us drop the assumption that the only way to deal with water quality problems is to reduce or limit waste discharges at individual outfalls.

ECONOMIC CONCEPTS RELATING TO REGIONAL WATER QUALITY MANAGEMENT SYSTEMS WITH COLLECTIVE FACILITIES

III

Our assumption that full efficiency could be achieved by water quality control measures at the individual waste outfall or water supply intake was useful for discussion of the maldistribution of costs resulting from technological external diseconomies, and probably descriptive of a significant number of real cases as well. But engineering-economic research has shown that there are many instances where economies can be realized by collective measures such as joint waste treatment, low-flow augmentation for quality improvement, stream reaeration, ground-water recharge for quality improvement, effluent diversion or redistribution to make better use of natural assimilative capacity, the specialized use of streams or stretches of streams, and combinations of these. Where facilities involve scale economies that cannot be efficiently realized at individual outfalls or intakes, it may be appropriate to have a regional authority with powers more extensive than those assumed in earlier chapters. At one extreme would be a river basin or sub-basin agency empowered to plan, design, construct, operate, and finance virtually all water quality control measures; at the other would be an agency that simply sees to it—through effluent charges or standards—that downstream costs are reasonably well reflected in the upstream decisions of managerially independent units.

In this part we emphasize the opportunities which a regional authority might have to improve the efficiency of water quality management by implementing various measures, such as those mentioned above, that cannot be efficiently instituted at individual points of waste generation and discharge. However, we also recognize the importance of the technologic and economic linkages between water quality improvement as an output from water resources systems and other outputs from such systems, such as hydropower, navigation, and water-based recreation. For example, operation of hydro facilities for "peaking" can reduce water quality significantly by causing extreme low flows during "off-peak" periods. Water released from the deeper parts of storage reservoirs which have "stratified" may be devoid of dissolved oxygen and have an effect on water quality downstream from the reservoir similar to the discharge of an organic waste. The installation of low head dams for slack-water navigation may result in substantial water quality deterioration. The dams reduce the velocity of flow and hold waste loads longer in a given reach of stream; at the same time they reduce the reaeration capacity in the given reach. Conversely, the operation of a storage reservoir to augment flows during summer periods to improve water quality may have adverse effects on water-based recreation on the reservoir, because of the resulting drawdown. These interrelationships suggest the desirability of a regional water resources management agency with responsibility for all aspects of water resources development and use. We return to this point in Part IV where we discuss more specifically the question of appropriate institutional arrangements for water quality management.

Within the context of both water quality management and over-all water resources management, a major problem is to integrate in an optimal way the decisions of fiscally independent units with those made directly by a regional agency. An agency concerned with water resources does not possess the scope, even in principle, to decide all courses of action bearing upon the way water resources are used. For example, if such an agency decided that a firm should be located at a particular site because the costs of handling its wastes would be low at that site, it might force the firm to incur transportation or other costs greater than the saving in waste management costs. Owing to such possibilities and even probabilities, decisions on location, production, and the character of production processes should *never* be based exclusively on considerations of water costs including waste disposal. Nevertheless, it is important to develop means whereby these considerations can be brought to bear on the water decisions of firms and of public agencies and on the decisions of agencies with broader responsibilities for land use planning. It is suggested in this section that systems of charges have special merit for this purpose.[1]

A number of the principles explored in conceptual terms in the following chapter are illustrated more concretely by means of case studies in subsequent chapters.

---

[1] While our emphasis will be on effluent charges as a central tool of water quality management, charges could well be used to cause other "external costs" of water resource use to be taken into account by decentralized decision makers. Certain waste reduction measures induced by effluent charges might under some circumstances themselves create other varieties of external cost. For example, waste treatment lagoons or underground disposal leads to actual depletion of the water-resource which in turn forecloses productive reuse of water downstream. To deal with such interdependencies, Blair T. Bower has proposed the possibility of a "Water Utilization" charge. See "The Economics of Industrial Water Utilization," in A. V. Kneese and S. C. Smith (ed.), *Water Research* (The Johns Hopkins Press, for RFF, 1966).

Collective Facilities in Water Quality Management

10

This chapter focuses on the economic criteria for planning a regional water quality management system that includes collective facilities as well as those that can be implemented efficiently at individual points of waste discharge or water intake and use. The chapter also includes some discussion of system operation because planning and operation are interdependent. The specific components of an optimal system are often quite sensitive to the operating procedures adopted.

A regional agency has a variety of potentially efficient collective measures to choose from: increasing streamflows during low-flow periods via releases from reservoir or groundwater storage; treatment of intake water and of municipal and industrial wastes in regional collective treatment plants in compactly developed areas; artificial or induced oxygenation of watercourses (including reservoirs and lakes); diversion of effluents via pipeline or other means; specialized stream use; artificial recharge of wastewaters to groundwater aquifers for quality improvement; and the construction of shallow oxidation reservoirs in the stream itself. These methods could supplement measures to control the generation and disposal of wastes at individual points. A regional agency seeking to minimize the over-all costs associated with waste disposal should plan and implement a system which equates the relevant incremental costs associated with water quality management in all directions. These costs include the costs of all manner of waste reduction and treatment and water supply treatment, the costs of flow regulation (including all opportunity costs that arise from the value of stored water for alternative uses), as well as the costs of conforming waste discharge to streamflow, changing industrial processes and outputs, and changing industrial location, and, finally, any damages which result from residual water quality deterioration.

This statement that the agency should equate the "relevant" marginal costs does not mean that the marginal costs of waste reduction should be equal at all points of waste discharge. Indeed, in an optimal system, as explained in earlier chapters, the costs of treatment or other waste reduction measures will tend to be higher at upstream points because upstream activities are reflected in downstream quality and costs. What the rule does mean is that it must not be possible to make marginal "trade-offs" and thereby reduce damage and waste reduction costs.

Ideally, the results of all relevant water resources systems and operating procedures would have to be considered and a solution derived which simultaneously indicated the optimum combination of systems elements and operating procedures. In industrial areas the solution would entail a system of charges and/or other measures such as effluent standards and zoning designed to secure the optimum amounts and locations of waste discharges. An "efficient" solution would enable the maximum net benefit to be obtained from the available water resources, and, as the latter implies, the over-all cost associated with the disposal of an optimum amount of wastes would be minimized.

As we explained in Chapter 5, in economic terms "cost" means the value of foregone opportunities. In regard to water quality management such opportunities may be associated with resources used, for example, to build and operate treatment plants or reservoirs which could be used productively in other applications, or they may consist of opportunities to use water for purposes other than waste carriage or assimilation. The development in this chapter is simpler to visualize if the only output of the system is water quality control, so that all costs associated with waste disposal consist either of resources devoted to control facilities (reservoir regulation of streamflows, treatment of wastes, process changes, effluent diversion facilities, etc.) or of damages associated with water quality deterioration. The principles are exactly the same, however, if some of the costs consist of foregone benefits from other water-related outputs such as peak power.

THE BASIN-WIDE FIRM AGAIN

The basin-wide firm is used here, as in Chapter 5, to illuminate economic principles. It is not put forth as a policy recommendation, for it would, in reality, have grave disadvantages: It cannot take account of uses that are not reflected in market prices; and, as a monopoly, it would present problems of regulation.

To illustrate some of the principles involved in taking account of the technical interdependencies in a river basin when economies of scale in water quality management measures are available, let us assume that a single firm (1) conducts all water-using industrial enterprises, all water and waste treatment facilities (no privately owned septic tanks, water softners, etc.), and all water transportation and related facilities; (2)

operates all hydroelectric facilities, owns all land and structures in the flood plain, and is the sole provider of flow regulation; (3) controls all recreational uses of the watercourse; and (4) operates in competitive markets or in ones where public regulatory authorities set prices equal to marginal costs at levels of output that just clear the market.

In order to maximize its profits the firm would select the combination of water quality control measures (water supply treatment, waste generation and treatment, flow augmentation, wastewater releases co-ordinated with streamflow, etc.) and downstream damages that would minimize the over-all costs associated with its waste disposal at its most profitable level of activity. This would be accomplished by equating the relevant incremental costs associated with waste disposal for all alternatives. As previously indicated, these costs would include any valuable outputs that are sacrificed to improve the efficiency of the waste disposal system.

If collective treatment costs are less than treatment at individual dis-charge points, the firm would transport effluent to collective treatment plants until the marginal costs of transportation and marginal treatment saved were equal. Since transporting wastes long distances and building scattered treatment plants are usually expensive procedures, the firm would weigh these and other diseconomies of scattered development against the economies (less congestion) to arrive at the optimum com-pactness of economic activities.

Compact economic development might be influenced by certain physi-cal characteristics of the stream. Since the rate of reaeration through the air-water interface is directly proportional to the oxygen deficit, the organic waste degradation capacity is a decreasing function of the dis-solved oxygen quality standards. This, plus the possibility of stream treatment to take advantage of economies of scale, emphasizes the possibilities of stream specialization (i.e., using some stream or stretches of stream more heavily for waste disposal and maintaining higher quality in others) as a means of reducing the costs associated with waste dis-posal. Again the firm would trade off such possibilities against alterna-tives such as additional flow augmentation, higher levels of treatment, and other means of waste reduction. In deciding upon the location of a new industrial plant, the firm would consider not only transportation costs and other factors affecting assembly, production, and distribution costs but also the increment of total waste reduction and damage costs of alternative locations. The location producing lowest costs would be the one at which the marginal costs of the alternatives bearing upon over-all costs are equalized.

While the point is expanded later, it is worth noting here that the firm "internalizes" all these costs. A water resources agency in a basin cannot internalize all of them, and *consequently it must attempt to have the opportunity costs of water resources use, including waste disposal, reflected in the decisions of entities that are simultaneously considering other resources costs.* This can be done by standards or, preferably, by charges.

The firm's general objective is to maximize profits, which implies that the costs associated with waste disposal will be minimized at the profit-maximizing level of output. If, for example, the firm could lower its costs by doing a little less waste treatment and permitting a little more damage, or by doing a little more water treatment and a little less waste reduction, or by a little more augmentation of low flows and a little less temporary storage of wastes, or a bit more process adjustment and a little less direct reaeration of the stream, etc., its over-all profit position could not be at a maximum. As part of its general profit-maximizing activities, the firm would integrate its waste control activities with other aspects of its water-related operations. One major linkage is through flow regulation.

Thus, in computing the costs of alternative water quality control devices, the firm would need to consider complementary and competitive relationships among different water uses and alteration of the stream's flow regimen. Accordingly flow-augmentation costs would have to be determined in light of the fact that this alternative is often complementary with navigation, for example, but at least partly competitive with irrigation, flood damage reduction, power, and recreation. Any net benefits associated with other uses foregone in using flow augmentation to improve water quality in the optimum system are counted among the costs associated with water quality improvement. Moreover, the firm would consider the full marginal costs of producing particular products including the costs imposed on other activities by waste disposal. If the market adequately registered the population's evaluation of all goods and services sold by the hypothetical firm, its solution to the waste disposal problem would be "efficient," as that term is understood in economic welfare theory.

Many extreme assumptions have been made in developing this example; hence the basin-wide firm is not put forward as a realistic policy alternative. Still, the concept has provided a useful vehicle for illustrating applicable systems and decision criteria. The following points concerning public policy merit particular emphasis.

First, public policies which explicitly recognize water quality management as a problem of optimizing an interdependent system in a region will find many alternative control measures to consider. Accordingly, a least-cost system is more likely to result from the implementation of such policies than from the adoption of narrowly circumscribed conventional approaches. The case studies in the next chapter show the savings that can result from a more comprehensive and flexible approach.

Second, implementing the regional approach requires the planning, design, and integrated operation of many interdependent elements in the system. The illustrative firm "internalized" all these elements and, under our assumptions, found their optimum planning and operation in its interest as a matter of seeking maximum profit.

A water management agency should not attempt to internalize more elements than needed for its objective. In one instance, an agency may plan, design, and operate only collective measures such as reservoirs and reaeration devices and use direct controls or incentives (charges) to integrate these with the rest of the relevant economic system. In other instances a regional agency may find that it serves efficiency to go much further and it may plan, design, and operate virtually all water-related facilities in a region including water and wastewater treatment plants. Even in this case it would still be necessary to influence industrial process design and plant location. This could be done by direct regulation or, again we think preferably, by an appropriate system of charges.

In the following section we develop these thoughts further by using a somewhat simplified example which nevertheless permits us to address some matters of planning incentives and financing in a system which includes collective measures. The major points are developed mathematically in the appendix.

A REGIONAL SYSTEM WITH FLOW REGULATION

We assume a system where the economically relevant alternatives are low-flow augmentation and waste reduction activities at individual points of waste discharge. The regional agency will design and operate a reservoir for flow regulation and use a system of effluent charges to control waste discharges at outfalls. If the reservoir is multipurpose we assume that the agency takes appropriate account of complementary and competitive uses of the water in determining the marginal cost of flow regulation for water quality management. For example, if navigation benefits occur in a fully complementary fashion with water quality benefits, the two must be summed and compared with the marginal costs of flow regulation.[1]

[1] If a system includes a variety of outputs and types of components, current techniques seldom permit an optimum solution by use of analytical procedures. In this instance, optimizing procedures based upon computer simulation of the system can be used. See Maynard Hufschmidt and Myron B Fiering, *Simulation of Water Resource Systems* (Harvard University Press, 1966). Each of the case studies presented in the following chapter used simulation methods in searching for (constrained) least-cost solutions.

Determination of the optimum amount of storage can be illustrated by a set of curves closely analogous to those used to illustrate optimum levels of waste reduction in Chapter 6.

Consider again a hypothetical streamflow-cost curve, as shown in Figure 31. Costs in this case are the total costs at various levels of flow of optimal combinations of downstream alternatives—for example, waste treatment, water supply treatment, and value of residual physical damages. We assume that these combinations are induced by an optimal system of effluent charges in accordance with the analysis presented in Chapter 6.

The effect of flow regulation is determined as follows. Starting with a natural (unregulated) flow frequency curve as in Figure 23, Chapter 6, the effect of different levels of regulation on the flow regime is estimated as shown in Figure 32. In this case, however, the downstream costs associated with a given flow remain the same, but flow regulation changes the frequency of occurrence of different flows. (By contrast, in Figure 24, Chapter 6, waste reduction reduced the damage associated with any *given* flow, but did not alter the probability of occurrence of the flow.) Figure 33 is analogous to the curves shown in Figure 24, and shows the results of two different levels of altering the flow regime, i.e., curves 2 and 3, where the damage associated with any given level of flow remains constant.

As before, the integrals of the curves are the expected values of the probability of costs. From a succession of such calculations a total down-

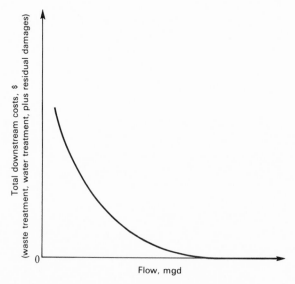

Figure 31.

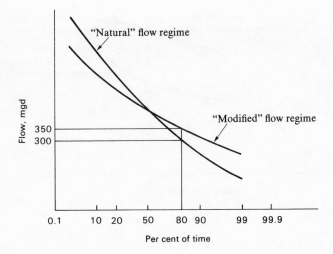

Figure 32.

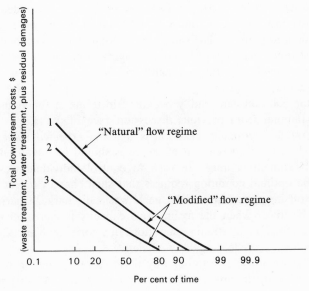

Figure 33.

stream expected value of costs-avoided function can be constructed analogous to that shown in Figure 25, Chapter 6, but in this case the damage reduction corresponds to increases in minimum flow[2] rather than reduction in residual waste material. A costs-avoided function is illustrated in Figure 34.

[2] "Increase in minimum flow" is used as a surrogate to represent the modification of the lower end of the flow frequency curve, as illustrated in Figure 32.

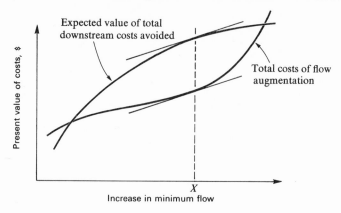

Figure 34.

A total cost function for the storage capacity necessary to produce the increases in minimum flow is also shown in Figure 34.[3] Minimum expected total cost (or maximum expected net benefit if avoided downstream costs are termed benefits) is achieved at an increase in flows corresponding to point X. The slopes of the total storage cost and downstream cost functions are equal to their respective incremental functions. Accordingly at point X the optimality condition (i.e., equality of incremental costs) prevails.[4]

The same solution can readily be stated in terms of functions which are more familiar from previous discussion (see Figure 35).

In general the optimality criterion is that the *expected value* of the incremental costs of all relevant alternatives should be equalized at the margin.[5] If effluent charges are used to control individual waste discharges, the optimal condition requires that such charges reflect the incremental offsite costs imposed by each waste discharge. Charges will of course be lower when the assimilative capacity is increased by flow augmentation and/or by stream reaeration. In a correctly planned system the lowered charges reflect a gain in efficiency.

It may be worthwhile restating why point X represents an optimum combination of upstream and downstream measures. At this point a

[3] Stream reaeration could be used instead of, or in conjunction with, flow augmentation to increase assimilative capacity. If reaeration is used, the relevant cost is the expected value.

[4] This result may also be stated in terms of the simple calculus. The slopes of the total functions are equal to their respective first derivatives. At point X the two derivatives are equal. If we were to construct a total (downstream costs and storage) cost function, the first derivative of that function would be equal to zero at point X, and total costs would accordingly be at a minimum.

[5] Expected value of costs will be a function not only of the per cent of the time particular flow (or temperature) conditions are expected to prevail but also of their duration. See the discussion on pp. 116–23 above.

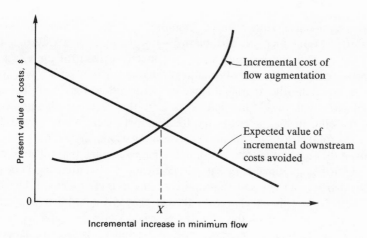

Figure 35.

small further increase in reduction activity at the outfall would cost more than the expected value of downstream water treatment costs and residual damages avoided by downstream users. The argument is symmetrical for a slight decrease in reduction activity at the outfall.

When costs associated with waste disposal are minimized, the incremental costs associated with waste disposal are equated at each outfall. This means that the marginal costs associated with waste disposal are equalized in all directions. However, it does not mean that the marginal cost of reduction will be the same at each outfall along a stream. This would only be the case if downstream costs per unit of waste were equal for different outfalls, as they might be when two outfalls are across the stream from each other; then strict marginal cost equality would be necessary for cost minimization.

EFFLUENT CHARGES AND COLLECTIVE MEASURES

Fortunately, devising an appropriate effluent charges policy for an agency which incorporates economically desirable collective measures in its system requires no new principles whatsoever. The ideal charge will still be equal to the marginal external cost imposed. The residual external marginal cost imposed by waste discharge, when control at relevant points of waste discharge is induced to an optimal level by effluent charges, is the measure of the marginal benefit of the collective quality improvement facility—say a flow-regulating reservoir.

Let us assume (unrealistically) that the agency creates the entire assimilative capacity of the river by producing a flow of water. Assume further that this flow can be produced at a constant marginal cost. Finally, assume that assimilative capacity can be increased efficiently in small increments. Under these assumptions, the agency, if acting efficiently, would increase assimilative capacity in such a way that the marginal cost of the last increment in capacity to control the effect of a waste would be equal to the effluent charge on that waste, which in turn is equal to the marginal cost of waste control at outfalls—our "equal marginal cost" principle again. In this instance the proceeds from the effluent charge reflecting the marginal external cost would just cover the total cost of producing the assimilative capacity.[6]

Given the same situation, except that we now assume that the marginal cost of further increments of capacity is rising, the relationship between the yield from charges and the total cost of the investment will change. The yield from effluent charges will now exceed the amount necessary to pay the total cost of the investment when optimum capacity is attained. Conversely, if the marginal cost of expanded assimilative capacity declines over the relevant range, the proceeds from the charge will be insufficient to cover the cost of the capacity expansion. This will be true even though the capacity expansion reduces the over-all costs associated with the regional waste disposal system.[7] If the regional agency decides not to augment assimilative capacity but to reduce waste loads by measures such as collective treatment, it should still follow the equal marginal cost rule and charge waste disposers the marginal reduction cost (which equals the marginal external cost) of handling the particular kind of waste involved.

The assumption that the regional authority created all of the assimilative capacity of the stream makes for a theoretically neat outcome, but it is unrealistic because a stream always has some natural waste assimilative capacity. This circumstance in no way affects the use of the marginal cost rule as the appropriate criterion for the agency's investment decisions, but it does affect the financial results. When the agency levies a charge reflecting marginal external costs in the presence of natural assimilative capacity, part of the payment made is a "pure rent" on the scarcity value of the natural capacity. As we have indicated earlier, this is analogous to a charge levied on the use of public lands for grazing, for example. Accordingly, when natural assimilative capacity

---

[6] To our knowledge Herbert Mohring was the first person to demonstrate that an optimal charge reflecting marginal external costs imposed by an activity is exactly analogous to a price reflecting short-run marginal cost in a firm in terms of its relationship to the desirability of and financing of investment. See Mohring, "Urban Highway Investment," in Robert Dorfman (ed.), *Measuring Benefits of Government Investments* (The Brookings Institution, 1965). The development with respect to water quality management in the appendix to this chapter in analogous.

[7] These propositions have been demonstrated rigorously for highways where the "toll" reflects marginal congestion costs. See Mohring, *op. cit.*

exists, the proceeds from the charge will be more than sufficient to pay for an economically justified augmentation of assimilative capacity produced under constant cost conditions. Any excess revenue should, in accordance with our discussion in Chapter 6, be used for general public purposes. If an agency implemented only economically justifiable facilities and levied charges equal to the marginal external cost, it might take rather sharply decreasing costs in the provision of collective facilities for the agency to incur a deficit if there is a large amount of naturally occurring assimilative capacity initially available.

The above discussion has assumed that collective facilities can be expanded more or less continuously. Since some of them, such as reservoirs, involve substantial indivisibilities, this is not very realistic for small systems. But the principles are the same even when durable and lumpy investments are made. Of course it will be necessary to make long-run projections of population and industrial production—and their related waste discharges—with their attendant uncertainties. Other measures such as mechanical reaeration can be expanded more or less continuously. Groundwater recharge operations represent an intermediate situation. Moreover, as a system becomes larger and more diverse, even absolutely large additions become small relative to the total system and can be implemented on the basis of comparatively short-run considerations.

The economic principles which we have discussed in this section are developed in a rigorous mathematical form in the appendix. Indeed, the appendix provides a compact synthesis of most of the economic principles which we develop in this book.

UNMEASURED VALUES AS
CONSTRAINTS ON THE OBJECTIVE

If there were no problems in the manner in which the market registers water quality values, the policies described above would produce a solution quite consistent with the general rationale of a market system. But the market provides no value, or no satisfactory value, for some aspects of water quality, and this creates a special problem for public bodies because they must take account of all aspects. Considerable progress has been made in finding ways to assess the worth of such matters as general aesthetic effects, public health, and recreation, but dealing with these unmeasured values is still far from being a routine matter.

Two ways of handling unmeasured values come to mind. One way would be to label them "intangible" and disregard them in planning and designing water quality management systems. Then, when the proposed systems are presented for consideration and authorization by representatives of the public, side information could be provided on aesthetic effects, public health, and other matters considered relevant to arriving at a decision in the public interest.

The second approach is to include hypotheses about such values in the process of system planning by expressing them in physical terms and treating them as constraints upon the cost-minimization objective. For example, if social choice should dictate that the oxygen level in a stream must be high enough to support fish life at all times, the system must be planned to minimize the real cost associated with waste disposal subject to the constraint, or "minimum D.O. standard." This may require a different combination of units with different operating procedures than a system planned without the standard or constraint. If the constraint is effective and not automatically achieved when measurable costs (including damage costs) are minimized, it will increase the cost of the system, the extra cost representing the limitation which the constraint places upon the objective.

To be consistent with efforts to achieve maximum welfare, the planning process should consider constraints "provisional" and view them as matters for research and study in order to discover how well they represent the preferences of society. One way of studying them from this point of view is to test their cost sensitivity. Varying a constraint by small amounts, redetermining the optimum system, and relating the change in costs to the associated physical changes in specific stretches of stream will provide information that will permit considered choices to be made by political representatives.

One useful way of stating the results of experiments with the constraints that are not valued directly by, or imputable from, the market is in terms of what they must "at least be worth." For example, a social judgment may be made that dissolved oxygen is to be maintained beyond the point indicated by the cost-minimizing solution in order to preserve or enhance a recreational fishery. A comparison of the system with and without the constraint will not establish precisely what preserving the fishing pleasure is worth, but it will indicate the *least* value that must be attached to it if the higher level of control procedures is to be worthwhile. Or the additional cost of a higher level of certainty of achieving the desired dissolved oxygen level can be estimated. If constraints are imposed representing goals not directly commensurable with the values stated in monetary terms in the objective function, marginal conditions analogous to those indicated earlier must still hold if the cost-minimization objective is to be fulfilled. The optimum system is not attained until a situation is reached in which it is impossible to make incremental "tradeoffs" between alternatives that will lower costs without violating the constraint.[8]

Once a combination of system elements has been decided upon, it will be necessary to utilize charges, effluent standards, or some other regulatory device to achieve optimum waste reduction at individual outfalls. The charge, if a charge is used, must be just high enough to achieve the standard, and it must not be possible to expand the large-scale measures at an incremental cost less than the incremental cost which can be avoided at the individual outfalls. If several wastes are involved, the expected value of all incremental costs avoided by an expansion in the large-scale measures must be added together and compared with the cost of expanding the measure.

We may generalize by saying that once a constraint is established by a duly constituted, well-informed political decision-making process, it may be viewed as representing a damage function which is perfectly inelastic at the specified quality level and degree of certainty. When this view is taken, the analysis with respect to appropriate levels of effluent charges and investment criteria presented in earlier sections and in the chapter appendix holds exactly.

Large amounts of data and extensive knowledge of physical and economic relationships are needed to implement the procedure outlined above. Rapid and flexible computational techniques for estimating the physical characteristics and patterns of water quality and for carrying out the actual minimization (maximization) procedure are also essential. Some of these techniques, as well as the specific character of the information required to make reasonably dependable analyses of complex river basin systems, including cost sensitivity analysis of constraints, are illustrated by the studies described in the next chapter.

Here we simply note that once a system is implemented the charges themselves are important sources of information about investment decisions in collective facilities. As was shown in Chapter 7, they indicate the marginal cost which waste disposers are incurring in order to meet

[8] In principle, the problem of finding an optimum system under constrained conditions is solvable by the use of differential calculus and the method known as La Grange multipliers. For a good exposition, see A. Enthoven, "The Simple Mathematics of Maximization," an appendix in C. J. Hitch and R. N. McKean, *The Economics of Defense in the Nuclear Age* (Harvard University Press, 1960), Pt. II. When the problem is set up in this form, the "multiplier" indicates the marginal cost of the constraint in terms of the cost included in the objective, i.e., an estimate of the cost-saving which would occur if the "standard" or constraint is reduced slightly. The problem can also be set up in the form of a mathematical or linear program. When this is done the so-called "dual" yields an estimate of the incremental cost of the constraints.

In some cases solutions are also possible by combinatorial or sampling methods. Computer simulation is necessary in many cases. Some of these methods were used in the studies reviewed in the next chapter.

the standard. This information can be used by the basin agency to determine whether a collective measure, either by capacity expansion or improved operation, can maintain the standard at a lesser incremental cost. Thus once the system is established the agency can obtain information on costs incurred by waste disposers without having detailed knowledge of their cost functions.[9]

Institutional Restraints. Where there is no regional agency with authority to plan and operate a comprehensive system of quality management, the type of cost-sensitivity analysis outlined above can be used to illuminate the desirability of institutional change. In most basins in the United States the only collective measures are industrial and municipal waste-treatment facilities and reservoirs operated for low-flow augmentation by federal or state agencies. By comparing a least-cost system restricted to these measures with one that incorporates all relevant alternatives, a price tag can be put on the restriction. Or, to put it another way, the comparison will provide an estimate of the economic gain that society can derive from an institutional mechanism with authority to implement a wider range of alternatives. This is illustrated by the Potomac case reported in the next chapter.

SOME "SHORT-RUN" ASPECTS OF SYSTEM OPERATION AND COST ASSESSMENT

At this point it is useful to introduce once more the distinction between "long-run" or "planning" costs and "short-run" or "operating" costs. There are two reasons for making this distinction in the present context: First, a system should be operated on the basis of its "current" opportunity costs, especially when certain elements such as dams must be introduced in "chunks." Second, hydrologic or meteorologic fluctuation may make it desirable, in terms of cost minimization, to operate the water quality control facilities in a variable manner. This indicates that, aside from any informational and administrative costs, effluent charges should be varied so as to maintain equality in the short-run marginal costs of alternatives.

So far the discussion has been primarily in terms of planning the regional system, and it was assumed that choices were not limited by past decisions. The view taken was sufficiently long-run, for example, to permit the building of dams *instead of* treatment plants. For planning, these are valid and appropriate concepts.

The point has been made several times that if the objective is to minimize the value of resources used internally and externally in con-

---

[9] For an empirical application of this concept, see E. L. Johnson, "A Study in the Economics of Water Quality Management," *Water Resources Research*, Vol. 3, No. 2 (Second quarter 1967), pp. 291–305.

nection with water quality management, the relevant cost for choosing a particular alternative is the value of the opportunities that must be foregone if it is chosen. This concept of "opportunity" costs has been used throughout, and methods of producing a better reflection of the value of foregone opportunities to society in decisions with respect to waste disposal were the subject of Part II.

The *concept* of opportunity costs does not change when a particular set of facilities has been decided upon and installed, but the *character* of the opportunities foregone does. When a dam is in the planning stage, all the labor, cement, steel, etc., needed for its construction can still be used in other activities, but once the labor, cement, etc., have been embodied in a dam they can no longer be used in alternative activities, and their price can no longer be considered an opportunity cost. The only costs that are still opportunity costs—and thus relevant for further decisions—are those that arise when a dam is operated for a particular purpose. If the dam is multipurpose, the opportunity costs may be largely "internal," representing the net value of the other uses foregone when its capacity is used for a particular purpose, although some operating costs will be involved, too.

In planning water quality management systems, therefore, the definition of costs should include all capital costs of new facilities. The system for water quality improvement should be expanded to the point where the cost of reducing an *additional unit* of any given waste—or combination of wastes if the reduction activity involves joint products —raises total reduction costs as much as it diminishes water quality damages. If there is a constraint, the system should be expanded until the constraint is met and the marginal total costs of all alternative measures for achieving the constraint are equalized.

However, after a water quality management system is established, only the currently variable costs and opportunity costs internal to a multipurpose system are relevant. For example, assume that a decision is to be made about whether to retain a waste treatment plant with excess capacity or replace it with a smaller plant. Comparison of total costs, including capital costs of both plants, would almost certainly lead to the wrong conclusion. If the original plant has no alternative use, the relevant costs include only the operating costs, the land, and portions of the existing investment for which there are alternatives uses. The value of such uses must, of course, be brought into the comparison because they represent genuine opportunity costs. The test is always whether there are currently feasible, valuable alternatives. From the point of view of allocating resources to their most productive use, only inputs which have alternative uses can be said to involve costs.

Since storage reservoirs ordinarily cannot be economically constructed in such a way as to add small increments to system capacity, a system adjusting to changing waste load conditions will have periods of excess capacity.[10] Under these circumstances the short-run opportunity costs of using the reservoir for flow augmentation for water quality improvement must be compared with the opportunity costs of alternative uses of the reservoir capacity. Appropriate operating procedures of the system would be based upon relevant marginal costs. Reliance upon flow augmentation would be heavier in the early period after the dam was built, and effluent charges or standards would be accordingly lower in those years.

This means that care must be taken to provide waste disposers with information on longer-run prospects so that investment decisions will not be based on the presumption that charges will continue to be low.

CONCLUDING COMMENTS

This chapter has focused on the integrated planning of various types of waste load reduction, flow regulation and in-stream measures; the incorporation of "unmeasured values"; and some "short-run" economic problems which stem from environmental variability. Attention was directed to the important role that can be played by effluent charges— either alone or in conjunction with other measures for regulating waste discharges—in articulating the decisions of individual waste dischargers efficiently into a regional system for water quality management. In addition, it was pointed out that the assessment of charges is important in financing the collective features of such a system.

It was indicated that, ideally, system planning would consider all alternative uses of water, including its use for waste disposal, the effects of the various uses on water quality, the losses imposed on other uses by quality deterioration, and the value of water-derivative uses. All feasible system plans and operating procedures would be considered, and a solution would be derived which would indicate the optimum combination of system elements and operating procedures in light of the objectives and constraints relevant to the system. The regional system view, taking cognizance of the efficiency of collective measures, did not require the introduction of any new economic principles. But there are practical reasons, including the inherent complexity of the problem and the primitive state or absence of much of the required data, why an optimum solution cannot be fully attained. Furthermore, some inevitable arbitrariness in the specification of constraints, the absence of fully satisfactory means of handling the risk inherent in natural phenomena,

---

[10] For a formal analysis of the considerations governing the optimum timing of the addition of system elements to a system serving expanding demands, see A. Maass *et al.*, *Design of Water Resources Systems* (Harvard University Press, 1962), Chapter 2.

and the uncertainty involved in forecasting future economic variables, militate against the achievement of fully optimum decisions. But with ingenious simplification, it is possible to develop workable procedures and mount investigations that will produce satisfactory, if not totally precise, results. This is illustrated by the case studies in the next chapter.

Nevertheless, an approach of the general type outlined in this chapter will improve decisions on water quality management. It emphasizes the importance of identifying interdependencies and viewing areas and economic functions tied together by "spillovers" in a "system" context; requires an explicit and unambiguous statement of objectives and constraints; stresses the identification and quantification of alternatives and their systematic testing in light of criteria of merit developed in terms of the objective or objectives of the system; and endeavors to cause the opportunity costs of water resources use to be reflected in decisions not controlled directly by the water resources management agency.

These features of the analysis represent a way of thinking about the problem of water quality management; they do not imply a specific procedure for solving it. When the situation is a complex one involving numerous alternatives and constraints, optimization procedures applied to formal mathematical models, often with the aid of computers, can be very helpful. This type of approach is illustrated by the cases in the next chapter.

APPENDIX TO CHAPTER 10

COLLECTIVE FACILITIES IN WATER QUALITY MANAGEMENT

By J. Hayden Boyd

This appendix presents a compact restatement of many of the economic principles explained in previous chapters, and it presupposes a considerable general knowledge of economic theory.[1]

The economic maximization model presented here treats the river basin as a multiple-product natural asset.[2] The products of this asset are flows of two types of services, a vector of *waste removal* services and

---

[1] A highly simplified water quality management situation is contemplated. It involves surface water only, and stochastic aspects of the problem are not explicitly considered. Nor is consideration given to situations in which joint outputs are involved, such as water quality improvement simultaneously with navigation water. The same basic economic principle would apply to more complex situations, however.

[2] An asset may be defined as something which yields a flow of services which contribute to the production of utility or of profit. If an externality has to do with water quality, the asset can be identified with certain attributes of a water course. The relevant asset may not always be readily identifiable as a physical entity, especially when complex urban externalities are involved.

one of *water quality* services. The quantity of the latter service available at a given location depends on the quantities of the former consumed at upstream points. In addition, it is recognized that the "natural" waste assimilative capacity of a river can be augmented by the investment of resources; for example, by constructing dams to provide dilution water or by mechanically aerating the river. This augmentation of capacity results in a higher level of downstream water quality for a given level of waste discharge. Both river-basin services are economic "goods," with positive marginal products (or utilities). Problems of allocation arise because these goods are scarce, in the sense that flows of waste removal services cannot be increased without decreasing flows of downstream water quality services, and conversely.

Properties of production functions involving water resources services will be discussed first. Next the relationship between water services will be formalized. These two sets of constraints are then incorporated into a welfare maximization model for water quality. The resulting efficiency criteria, which are in the form of marginal conditions for a Pareto optimum, can be used to derive optimum prices at each location for the river basin's waste removal and water quality services.

The optimization criteria also include one for the optimal level of investment. (The prices derived for river-basin services are for the river as augmented by this investment.) These prices, when levied, yield an income to the taxing authority which can be regarded as a quasi rent on the investment and a rent on the "natural capacity" of the river basin asset. The final part of the appendix will derive conditions under which the income from charges for waste removal services will cover the costs of an optimal level of investment in river-basin capacity.

Production Functions of Firms Using River Basin Services

Let the production function for a typical firm be written:

(1) $$Y_i = Y_i(X_i, Z_i, Q_i, S_i),$$

where:

Y_i = output of ith firm,
X_i = conventional input used by i^{th} firm,
Z_i = quantity of waste removal services used by i^{th} firm,
Q_i = water quality enjoyed by i^{th} firm,
S_i = quantity of normalized site advantage at location i, as explained below.

Although each of these variables could be a vector, they will be treated here as unidimensional. Y_i and X_i are assumed to be perfectly divisible, and always to have positive prices. Z_i is assumed to be perfectly divisible, but the model places no *a priori* restrictions on its price.

S_i represents capital specific to the ith site, that is, attributes of the site which cannot be varied in the period relevant to the analysis. If the analysis is long-run, and each capital plant is allowed to vary in size, then S would include such comparative advantages as location, soil fertility, climate, and the like. In this case, capital inputs would be included in X. If the analysis is short-run, with plant size fixed, then S would include the plant, and X, the variable factors alone. In either case, the level of S_i is, by definition, fixed. Any income from the sale of Y not spent on purchases of the first three inputs is assumed to accrue to S as a residual site rental.

X_i, Z_i and S_i are assumed to have the following properties:

(2) $$\alpha > 0 \text{ if } Y_i > 0, \text{ and } \alpha = 0 \text{ if } Y_i = 0;$$

$$\frac{\delta Y_i}{\delta \alpha} \gtreqless 0; \frac{\delta^2 Y_i}{\delta \alpha^2} < 0; \frac{\delta^2 Y_i}{\delta \alpha \delta \beta} > 0; \alpha \neq \beta;$$

where α and β are any of X_i, Z_i and S_i. These conditions state that the three inputs are "goods." They would be sufficient to insure that all positive levels of production would use positive amounts of each of these inputs if the production function did not involve Q_i. The conditions are purely formal for the site S_i since it is defined as fixed in quantity.

Water quality cannot enter into the production function symmetrically with the other inputs, however. The production relation between upstream waste discharges and downstream water quality expresses the latter as *concentrations* of various constituents, as, for example, parts dissolved oxygen per million parts water. The physical intake of these constituents depends both on their concentration and on the quantity of water used. Specifically, if W_i is the quantity of water withdrawn, used, and discharged back into the river (neglecting consumptive use), then the amount of the quality constituent taken in is $Q_i W_i$, and the production function may be rewritten as:

(3) $$Y_i = Y_i^*(\ldots W_i, Q_i W_i).$$

If W_i and the other inputs are held constant, it seems reasonable to assume that Q_i variations yield the usual diminishing marginal returns. However, if Q_i is held constant and the other inputs are varied proportionally, the quality constituents input, $Q_i W_i$, also is varied proportionally. All physical inputs are therefore varied proportionally, and it is not reasonable to speak of diminishing marginal returns to the other variables (taken as a unit), when quality is held constant. Water quality enters the production function as a parameter rather than a physical input. Unfortunately (from the standpoint of analytical ease), Q_i, not W_i or $W_i Q_i$, is the economic good whose "production" by the sale of fewer upstream pollution removal services requires the sacrifice of valuable alternatives.

The firm's level of W_i, as defined above, does not represent the utilization of an economic resource. Paradoxically, while W_i may be limited in amount for firm i, its level has no effect on the operations of upstream or downstream firms. If the firm's water intake is upstream from its outfall, the rate of withdrawal is limited by the river's rate of flow. Even if this constraint were binding, perhaps because a very large plant had located on a very small stream, the relevant scarcity would be automatically internalized. The profit maximizing firm would optimally allocate the available rate of water flow among alternative uses, and no public policy problems of allocation would arise.[3] Downstream from the outfall, the river's quantity and quality will be unaffected, *except* insofar as pollutant removal services, Z_i, have been consumed. Of course, it is possible for a firm to consume Z_i without using water (as by dumping) or to "use" all of the flow without polluting (as a recreation area or bathing beach).

If equation (3) is linear-homogeneous in the arguments as written, then it will not be linear-homogeneous when each element is written as a separate argument. In particular, it will be linear-homogeneous in all inputs *except Q*. Although this fact is true for all such linear-homogeneous functions, it is most easily illustrated for a Cobb-Douglas production function:[4]

(4) $$Y_i = X_i^\alpha Z_i^\beta W_i^\gamma (W_i Q_i)^\delta S_i^\epsilon = (Q_i^\delta) X_i^\alpha Z_i^\beta W_i^{\gamma+\delta} S_i^\epsilon,$$

where

$$\alpha + \beta + \gamma + \delta + \epsilon = 1.$$

Water Quality as a Public Consumption Good

It is interesting to note that water quality is a public or collective consumption good. Samuelson defines a public good[5] as one which satisfies the following relationship:

[3] Increasing the river's flow during the dry season is one way of augmenting its waste assimilative capacity. In the unlikely event that W_i is scarce for some i, an additional benefit, not considered in this appendix, would arise from this activity.

[4] It should not be inferred that a Cobb-Douglas production function is a useful tool for the analysis of water quality.

[5] Paul Samuelson, "The Pure Theory of Public Expenditure," *Review of Economics and Statistics*, Vol. 36 (November 1954), p. 387; "Diagramatic Exposition of a Theory of Public Expenditure," *Review of Economics and Statistics*, Vol. 37 (November 1955), p. 350; "Aspects of Public Expenditure Theories," *Review of Economics and Statistics*, Vol. 40 (November 1958), p. 332.

Public goods are sometimes described as goods whose consumption involves externalities or spillover effects [Alan Williams, "The Optimal Provision of Public Goods in a System of Local Government," *Journal of Political Economy*, Vol. 74 (February 1966), pp. 18–19]. The concept of externality is confused enough without applying it to yet another economic phenomenon. I use the term external diseconomy to imply the presence of a capital asset outside the sphere of property ownership, and the term public good to refer to a commodity subject to a joint supply constraint, as defined below.

(5) $X_2 = X_2^i$ $(i = 1, \ldots, n)$,

where

$X_2 =$ quantity of public good produced,
$X_2^i =$ quantity of public good consumed by i^{th} consumer.

It can be shown that welfare maximization conditions for a public good differ from those for a private good. Vertical addition of individual demand curves or marginal-rate-of-substitution curves is necessary to derive the corresponding aggregate curves for a public good. For a private good, horizontal addition is called for.[6] This vertical addition of demand curves is the hallmark of the joint product. The public good differs from the usual joint product in that it involves simultaneous provision of a product to different *individuals* rather than the simultaneous production of several different (private good) outputs.

Thus, a public good is one which is characterized by a *joint supply constraint*. That is, supplying the good to one individual is not possible without simultaneously supplying it to other individuals. The classic examples are national defense and broadcasting. Samuelson's definition (equation 5 above) can be extended to the more general case in which equal amounts are not supplied to all individuals. Using his notation, if X_2 of the public good is produced, then a_iX_2 goes to individual i; a_i can be either a fixed coefficient, or, more generally, a function of X_2. The feature which distinguishes X_2 from a private good is that no a_i can be varied, given a level of X_2.

Production of higher quality water requires either the sale of fewer upstream waste removal services, through a higher (implicit or explicit) price for these river services, or the investment of resources to augment the river's capacity. But high quality water cannot be supplied selectively to some firms and not to others. Moreover, not only the water used by a firm, but also all of the water flowing past the firm's intake must be simultaneously improved in quality.

The joint supply constraint means that market mechanisms cannot be used to determine the optimal amount of a public good to be produced. A person contracting for some national defense, a broadcast, or water quality cannot, because of this constraint, avoid having some of these services delivered to others. Thus, it would be foolish for him to attempt to buy his "share" of any public good.

Alternatively, a supplier could ask each beneficiary what price he would be willing and able to pay for various amounts of the public good, with the proviso that the prospective consumer would have to make the stated payment for the amount actually supplied to him. Each consumer

[6] Samuelson, *op. cit.*, 1954.

would have a strong incentive to understate his true demand curve if he were required to pay, since the amount actually supplied him depends on statements by others as well. If he were not required to pay, he would have a strong incentive to overstate his demand. In short, there is no easy way to ascertain an individual's demand for a public good, because of the joint supply constraint. Among other things, this means that ascertaining benefits from public goods, in comparison to benefits foregone by devoting resources to their production rather than to some alternative use (i.e., opportunity cost), is extremely difficult.

Water quality is a public good, and it is also something which enters into a production function with other goods asymmetrically. The same kind of difficulty occurs with national defense and broadcasting. On the one hand, increments in the amounts of these two public goods ought to entail diminishing marginal returns; on the other hand, proportional increments in all other inputs need not result in diminishing marginal returns. It is impossible to conceive of using one of these public goods more "intensively," as that term is generally understood.

The Technological Relationship Between Waste Loads and Water Quality

It can be shown that the relation between any Z_i and Q_j (for several major kinds of waste and quality constituents)[7] may, in the absence of any man-made investment, be represented by the matrix equation:

$$(6) \qquad Q = AZ + Q^o,$$

where Q and Z are $(1 \times n)$ vectors whose elements are the corresponding river-basin services, A is an $(n \times n)$ matrix of constants whose elements on and to the right of the diagonal are zero, and Q^o $(1 \times n)$ represents the level of quality which would be present without waste discharges.

Consider for illustrative purposes an investment which somehow doubles the physical volume of the watercourse at all locations in a way that does not alter the rate of flow, temperature, and reaeration coefficient. Then, water quality at every location would be unchanged if, at the same time the water course is doubled in volume, all firms were to double their discharge of wastes. If each firm were to double its inputs (X_i, Z_i, W_i, S_i) then, quality unchanged, the vector of physical inputs $(X_i, Z_i, W_i, Q_iW_i, S_i)$ would also be doubled.[8] If

$$(7) \qquad Y_i = Y_i^*(X_i, Z_i, W_i, Q_iW_i, S_i)$$

is linear-homogeneous, then Y_i would also be doubled for each firm.

---

[7] See Chapter 2.

[8] Of course, S_i, by definition, is fixed.

The doubling of capacity of a joint product firm usually implies that all outputs are potentially doubled. This might be interpreted for the river-basin authority as a doubling of both water quality and waste removal services at each location. Yet, since water quality is a parameter rather than a physical input in the usual sense, the doubling of river-basin volume discussed above can meaningfully be termed a doubling of river-basin capacity.

Write, therefore, the river services constraint as

$$(8) \qquad Q = \left(\frac{1}{1+I}\right)AZ + Q^o,$$

where Q, Q^o, A, and Z have the same definitions as in equation (6) and I is the scalar which appears in the benefit expression, equation (15). If $I = 0$, the river basin is in its natural state; if $I = 1$, its capacity has been doubled as discussed above; etc. While I, as defined, probably does not correspond exactly to any feasible capacity augmentation, it is perhaps the conceptually simplest form of man-made investment.

Collective Facilities for Waste Treatment

Because of economies of scale in waste treatment or for other reasons, it may be desirable for firms to utilize collective treatment facilities. The most obvious example is furnished by regional sewerage and treatment systems, which collect and process wastes for many different economic units. These collective treatment facilities will be considered briefly in the context of questions of efficient allocation of resources raised in the next section.

The cost of treating wastes may be expressed in terms of the amounts of polluting materials contained in the wastewater, the amount of water to be treated, and the residual wastes discharged after treatment. Other things equal, treatment costs increase with increases in influent wastes or water flow and with decreases in pollutant removal services consumption. The costs and appropriate efficiency prices for the collective facility's services may be derived.

Assume, for simplicity, that the facility, located at site j, treats waste water containing a single waste.

$$(9) \qquad C = f(B, W, Z_j),$$

where

> C = treatment costs,
> B = waste load (in physical units, e.g., pounds of BOD),
> W = wastewater volume,
> Z_j = waste removal services consumed by the treatment facility from the river basin.

This can be rewritten, using the same terminology as for the Y firms above, as:

(10) $$X_j P_x + R_j = f(B, W, Z_j),$$

where

$X_j P_x$ = expenditures on variable inputs,
R_j = residual accruing to fixed capital.

In turn, equation (10) implies a production function of the form:

(11) $$(B, W) = g(X_j, Z_j, S_j).$$

Even though a collective treatment facility is operated by the river-basin authority that controls the allocation of waste removal and water quality services, it is useful to consider it as autonomous in the sense that it faces a price for waste removal services in the same manner as other firms. This assumption may be more realistic than it seems at first glance, because most large corporations use inter-division sales and set exchange prices as a management tool.[9] The purchase of Delco batteries by the Chevrolet Division, for example, serves most of the functions of a similar transaction between two independent companies.

The production functions for each firm using the combination of waste load and water handling services of the facilities, together with demand and supply conditions for the firm's outputs and inputs, determine a joint demand function for the vector of services (B, W):

(12) $$(B, W)_d = d(P_B, P_W).$$

It can be readily shown that Pareto optimality requires that:

(13) $$\frac{P_X}{\delta B/\delta X_j} = \frac{P_{Zj}}{\delta B/\delta Z_j} = MC_B = P_B,$$

$$\frac{P_X}{\delta W/\delta X_j} = \frac{P_{Zj}}{\delta W/\delta Z_j} = MC_W = P_W.$$

Note also that, by a suitable rearrangement:

(14) $$\frac{\delta B/\delta X_j}{\delta W/\delta X_j} = \frac{\delta B/\delta Z_j}{\delta W/\delta Z_j} = \frac{\text{Marginal rate of trans-}}{\text{formation of } W \text{ into } B} = \frac{P_W}{P_B}.$$

In summary, then, the collective treatment facility should charge a marginal cost price for each of the services, waste removal and water handling, it provides. This price will induce the most socially efficient reduction of both water intake and waste production. The analysis would be similar if more than one waste were considered, and also the conclusions with respect to the appropriate vector of prices for the vector

[9] See the discussion of in-plant charges in Chapter 8.

of waste and water loads, i.e., they would be set equal to the marginal costs of each of these elements.

River-Basin Maximization Model

Let there be a watercourse used by n firms located along it. All firms benefit from water quality improvements, and from being allowed to discharge wastes into the river. These firms produce an output Y using a common purchased input X. The watercourse has no alternative uses, all firms view all prices parametrically, industry demand for Y is given, and X is available at constant cost to all firms. The river basin asset is controlled by an authority which wishes to invest a Pareto-optimal level of resources in river-basin capacity, and, given this capacity at any moment in time, to allocate its services in a Pareto-optimal fashion.

Benefits from the river-oriented production may be written as the sum of revenues and consumers surplus from the production, minus the cost of resources withdrawn from the rest of the economy, as constrained by the firms' production functions and the relationship among the water resources services:

(15)
$$G = \int_0^Y P(y)dy - XP_X - C(I)$$

$$- \sum_{i=1}^{n} \lambda_i[Y_i - Y_i(X_i, Z_i, Q_i, S_i)]$$

$$- \sum_{a=1}^{n} \alpha_a[Q_a - Q_a(Z_1, Z_2, \ldots, Z_{a-1}, I)].$$

where

G = benefits from river-oriented production,

Y = $\sum_{i=1}^{n} Y_i$,

$P(Y)$ = market price of $Y = P_Y$,
X_i = conventional input used by ith firm,
P_X = price of X = constant,
Z_i = waste removal services consumed by ith firm,
Q_i = water quality at location i,
S_i = quantity of site advantage or specific capital at location i,
I = level of investment in river capacity,
$C(I)$ = cost of I.

Equation (15) has $4n + 1$ variables (n Y_i's, n X_i's, n Z_i's, n Q_i's, and I) and $2n$ constraints which are incorporated by the LaGrangian multipliers (n λ's and n α's), leaving $2n + 1$ degrees of freedom. The necessary number of optimization relations can be derived in terms of marginal conditions for the n X_i's, the n Z_i's, and I. Differentiating G with respect to Y_i ($i = 1, \ldots, n$) and X_i ($i = 1, \ldots, n$), and substituting for the λ's yields the following condition for employment of X_i:[10]

(16) $$P_X = P_Y \left(\frac{\delta Y_i}{\delta X_i} \right). \qquad (i = 1, \ldots, n).$$

Equation (16) states that X ought to be employed by each firm in an amount such that its marginal product is equal to its price. This equation would describe optimum conditions for X allocation regardless of whether the river-basin services were optimally allocated; if they were not, (16) would indicate a second-best solution.

Differentiating with respect to Z_i and Q_i ($i = 1, \ldots, n$) and substituting for the LaGrangian multipliers yields:

(17) $$P_Y \frac{\delta Y_i}{\delta Z_i} = - \sum_{b=i+1}^{n} P_Y \frac{\delta Y_b}{\delta Q_b} \frac{\delta Q_b}{\delta Z_i}.$$

Equation (17) states that waste discharge at each location ought to be allowed up to the point where the incremental benefits to the discharging firm are just offset by decrements in downstream benefits. Note that the term on the right is a weighted negative sum of marginal products of water quality, and that the term on the left is equivalent to the negative of the marginal cost of this weighted sum. Equation (17) is therefore analogous to the result of a weighted vertical addition of demand curves necessary to derive the "price" of a public good.

The derivatives on the right of equation (17) are, as a practical matter, very difficult to evaluate. This difficulty stems primarily from the public good character of water quality. Lacking precise information as to the incremental benefits of water quality, the authority may wish simply to achieve a certain vector of water quality at least cost. This procedure is formally equivalent to specifying a completely inelastic demand for quality at each location b, at the Q_b^* selected by the authority.

In other words, the constraint implicitly states that increments in quality above Q_b^* are valueless, and that incremental damages due to quality below Q_b are infinite. The derivatives $\delta Y_b / \delta Q_b$ in equation (17)

---

[10] Note that efficiency conditions (16), (17), and (18) make no use of an assumption as to returns to scale in the firms' production functions. The property of linear homogeneity is utilized in this appendix only to derive relationships among aggregate inputs and outputs, as in the last section concerning the relationship between the income from effluent charges and the costs of capacity augmentation.

would be indeterminant[11] at the specified Q_b^*, but (17) does specify the interrelationships among the Z_i's necessary to achieve the constraint at least cost. For any downstream location b where the constraint is binding, the same numerical value of $\delta Y_b / \delta Q_b$ would appear in the optimization equation (17) of each upstream firm.

Finally, differentiating with respect to I and substituting as before for the LaGrangian multipliers:

$$(18) \qquad C'(I) = \sum_{a=1}^{n} P_Y \frac{\delta Y_a}{\delta Q_a} \frac{\delta Q_a}{\delta I}$$

Equation (18) states that the marginal product of investment in river-basin waste assimilative capacity ought to be equated to its marginal cost.

All inputs could, in principle, be allocated via the price mechanism. Since each Y firm is assumed to be a perfect competitor, the conventional theory of the firm suggests that the ith firm will adjust its purchases of inputs so that:

$$(19) \qquad P_{Xi} = P_Y \frac{\delta Y_i}{\delta X_i},$$

$$(20) \qquad P_{Zi} = P_Y \frac{\delta Y_i}{\delta Z_i},$$

$$(21) \qquad P_{Qi} = P_Y \frac{\delta Y_i}{\delta Q_i}.$$

Implicit in these three equations is the assumption that the quantity purchased of each of these factors is under the control of the firm. This assumption is, of course, realistic as far as the conventional input X is concerned. Similarly, the amount of Z purchased can be altered, as by changing the mode of production or the degree of waste treatment.

At first glance, it may appear that Q_i cannot be varied by firm i. It is true that Q_i depends only on Z_j $(0 < j < i)$ and I. Hence, once these are determined, Q_i is given. The situation is not unlike that of a householder who has milk delivered to his home. His contract with the dairy implies an indirect control over other economic units, such as farmers and deliverymen. A contract for a certain level of water quality with the same river basin authority which has the power to tax upstream waste discharges is easy to visualize. Unfortunately, however, water quality

---

[11] The term $\delta Y_b / \delta Q_b$ is indeterminant in the same sense that demand price is indeterminant for an inelastic demand curve at the relevant quantity in the standard competitive model. The equilibrium price in that case is one which will call forth the specified quantity from suppliers. In equilibrium, all firms are producing quantities such that each one's marginal cost is equal to the market price and, hence, to each other's marginal cost.

is a public good and hence subject to a joint supply constraint. For this reason, and not because water quality is given at any moment in time, it would be difficult if not impossible to contract for water quality.

It was argued above that the firm's production function:

$$(22) \qquad Y_i = Y_i(X_i, Z_i, Q_i, S_i) = Y_i^*(X_i, Z_i, W_i, W_iQ_i, S_i),$$

written as Y^* could reasonably be assumed to be linear-homogeneous, such that for any arbitrary constant c:

$$(23) \qquad cY_i = Y_i^*(cX_i, cZ_i, cW_i, cW_iQ_i, cS_i).$$

Also, if the ith firm has such a linear-homogeneous production function and maximizes its profits, then payments to X_i, Z_i, W_i and S_i of their marginal products will exactly exhaust the total revenue $(P_Y Y_i)$.

It is worth noting that the equality $P_{Si} = P_Y \dfrac{\delta Y_i}{\delta S_i}$, occurs by an adjustment of the residual site rental R, where:

$$(24) \qquad R_i = S_i P_{Si} = Y_i P_Y - X_i P_X - Z_i P_{Zi} - W_i P_{Wi},$$

rather than by variations in S_i. W_i, as defined, is a free good, so the appropriate efficient $P_{Wi} = 0$ for all i. Water is withdrawn, circulated through the plant, and discharged (neglecting consumptive use), to the point where its marginal product is zero.

If the river basin chooses to levy a charge P_{Qi} for water quality, the site S_i will receive $P_{Qi} Q_i$ less than its marginal product, given the above assumption of linear homogeneity. If P_{Qi} is set equal to $P_Y (\delta Y_i/\delta Q_i)$, then the residual site rental will be non-negative if, and only if, the value of the marginal product of the site is at least as large as that of water quality. $P_{Qi} \leqq (S_i/Q_i) P_{Si}$ will not alter the firm's actions and $P_{Qi} > (S_i/Q_i) P_{Si}$ will cause the firm to shut down if doing so will enable it to cease the payments for water quality.

In fact, most discussions of public goods assume either implicitly or explicitly that the amount of these goods produced is decided by some agency, and that the recipients of the public goods exercise no direct market control over the amounts they receive.[12]

The following section assumes, therefore, that a vector of P_{Zi} is established by the river-basin agency and that each of the n firms must accept the resulting water quality at its location as given and outside its control. The agency allocates waste removal services so that (17) holds.

[12] Howard R. Bowen, "The Interpretation of Voting in the Allocation of Economic Resources," *Quarterly Journal of Economics*, Vol. 63 (November 1943), p. 27. Richard A. Musgrave, "The Voluntary Exchange Theory of Public Economy," *Quarterly Journal of Economics*, Vol. 53 (February 1939), p. 213. See also Samuelson, *op. cit.*, 1954, 1955, and 1958.

Relationship Between Effluent Charge Income
and Costs of Capacity Augmentation

By investing I in river capacity augmentation, the river-basin agency incurs costs of $C(I)$. The conditions under which $\sum_{i=1}^{n} P_{Z_i} Z_i \geqq C(I)$ will be examined next, since financing of I would be greatly facilitated whenever income from effluent charges at least covers the cost of such investment.

Assuming that the river-basin agency allocates river-basin services efficiently among the firms in the industry, an industry production function for Y may be written:

$$(25) \qquad\qquad Y = Y(X, S, 1 + I),$$

where
$$Y = \sum_{i=1}^{n} Y_i,$$

$$X = \sum_{i=1}^{n} X_i,$$

$S = S(S_1, S_2, \ldots, S_n)$ where $\lambda S = S(\lambda S_1, \lambda S_2, \ldots, \lambda S_n)$,
$1 + I = $ natural $+$ man-made capacity of watercourses.

It has been intuitively argued that if each firm's production function (22) is homogeneous of order one, then the industry production function is also linear-homogeneous. Euler's theorem then implies that:

$$(26) \qquad\qquad Y = X \frac{\delta Y}{\delta X} + S \frac{\delta Y}{\delta S} + (1 + I) \frac{\delta Y}{\delta I}.$$

It was shown earlier that if $P_{Q_i} = 0$, Q_i is outside the firm's control, and Z_i is paid its marginal product, then the residual rent accruing to S_i is equal to its marginal product in the case where returns to scale are constant. Write:

$$(27) \qquad\qquad Y = \sum_{i=1}^{n} X_i \frac{\delta Y_i}{\delta X_i} + Z_i \frac{\delta Y_i}{\delta Z_i} + W_i \frac{\delta Y_i}{\delta W_i} + S_i \frac{\delta Y_i}{\delta S_i}.$$

The efficient allocation assumption means that:

$$(28) \qquad \delta Y / \delta \alpha = \delta Y_i / \delta \alpha_i, \qquad\qquad \text{where } \alpha \text{ stands for any of } X, Z, \text{ or } W.$$

S is defined so that proportional increases in each S_i will proportionally increase S. By Euler's theorem,

$$S = \sum_{i=1}^{n} S_i \frac{\delta S}{\delta S_i},$$

and

$$(29) \qquad\qquad S \frac{\delta Y}{\delta S} = \sum_{i=1}^{n} S_i \frac{\delta S}{\delta S_i} \frac{\delta Y}{\delta S} = \sum_{i=1}^{n} S_i \frac{\delta Y}{\delta S_i}.$$

Substituting (28) and (29) into (26) and subtracting from (27) yields:

(30) $$(1+I)\frac{\delta Y}{\delta I} = \sum_{i=1}^{n} Z_i \frac{\delta Y_i}{\delta Z_i} = \sum_{i=1}^{n} Z_i \frac{P_{Zi}}{Py}.$$

Equation (30) states that the revenues from an effluent charge, given universal constant returns to scale and efficient allocation of all resources and given the scalar definition of river-basin capacity, will just equal the value of the marginal product of river-basin capacity.

The payment to the river basin of its marginal product by collecting the optimal P_{Zi} at each location is analogous to the "sale" of units of natural and man-made capacity at a price P_I. For, by Euler's theorem,

$$Y = X\frac{\delta Y}{\delta X} + S\frac{\delta Y}{\delta S} + (I+1)\frac{\delta Y}{\delta I}$$

and

(31) $$P_Y Y = XP_X + SP_S + (I+1)P_I.$$

If $C(I)$ is the cost of man-made capacity, then $C'(I) = P_I$ is the condition for the efficient level of investment. Assume $C(0) = 0$. If $C''(I) = 0$ then $C'(I) = \beta$ (capacity expandable at constant marginal cost). $C(I) = \beta I$, and, when I is adjusted to the optimal level, $P_I = \beta$. In this case, when the level of investment is optimal,

(32) $$C(I) = IP_I,$$

leaving P_I as a pure rent accruing to the "natural" capacity of the river basin. If $C(I)$ is an increasing function of I, more than the marginal product of natural capacity will accrue to the river basin agency as pure rent. A deficit could occur, given the scalar definition of I in equation (8) above, only if $C(I)$ declines as a function of I; that is, only if marginal increments in river-basin capacity decline in cost as capacity is increased.

U.S. Cases of Regional Water Quality Systems Analysis

11

Regional water quality management systems that incorporate the full range of alternatives are still in the planning stage in the United States, although collective regional-scale measures for water quality improvement have been instituted in a few cases by local, state, private, and/or federal agencies.[1] However, more systematic planning for regional water quality management is evolving, and progressively more comprehensive and sophisticated planning approaches are being taken. Because the plans involve a greater variety and number of components, the systems are more intricate in terms of both planning and operation, and questions of the institutional means for implementation become increasingly critical. The need is especially acute in situations where coordination of the decisions of many public and private parties is needed and where the financing of various alternatives presents diverse problems. Furthermore, where information on the benefits and costs— especially the benefits—associated with various water quality objectives is limited, mechanisms are needed to gauge public preferences and to see that the interests of affected parties are appropriately reflected in decision making.

[1] Early examples of these measures include the provision for low-flow augmentation for water quality improvement in the Youghiogheny and Tygart reservoirs in the Monongahela River Basin, and addition of oxygen to streams by turbine aeration in Wisconsin. See E. W. Landenberger, "Multi-purpose Reservoirs and Pollution Control Benefits," Ohio River Valley Water Sanitation Commission (ORSANCO), Cincinnati, 1953; and A. J. Wiley, *et al.*, "Commercial-scale Operation of Turbine Aeration on Wisconsin Rivers," *Journal of the Water Pollution Control Federation*, Vol. 32, No. 2, 1960, pp. 186–94. For many years releases have been made from Shasta Reservoir, of the Central Valley Project (California), to reduce salinity intrusion in the Sacramento San Joaquin Delta. More recently initiated collective measures include the wastewater reclamation operations at Whittier Narrows and Santee, California. With respect to the former, see J. D. Parkhurst, "Progress in Waste Water Re-use in Southern California," *Journal of the Irrigation and Drainage Division, Proceedings ASCE*, Vol. 91, No. IR1 (1965), pp. 79–91; the latter, R. L. Stoyer, "Special Uses for Water Reclaimed from Sewage" (Paper presented at 21st Annual Meeting, Soil Conservation Society of America, 1966).

The planning studies reported in this chapter illustrate the advances that have been made in developing analytical techniques, and at the same time point up the influence of institutional arrangements at both the planning and operational stages. In the studies of the Potomac and Delaware estuaries (examined in greater detail later in the chapter), efforts were made to achieve economic objectives through planning on a regional basis, and at least some attention was given to alternatives in addition to control at the source. A research study made after the planning study for the Potomac provided particularly useful information for our purposes.

In a resolution of January 1956 (amended in 1959 and 1960), the Congress requested review of existing reports on the Potomac Basin with a view to preparation of a comprehensive plan for water supply, water quality control, and water-based recreation in the basin. In 1963 the U.S. Corps of Engineers submitted to the Board of Engineers for Rivers and Harbors the *Potomac River Basin Report*. This was the first time that a federal water resource agency had submitted a comprehensive report in which water quality management was a major consideration. The plan took a quality objective stated in physical terms as given and recommended a program that combined waste treatment at individual outfalls with low-flow augmentation. While it was a pioneering effort, the plan fell far short of analyzing the full range of alternatives—including alternative quality objectives. Basically it was limited to considering those water quality improvement facilities which could clearly be implemented through existing institutions, and therefore avoided facing the question of institutional design for implementation of an efficient system for regional water quality management, within the context of efficient over-all water resources management.

Subsequently, Robert Davis of the RFF staff used the Corps data plus considerable additional information to expand the range of alternatives for water quality management in the Potomac estuary in the neighborhood of Washington, D.C., the locus of most of the quality problem.[2]

The Delaware study was made by the Federal Water Pollution Control Administration[3] under the provisions of the Federal Water Pollution Control Act of 1956 which provides that comprehensive programs are

---

[2] R. K. Davis, *The Range of Choice in Water Management: A Study of Dissolved Oxygen in the Potomac Estuary* (The Johns Hopkins Press, for RFF, 1968).

[3] The study was started by the Division of Water Supply and Pollution Control, U.S. Public Health Service, which was responsible for administering water pollution control until the Federal Water Pollution Control Administration was established in 1965. In 1966 the FWPCA was transferred from the Department of Health, Education, and Welfare to the Department of the Interior.

to be devised for eliminating or reducing the pollution of interstate waters and their tributaries and improving the sanitary condition of surface and underground waters. Such plans are to be prepared or developed in co-operation with other federal agencies, state and interstate water quality control agencies, and the municipalities, industries, and other water users involved.

The highly industrialized Delaware estuary area has a severe water quality problem, even though quality has been somewhat improved by the efforts of an interstate body, the Interstate Commission on the Delaware (INCODEL), since superseded by the Delaware River Basin Commission. Institutional arrangements in the Delaware Basin are covered more fully in Chapter 13; here we simply note that the basin is the only area in the United States where there is an agency fully qualified by law to implement a thoroughgoing system of regional water quality management. The study of the Delaware estuary is also notable as a technical achievement. Although the study placed heavy emphasis on conventional waste treatment, it did analyze a range of alternative objectives and systems. Of particular interest in the present context is the fact that the study sheds some light on the economies which may result from the implementation of collective measures for water quality management, and that it explores the incremental cost associated with various levels of water quality objectives.

It is perhaps not altogether coincidence that in its Potomac plan the agency which views its mission as regulating the flow of the nation's rivers (the U.S. Corps of Engineers) concluded that flow regulation should be the major device for dealing with the water quality problem, whereas in the Delaware the agency which views its mission largely as stopping pollution at its source (the Federal Water Pollution Control Administration) found waste load reduction at individual outfalls to be the solution. In both instances consideration of realistic alternatives was rather cursory. Agency perceptions of water problems and their solutions are almost inevitably reflected in the approaches to planning. When an agency's "mission" is rather narrow, its capability to identify and consider the full range of alternatives is limited.

More important perhaps in limiting the range of alternatives is the conception of the planners as to what it is feasible to implement.[4] At the federal level, responsibility for planning is sharply separated from operating responsibility for at least certain types of measures; and operating responsibilities which should be integrated in an efficient system are separated. These points are well illustrated in planning for water quality management. The Corps of Engineers could design a water quality

[4] Perception of feasibility of implementation cannot, of course, be completely separated from perception of water problems.

management system (as part of a water resources development plan), based in part on such alternatives as waste treatment in collective plants, diverting wastes to new locations, and mechanical reaeration of rivers. Since these activities are not normally conducted by the Corps, Corps planners are not likely to conceive of these as realistic alternatives for which they should present plans.

The same point holds in regard to system operation. In theory the Corps could plan a water resources management system based upon the integrated operation of reservoirs and waste treatment facilities. Since the Corps does not operate waste treatment facilities or have the authority to levy variable effluent charges, it tends to question the practicability of making plans that require an activity to be highly coordinated with the actions of another agency. Again, this view, which is narrow but consistent with institutional arrangements in most regions, limits the range of alternatives considered and the efficiency of the systems which are planned. In this context, too, institutional problems are critical.[5]

Before proceeding to a detailed discussion of the Potomac and Delaware cases, we wish to mention three other studies that were proceeding as this chapter was written. The first is a study of the Miami Basin in Ohio being conducted by a team of researchers from Carnegie-Mellon University. This small but highly industrialized basin already faces severe water quality problems. It has, however, a well-established river basin institution—the Miami Conservancy District—which has so far devoted itself to reducing flood damage and developing water-based recreation. This organization is highly respected locally and might take responsibility for implementing a well-articulated water quality management system which included collective measures. Preliminary results of the Carnegie-Mellon study indicate that a system with collective measures could achieve major economies vis-à-vis one dependent solely on treatment at individual points of waste discharge.

The second study, under the aegis of the Federal Water Pollution Control Administration and the State of Texas, focuses upon Galveston Bay and its tributary areas. Galveston Bay is the largest (520 square

---

[5] The situation in terms of planning perspective is similar to the history of Corps planning with respect to flood damage reduction. Until the past few years the Corps restricted its purview to structural measures for reducing flood damage— reservoirs, levees, channelization. Only with the stimulus of outside research efforts has the Corps begun to consider alternatives for flood damage reduction such as flood plain zoning and flood proofing. These alternates, as with many water quality improvement measures, are the responsibility of agencies or governmental units at other levels, or of private parties, or of no one at all. For a discussion of institutional problems in flood damage management, see Gilbert F. White, "Optimal Flood Damage Management: Retrospect and Prospect" in A. V. Kneese and S. C. Smith (ed.), *Water Research* (The Johns Hopkins Press, for RFF, 1966).

miles), most heavily used, and most productive bay on the Texas Gulf Coast. It is also, however, plagued by waste discharges from some of the nation's fastest growing municipal and industrial areas.

The third is the San Francisco Bay-Delta study sponsored by the State of California. This study encompasses about 40 per cent of the state and will deal with its most complex and heavily used water body.

The Galveston Bay and San Francisco Bay-Delta studies appear to be the most comprehensive water quality planning studies ever undertaken. They aim to examine the full range of alternatives including various collective measures, assign benefits and costs to alternate levels of water quality, and recommend appropriate institutional arrangements for implementation.[6] Two facts help to account for the pioneering character of these studies: *no operating* agencies have major responsibilities in the planning; and the studies deal with intrastate bodies of water over which an individual state has sovereignty to the point of creating an appropriate management authority.

THE POTOMAC ESTUARY

The watershed of the Potomac River includes an area of about 14,000 square miles, lying in portions of four states and the District of Columbia. Over 2 million people—three-fourths of the population in the basin—live in the Washington metropolitan area, which extends beyond the District of Columbia into Maryland and Virginia, and is one of the most rapidly growing metropolitan areas in the nation. The Washington area surrounds the head of the Potomac estuary which is heavily used for recreation. Water supply for the area is taken from the Potomac River upstream from the estuary. The estuary periodically experiences low dissolved oxygen—a condition which could get much worse as waste loads from the metropolitan area and upstream sources mount.

The Corps of Engineers' Study

In its planning effort the Corps of Engineers projected waste loads (see Figure 36) and water withdrawals for the year 2010.[7] Given water quality improvement in the estuary as one of the central targets, the effects of the projected waste loads would have to be controlled. In planning control, the Corps assumed that reduction of waste loads at individual outfalls would be achieved by conventional secondary sewage

[6] See "The Galveston Bay Work Plan," prepared by Texas A & M University, the University of Texas and Texas Technological College, October 31, 1966, and "San Francisco Bay-Delta Water Quality Control Program," The State of California, The Resources Agency, February 1966.

[7] Although not directly germane to our discussion, it should be noted that the planning or investment decision can be significantly affected by the assumptions made in these projections, as well as by the range in choice of alternatives to meet the specified conditions and objectives. The latter point is elaborated below.

treatment, with a maximum of about 90 per cent BOD removal. The residual waste load based on the projected loads and the assumed degree of treatment would result in D.O. concentrations in portions of the estuary less than the 4 ppm objective (24 hour monthly mean for the minimum month).[8]

The plan, made public in 1963, recommended the construction by the year 2010 of sixteen major reservoirs in the Potomac Basin and more than 400 headwater structures. These were meant to meet the projected municipal and industrial water supply and water quality targets, reduce flood damage, and provide water-based recreation opportunities. Of the sixteen major reservoirs proposed, ten were to meet projected upstream targets for water supply and water quality control. Simultaneously, this group of reservoirs would provide a sufficiently higher sustained flow at Washington to meet the projected municipal water diversions there. The remaining group of six reservoirs (providing sixty per cent of the estimated yield—2,340 cfs out of 3,930 cfs) was designed to augment flows into the estuary sufficiently to maintain 4 ppm of D.O., given the 2010 waste loads remaining after 90 per cent BOD removal by treatment. The estimated storage capacity required was based on a presumed replication of thirty years of observed river flows into the estuary.

A benefit-cost analysis was presented which indicated that the benefits from flow augmentation for water quality improvement would be greater than the costs. But this analysis does not do what benefit-cost analysis is intended to do—assist in deciding whether a proposed investment is socially worthwhile. First, the physical quality target of 4 ppm of D.O. was taken as given; no other levels of quality were investigated. Second, the only method seriously investigated as a means of meeting the D.O. objective was flow augmentation to improve the waste assimilative capacity of the estuary. Third, benefits from low-flow augmentation were taken to be the costs of a single-purpose reservoir designed to meet low-flow targets at each point of projected need without regard to the complementary effects of meeting upstream needs. Moreover, a higher rate of interest was used in calculating the costs of the alternative reservoirs—an incorrect procedure from an economic point of view—presumably because it was assumed they would be constructed by state or local governments which have to pay higher rates of interest than those the federal agencies use in their own calculations.

---

[8] Initial target objectives for water quality in the estuary were based solely upon dissolved oxygen levels. Control of discharges of nutrients has more recently been given attention (Inter-Departmental Task Force on Project Potomac, Sub-Task Force on Water Quality, *Final Report*, February 1967).

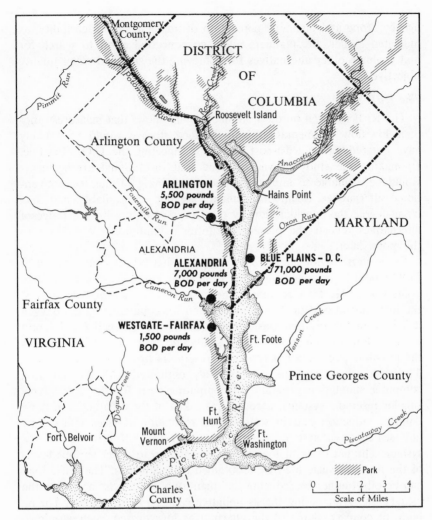

Figure 36. Upper Potomac River estuary with projected residual waste loads for the year 2010 (after 90 per cent removal).

This string of planning assumptions was bound to produce positive net benefits for water quality improvement without even addressing the real benefit question: Is the 4 ppm objective justified by the willingness of beneficiaries to pay at least as much as it costs to achieve and maintain it? Clearly, the benefit-cost analysis as performed is not helpful in deciding whether the plan is justified. Moreover, the comparison of the costs of alternatives which is implicit in the benefit-cost analysis as conducted does not even provide assurance that the least-cost system for meeting the given quality objective has been identified. Because of agency scope and planners' perception of implementation feasibility, as indicated earlier, the planners made no concerted effort to search for and evaluate other alternatives for achieving the specified water quality objective.[9]

The RFF Study

The RFF research on the Potomac estuary shows that measures other than low-flow augmentation from surface storage would very likely have entered into a least-cost system for meeting the D.O. objective. In making the study it was assumed that institutional arrangements would be available to implement plans containing various less conventional alternatives. Such arrangements are not yet available, and to a large degree the consideration by the Corps of only a limited range of alternatives reflects the present institutional limitations. We return to this point later.

Davis started with the Corps assumption that 90 per cent removal of BOD would be achieved for waste discharges in the Washington metropolitan area. He then compared the costs of other alternatives against the incremental cost of flow augmentation for counteracting the oxygen deficit from the residual waste load. Costs were obtained for different levels of low-flow augmentation by scaling down by successive amounts the low-flow augmentation system of reservoirs proposed by the Corps. The scaled-down systems were roughly optimized with the aid of a computer simulation program. In computing costs for the successively smaller reservoir systems, account was taken of the differences in flood damage reduction and in water-based recreation services realized by any scaled-down system in comparison to the full proposed Corps system. The net costs of low-flow augmentation to offset various levels of the residual waste load were obtained by this means. The waste load can be offset either by reducing the quantity of wastes discharged to the estuary or by increasing the assimilative capacity of the estuary (or by both, of course). Some of the alternatives investigated, such as microstraining, operate in the former manner; some, such as low-flow augmentation and reaeration, in the latter.

[9] In a memorandum entitled "Reservoir Storage and Releases for Flow Regulation for Quality Control," June 16, 1967, Secretary of the Interior Udall stated a new departmental position on various aspects of the evaluation and reimbursement of federal low-flow augmentation projects. In general these constitute a great improvement over previous policies. Points of major interest in regard to the present discussion are: (1) Alternative costs of single purpose reservoirs will no longer be an acceptable basis for benefit evaluation; (2) Emphasis is to be placed on the analysis of a wider range of alternative facilities for managing water quality; and (3) It is recommended that the Federal Water Pollution Control Act (see Chapter 13) be amended to require states or interstate agencies to provide 50 per cent of the separable and allocated costs of reservoir storage for quality control.

With the assistance of consulting engineers and personnel of the Advanced Waste Treatment Research Program at the Robert A. Taft Sanitary Engineering Center, Cincinnati, costs were developed for several alternate ways of equivalently offsetting the waste load. These included: processes for further treatment of the waste load such as microstraining, step aeration, chemical polymers, powdered carbon, and granular carbon;[10] effluent distribution along the estuary to enable better use of its natural assimilative capacity; and reoxygenation of the estuary which, like low-flow augmentation, would improve assimilative capacity.

Using a mathematical model of the waste assimilation and transport capacity of the Potomac estuary, similar to the model developed for the Delaware by Thomann and his colleagues,[11] the effects of the various methods were evaluated by computer simulation, using sets of 500 years of generated hydrologic sequences of monthly flows. The analysis showed that the processes would have to be operated, on the average, for only 2.5 months per year to meet the D.O. target.

Establishing combinations which would meet the quality standard required that if one process were reduced another had to be equivalently increased. It was possible to use computer simulation to exhaust all possible combinations of the feasible and sufficient processes, given the relatively large increments defined for the processes. The computer program gave a complete listing and cost ranking of all systems—some 300 in all. A sampling of alternative feasible and sufficient systems for meeting the dissolved oxygen objective is shown in Table 10.

It should be noted that there is considerable uncertainty about cost and performance. For some of the alternatives, estimates of both cost and performance were based on pilot operations, as no full-scale installations are in operation. For low-flow augmentation, costs can be estimated with a reasonable degree of accuracy, but not performance. First, there is as yet an incomplete understanding of the natural system of the estuary, i.e., the manner in which dissolved oxygen responds to all the factors involved—streamflow, waste loads, temperature, tidal variations, and so on. Second, the efficient operation of a system of reservoirs at a considerable distance from the estuary depends on the ability to forecast streamflows, and as yet it is almost impossible to forecast more than a few days in advance. Consequently there is likely to be less than perfect performance from any reservoir system. In contrast again, the alternative involving reoxygenation is one which can respond very

[10] The costs of these processes represent advanced or tertiary waste treatment assuming a prior 90 per cent waste load reduction by conventional secondary treatment.

[11] See discussion of the Delaware model in Chapter 2 and below in this chapter. The Delaware model was adapted for the Potomac by the Federal Water Pollution Control Administration.

Table 10.   Costs of Some Alternative Systems for Meeting the Dissolved
Oxygen Objective of 4 ppm in the Potomac Estuary

(*million*)

System	Cost[1]
1. Single Process Solutions	
Reoxygenation	$ 29
Effluent distribution	$ 85
Low-flow augmentation	$115
2. Multiple Process Solutions	
Various combinations of low-flow augmentation, reoxygenation, polymer precipitation, step aeration	$22 to $35
Combinations using effluent distribution or microstraining or step aeration with low-flow augmentation and/or reoxygenation	$35 to $47
Combinations using lime-alum coagulation and higher degrees of low-flow augmentation or effluent distribution	$48 to $78
3. Systems using powdered carbon adsorption	$79 or more
4. Systems using granular carbon adsorption	$127 or more
5. The complete range of system costs	$22 to $146

[1] Costs are present value (1965 dollars) of capital, operating, and routine maintenance discounted at 4 per cent for a fifty-year life. Costs of processes other than low-flow augmentation are based on 2.5 months operation per year.

rapidly to charges in streamflow and waste loads. Whether the uncertainties on both sides of the cost-effectiveness relationship for low-flow augmentation are greater than, less than, or about the same as the uncertainties relating to the other alternatives cannot be conclusively determined.

The Davis analysis is a step toward the planning and operation of a regional water quality management system that takes systematic account of variations in environmental factors affecting natural waste assimilative capacity. This approach seems to hold considerable promise, particularly when quality objectives cannot be met by conventional treatment alone. Clearly, many combinations of processes, all of them involving collective measures in our sense of the term, could achieve the objective for the Potomac estuary at less cost than the system of conventional treatment and flow augmentation proposed by the Corps. Because the alternative systems have higher operating costs and lower capital costs than low-flow augmentation, they can be relatively efficient if operated only as needed, but they would not be competitive if operated continuously.

Two additional points merit emphasis. First, all alternatives except flow augmentation require the construction and closely articulated operation of facilities—such as stream aeration equipment and regional effluent distribution systems—which traditionally have not been in the purview of either the federal or local governments involved. The Interstate Compact Commission for the Potomac Basin (INCOPOT), which might be a candidate for implementing the system, is only an information and advisory body.[12] Second, low-flow augmentation is actually much more costly than reoxygenation or some of the other alternatives, but from the viewpoint of the people in the Potomac basin it costs much less. Low-flow augmentation for water quality improvement is a fully non-reimbursable purpose of federal water resources development, while no subsidy at all is available for measures like reoxygenation and waste diversion. Both of these factors were undoubtedly implicit considerations in the plan recommended. Implementation of other components of systems which efficiently meet water quality objectives would require rather far-reaching institutional changes. We return to this point in Parts IV and V.

We now turn to another matter discussed in the previous chapter which the Davis study illuminates in a quantitative way. This is the procedure for analyzing the cost sensitivity of objectives stated in physical terms when no explicit benefit measure is available. The results of cost sensitivity analysis of alternative D.O. objectives are extremely interesting. Table 11 shows the costs of achieving alternative D.O. objectives from 2 ppm to 5 ppm, first, by means of a low-flow augmentation system in accordance with the Corps concept, and, second, with a least-cost system.

Table 11.   Costs of Alternative Systems for Achieving Alternative
Water Quality Goals*

(million)

D.O. Target	Cost of flow augmentation	Cost of least-cost alternative
2 ppm	$ 8	$ 8
3 ppm	27	18
4 ppm	115	21
5 ppm	—	27

* Present value of capital and O & M costs with 4 per cent discount rate and fifty-year time horizon.

Some really striking results emerge from these calculations. If the low-flow augmentation system is used, costs increase by almost $90 million when the objective is raised from 3 to 4 ppm. In contrast, the least-cost system permits an increase from 3 to 5 ppm for only about $10 million and imposes a total cost at 5 ppm which is only about one-fourth of the cost of the flow augmentation system at the 4 ppm quality level. The important point here is that when we concern ourselves with efficient systems the matter at issue is not only what combination of facilities will best accomplish a *given* objective, but what the *appropri-*

[12] Expansion of INCOPOT's functions is currently under consideration.

ate objective is, as well. The latter is a function of the costs of achieving different levels of quality, and, in turn, the cost for any specific quality level is a function of the type of management system.

The relationship between means of achieving the objective and the objective can be conveniently shown on the assumption that we can measure a suitable benefit function. Figure 37 illustrates a hypothetical situation analogous to that found in the Potomac estuary. The efficient system provides higher quality at equivalent or lower costs.

The same point holds even when we do not have a measured benefit function but a budget limitation exists, as it does in regard to all economic activities. Since costs vary with the type of system, the type of system we find institutionally possible to implement will affect the quality of the water we have.

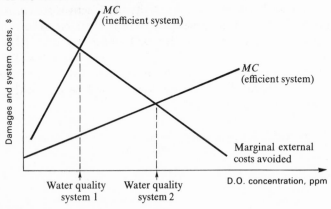

Figure 37.

THE DELAWARE ESTUARY STUDY

The Delaware River Basin, though small by American standards and draining an area of only 12,765 square miles, has a population of over six million. Portions of the basin, especially the Lehigh sub-basin and the Delaware estuary area, are among the most highly industrialized and densely populated regions in the world, and it is in these areas that the main water quality problems are encountered. The Delaware estuary, an 86-mile reach of the Delaware River from Trenton, New Jersey, to Liston Point, Delaware, is most important in terms of the quantity of water affected, the area involved, the extent of industrial activity, and the number of people affected.

Despite early industrial and municipal development in the basin, very little was done to deal with water quality problems until the last few decades. The Interstate Commission on the Delaware River Basin (INCODEL), was formed in 1936, and under its auspices the states in the basin signed a reciprocal agreement on water quality control. This provided the legal basis for construction of treatment plants by municipalities after World War II. The standards of treatment achieved were not particularly high (on the average not much more than- primary treatment), and the residual waste load from the plants, together with industrial discharges, continued to place very heavy oxygen demands on the estuary. Especially during the warm summer months, D.O. falls to low levels or becomes exhausted in a few portions of the reach of the estuary from Philadelphia to the Pennsylvania-Delaware state line.

Features of the Study

In 1957–58, at the request of the Corps of Engineers, the U.S. Public Health Service made a preliminary study of water quality in the Delaware estuary. The data it produced regarding the quality of the estuary led state and interstate agencies concerned with water quality to request a comprehensive study of the estuary under the provisions of the Federal Water Pollution Control Act. The study was begun in 1961 by the Water Supply and Pollution Control Division of the Public Health Service, and in the summer of 1966 a report was issued by the Federal Water Pollution Control Administration—*Delaware Estuary Comprehensive Study: Preliminary Report and Findings*.

The study provides an excellent opportunity to illustrate points developed earlier.

1. It provides some insights into the possibilities for large-scale collective measures in a regional system for water quality management. However, the limited consideration given to alternatives to conventional treatment at individual points of waste discharge is a weak part in an otherwise very strong report. Several possibilities were noted, but they were not analyzed in the detail that study of treatment possibilities was.

2. It is a good illustration of how cost-sensitivity analysis can be applied to alternative physical goals.

3. Most important from our point of view, the study provided the basic data for an analysis of effluent charges as a means to induce an efficient pattern of waste reduction.[13]

Among the notable contributions of the estuary study was the development and application of a rigorous mathematical representation of the causal relationships defining the waste assimilative and transport characteristics of the estuary. The model, as described in Chapter 2, permits estimating the effects of increases or decreases in the waste load discharged in a particular section on all other sections throughout the

[13] The effluent charges study of the Delaware estuary is described in Chapter 8.

estuary area. A model of this character is an essential element in a systematic analysis for regional water quality management, whether or not an estuary is involved. This model, which characterizes physical, biological, and chemical relationships in the estuary, was wedded to an economic optimization (linear programming) model. This permitted the identification of cost-minimizing solutions which could then be compared with other solutions more consistent with conventional administrative modes of water quality control.

The strategy of the study was to use the model to analyze the total and incremental costs of achieving five "objective sets," each representing a different package and spatial distribution of water quality characteristics, with the level of quality increasing from set 5 (representing 1964 water quality) to set 1. The water quality characteristics and associated levels and the areas to which they apply, are shown for objective set 2 in Table 12. The 30 sections referred to in the table are shown on the map in Figure 38. An effort was then made to measure benefits associated with the improvement in water quality indicated by the successive objective sets. At the same time, limited analysis was made of collective measures which might substitute efficiently for waste treatment over certain ranges. These included the dredging of bottom deposits that exert an oxygen demand, reoxygenation of the estuary, and diversion of wastes from the estuary. In general, the figures on costs and benefits cannot be credited with great accuracy. However, as we shall explain later, we believe the analysis suffices to launch a program leading toward an efficient and effective management of water quality in the Delaware estuary.

Water Quality Objectives Analyzed

Analysis of the benefits associated with the objective sets is constrained by two facts. First, each set of objectives calls for primary treatment at all discharge points. Second, all but objective set 5 (which would maintain 1964 quality conditions) project an improvement in dissolved oxygen levels that would make septic conditions in the estuary highly unlikely. Thus, there will be little or no improvement in general aesthetic conditions after set 4. It is true, however, that some finite but small probability of septic conditions exists with the lower sets. It should also be noted that each set, except 5, would involve negligible quantities of toxic materials in the estuary. We make these points to indicate that aesthetic and health considerations are not important in making choices among the objective sets—especially the upper three. This narrows the basis of choice to benefits associated with municipal and industrial water use, recreation, and commercial fishing. While still presenting significant and difficult problems, these are comparatively easier to

Table 12.   Water Quality Goals for Objective Set 2

WATER QUALITY PARAMETER: [a,b]	Trenton 1	2	Bristol 3	4	Torresdale 5	6	7	8	9	10	11	12	13	14	15	16	Chester 17	18	19	Wilmington 20	21	22	23	New Castle 24	25	26	27	28	29	Liston Point 30
Dissolved oxygen [c]	5.5													5.5	4.0				4.0	5.0								5.0	6.5	
D.O. [i] 4/1 – 6/15 and 9/16 – 12/31	6.5																													6.5
Chlorides [d]															50		250													
Coliforms (#/100 ml.)	5,000 [e]													5,000 [e]	5,000 [f]														5,000 [f]	
Coliforms 5/30 – 9/15	4,000 [e]				4,000 [e]		5,000 [e]							5,000 [f]										5,000 [f]					4,000 [e]	
Turbidity (Tu)	N.L.+30																													N.L.+30
Turbidity 5/30 – 9/15	N.L.				N.L.		N.L.+30																	N.L.+30	N.L.					N.L.
pH [g] (pH units)	6.5-8.5																													6.5-8.5
pH [g] 5/30 – 9/15	7.0-8.5				6.5-8.5																			6.5-8.5					7.0-8.5	
Alkilinity [g]	20-50						20-50	20-120																						20-120
Hardness [h]	95						95	150									150													
Temperature [g] (°F)	Present levels																												Present levels	
Phenols [h]	.001						.001	.005								.005	.01													.01
Syndets [h]	.5						.5	1.0																						1.0
Oil and grease, floating debris	Negligible																													Negligible
Toxic substances	Negligible																													Negligible

SECTION: 1 2 3 4 5 6 7 8 9 10 11 12 13 14 15 16 17 18 19 20 21 22 23 24 25 26 27 28 29 30

a. mg/l unless specified.   b. Not less stringent than present levels.   c. Summer average.
d. Maximum 15-day mean.   e. Maximum level.   f. Monthly geometric mean.   g. Desirable range.   h. Monthly mean.   i. Average during period stated.   N.L. = Natural levels.

measure, and efforts were made to provide reasonable estimates for them.

Table 13 shows several water quality parameters with the associated levels for the five objective sets. A few further comments about the objective sets may be useful.

Objective Set 1. This is the highest objective set. It makes provision for large increases in water-contact recreation in the estuary. It also makes special provision for 6.5 ppm levels of dissolved oxygen to provide safe passage for anadromous fish passage during the spring and fall migration periods. Thus this objective set should produce condi-

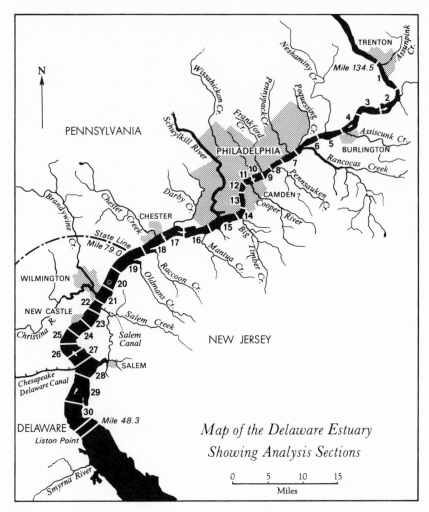

N

PENNSYLVANIA

Wissahickon Cr.

Schuylkill River

Neshaminy Cr.

TRENTON

Assunpink Cr.

Mile 134.5

1

3

2

4

Pennypack Cr.

Poquessing Cr.

Frankford Cr.

PHILADELPHIA

Assiscunk Cr.

5

6

BURLINGTON

7

Rancocas Creek

10

8

11

9

12

CAMDEN

Pennsauken Cr.

13

Cooper River

Darby Cr.

CHESTER

Chester Creek

Brandywine Cr.

14

15

State Line
Mile 79.0

17

16

18

Big Timber Cr.

Mantua Cr.

19

Raccoon Cr.

WILMINGTON

20

22

21

NEW CASTLE

23

Oldmans Cr.

Salem Creek

Christina R.

25

24

26

27

*Salem
Canal*

NEW JERSEY

SALEM

28

*Chesapeake
Delaware Canal*

29

30

Mile 48.3

DELAWARE

Liston Point

Smyrna River

*Map of the Delaware Estuary
Showing Analysis Sections*

0   5   10   15

Miles

Figure 38.   Source: FWPCA, *Delaware Estuary Comprehensive Study.*

tions in which water quality is basically no obstacle to the migration of
shad and other anadromous (migratory) fishes.

Objective Set 2. Under this objective set the area available for water-
contact recreation is constricted somewhat. Some reduction in sport and
commercial fishing would also be expected because of the somewhat
lower dissolved oxygen objective. This set, like objective set 1, makes
special provision for high dissolved oxygen during periods of anadromous
fish passage.

Objective Set 3. This set is similar to set 2. Although there is no
specific provision for raising dissolved oxygen during periods of

Table 13. Comparison of Water Quality Goals for Objective Sets 1–5
(Set 5 represents conditions in 1964)

SECTION header regions: Trenton (1), Bristol (4), Torresdale (6), Philadelphia–Camden (7–14), Chester (17), Wilmington (19), New Castle (21), Liston Point (30).

WATER QUALITY PARAMETER	SET	1	2	3	4	5	6	7	8	9	10	11	12	13	14	15	16	17	18	19	20	21	22	23	24	25	26	27	28	29	30
Dissolved oxygen, mg/l, summer average	1	6.5						6.5			5.5				4.5			4.5	5.5		5.5	6.5							6.5	7.5	7.5
	2	5.5									5.5		4.0						4.0	5.0					5.0				6.5		
	3	5.5									5.5		3.0							3.0	4.5				4.5				6.5		6.5
	4	4.0									4.0		2.5								2.5				3.5				5.5		
	5		7.0		5.1			5.8							1.0				1.0			4.2								7.1	
Chlorides, mg/l, max. 15-day mean	1															50			250												
	2														50		250														
	3														50		250														
	4													50		250															
	5											50			100	250	400		1,340		2,400										
Coliforms, #/100 ml, 5/30 – 9/15, Monthly geometric mean	1	4,000[a]						4,000[a]			5,000[a]							5,000[a]			5,000[b]	4,000[a]									4,000[a]
	2	4,000[a]			4,000[a]			5,000[a]			5,000[b]														5,000[b]				4,000[a]		
	3		4,000[a]					5,000[b]																	5,000[b]				4,000[a]		
	4	5,000[b]						5,000[b]																	5,000[b]				4,000[a]		
	5		2,600			2,700		6,800			25,000					63,000		66,000	51,000		22,000	7,000							1,900		700
Turbidity, turbidity units, 5/30 – 9/15	1	N.L.						N.L.			N.L.+30										N.L.+30	N.L.									N.L.
	2	N.L.				N.L.		N.L.+30																	N.L.+30				N.L.		
	3		N.L.					N.L.+30																	N.L.+30				N.L.		
	4	N.L.+30																							N.L.+30				N.L.		
	5 (Maximum level)		23			28		29			24					22		24	27		27				37				43		43
pH, pH units, desirable range, 5/30 – 9/15	1		7.0-8.5								6.5-8.5										6.5-8.5				7.0-8.5						
	2	7.0-8.5				6.5-8.5																			6.5-8.5				7.0-8.5		
	3	7.0-8.5				6.5-8.5																							7.0-8.5		
	4	6.5-8.5						6.5-8.5			Present levels										Present levels				6.5-8.5				7.0-8.5		
	5 (Present range)		7.0-8.7					6.9-7.6							6.6-7.3				6.4-7.0						5.6-7.6						6.1-7.8
Alkalinity, mg/l, desirable range	1	20-50									20-50		20-120																		20-120
	2	20-50									20-50		20-120																20-120		
	3	20-50									20-50		20-120																		20-120
	4	20-50									20-50		Present levels																Present levels		
	5 (Present range)		25-51					33-46							34-50				13-41						4-25						10-49
Hardness, mg/l, monthly mean	1	95									95		150						150												
	2	95									95		150				150														
	3	95									95		150				150														
	4	95									95		150		150																
	5		83								122								467												
Phenols, mg/l, monthly mean	1	.001																	.001		.01										.01
	2	.001						.001			.005							.005	.01												.01
	3	.001						.001			.005							.005	.01												.01
	4	.005																.005	.01												
	5		.01			.02		.03			.04					.03		.05	.05		.06										

SECTION: 1 2 3 4 5 6 7 8 9 10 11 12 13 14 15 16 17 18 19 20 21 22 23 24 25 26 27 28 29 30

a. Maximum level.   b. Monthly geometric mean.   N.L. = Natural levels

anadromous fish migrations, there is comparatively little difference in the survival probability under objective sets 2 and 3. Under the waste-loading conditions envisioned for objective set 3, the estimated survival twenty-four out of twenty-five years would be at least 80 per cent—compared with 90 per cent for set 2.

Objective Set 4. This provides for a slight increase over 1964 levels in water-contact recreation and fishing in the lower sections of the portion of the estuary studied. Generally, water quality is improved slightly over 1964 conditions and the probability of anaerobic conditions occurring is greatly reduced.

Objective Set 5. This would maintain 1964 conditions in the estuary. It would provide for no more than a prevention of further water quality deterioration.

Costs of Alternative Programs

The costs of achieving objective sets 1 through 4 by various combinations of treatment and other measures for the waste-load conditions expected to prevail in 1975–80 are shown in Table 14.

It is estimated that achieving objective set 1, which calls for an average dissolved oxygen level of about 4.5 ppm in the summer and 6.5 ppm during spring and fall fish runs in critical zones, would require about

Table 14.   Summary of Total Costs of Achieving Objective Sets 1, 2, 3, and 4
(Costs include cost of maintaining present (1964) conditions and reflect
waste-load conditions projected for 1975–80.)
Flow at Trenton = 3,000 cfs

(million 1968 dollars)

Objective set	Uniform treatment			Zoned treatment			Cost minimization		
	Capital costs	O&M costs[1]	Total costs	Capital costs	O&M costs[1]	Total costs	Capital costs	O&M costs[1]	Total costs
1	180	280 (19.0)	460[2]	180	280 (19.0)	460[2]	180	280 (19.0)	460[2]
2	135	180 (12.0)	315[3]	105	145 (10.0)	250[3]	115	100 (7.0)	215[3]
3	75	80 (5.5)	155[3]	50	70 (4.5)	120[3]	50	35 (2.5)	85[3]
4	55	75 (5.0)	130	40	40 (2.5)	80	40	25 (1.5)	65

[1] Operation and maintenance costs, discounted at 3 per cent, twenty-year-time horizon; figures in parentheses are equivalent annual operation and maintenance costs in millions of dollars/year.

[2] High-rate secondary to tertiary (92–98 per cent removal) for all waste sources for all programs. Includes in-stream aeration cost of $20 million.

[3] Includes $1–$2 million for either sludge removal or aeration to meet goals in river sections #3 and #4.

92 to 98 per cent removal of all carbonaceous waste plus in-stream aeration. The estimated cost of achieving this objective set is $460 million, regardless of the type of program utilized. This cost includes capital plus operation and maintenance costs, discounted to present value at 3 per cent over a twenty-year period. All other costs given in this description were similarly arrived at. Those responsible for the study admit considerable uncertainty concerning the accuracy of the cost figure for objective set 1.

Very little basis was found for claiming benefits to municipal and industrial water users from higher levels of D.O. In fact, some industries reported that they would suffer increased costs because of corrosion if dissolved oxygen levels were raised. Some benefits to municipal water treatment and commercial fishing were found, but the great bulk of benefits claimed stemmed from improved water-based recreation opportunities.[14]

Achieving objective set 2 would require about 90 per cent removal of carbonaceous wastes and would cost between $215 and $315 million depending upon whether uniform treatment (most costly), zone treatment (intermediate), or cost minimization programs were employed.

Objective set 3, as previously indicated, is similar in most respects to objective set 2. Perhaps the major difference is that it calls for summer average dissolved oxygen of 3 ppm in the critical sections rather than 4 parts per million as in objective set 2. It is estimated that this program would cost between $85 and $155 million.

Objective set 4 calls for summer average dissolved oxygen in the critical sections of 2.5 ppm. It is significantly less effective in enhancing recreational and commercial fishing opportunities. The range of costs for this objective set is from $65 to about $130 million.

Objective set 5 would maintain 1964 conditions for the period to 1980 at a cost of about $30 million.

Benefits of Improved Water Quality

The Delaware Estuary Comprehensive Study pioneered by broadening the range of benefits considered in the water quality planning process and by introducing quantitative estimates of recreation benefits into the process. While the benefit figures were necessarily rather rough, they appear to be sufficiently accurate to comprise a general guide to the decision-making process.

Three general categories of recreation benefits were considered: (1)

---

[14] This is consistent with our general analysis of water quality benefits. However, with respect to chloride concentration, substantial benefits to industrial users would result if average concentrations were decreased. See footnote 17, this chapter.

swimming, (2) boating, (3) sport fishing. Analyses conducted at the University of Pennsylvania, and based on a highly simplified model of recreation participation, indicated a large latent recreation demand in the estuary region. Another study, separately sponsored, tended to confirm the order of magnitude of the estimates.[15] In computing the monetary values associated with recreation demand under each objective set, a number of factors were considered—including recreation-bearing capacity of the estuary as influenced by improved quality.[16] A range of benefits was calculated by the application of alternative monetary unit values to the total use projected for the estuary. The analyses indicated that the increase in direct quantifiable recreation benefits for set 1 would range between $160 million and $350 million, for set 2 between $140 million and $320 million, for set 3 between $130 million and $310 million, and for set 4 between $120 million and $280 million. Since municipal and industrial benefits were deemed to be small and to some extent cancelled by negative features in regard to industrial water use, these ranges were taken to be rough estimates of the total benefits from improved water quality in the estuary.[17]

A comparison of the recreation benefits with the cost estimates (Table 15) shows that objective set 4 appears to be justified, even when the lowest estimate of benefit is compared with the highest estimate of cost. The incremental costs of going from set 4 to set 3 suggests that the justifiability of set 3 is marginal. On the assumption that some of the more widely distributed benefits of water quality improvement may not have been appropriately taken into account, it can probably be justified. Clearly, however, the incremental benefits of going to sets 2 or 1 are vastly outweighed by the incremental costs.

It is interesting to note that a water use advisory committee, composed of representatives of the general public, industry, local government and planning agencies, and recreation, conservation, and fish and wildlife interests, recommended objective set 3. In hearings on quality objectives

[15] Paul Davidson, F. Gerard Adams, and Joseph Seneca, "The Social Value of Water Recreational Facilities Resulting from an Improvement in Water Quality: The Delaware Estuary," in Allen V. Kneese and Stephen C. Smith (ed.), *Water Research* (The Johns Hopkins Press, for RFF, 1966).

[16] However, no consideration was given to whether or not regulation of land use in areas adjacent to the estuary would enable taking advantage of the improved water quality in the estuary. (See the discussion of related land and water management in Chapter 14.)

[17] Larger benefits were found to accrue from the reduction in chloride concentration by flow augmentation into the estuary, but this is a somewhat separable issue since water quality aspects associated with oxygen-demanding waste discharge are not improved by flow regulation except at very high flows. At flows ranging up to about 10,000 cubic feet per second (at Trenton), the increased flow results primarily in a shift of the dissolved oxygen water quality problem downstream to other water-use areas.

Table 15.   Costs and Benefits of Water Quality Improvement
in the Delaware Estuary Area[1]

(million dollars)

Objective set	Estimated total cost	Estimated recreation benefits	Estimated incremental cost		Estimated incremental benefits	
			minimum[2]	maximum[3]	minimum[2]	maximum[3]
1	460	160–350				
			245	145	20	30
2	215–315	140–320				
			130	160	10	10
3	85–155	130–310				
			20	25	10	30
4	65–130	120–280				

[1] All costs and benefits are present values calculated with 3 per cent discount rate and twenty-year time horizon.
[2] Difference between adjacent minima.
[3] Difference between adjacent maxima.

held by the Delaware River Basin Commission on January 26, 1967, virtually all representatives of industry, and some representatives of municipalities in the area supported objective set 3. Conservation groups and publicly elected officials generally supported objective set 2. The study provided alternatives for public debate and much information which participants could use. The atmosphere during the hearings was one of intelligent men reasoning together. Fifty persons testified and virtually each statement contained information and viewpoints useful to the decision-making process. It is notable that nearly all discussion related to objective sets 2 and 3; the other sets were recognized by almost everyone as not being in the public interest. The quality of the hearings was unique, and fully justified the concept of illuminating alternatives embodied in the Delaware Estuary Study.[18]

Collective Measures for Water Quality Improvement

Some attention was given to the possibility of achieving improved water quality by means of collective measures such as dredging the estuary to reduce benthal oxygen demand, collecting wastes for treatment in regional treatment plants, diverting wastes from critical reaches of the estuary to Delaware Bay or to the Atlantic Ocean, and providing mechanical reoxygenation of the estuary. Some of these measures looked quite promising on the basis of preliminary reconnaissance, but they received very little emphasis in the study. For example, it appeared that even the great cost of collecting certain industrial wastes and

[18] The Commission subsequently adopted an objective set falling between 2 and 3.

piping them from the estuary to the Atlantic Ocean would reduce the over-all costs of achieving at least the higher objective sets, but this result is not stated in the report proper.

Rough estimates of the total cost of reaching various D.O. objectives by mechanical reoxygenation produced perhaps the most spectacular results. These are shown below, the costs being present values calculated with 3 per cent discount rate and twenty-year time horizon:

Objective set	Cost (*Millions*)
1	$70
2	$40
3	$12
4	$10

The D.O. conditions of objective set 2—namely, 4 ppm of dissolved oxygen in the critical reaches during the summer and 6.5 ppm during anadromous fish passage—could be reached through reoxygenation at not much greater cost than simply maintaining present conditions with even the least-cost waste treatment alternative. However, as reoxygenation would meet only the D.O. objective, and the additional costs of meeting other water quality objectives were not presented, it is impossible to tell how reoxygenation might enter into the efficient achievement of the various objective sets.

It is unfortunate that these collective measures were not adequately explored. Enough was done, however, to suggest that such measures should enter into a strategy for dealing with the water quality problems of the estuary. In the next section we discuss a possible or potential strategy based upon what has already been learned.

Outline of a Strategy for the Delaware Estuary

Despite all the uncertainties involved, we believe that the results of the economic analyses made of the Delaware estuary provide a basis for a strategy leading toward efficient water quality management in the area. The central elements in an appropriate strategy for the Delaware River Basin Commission appear to us to be the following:

1. Adopt objective set 3 as the provisional water quality objective for the Delaware estuary.

2. Extend the effluent charges analysis reported in Chapter 7 to water quality characteristics other than BOD and enact a system of charges.

3. Implement a program of further research and planning to improve understanding of water quality problems in the estuary, opportunities for effective management of the problems, and estimates of benefits from water quality improvement. Use proceeds from the effluent charges for this purpose to the extent that appears appropriate.

4. Make a more systematic search for efficient collective measures for water quality management.

5. Implement those collective measures which will lower the over-all costs associated with achieving the quality objectives.

6. Reconsider the provisional quality objectives and the system of charges in light of further research, experience, and changing conditions.

CONCLUSIONS

The cases presented in this chapter show that contemporary techniques permit useful economic analysis of even highly complex water quality management situations. They also indicate that provision of collective facilities and integrated operation of systems can achieve major economies over conventional approaches which encompass only a limited range of alternatives. The Delaware example further shows that with careful attention to communication the results of sophisticated analysis can be understood and used by representatives of affected parties in decision making. The central problem is rapidly becoming one of developing institutions for management rather than analytical techniques for planning, even though much remains to be accomplished in the latter area.

In the next chapter we present a case study which can be viewed as a bridge between the economic-engineering analysis which has been our focus so far and the institutional analysis which is the subject of the next part.

Water Management in the Ruhr:

A Case Study of the *Genossenschaften*

12

This chapter is a case study of an existing regional system of water resources management primarily directed toward the problems of water quality. The subjects are the eight large water resources associations operating in the Ruhr industrial area of West Germany: the Ruhrverband, the Emschergenossenschaft, the Ruhrtalsperrenverein, the Lippeverband, the Wupperverband, the Niersverband, the Linksniederrheinische-Enterwaesserungsgenossenschaft (Lineg), and the Erftverband (see Figure 39). These associations, generally referred to as *Genossenschaften*, are the only organizations in the world that have designed, built, and operated *regional* systems for waste disposal and water supply. Of equal interest, they have developed comparatively sophisticated methods of distributing the costs of their water quality operations by levying charges on the effluents discharged in their respective regions. The important role that such charges can play in attaining efficient systems has been described earlier. In this chapter the activities of the *Genossenschaften* are studied with reference to the economic concepts and criteria developed in this study.[1]

[1] For a discussion of the history and legal character of these associations, see Chapter 13.

The only general description on the *Genossenschaften* in English known to the authors is Gordon M. Fair, "Pollution Abatement in the Ruhr District," in Henry Jarrett (ed.), *Comparisons in Resource Management* (The Johns Hopkins Press, for Resources for the Future, 1961). There is a vast German literature on the *Genossenschaften*. General treatments include Helmut Moehle, "Wasserwirtschaftliche Problems an Industriefluessen" (Problems of Water Management on Industrial Streams), *Die Wasserwirtschaft*, Vol. 45, No. 4 (1954); *Fuenfzig Jahre Emschergenossenschaft 1906–1956* (Fifty Years of the Emschergenossenschaft) Selbstverlag der Emschergenossenschaft, Essen, 1957; Max Pruess, "Der Ruhrverband und Ruhrtalsperrenverein als Muster gemeinwirtschaftlicher Wasserwirtschaft" (The Ruhrverband and Ruhrtalsperrenverein as a Pattern for Collective Water Economics), *Staedtehygiene*, Heft 9 (1954); H. W. Koenig, "Wasserverbaende als rationelle Loesung fuer den Gewaesserschutz" (The Water Association

There are thousands of water associations in Germany, most of them established for special purposes such as drainage or flood protection of specific plots. The eight large *Genossenschaften* in the Ruhr, however, were established by special laws (Sondergesetzen) between 1904 and 1958 and given almost complete multipurpose authority over water quantity and quality.[2] These organizations are henceforth referred to simply as the *Genossenschaften*. For up to sixty years they have made and executed comprehensive plans for waste disposal, water supply, and flood damage reduction, as well as for land drainage which is a problem of great significance in the coal-mining areas. This has involved the planning, design, construction and operation of a large array of water quality management facilities, including large-scale measures of various types and most of the conventional wastewater treatment plants in the region. The *Genossenschaften* are comparable to co-operatives in the Anglo-American sense, but voting power is distributed in accordance with the size of the contribution to an association's expenses, and membership is compulsory. Members of the associations are principally the municipal and rural governmental districts, coal mines, and industrial enterprises.

General public supervision is in the hands of the Ministry of Food, Agriculture, and Forestry of the State of North Rhine-Westphalia in which the *Genossenschaften* are located. The Ministry's supervision is, however, largely limited to seeing that the associations comply with the provisions of the laws which created them.

The statutes creating the *Genossenschaften* set forth goals and responsibilities in highly general terms. This has left the staffs and the members comparatively free to adapt to changing conditions and to develop procedures and elaborate concepts in line with experience. One general provision of the statutes that has played a large role in successful and efficient operation is the requirement that the costs of constructing and operating the system are to be borne by the members responsible for them as well as by those who benefit. Over the years, comparatively sophisticated procedures have been developed for assessing costs, especially of land drainage and waste disposal.

The Ruhr area is one of the most concentrated industrial areas in

---

as a Rational Solution for Protection of Water Supplies), *Plan—Schweizerische Zeitschrift fuer Landes, Regional-und Ortsplanung* (Zuerich, September/October, 1960), p. 157; *Wasserwirtschaft in Nordrhein-Westfalen* (Water Economics in North Rhine-Westphalia) (Frankfurt/Main: Verwaltungsverlag G.m.b.H., 1960); and H. W. Koenig, "Die Wasserwirtschaft im Ruhrgebiet" (Water Management in the Ruhr Area), *Die Wasserwirtschaft* (August 1965), pp. 351–55.

[2] All but one of the *Genossenschaften* were established before 1930. The Erftverband (*Verband* and *Genossenschaft* are used interchangeably) was created in 1958 primarily to deal with problems resulting from a massive decline of groundwater tables in the Erft basin from pumping by the coal industry.

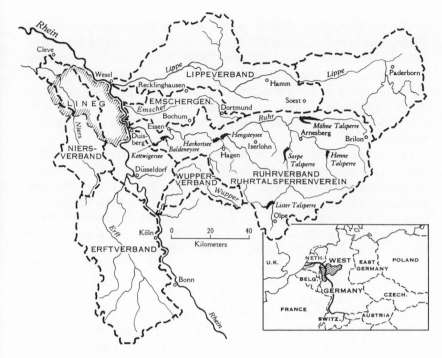

Figure 39. River basins of the Ruhr district.

the entire world. It contains some 40 per cent of total West German industrial capacity and between 70 and 90 per cent of West German production of coal, coke, iron and steel. There are some 10 million people in the Ruhr region's 4,300 square miles—roughly one-third the size of the Delaware River watershed in the United States.

Water resources are extremely limited if one excludes the Rhine River, into which the streams of the Ruhr area flow. Although the Rhine has a mean flow roughly comparable to that of the Ohio River, it is drawn upon to supply water to the Ruhr area only during periods of extreme low flow. Not only is the Rhine itself of very poor quality at the point where the Ruhr enters it, but the water from the Rhine must be *lifted* into the industrial area. Pumping stations have been installed in the dams that were built to create a series of shallow reservoirs in the Ruhr, and water from the Rhine has been pumped back up the Ruhr as far as Essen in periods of extreme drought. Development of a large new reservoir (the Biggetalsperre) for the augmentation of low flows by the Ruhrtalsperrenverein should end the area's already modest dependence on water from the Rhine for a rather lengthy period at least.

The Ruhr area is much more dependent upon the Rhine for its waste carriage capacity than for water supply. A large proportion of the wastes discharged from the industrial region into the Rhine via the Emscher River now receive comparatively little treatment. However, a large biological treatment plant, which will extensively treat the entire flow of the Emscher before it enters the Rhine, is now under construction. When this plant is completed, virtually all effluents reaching the Rhine will have been given far-reaching treatment, and the contribution of this area to the organic pollution of the Rhine will be comparatively modest.

Five small rivers constitute the water supply and the water-borne waste carriage and assimilative capacity of the industrial area proper. In descending order of size, these are the Ruhr, Lippe, Wupper, Emscher, and the Niers. Their combined *annual* average low flow is only about one-fourth of the *low flow of record* of the Delaware River near Trenton, New Jersey, or about one-half of the low flow of record on the Potomac River near Washington, D.C.

The amazing waste load which these rivers carry is indicated by the fact that the annual average natural low flow in the Ruhr, which is heavily used for household and industrial water supply and recreation, is less than the volume of effluent discharged into the river.

The *Genossenschaften* have made this small supply of water serve the needs of the mines, factories, and households of the great industrial complex, while permitting the use of streams for recreation and waste disposal. And they have achieved this at relatively modest cost. Despite rather impressive attention to appearance and recreation, the combined expenditure of the *Genossenschaften* on building and operating all waste-water treatment plants, dams, pump stations, etc., amounts to about $60 million a year, somewhat over half of which is for land drainage. The largest waterworks in the area is a profit-making enterprise which delivers water for household use at 30 cents per thousand gallons and for industrial use at 20 cents per thousand gallons. These are among the lowest water prices in any of the German metropolitan areas, despite the fact that the waterworks pays a share of regional water supply and quality improvement costs.[3]

[3] See George Mueller and Franz-Josef Hessing, *Kostentraeger der Wasserversorgung und Abwasserbeseitigung* (Cost Incidence—Water Supply and Wastewater Disposal) (Bad Godesberg: Institut fuer Raumforschung, 1962), p. 137. Water companies pay via a charge levied on the Ruhrtalsperrenverein (supported by the water users) by the Ruhrverband (which supplies the water quality improvement facilities). The charge equals 45 per cent of the costs of facilities strictly necessary to maintain the quality of the Ruhr, from which about 70 per cent of the water used in the entire industrial area is withdrawn. The base excludes works (conveyance facilities, for example) which are constructed primarily in the interest of particular waste dischargers and for which they pay individually. See, for example, *Veranlagung zum Ruhrverband* (Charging System of the Ruhrverband), January 1, 1965.

The success of the *Genossenschaften* stems from institutional arrangements which permitted them to plan and operate a relatively efficient
regional system. Because of the regional purview of the associations,
their authority to implement a wide range of alternatives, and the dense
development of their areas, far-reaching use is made of collective water
quality improvement measures and stream specialization. Moreover, as
will be seen later, so-called indirect measures such as materials recovery,
by-product production, and process engineering play a large role in
controlling the generation of industrial wastes.

In the rest of this chapter, references to the *Genossenschaften* may be
taken to mean either the Ruhrverband-Ruhrtalsperrenverein or the
Emschergenossenschaft-Lippeverband unless a specific organization is
indicated. Nominally four organizations, they are linked in two pairs,
each under a single management. These are by far the largest *Genossenschaften*, and they have both the most complex engineering systems and
the most sophisticated methods of assessing costs.

Although little or no explicit attention was given to formal optimizing
procedures, the systems were designed with the explicit objective of minimizing costs of attaining certain water quality levels in the rivers, and
there was explicit recognition of the role played by the equi-marginal
principle in achieving minimum costs.

In the Ruhr River Basin itself the general objective of the system is
to maintain water quality suitable for water supply—about 70 per cent
of the water intake in the industrial area comes from this stream—and
recreation. In the Lippe Basin the objective is much the same. The
Lippe River, however, is made largely unsuitable for drinking purposes
by salinity arising both from natural sources and from the saline water
pumped from coal mines. Some of the tributaries of the Lippe, notably
the Stever and Muehlenbach, are used extensively for potable supply.

Water quality in the Ruhr is controlled by a variety of measures including waste treatment in over one hundred plants, regulation of river
flow by upland reservoirs, and a series of shallow oxidation lakes in the
Ruhr itself, one of which is mechanically reaerated during critical flow
and temperature periods.[4] Neutralization, precipitation and oxidation
occur in the Hengsteysee, and further stabilization takes place in the
Harkortsee, a similar in-stream oxidation lake. By the time the water
reaches the Baldeneysee (a third such lake) at Essen, the quality has
improved to such an extent that the water is suitable for general recre-

---

[4] A good description of these various activities is found in G. Rincke,
"BSB-Abbau und Sauerstoffverbrauch in der Ruhr" (BOD Assimilation and D.O.
Demand in the Ruhr), Ruhrverband, mimeo., 1966.

ation use.[5] The heavy discharges between the Hengsteysee and the Baldeneysee have generally had far-reaching treatment, frequently by means of treatment plants with double biological stages.

The Emscher, by far the smallest of the three major streams, is used exclusively for waste dilution, degradation, and carriage. Actually, as an aid to protecting the quality of the Ruhr, a small portion of the wastes generated in the Ruhr basin are pumped over into the watershed of the Emscher.

The Emscher has been fully lined with concrete and converted into a single-purpose stream—sometimes referred to as the *cloaca maxima* of the Ruhr area. The only quality objective is the avoidance of aesthetic nuisance. This has been achieved by mechanical (primary) treatment of effluents entering the stream and by the rather slow rate of biological degradation in the stream itself, and also by attractive plantings, gentle curves in the canalized stream, and well-designed bridges. Since the Emscher can be used only for effluent discharge, the area is dependent upon adjoining watersheds for water supply and water-based recreation opportunities. This presents little hardship because the distances are small and the streams are parallel.

Near its mouth the entire flow of the Emscher up to about 1,000 cfs is given primary treatment to remove most of the suspended matter, thus making possible the realization of scale economies to a far-reaching extent. The heavy waste load discharged to the Rhine both from upstream sources and from the Ruhr industrial area (largely via the Emscher) has caused great costs downstream, especially in Holland. Consequently, the Emschergenossenschaft now has under construction a plant for biological treatment of the Emscher, which experiments indicate will be highly successful. A test plant is achieving 98 per cent degradation of phenols, which are one of the most expensive and difficult substances to deal with in treating raw water supplies. When the entire Emscher flow is subjected to biological treatment, the contribution of the Ruhr industrial area to the Rhine River pollution will be substantially mitigated,[6] and, with the increased upland reservoir capacity, the area will be essentially a closed water supply and wastewater system.

---

[5] Ruhrverband records show that the oxidation lakes assimilate a significant share of the residual wastes discharged to the river. See Rincke, *op. cit.* Bacteriological standards for swimming are lower in Germany than in the United States. There is a feeling among some water quality experts that the higher U.S. standards do not have a rational basis.

[6] Except for saline pollution from the coal mines in the area. The Lippe carries considerable natural salinity and additional saline water is pumped up from the mines. Another major source of salinity in the Rhine is the potash industry, particularly in France. Effective arrangements for reducing salinity have not yet been made.

Without using thoroughgoing formal optimization procedures, the *Genossenschaften* have probably achieved the major benefits to be gained from such procedures by viewing the problem of waste disposal and water supply as one of integrated system planning and design. They have staged the construction of quality management facilities according to *Lastplaene* (plans based on the burden in the river), which call for such facilities to be built at sites and in a sequence so that their over-all effect in the regional system will be greatest. They have co-operated with the Siedlungsverband, the association responsible for land use planning in the Ruhr industrial area, to assure that considerations of water and waste disposal costs enter the land use planning process. They have made extensive use of collective treatment facilities by linking several towns and cities to a single plant in cases where scale economies more than offset the cost of transporting effluents to the plants. In the case of the Emscher they have linked an entire watershed to a single treatment plant. They have combined industrial and household wastes when joint treatment is more efficient. They have made use of stream specialization for recreation and water supply purposes and of artificial groundwater recharge for quality improvement purposes. They have at various times and places used flow augmentation and direct aeration of streams. Where scale economies or the special technical competence of their staff merited it, they have established their own materials recovery plants. In other instances, they have induced materials recovery or process changes by levying effluent charges based on the quantity and quality of the waste-water and by acting as a co-operative marketing agency for recovered waste products. They have built central stations for the detoxification of industrial sludges, and are contemplating other unusual water quality management devices.[7]

Decisions among alternative ways of achieving objectives have, at least in a rough and ready fashion, been based upon consideration of the cost "trade-offs" between them.[8] Finally, and of considerable importance, the associations have provided for monitoring stream quality, especially in streams used for water supply, and for operating facilities to take account of changing day-to-day and seasonal conditions in a more or less continuous fashion.[9]

[7] See Koenig, "Die Wasserwirtschaft im Ruhrgebiet," *op. cit.*

[8] An excellent illustration is the analysis of aeration systems which is still going forward. See Rincke, "BSB-Abbau und Sauerstoffverbrauch...," *op. cit.*

[9] Sanitary engineers in the United States claim that individual municipalities and industrial plants often operate their treatment plants inefficiently, and rarely take account of changing conditions in the stream. Institutional constraints often preclude modification of operation in relation to stream conditions. Permits granted by water quality control agencies often require continuous operation of all plant facilities to achieve a specified percentage reduction of waste load regardless of stream conditions.

Other economies result from integrated operations of facilities. Great emphasis is placed on the economies that can be achieved when a single staff is in charge of planning, building, operating, and supervising the water resources facilities of an entire basin. In 1966 the Ruhrverband-Ruhrtalsperrenverein system included 106 effluent treatment plants (on the average, 4 new plants are added each year); 4 large detention lakes; 30 pumping stations; over 300 km. of trunk sewer; several run-of-the-river power plants; and 7 upstream flow-regulating dams with their own power plants and electrical distribution systems. The total staff, including laborers, apprentices, and janitorial help, numbered only 850 persons.[10]

Whether the use of the Emscher as a waste conveyance channel or the heavy use of waste degradation capacity on certain stretches of the Ruhr is optimal cannot be conclusively determined, partly because economic evaluations of recreation use have not been made. Actually, however, outdoor recreation is quite impressively catered to in the Ruhr area, partly because of the considerable power which the communities and counties exercise in both the water associations and the Siedlungsverband. Co-ordination between the work of the Siedlungsverband and the *Genossenschaften* has contributed to the explicit weighing of recreational and aesthetic values against costs in the development and use of water resources.

THE EFFLUENT CHARGES

The *Genossenschaften* have worked out procedures for levying fees in accordance with their mandate to charge those who benefit and those who make it necessary for the associations to take action. The fee systems relating to water quality management, water supply, flood damage reduction, recreation, and hydroelectric power all reward study, but our interest here is primarily in the effluent charge systems.[11] Even these systems are so varied that we do not attempt detailed coverage. To illustrate central concepts we describe the system used by the Emschergenossenschaft-Lippeverband and then indicate the ways in

---

[10] See Ruhrverband-Ruhrtalsperrenverein, *Jahresbericht* (Annual Report), 1966.

[11] In several instances, the charges are framed in such a way as to be generally conducive to over-all economic efficiency. For example, the very high costs associated with counteracting subsidence are levied on the coal industry in such a way that companies have an incentive to consider these "external" costs when making decisions about which areas to mine. See Allen V. Kneese, "Water Quality Management by Regional Authorities in the Ruhr Area, with Special Emphasis on the Role of Cost Assessment," *Papers and Proceedings of the Regional Science Association*, Vol. 11 (1963).

which the Ruhrverband method differs.[12] In both cases, only the general principles will be outlined.

In practice, the charging schemes are applied somewhat flexibly to take account of particular circumstances. For example, whenever a new plant in the jurisdictional area of the *Genossenschaften* chooses a location that entails extra costs, such costs may be laid upon the waste discharger. These costs might include the cost of building a special treatment plant to handle the new plant's waste or the cost of transporting the waste to existing facilities. A city or municipality may also request special facilities which would not otherwise be included in the management system. In these instances, the costs do not enter into the general effluent charge system but are assessed directly on the industry or municipality.[13] The following description relates to the way in which charges are devised to spread the cost of the general systems operations among all the members.[14]

Emschergenossenschaft-Lippeverband
Effluent Charge Assessment Method

Both the Emschergenossenschaft and the Ruhrverband endeavor to distribute the costs of the water quality management system in some reasonable proportion to the quantity and quality of the individual effluents which cause the costs to be incurred. No effort is made here to describe in full detail the laboratory tests upon which the Emschergenossenschaft-Lippeverband method is based. Some under-

[12] There is a considerable literature on the effluent charge system. Details can be obtained from the annually published instructions to the *Genossen* concerning preparation of reports on which the charge will be based. (For example, *Veranlagung zum Ruhrverband*, January 1, 1965.) Selected general discussions are E. Knop, "Die Schaedlichkeits-bewertung von Abwaessern" (Evaluating the Damaging Effects of Effluents), *Technisch-Wissenschaftliche Mitteilungen*, Heft 4, Juli 1961 (Essen: Vulkan Verlag); W. Bucksteeg, *Verfahren zur Bestimmung des Einwohnergleichwerts beliebiger Abwaesser* (Procedure for Determination of the Population Equivalence of Varied Effluents), Ruhrverband, Essen, mimeo.; W. Bucksteeg, "Problematik der Bewertung giftiger Inhaltsstoffe im Abwasser und Moeglichkeiten zur Schaffung gesicherter Bewertungsgrundlagen" (Problems in the Evaluation of Toxic Substances in Effluents and the Possibility of Obtaining Secure Evaluation Standards), *Muenchner Beitraege zur Abwaesser-, Fischerei-, und Flussbiologie* (Muenchen: Verlag von R. Oldenbourg, 1959), Band 6. Much of the following description is also based upon conversation with the staffs of the *Genossenschaften* and upon correspondence with Dr. Knop, Executive Director of the Emschergenossenschaft-Lippeverband, and with Dr. Koenig, Executive Director of the Ruhrverband-Ruhrtalsperrenverein.

[13] Specifically, Essen met part of the cost of the Baldeneysee because at its urging the lake was moved closer to Essen and enlarged so that it could serve as a civic recreation facility, which it has done most successfully. Similar negotiations are now going on between the Ruhrverband and the city of Dortmund.

[14] Capital investments are financed by loans. Annual costs consist of interest, operation, maintenance, and normal replacement.

standing of the chemical-biological underpinnings is essential, however, if the economic merits and shortcomings of the method are to be understood. The basic principles of the method are readily explained by the use of the following formula:

$$D = -1 + \frac{S}{S_p} + \frac{1}{2}\frac{B}{B_p} + \frac{1}{2}\frac{P-30}{P_p} + F$$

D = dilution factor,
S = materials subject to sedimentation in cm_3/l,
S_p = permitted S in cm^3/l,
B = BOD_5 in mg/l after sedimentation,
B_p = permitted BOD_5 in mg/l,
P = potassium permanganate oxygen used in mg/l after sedimentation,
P_p = permitted potassium permanganate use in mg/l,
F = toxicity to fish as determined by dilution method.

The characteristic that permits different wastes to be handled as commensurables in the formula is their damaging effect on fish. Indeed, the formula indicates the amount of clean water required to dilute the effluent in order to avoid harm to fish.[15] On this basis, the degree of pollution (fish damage) caused by greatly differing types of wastes can be expressed as single, commensurable numbers. The effluent is tested before it is treated in the system treatment plant but after any pretreatment by the manufacturers. Communities do not provide any type of pretreatment.

In each term of the equation the numerator indicates the actual amount of a polluting substance found in the effluent sample, and the denominator indicates a permitted amount of the substance. The ratio, of course, represents a dilution factor. It is important to note that the individually derived dilution factors are held to be additive in character. To this end, the water is aerated during the toxicity dilution test to prevent oxygen shortage from developing and influencing the result. The product of the aggregate dilution factor and the quantity of effluent as compared with all other similarly obtained products indicates the share of over-all costs which an individual effluent discharger is to pay. This indicated procedure is not regarded as ideal, but it produces usable results while requiring only a comparatively modest number of relatively simple chemical and biological tests. The described procedure, though something of an idealization of the procedures actually used, illustrates the principle favored by the Emschergenossenschaft-Lippeverband. A

[15] See below and the discussions of fish damage in Chapter 2. The Emscher does not support fish so the formula is used merely as an index.

somewhat more detailed discussion of the reasons for the individual terms in the formula will aid in understanding its over-all rationale.[16]

The second term relates to suspended materials that will settle out of the effluent. These substances may be either degradable (oxygen-consuming) organics or nondegradable material. Unless the non-degradable material is removed from the effluent, it can cause substantial biological damage by settling out, covering the bottom of the stream, and killing organisms entering the food chain of fish. On this ground, the rule of thumb is adopted that substances subject to sedimentation, whether organic or inorganic, require the same amount of dilution. The permitted quantity in cm^3/l is one which is deemed to be just low enough not to harm fish life under the conditions of the area. For the organic materials (which provide the standard for the inorganics) permissible quantity is determined on the basis of oxygen demand (see below).

The next two terms relate to dissolved degradable organic substances left in the effluent after "primary" (or, as it is termed in Germany, "mechanical") treatment without the addition of chemical precipitating agents. Each of these terms is given one-half weight because each of the two methods for testing the biochemical oxygen demand of degradable organic wastes is biased unless the stream and the effluent contain the same amount of toxic material. The BOD_5 test establishes the amount of oxygen consumed by bacteria in a sample of effluent incubated over a period of five days under controlled temperature and light conditions. When toxic substances are present in the effluent, bacteriological action may be slowed down, and the test will yield too low a BOD value. When such an effluent is put into receiving water which contains a smaller amount of toxic material than the effluent sample, biological activity is more intense than it was in the sample, and the demand for the dissolved oxygen in the stream exceeds the demand in the laboratory.

The potassium permanganate test, on the other hand, is based upon chemical oxidation of materials in the effluent and is therefore not influenced by the presence of toxic materials. The potassium permanganate oxidizes some inorganic materials which would not be degraded by bacteria in a stream, even under ideal conditions for biological action. Thus this test is not a direct indication of the decomposability of the organic matter in the effluent, but it yields an estimate of total oxidizable material including some inorganic material and some organic material which does not oxidize in the stream.

The equation indicates that 30 is to be subtracted from P in the

---

[16] The following discussion is based upon the article by E. Knop, "Die Schaedlichkeitsbewertung von Abwaessern," *op. cit.*, and upon discussion with Dr. Knop and members of his staff, particularly, Drs. Husman, Philipsen, and Sons.

numerator of the fourth term. This is an estimate of the amount of *non-biologically* degradable material registered by the permanganate test. It will be noticed that the third and fourth terms are each given one-half weight in the equation. This results from the fact that the combined effect of the two tests (with the result of the potassium permanganate test adjusted as indicated) is held to provide an approximation of the degradability of organic wastes in a receiving water containing some toxic materials. The permissible amount of oxygen demand (the denominators of the third and fourth terms) is set at a level that is calculated to prevent dissolved oxygen from falling below the 3 to 4 mg/l which is necessary to sustain the types of fish life found in the area.[17]

The fifth term in the formula indicates the necessary dilution for toxic materials, and its value is derived directly from a fish toxicity test. During the test the effluent is constantly aerated to compensate for the action of the oxygen-consuming waste. The dilution standard is determined on the basis of absence of noticeable damage to the fish during the 48-hour test period.

The initial term (-1) compensates for the fact that the discharge of waste products includes a volume of dilution water.

Several additional calculations are made in finally establishing the share of costs to be attributed to a specific waste discharger. Two of these relate to strength and heat of the effluent. It is considered that the costs of dealing with wastes do not rise in one-to-one correspondence with the strength of the effluent, and stronger wastes are assessed at a proportionately lower rate than more dilute wastes. For hot effluents, an additional cost is assessed to cover the extra dilution that is required because heat not only stimulates BOD but reduces the oxygen saturation level of the receiving water.

Ruhrverband Effluent Charge
Assessment Method

The Emschergenossenschaft system achieves commensurability between varied effluents by determining their propensity to kill a given type of test fish. This permits all effluents to be evaluated in terms of a single numerical scale. The choice of the objective of maintaining fish life does not necessarily mean the absence of other objectives; it is simply considered a useful summary surrogate for a wide range of values. Thus it may well be held that such other objectives as

---

[17] The actual p values used in the equation are as follows:

$$D = -1 + \frac{S}{0.4} + \frac{1}{2}\frac{B}{40} + \frac{1}{2}\frac{P-30}{42} + F.$$

aesthetics and public health are adequately met if the fish objective is met.

The Ruhrverband also achieves commensurability between various types of waste materials by basing its procedure on a single physical objective, but a somewhat different one.[18] In essence, the objective is to maximize the self-purification capacity of the stream (and the organic waste degradation capacity of biological treatment plants). With this objective in view, a method was developed which is capable of integrating into a single measure the effects of organic wastes and of toxic wastes. The measure used is a special form of the population equivalent BOD.

Population equivalent BOD is a common measure of organic waste load both in the United States and in Europe. One population equivalent is the oxygen demand exerted, on the average, by the untreated daily wastes of one person over a specified time period (usually five days) and at a specified temperature. Population equivalent BOD tends to be a very undependable measure of industrial waste loads because it does not comprehend the destructive effects of substances other than oxygen-demanding organic materials found in industrial wastes. The Ruhrverband has, however, developed a population equivalent measure which aims to include both oxygen-demanding and toxic wastes. The character of this measure, and its rationale, has been stated as follows:

. . . it was possible, in the course of recent years, to develop a test which makes it possible to judge every effluent, regardless of its composition, by its population equivalent. In doing this we start with the presumption that household (and other oxygen-demanding) wastes, as well as toxic wastes, work themselves out in a very similar fashion even though through different mechanisms. The self-purification of a stream over a given stretch is similarly affected by both types of effluents, in the one case due to additional pollution, in the other through inhibition of the self-purification process. The opportunity thus presents itself to form an equivalence between these two effects and to assign a population equivalent value of 3 to the quantity of industrial effluent that has the same inhibiting effect on self-purification as a household effluent of 162 grams (54 grams BOD = 1 population equivalent). Clearly, this method is contestable at many points; still it seemed to us a usable point of departure, and we have developed an easily executed test on this basis which has already yielded numerous good results . . . about the test itself I would just like to say that we use two rows of Erlenmeyer flasks which contain a standard solution of an organic substance of known degradability and a small amount of activated sludge. To one row are added increasing

[18] The following discussion is largely based upon W. Bucksteeg, "Teste zur Beurteilung von Abwaessern" (Tests for the Judgment of Effluents), *Staedtehygiene*, 9, 1961, and "Problematik der Bewertung . . .," *op. cit.*, and conversation with Drs. Bucksteeg and Thiele of the Ruhrverband laboratories.

amounts of household effluent of which the BOD_5 is simultaneously determined, and to the other increasing amounts of the effluent to be tested. The flasks are then shaken for three days on a shaking device and after this time the potassium permanganate demand of the filtered contents of the bottles is determined.

If the differences between the $KMnO_4$ use of the individual concentrations (the concentration of the known household effluent measured in additions of mg BOD_5/l and the test effluent in additions of ml/l are carried into a co-ordinate system, we obtain the type of curves indicated in the illustration [see Figure 40]. These curves are used in the following way: we find the points for 54, 108, and 162 BOD (1, 2, and 3 population equivalents, respectively) on the A-curve, carry them to the B-curve and from there read to the abscissa. In the illustrated case, the corresponding values are 18, 34, and 42 mg/l. Accordingly, $\frac{94}{6} = 15.7$ liters of the test effluent are to be valued at one population equivalent. The main advantage of this procedure is that all factors influencing self-purification, including oxygen-demanding and toxic qualities, are comprehended simultaneously.[19]

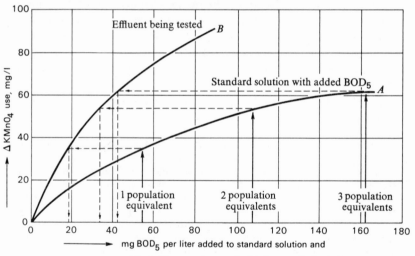

Figure 40. Determination of the population equivalent of industrial effluents.

An additional merit of the described test is, according to Dr. Bucksteeg, that biological degradation processes are unusually sensitive to toxins, more sensitive than fish, for example.

[19] Translated from W. Bucksteeg, "Teste zur Beurteilung von Abwaessern" *op. cit.*, p. 4. A detailed set of laboratory instructions is found in W. Bucksteeg, *Verfahren zur Bestimmung des Einwohnergleichwertes beliebiger Abwaesser, op. cit.* In practice, the charge levied upon individual polluters is made contingent upon some simple indicator of production or waste discharge with adjustments made when the quality and/or quantity of waste discharge changes.

As indicated earlier, both the Emschergenossenschaft and the Ruhrverband are able to measure the "pollution effect" of varied wastes along a single scale because their procedures are contingent upon the effects of varied effluents upon a single physical phenomenon. As will be indicated subsequently, the principle underlying the cost allocation technique is not precisely consistent with the objective of the water quality management activities of the *Genossenschaften*, but it provides a useful rule of thumb.

COMMENT ON THE EFFLUENT CHARGE PROCEDURES

From the point of view of strict economic theory there is an objection to the charge procedures described above—they violate the principle of marginal cost pricing. In a system where waste treatment and other quality management measures are undertaken collectively to achieve a specified stream standard, each waste discharger should be charged the incremental cost that his waste discharge imposes upon the system. This would require assessing wastes in terms of the differential costs they impose on the system—not in terms of a concept of physical equivalence. Also, wastes discharged at different locations impose different costs, which means that the waste assimilative capacity of the stream must be considered not only in the basic system plan and operation (which it is in the *Lastplaene*), but in the charges scheme as well, and that a concept of incremental, rather than average, cost must be used. The fact that incremental costs are affected by variable environmental factors such as streamflow and temperature would have to be reflected in the charging scheme. A charges system based on these principles would only cover the annual cost of the management system if constant returns to scale prevailed in the control measures (see the Appendix to Chapter 10).

It must be recognized, however, that certain costs of implementation that are ordinarily and properly neglected in reasoning about the character of ideal procedures cannot be neglected in practice. Methods that are less than theoretically ideal may be optimal in practice, since an important element in determining the best method for actual use is the cost of making marginal refinements. A comparatively crude method that is generally correct in principle will often realize the major share of the gains that could be achieved by more complex and conceptually more satisfying techniques. The methods used by the *Genossenschaften* recognize that the effluent charge is a price which provides an incentive to economize in the use of scarce resources—in this case, the waste assimilative capacity of the streams and the inputs to the collectively provided water quality management system. Alternative financing arrangements such as property taxes would not provide a similar incentive.

It should be pointed out once more that from the point of view of resource allocation the method of charging adopted—or indeed whether effluent charges are made at all—would be relatively unimportant if waste loads delivered to the system were unresponsive to the charges imposed on them. However, as we showed in Chapter 4, through process and product adjustments, through materials recovery and by-product production, through separation of wastes and various forms of pretreatment, industrial waste loads can be altered over very wide ranges. As might be expected, waste loads have responded to effluent charges and other complementary measures used to diminish them.

In general, the associations consider indirect methods of reducing wastes such as recovery and process changes on a par with treatment. The phenol recovery plants operated by the Emschergenossenschaft recover about 65 per cent of the waste phenols in the basin[20] and are virtually self-sufficient economically. A comparable job could probably have been done through private action; even a modest effluent charge might have caused individual firms to operate such plants. However, economies in marketing, staff, and research are thought to have been achieved by centralized operation.

Salvage of iron sulfate and sulfuric acid from the wastewater of the Ruhr's iron and steel industry is another example of intensive waste recovery. Of the total amount of industrial acid used in the Ruhr Valley, almost 40 per cent was recovered in 1966.[21] Recovery is usually carried on at a loss, but it still tends to be a considerably cheaper method than treatment by neutralization.[22] The incentive for recovery is a combination of effluent charges and technical marketing assistance offered by the Ruhrverband. One steel plant at Dortmund introduced water recirculation, internal treatment, and materials reuse processes and virtually eliminated effluent from the plant. The incentive in this case was a combination of intake water costs and effluent charges.[23] Other iron and steel plants in the area are gradually adopting measures to reduce their water intake and wastes generation.

[20] *Fuenfzig Jahre Emschergenossenschaft, op. cit.*, p. 256.

[21] Ruhrverband-Ruhrtalsperrenverein, *Jahresbericht, op. cit.*

[22] W. Husman, "Die Abwaesser der metallverarbeitenden Industrien" (The Effluents of the Metal Working Industries), *Beseitigung und Reinigung industrieller Abwasser* (Basel, 1958), p. 8.

[23] Based on a conversation with Maximilian Zur who is in charge of water management at the Hoesch-Westfalenhuette. See also Maximilian Zur, "Die Wasserwirtschaft der Hoesch-Westfalenhuette A. G., Dortmund" (The Water Management of the Hoesch-Westfalenhuette, Inc., Dortmund), *Stahl und Eisen*, Heft 17, 1958. Among the more interesting of the water saving procedures incorporated in the Westfalenhuette is the use of high-pressure boiler feedwater in several of the cooling systems—including blast furnace cooling. The water is evaporated in the cooling process, the steam is heated further, and is then fed into the high pressure steam system. In this way the plant conserves both water and heat.

CONCLUDING COMMENTS

The foregoing critique of the procedures used by the *Genossenschaften* contains no information about the administrative costs of achieving a more precise and theoretically correct system of cost assessment. This being the case, it cannot be conclusively established that the systems presently in use are inferior to more refined procedures. Where the primary objective of water quality works is protection of the Rhine and there is relatively little degradation of wastes, as is the case with the Emscher, efforts at discriminating on the basis of location may be of minor value. Also, where there is little variation in flow, as in the Emscher, peak load pricing would be of limited utility. Moreover, peak load pricing would no doubt require substantially higher expenditures for monitoring.

Because of considerations of this kind the above critique should be considered not so much as a demonstration that the procedures in the Ruhr area should be changed but as a reiteration of the fact that the assessment of costs is really *an important part* of system planning and should be considered with the same care as other elements of the system. It is an important device for inducing efficient behavior in the absence of full centralization of decisions, and its potentials in that regard should be fully identified and evaluated.

Furthermore, questions about specific features should not be permitted to obscure the achievements of these organizations in planning, designing, and operating a regional system of water quality and water supply management. They have taken extensive advantage of the economies realizable through integrated planning and operation, they have achieved economies by causing industries to consider regional waste disposal costs in their location and process design decisions, and they have incorporated cost assessment systems based upon concepts of water quality damages and independent of specific system elements. All this is a pioneering achievement of the highest order. The work of these organizations merits the close attention of all those concerned with the difficult set of problems presented by water resources management in basins containing urban-industrial complexes.

INSTITUTIONAL AND ORGANIZATIONAL APPROACHES TO REGIONAL WATER QUALITY MANAGEMENT

IV

Studies of the economic-engineering aspects of water quality management have demonstrated that a regional system can achieve major economies that cannot be realized by the conventional approach to water quality control. But little is known about how to devise legal and institutional arrangements that will permit efficient and politically responsible implemenation of water quality management programs. Compared with engineering and even economic studies, institutional studies of water quality management are in their infancy. For this reason, we have concentrated up to this point on questions of economics and technology largely within an economic efficiency framework. Not until the preceding chapter did we take a tentative step toward recognizing that economic and technological analysis can only find its ultimate meaning in a political and institutional context. Political and institutional forces cannot by themselves produce efficiency, but they can prevent it. Moreover, certain institutional arrangements may channel political forces in a way that is conducive to efficiency. In this Part we take a long but uncertain stride into the realm of institutional arrangements for implementing water quality management programs.

Water quality has received increasing political attention in the postwar period, and during the last few years a number of major industiral countries have enacted new water quality control legislation. Most of the new laws emphasize the river basin as the geographic unit for water quality control programs. England and France have adopted this approach and established regional institutions to implement it, and a new law in Germany requires water quality planning on a regional basis. Contemporary law in the United States also calls for regional planning and provides some financial encouragement for setting up water quality programs on a regional basis. At the same time there is a trend in all of these countries toward much deeper involvement on the part of central government in the development and allocation of water resources.

In the following chapter we discuss instances of regional approaches to water quality management in several western countries. At the end of the chapter we expand on some aspects of these approaches, and assess them in terms of the concepts of economic efficiency developed in earlier chapters.

The Approaches

13

The instances of water quality management chosen for discussion in this chapter are those that appear to be the most highly developed regional approaches. In some cases, the laws are so new that there is little to report but good intentions. In others, there is a long history of activity on a regional basis.

Obviously, these two situations have to be assessed somewhat differently. Many factors other than the "inherent merit" of legal and institutional arrangements will influence outcomes. Despite the limitations imposed by the difficulty of making comparisons at this time, we feel that the discussion will be useful. It is clear from legal developments and from professional and lay debate that we in the United States are trying to find our way toward suitable institutions for dealing with the water quality problem. In this regard, it is useful to review the experience of other areas, some of which have long had to face problems of an intensity we are just beginning to meet.

The particular regional approaches discussed are: (1) the *Genossenschaften* (river associations) in the Ruhr area of Germany, which have been in operation for various lengths of time up to sixty years; (2) the English River Authorities, created by Parliament in 1963 to supersede the existing River Boards established in 1948; (3) the French river agencies created by a law passed in 1964; and (4) the Delaware River Basin Commission which was established by an interstate-federal compact in the United States in 1961 to supersede an earlier interstate commission.[1]

Regional authorities have also been established in Belgium, in Holland, and in Ontario, Canada, and a current research project points toward a regional approach in Upper Silesia in Poland. In the United

[1] The sources consulted in the preparation of the following discussion of water quality management in the Ruhr, in England and Wales, in France and in the Delaware River Basin are listed at the end of the chapter.

States the Ohio River Valley Water Sanitation Commission has a record of some twenty years of productive effort.[2]

At the end of the chapter we list some capabilities which a regional water quality management agency would seem to need to achieve economic efficiency. These provide us with a rather loose but useful framework for comparative discussion of the cases.

THE RUHR AREA *GENOSSENSCHAFTEN*

The *Genossenschaften*, as described in the preceding chapter, have implemented a wide array of measures to improve water quality. These include treatment in large collective plants, waste treatment at individual municipal and industrial outfalls, mechanical reaeration of streams, retention ponds, diversion of a stream through a treatment plant, low-flow augmentation by releases from upland reservoirs, and specialized use of certain streams or stretches of streams. The costs of these facilities attributable to water quality management have been met largely from charges levied upon all waste dischargers according to the quality and quantity of waste they discharge whether it goes directly to treatment plants or into the river. (The river basins of the Ruhr district are shown in Figure 39, Chapter 12.)

Historical Background. Critical conditions in the Emscher area at the turn of the century led to the formation of the Emschergenossenschaft—the first of the *Genossenschaften*, and the one on which the others were modeled. The naturally poor drainage situation in the Emscher valley became steadily worse after 1860 when coal mining began moving into the area, followed by steel, steel-finishing, and chemical industries. Subsidence in the mining areas soon created depressions that filled with the waste of industries and municipalities, and efforts by individual mining enterprises and small associations had little effect on over-all drainage conditions. A regional drainage plan that might have improved the situation was proposed in 1883, but abandoned when no agreement could be reached on membership arrangements.

Population in the area rose from 350,000 in 1870 to over 1,250,000 by 1900; industrial expansion accelerated; and the increasing waste discharges overburdened the rivers and streams. Individual communities and industrial enterprises began to pump water from the Ruhr watershed, and court cases involving claims of damages resulting from upstream waste discharges became frequent. Despite a few municipal treatment plants, sanitary conditions became worse, and when a typhoid epidemic swept the country in 1901 the Emscher area was particularly hard hit.

[2] See E. J. Cleary, *The ORSANCO Story* (The Johns Hopkins Press, for RFF, 1967).

Towards the end of the nineteenth century it became obvious that forbidding mines, mills, or municipalities to discharge their wastewater into the rivers was a futile approach, and that substantial improvement could be obtained only by unified regulation of the Emscher from its headwaters to its mouth. In 1899 various industrial and municipal officials met in Bochum and appointed a commission, made up of representatives of municipalities, industries, and members of the scientific and technical community, to devise a technical plan for the area. The commission was also confronted with the question of how to form an organization that could successfully carry through the needed works. There was no organization that could be taken as a model, and the fact that the Emscher area was divided into some 200-odd political jurisdictions created additional problems. The commission was convinced that the plan could succeed only if a feeling of community could be established among the involved groups. This, in their view, required a self-governing organization with a carefully structured political representation. A higher unit of government would have to assume some supervisory responsibility, but it was argued that a continuing self-governing management agency would be the best means for economical operation; it would be in a position to adapt to the changing conditions of a dynamic industrial area and would have a close association with the technical and economic resources of the region. At this early stage, the need for technical competence and research work was stressed.

A question of great importance was who the members of the association should be. It was decided that the membership should consist of all dischargers of wastewater and those benefiting from the regulation of the stream. Not surprisingly, the matter of distribution of costs was prominently discussed by the commission, and the principle was established that costs should be distributed on the basis of the benefits received from the operation of the organization and the costs made necessary by the activities of the membership. In the Emscher, the most important costs were those related to subsidence in coal mining areas and those imposed by the discharge of wastewaters.

The proposed law passed the Rhennish and Westphalian Landtags and in 1904 was signed by the King of Prussia. The law sets out the duties of the Emschergenossenschaft in general terms as the regulation of the stream and treatment of wastewaters in the area. The statute indicates that this is to be done in accordance with a general plan, but it also provides for adaptation to changing circumstances.

The Emschergenossenschaft proved so effective that the other *Genossenschaften* were patterned after it, although none of them faced such critical problems at the time of their establishment. The organizational and membership arrangements are not precisely the same for all the associations, but on the whole the members fall into three groups: mines, industrial and business establishments; railroads and other productive facilities; and communities.

Present Organizational Arrangements. Because the *Genossenschaften* are organized along such similar lines, much of the following description of the Ruhrverband-Ruhrtalsperrenverein can be taken as generally descriptive of them all. The Ruhrverband was formed in 1913 to regulate water quality of the Ruhr River and to support the water supply functions of the already existing Ruhrtalsperrenverein (Ruhr reservoir association). The two organizations have separate boards of directors, but since 1939 they have had a single director and staff (see Figure 41).

Organization of the Ruhrverband and the Ruhrtalsperrenverein

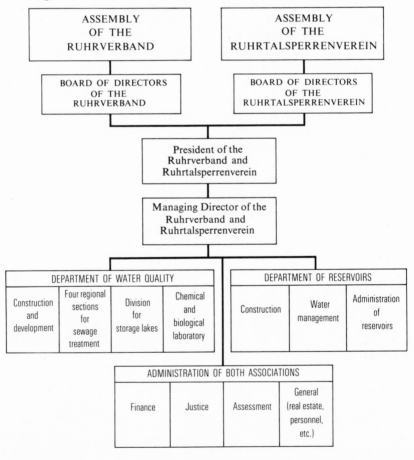

Figure 41.

The basic political power in the Ruhrverband lies in the governing board which is made up of: (1) the owners of business and industrial establishments and other facilities that lie in the Ruhrverband area and that contribute to water quality deterioration in the Ruhr or its tributaries, and those who benefit from the activities of the Rhurverband to the extent that they make a specified minimum financial contribution to its activities; (2) communities within the Ruhrverband area; and (3) the Ruhrtalsperrenverein as a representative of the waterworks and other water withdrawal facilities.

The political organs are the assemblies and the board of directors. The assembly members (about 1,500) elect the board of directors, approve or disapprove the plan for water quality management, approve or disapprove the assessment of charges, and decide upon the basic method for calculating the level of charges. The assembly reaches its conclusions on the basis of absolute majority with the number of votes cast by each member being dependent upon the amount of financial contribution.

The board of directors consists of a chairman, his deputy, and seven additional members—all elected by the assembly from among its membership. The business establishments, the communities, and the Ruhrtalsperrenverein must all be represented on the board of the Ruhrverband.

Since the board members serve only part-time and are not necessarily skilled in technical water resource matters, they appoint a staff director to manage the program. The staff of the Ruhrverband-Ruhrtalsperrenverein now comprises about 450 professionals and 400 other workers.

In the course of its roughly fifty-year history, the Ruhrverband has built over 100 waste treatment plants on the Ruhr and its tributaries. The Ruhrtalsperrenverein has built and/or manages seven large upland reservoirs. The Ruhrverband also operates waterpower facilities and a series of shallow oxidation lakes in the Ruhr itself. The costs of these activities have been considerable. Construction funds are obtained from the capital market, while the annual expenses for interest, operation, maintenance and replacement are met by a system of charges. The basic charge for the Ruhrverband quality management activities is contingent upon the amount and quality of the effluent discharged by the industries and municipalities in the region.[3] The staff prepares lists of charges based on waste discharge information. The lists show the name of the member and an estimate of the charge he must pay. The member may appeal his charge to a commission established by the Ruhrverband or finally to the courts. The Minister of Food, Agriculture, and Forests of North

[3] See Chapter 12 for a detailed discussion.

Rhine-Westphalia has general supervisory powers and must approve the lists, but his responsibility is limited to determining whether they follow the form prescribed in the laws creating the association.[4] The assessments on the individual members established through the indicated procedure are public obligations and can be enforced by law as taxes. However, because of particularly good relationships between the *Genossenschaften* and their members, there has been little need for enforcement. This favorable experience, plus the public character of the obligations, has given the *Genossenschaften* such a strong credit rating that there is an international market for their bonds.

THE RIVER AUTHORITIES IN ENGLAND AND WALES

In England and Wales uniform water policies are now laid down by the central government and administered in large measure by regional authorities.

The British contributed heavily to the development of the basic biological sewage treatment processes and over the years constructed many plants. Indeed, most urban households are connected to some form of treatment plant. However, overloading and failure to deal effectively with industrial wastes in many instances have left the country with severe water quality problems.

A 1958 survey of stream and estuary water quality showed that 73 per cent of total river mileage was "unpolluted or recovering from pollution," 15 per cent was of "doubtful quality," 6 per cent was of "poor quality," and 6 per cent was "mostly polluted." At first sight these figures seem encouraging. But they fail to reveal that the long stretches of rivers with water of good quality are mostly in upland areas, that many estuaries are grossly polluted, and that the water in the middle and lower reaches close to urban areas tends to be of doubtful quality at best. These facts make the picture look quite different, for it is in the highly populated areas that the rivers are becoming increasingly important for water supply and for recreation.

The idea of entrusting the management of water resources to comprehensive authorities with jurisdiction over a whole river basin or group of basins is not new in Britain. It has been put forward from

---

[4] The Ruhrrheinhaltungsgesetz of 1913 sets forth the relationships between the Ruhrverband and the government of the *Land* (state). In addition to approving the list of charges, a supervisory board responsible to the Minister must license individual installations and approve loans. In general, a ministerial license for a Ruhrverband waste treatment plant cannot be refused, but the conditions under which a license will be given could come under dispute. Such disputes have not arisen. Later *Land* and federal laws (the most important of which is the Wasserhaushaltsgesetz of July 1957) have not altered the operations of the *Genossenschaften* in any essential respect.

time to time over the years by Royal Commissions and government committees as well as by professional groups. Moreover, English law had been moving toward river basin management for some time. Several river basins, notably the Thames, have long had conservancy boards empowered to deal with navigation and pollution control. In 1930, Catchment Boards were set up in every drainage district in England and Wales to carry out land drainage and flood control works, and in some river basins there were agencies with authority to enforce pollution control laws. But extremes of drought and flood plus mounting pollution problems in the postwar period emphasized the shortcomings of the limited approach to basin management, and prompted the far-reaching legislation of 1963, which created the River Authorities. These agencies, which have broad powers for water management, began to function in 1965.

Historical Background. Stream deterioration really began in England early in the nineteenth century. Industrialization itself produced massive amounts of wastes and gave rise to an explosive increase in the size of the cities. At about the same time, the water carriage system of sewage disposal was introduced; wastes were no longer disposed of in the streets but carried into the rivers. This, combined with direct discharges to the rivers by industrial establishments, meant that large amounts of untreated municipal and industrial waste began to find their way into the streams.

By the middle of the nineteenth century, pollution had become a serious public health problem, particularly in such densely populated areas as Lancashire, Yorkshire, the Midlands, and London. Epidemics, destruction of fish life, and grossly offensive river conditions prompted the appointment of Royal Commissions in 1865 and 1868 to study and report on the problem of river pollution. Their work led to the Public Health Act of 1875. This was followed by the Rivers (Prevention of Pollution) Act of 1876, which was the basic pollution control law until 1951. The Act contained strong provisions forbidding the discharge of solid and liquid wastes, but it also stipulated that no action could be taken unless the local government board was satisfied that "no material injury will be inflicted by such proceedings on the interests of such industry. . . . " This and certain other provisions hindered enforcement, and in the course of time it became clear that the Act was not being successfully implemented. River agencies of various kinds were then set up in some of the most heavily developed watersheds to administer the 1876 Act. Between 1891 and 1932, the Mersey and Irwell Joint Commission (in Lancashire), the Ribble Joint Committee, the West Riding of Yorkshire Rivers Board, and the River Dee Joint Committee were established. Two other boards, the Thames Conservancy Board formed in 1857 and the Lee Conservancy Board of 1868, were originally intended to control navigation but were later given anti-pollution powers which in many respects were wider than those provided by the 1876 Act. The Thames Board had the most far-reaching water quality control powers and seems to have conducted its water quality control activities rather successfully.

After World War II, a feeling emerged that previous legislation had in large measure been a failure. The situation has been described by Craine as follows: "The administration of regulatory law prior to the end of the Second World War tended to favor established uses giving dominance to the doctrine of protecting individual rights unless the exercise of such rights implied a flagrant violation of the public interest. With the war and throughout the immediate post-war period, a rapid shift in public attitude gave greater weight to the collective interest in the quality of the natural waters of the nation."[5] In 1948, Parliament passed the River Boards Act, which established thirty-two river boards— one in each basin in England and Wales—and conferred on the boards, or transferred to them, functions relating to land drainage, fisheries, and water quality, and recognized them as local authorities so they could prosecute under the 1876 Act. When the Rivers (Prevention of Pollution) Act of 1951 was passed, the River Boards were given the authority to enforce it.

The 1951 Act basically repeated the 1876 Act's general prohibition against waste discharges. It also made it an offense for any person to create or substantially alter an outlet for the discharge of industrial or municipal effluent to a stream or to make any increased discharge of industrial or municipal effluent without the consent of the river authority. It further provided that such consent was not to be withheld unreasonably. This licensing authority was the primary new feature of the act. The act also permitted the River Boards to enact by-laws to restrict existing discharges, but the boards were unable to achieve agreement with the Ministry of Housing and Local Government which had general review authority on this matter.

The 1948 River Boards Act and the 1951 Rivers (Prevention of Pollution) Act proved comparatively unsatisfactory. The 1951 Act had two main weaknesses. First, the discharge license powers exercised by river authorities over industrial effluents basically applied only to new outlets or significant alterations in existing discharges; no standards were specified for established outlets. This loophole was not closed until ten years later when the Rivers (Prevention of Pollution) Act of 1961 was

[5] Unpublished notes prepared by Lyle Craine, School of Natural Resources, University of Michigan.

passed as a supplement to the 1951 Act. Second, despite the River Boards, there still was no agency within the region charged with the general duty of providing for the development and efficient use of water resources generally. One small step in this direction was a provision enabling the Minister of Housing and Local Government to set up, where necessary, a regional sewage board for centralizing the treatment of municipal and industrial waste. In the course of time, one such board was set up in the Mersey area. This board replaced fifteen obsolete waste treatment facilities with a central plant, which also serves a large number of industries that formerly discharged their wastes directly to the Irwell River.

Present Organizational Arrangements. The new Water Resources Act of 1963 had its immediate origins in a series of three reports issued by a subcommittee of the Central Advisory Water Committee, created by the Water Act of 1945. The first report was a general assessment of the water situation. The second, which followed a severe drought during the 1959 crop season, found the potential irrigation demand sufficient to establish a need to control withdrawals from surface waters. The third and final report, the so-called Proudman Committee Report, set forth in some detail proposals for comprehensive water policy and unified administration of water use and development activities in river basin areas. The government's White Paper followed quickly, and the ground was laid for the Water Resources Act of 1963. The Act was drafted and passed with a minimum of controversy. Such issues as did develop related largely to matters of financing and organization.

The Water Resources Act of 1963 endeavors to deal with the whole problem of water management in a comprehensive manner. It has very little additional to say about water quality management, but it is expected that the regulatory powers of the Rivers (Prevention of Pollution) Acts of 1951 and 1961 will be more vigorously exercised by the new River Authorities which have broader responsibilities for water management than their predecessors, the River Boards. (Figure 42 shows the jurisdiction of the twenty-seven River Authorities, and of the Thames and Lee Conservancies which continued as separate and different regional agencies.)

Among the regulatory powers given to the River Authorities the following are particularly significant: authority to operate a comprehensive system for licensing water withdrawals from surface and groundwater sources; authority to introduce "charging schemes" under which water withdrawers will be charged on the basis of the quantity they have been authorized to withdraw, with some adjustment for source of supply, season of the year, uses to which water will be put, and the

Areas of River Authorities in England and Wales

Figure 42. Source: Water Resources Board.

way water is disposed of after use; and authority to license *all* discharges of wastewater—to underground strata as well as to streams.

These regulatory provisions in the Water Resources Act are associated with extensive multipurpose development powers which now reside in the River Authorities. The functions and power to carry out development works relating to land drainage, flood damage reduction, and fisheries were transferred from the River Boards, and, in addition, the River

Authorities were given new powers to construct, operate, and finance multipurpose facilities, including water storage for municipal, industrial, and agricultural uses. The 1963 Act further strengthens River Authorities by giving them a key role in the collection and analysis of basic data and information and in the formulation of specific development proposals. Methods of financing the various activities are shown in Figure 43.

Of particular interest for our purposes is the provision that each River Authority is required to determine a minimum acceptable flow at each of the designated and agreed upon control points. "In determining the flow to be specified . . . the River Authority shall have regard to the character of the inland water and its surroundings (and, in particular, any natural beauty which the inland water and its surroundings may possess) and the flow so specified shall not be less than the minimum which in the opinion of the River Authority is needed for safeguarding the public health and for meeting (in respect both of quantity and quality) the requirements of existing lawful uses . . . whether for agriculture, industry, water supply or other purposes, and the requirements of land drainage, navigation and fisheries. . . ." [Sec. 19(5)]

At the national level, the Ministry of Housing and Local Government and the Ministry of Agriculture have long been the dominant cabinet agencies concerned with water. Under the new law, they continue to play a major role in their respective areas of concern. In addition, a new Ministry of Land and Natural Resources has been created to give supervision to data collection, surveys, and research related to water resources. A fourth agency of major significance is a newly established Water Resources Board, located administratively under the Minister of Land and Natural Resources, but with wide-ranging water policy, planning and advisory authority, particularly with regard to inter-basin transfers of water. The Board also has specific approval and directive authority over river authorities in performing their functions regarding hydrologic measurement schemes, minimum acceptable flows, water quality control and proposals for action.

Craine has commented as follows about the over-all situation: "River Authorities, however, are central to the new British scheme. The law provides that their managing boards will be composed of representatives of local governments and of the central government in such proportions as to always assure local governments a bare majority and no more. It is in these 27 semi-independent authorities that the grass-roots issues of water management are faced."[6]

[6] From "The River Authorities in England and Wales," an unpublished paper prepared by Lyle Craine for the American Society of Public Administration meetings in Washington, D.C., April 15, 1966.

Methods of Financing River Authorities in England and Wales

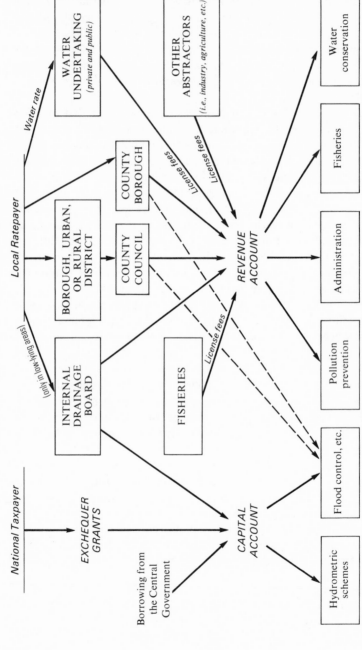

Dashed lines represent payment to River Authority when the River Authority is working as agent for the Local Authority concerned on rivers which are not under direct River Authority control (i.e., are not "Main River" as defined in the Acts).

Figure 43.

THE FRENCH BASIN AGENCIES

In France, as in Britain, regional water management agencies are creatures of national law. Prior to the Act of 1964, responsibility for formulating standards for water quality control and supervising their application was scattered among a number of agencies, both national and local.

Historical Background. The central authority for industrial waste control appears to derive from the Dangerous, Objectionable, and Unhealthy Establishments Act of December, 1917, and its various implementing decrees. The 1917 Act placed all industrial and commercial establishments endangering the safety, health, or amenities of the community under the authority of the Prefect (chief administrator of a department, or administrative district). All these establishments are inspected by civil servants known as Inspectors of Classified Establishments. They operate under the instructions of the Prefect, and their recommendations usually carry considerable weight. Emphasis seems to have been put upon negotiations and advice to the industries on a case by case basis. Should negotiations fail, there are legal arrangements to compel compliance. This approach has not prevented the development of a severe industrial waste disposal problem.

Other water quality control laws relate to fish life, protection of drinking water, and protection of public and private watercourses. Under the Rural Code, any discharge harmful to fish life, reproduction, and nutritive value is punishable by a fine of 50,000–500,000 francs and/or imprisonment for ten days to one year. Water and forestry officials are responsible for enforcement, and because the penalties are heavy, they have tended to enforce the law with considerable restraint. The Public Health Code, in addition to some more specific provisions, provides penalties for any person who allows substances injurious to health to enter the public drinking water supply.

The engineers of the Navigation Service enforce the water quality control regulations pertaining to public (navigable) watercourses. Authorization must be obtained for any discharges into these watercourses. Infractions are dealt with by the administrative courts.

On so-called private (non-navigable) watercourses, the Civil Code stipulates that a riparian owner has the right to use the water flowing along or through his property, but not to impair its quality—it must leave his land in its initial condition. As in other countries having riparian law, this provision is ignored more often than it is observed. Additional provisions of the Rural Code entrust the Rural Engineering Service with water quality control functions on the private watercourses.

Evaluations of pollution control in France vary. Still, the preponderance of evidence seems to be that it has been rather ineffective. In 1961, the French government indicated that a large number of industrial concerns were discharging harmful effluents. The breakdown by watershed was estimated as follows: Seine, 1,000; Loire, 600; Garrone, 300; Rhone, 750; Rhine-Moselle, 500; Adour, 75; northern rivers, 350; watercourses flowing to the Brittany and Normandy coasts, 400; Atlantic Coast watercourses, 100; Mediterranean watercourses, 150. As of 1965, only 3 million people out of 25 million people in towns and cities with populations of over 2,000 were provided with any treatment facilities. Despite nominally stringent pollution control laws, this is a smaller proportion than in any of the other countries discussed in this chapter.

Discontent with the previous record of pollution control and the fragmentation of responsibility played a large role in the creation in 1959 of a Commission on Water, attached to the Commissariate Général du Plan. As the result of the work of this Commission, a comprehensive new law was passed by Parliament in December 1964.

Present Organizational Arrangements. The law of 1964 might be described as revolutionary. While France has had less experience with regional approaches to water quality management than any of the other countries considered in this study, the new law foresees going beyond what has been done elsewhere, particularly in the area of using economic incentives for water quality management.

Three features of the law are of particular importance: (1) it established agencies in each of the six river basins of France (see Figure 44) to serve as regional branches of the national government; (2) it gives these agencies powers to implement regional programs of water quality management; and (3) it places primary emphasis on charges, particularly effluent charges, to finance the program and to co-ordinate private and local government waste discharge decisions with the objectives of the regional agency. In other words, it views charges levied on effluents as the primary means for inducing private and local governmental control of waste discharges. The act does not repeal previous water quality control legislation, but it anticipates that most of it will be displaced as the provisions of the new law become effective.

The act is extremely general, indeed it is what the French term a skeleton enactment. This means that Parliament has defined broad principles, and the administration is to state the provisions of the act in the form of rules (decrees in the Council of State). As of mid-1967, very few such decrees had been published, and consequently much of what the law intends must be inferred from the statements of those who helped frame it.[7] The Act takes a very broad view of the water

---

[7] Largely Hubert Levy-Lambert who was rapporteur for the Commission and who commented extensively on the law in a chapter prepared for Allen V.

French River Basins

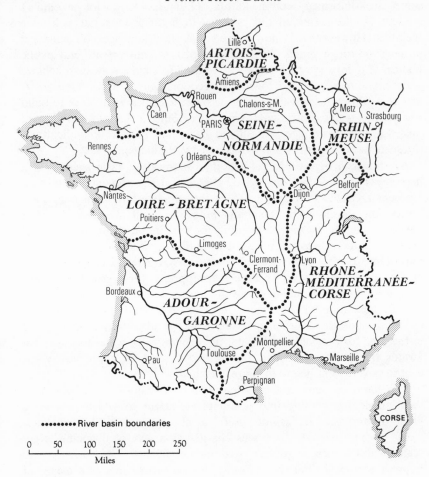

Figure 44.

quality problem as involving "any occurrence liable to cause or increase the pollution of water by altering the physical, chemical, biological, and bacteriological problems of surface water, groundwater or seawater within territorial limits." It also sees the water quality problem within the context of over-all water resources management and gives the basin agencies general water resources management powers.

The generalities of the act have given rise to some disagreements over

Kneese, *Economie et Gestion de la Qualité des Eaux* (Paris: Dunod, 1967), translated and adapted for French readers by Hubert Levy-Lambert. The projections concerning what will be done to implement the act presented in the following discussion are Levy-Lambert's.

its proper interpretation with respect of collective facilities. At first, some well-informed commentators (Levy-Lambert, for example) thought that it permitted the agencies to build and operate collective facilities. However, it is now agreed that the basin agencies must act primarily through grants, loans, and contracts with private and public bodies. It is foreseen that these will be used in such a way as to achieve scale economies and lead toward an economically efficient solution. A new law will be needed to enable the basin agencies themselves to build and operate water control quality measures. Since it is now widely agreed that the new basin agencies should have this power, no difficulty is foreseen in getting such a law enacted by Parliament.

As shown in Figure 45, the activities of the river basin agencies will be supervised and co-ordinated by the central government. Each management area will be mapped out by the standing interministerial committee on development planning problems, and a national water committee under the direct authority of the Premier will advise on all water resource development and distribution projects that are of major importance or that affect several basins. A River Basin Committee will be set up for each basin or, where appropriate, for a group of basins. The water users (including waste dischargers), local communities, and the administration will be equally represented on it. The committees are to advise upon the desirability of any works or alterations contemplated in the area for the common benefit, but programs for water management (water quality improvement, for instance) must be approved by the central government before they are executed.

The basin agencies will be allowed to levy charges on corporations and individuals "taking into account the extent to which they have made the provision of facilities useful or necessary or will benefit therefrom." While the 1964 Act sees charges as a way of financing large-scale facilities such as reservoirs, treatment facilities, and measures to improve stream assimilative capacity, it also views them as a means of compelling waste dischargers to compensate for the "external" costs they impose on the general economy. The original plan of setting up organizations only in areas where there seemed to be particular problems was abandoned, and basin agencies were established throughout the country, each encompassing a whole hydrologic area. It was felt that interdependence between the users of the basin from the source to the mouth could no longer be neglected; at the same time it was recognized that some geographical decentralization might be desirable in the larger basins, and the matter of sub-basin authorities was left open. Such authorities, if set up, would have considerable freedom of action, but would remain under the general authority of the agency in charge of the whole basin.

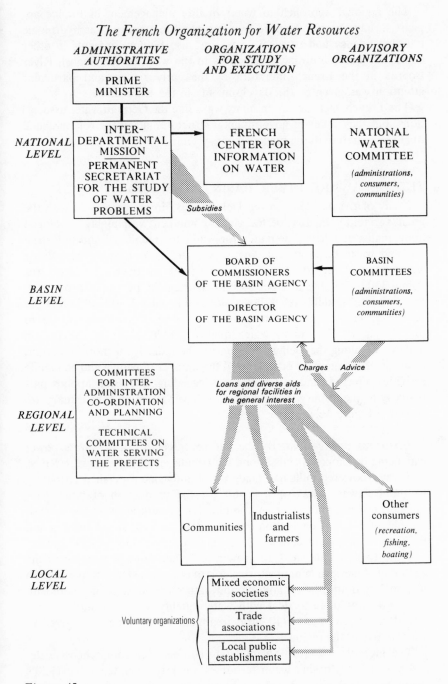

The French Organization for Water Resources

Figure 45.

The regional approach to water quality management in France appears to have been influenced by conceptual matters such as hydrologic interdependency and external costs, and also by developments in other countries. There are many references to the work of the English River Boards in the French literature of the early sixties, and particular attention was given to the developments in the Ruhr area.

The French agencies are in many ways like the German water associations, but they differ in governmental structure and in the role assigned to effluent charges in the management systems.

THE DELAWARE RIVER BASIN COMMISSION

Many of the problems in the Delaware Basin are associated with the great variability in flow of the river, combined with highly developed flood plains and heavy demands for water for municipal and industrial use and waste disposal. On August 19, 1955, the date of the valley's worst flood of record, the peak discharge of the river at Trenton was about 330,000 cubic feet per second. During the persistent drought of the early and middle sixties flows were well under 1,500 cubic feet per second at Trenton every summer and fall, despite reservoir releases to increase flows. The main water quality problems are in the Lehigh Valley and along the Delaware estuary. The latter is far more important in terms of the quantity of water and the number of people and economic activities affected, and much of the succeeding discussion applies particularly to the estuary. (The Delaware River Basin and the estuary are shown in Figure 46.)

Historical Background. By the late seventeenth century, waterpower was being developed at falls along the tributaries of the Delaware River, and water-powered mills had made the Brandywine watershed (tributary to the Delaware estuary) a center for the production of flour, gunpowder, textiles, and paper. A combination of natural resources, including plentiful water, navigation opportunities, and advanced cultural and political development enabled the Delaware area, especially the estuary and the Lehigh watershed, to grow rapidly and hold its position as the center of American manufacturing for many years. Despite the growth in population and the magnitude and nature of industrial development, very little was done to deal with water quality problems until the last few decades. Even in 1940 little treatment of any kind was given to wastewaters in the region.

The idea of setting up an interstate compact for comprehensive development of the basin's water resources was first suggested in the 1920's when New York City wanted to withdraw 600 million gallons of water a

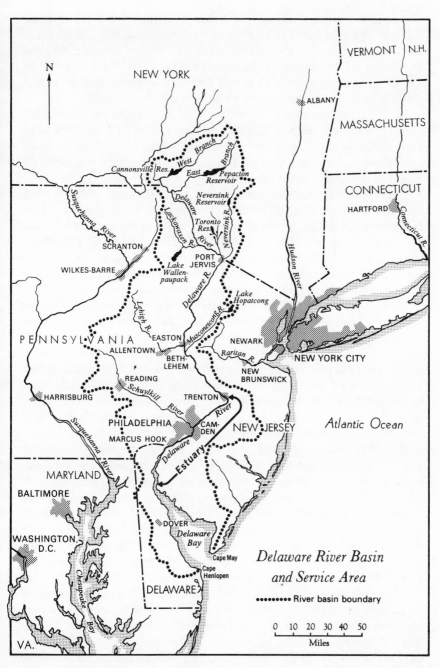

N

VERMONT   N.H.

NEW YORK

ALBANY

MASSACHUSETTS

West Branch
East Branch
Cannonsville Res.
Pepacton
Reservoir

CONNECTICUT

Delaware R.
Neversink
Reservoir
HARTFORD

Susquehanna River
Lackawaxen R.
Toronto
Res.
Neversink R.
Connecticut R.

SCRANTON
PORT
JERVIS
Hudson River

WILKES-BARRE
Lake
Wallen-
paupack

Delaware R.
Lake
Hopatcong

Lehigh R.
Musconetcong R.

PENNSYLVANIA
EASTON
NEWARK

ALLENTOWN
Raritan R.
NEW YORK CITY

BETH-
LEHEM
NEW
BRUNSWICK

READING
Schuylkill River
TRENTON

HARRISBURG
Delaware River

PHILADELPHIA
CAM-
DEN
NEW JERSEY
Atlantic Ocean

MARCUS HOOK
Delaware Estuary

Susquehanna River

MARYLAND

BALTIMORE

WASHINGTON
D.C.
DOVER
*Delaware
Bay*

Chesapeake Bay
Cape May
Delaware River Basin
and Service Area

Cape
Henlopen

DELAWARE
•••••••• River basin boundary

VA.
0 10 20 30 40 50
Miles

Figure 46. Source: Water Research Foundation for the Delaware River
Basin.

day from the upper Delaware Basin. However, the New York proposal led not to a compact but to a Supreme Court case and a decision in 1931 that permitted a diversion of up to 440 million gallons a day, and authorized a development of the upper Delaware designed for New York City's water supply with incidental low-flow augmentation to reduce claimed downstream damages in the basin itself.

In 1936, the Interstate Commission on the Delaware River Basin (INCODEL) was formed. The Commission was not an interstate compact agency as such but an agency created by parallel legislation enacted by Delaware, New Jersey, New York, and Pennsylvania, and operated from the beginning on the principle of voluntary interstate cooperation.

INCODEL had two main committees: one to deal with water quantity and one with water quality. The Committee on Water Quality, whose members represented the departments of health in the four states, came to dominate the activities of INCODEL. The committee's orientation was not toward comprehensive planning of the water resources of the basin but toward dealing with immediate water quality problems. For this purpose, the committee prepared a reciprocal agreement on pollution control, which classified the waters of the river and its tributaries into four categories or zones based on use, and prescribed standards of treatment for each. The agreement was promptly adopted by the department of health in each of the four states. The committee also drafted a uniform pollution control law which was passed in all states except Pennsylvania by 1941. The strong opposition in the Pennsylvania legislature reflected both the atttiude of industry and the fact that the City of Philadelphia accounted for a substantial portion of the untreated sewage discharged into the Delaware.

In 1945, when INCODEL offered its plan again, the measure was passed by the Pennsylvania legislature, and construction of waste treatment plants by municipalities commenced immediately after the war. This was counted as a major victory by INCODEL, and the agency then appears to have rested on its laurels. The importance of waste treatment plant construction is by no means to be minimized, but on the average not much more than primary treatment was provided, and the residual municipal wastes together with industrial discharges from a growing economy continued to place heavy oxygen demands on the stream.

For a number of years INCODEL did comparatively little in the way of multipurpose planning. It displayed a preference for parallel state legislation, and not until the late forties and early fifties did INCODEL attempt to initiate broader planning in the basin. Engineering firms were engaged to survey the situation, and they presented a plan for the states to join in a compact for the construction of a number of reservoirs. Pennsylvania once more proved to be the critical state. Upon the negative recommendation of a special study committee, which decided that the benefits to Pennsylvania were not worth the costs, the Pennsylvania legislature did not pass the plan.

While the Pennsylvania study was going on, New York filed a petition with the Supreme Court in 1951 for modification of the 1931 decree to permit diversion of 800 million gallons per day. The Supreme Court appointed a special master to conduct hearings among the litigants and to make recommendations to the Court. Agreement was finally reached on a plan which would permit New York to divert 800 million gallons per day with compensating releases during low-flow periods from reservoirs, which New York would construct.

In 1954, the Supreme Court without opinion adopted a decree as agreed upon among the party states and recommended by the master. By this time, the INCODEL proposal was virtually dead.

In 1955, two severe hurricanes struck the Delaware Basin causing floods which took about 100 lives and caused some $125 million of damage. This set in motion a study by the U.S. Corps of Engineers. Even before the flood and the initiation of the Corps of Engineers planning study, the governors of the four basin states and the mayors of New York and Philadelphia had organized the Delaware River Basin Advisory Committee and given it responsibility for assessing water problems in the basin. The Committee, working with leading citizens of the basin, stimulated the formation of a private nonprofit corporation, Delaware River Basin Research, Inc., which financed a study of governmental organization for water resources administration at Syracuse University. Upon completion of the study in late 1959, the Advisory Committee drafted a compact to establish a regional water management agency, which would be an agency of the four states and the federal government. The states and federal agencies acted quickly, and in 1961 Congress approved the federal-interstate compact establishing the Delaware River Basin Commission.

Before turning to an actual description of the compact and its provisions, it should be noted that, when the Advisory Committee was drafting the compact and the Corps of Engineers was preparing its plan for the basin, municipal and industrial water supply, flood damage reduction, and water-based recreation were regarded as the main considerations, although salinity and other water quality problems commanded some attention. It now appears to the staff of the Commission and to the Water Resources Association of the Delaware River Basin (a nonprofit corporation founded in 1959 to represent a number of citizens' associations) that the water quality problem is the most serious one in the basin.

Another necessary background item is a brief history of federal laws concerning water quality. The successful completion of the INCODEL program of providing basic (at least primary) treatment—like similar endeavors by ORSANCO in the Ohio Valley and by a number of important states—largely preceded any effective national legislation in water quality matters. Also, the development of the Delaware River Basin Compact was independent of federal initiative in water quality matters. Nevertheless, the national scene has been characterized by vigorous law-making activity in recent years and it is within the resulting legal context that regional agencies must, at least for the time being, operate.

With the passage of the Water Pollution Control Act in 1948, the federal government took its first step into what had been an exclusive area of state sovereignty. The details of the act need not detain us. It primarily supplemented state and interstate efforts with technical aid and services. Federal enforcement action was authorized, but only in interstate situations and with the consent of the states in which waste discharges causing water quality degradation were deemed to originate. In 1956 the act was rewritten. The new act strengthened federal enforcement authority in connection with interstate water quality problems and introduced grants-in-aid to subsidize municipal waste treatment plant construction, although the amount authorized was comparatively small ($50 million a year) and the limit for individual projects relatively low ($600,000). The law also aimed to encourage state and interstate efforts by various means—primarily subsidies for administration—and it initiated a program of comprehensive water quality surveys. (The Delaware Estuary Comprehensive Survey described in Chapter 11 was part of this program.)

The Water Pollution Control Act was amended again in 1961. Enforcement authority was broadened to include all "navigable" waters, and subsidies for the construction of municipal waste treatment plants were increased. The 1961 Act also provided for the inclusion of storage in federal multipurpose reservoirs to augment low flows for water quality improvement. In general, the costs of such storage were to be considered nonreimbursable.

The law was once again amended in 1965. The 1965 Water Quality Act was highly significant because it broadened federal jurisdiction through a provision requiring the establishment of standards of quality for all interstate waters. The states were required to set such standards (to be approved by the Secretary of Health, Education, and Welfare) by June 30, 1967, or face the imposition of federal standards. Federal subsidies for municipal waste treatment plant construction were once more increased. Also, a new agency—the Federal Water Pollution Control Administration (FWPCA)—was created to replace the U.S. Public

Health Service Division of Water Supply and Pollution Control. This represented an effort to broaden and improve the status of the federal water quality effort. The FWPCA was subsequently moved from the Department of Health, Education, and Welfare to the Department of the Interior. The intention was to broaden the presumably narrow public health view of water quality control.

The most recent law is the Clean Water Restoration Act of 1966. The feature of primary interest to us is a further large increase in the federal subsidies available for municipal waste treatment facilities. It authorizes $3.4 billion for construction grants for the fiscal years 1968 through 1971. The former limitation on individual grants is modified. If certain conditions are favorably met, the federal share can now rise to as high as 55 per cent of capital costs. To provide incentives for developing comprehensive water quality planning for entire watersheds, the act offers assistance in the financing of such undertakings up to 50 per cent of the cost of the expenses of a planning agency for a period of three years if it is requested by the relevant governors and certain conditions for representation are met.

The central elements of current federal law of interest here are: (1) heavy subsidization of waste treatment plant construction; (2) technical and planning assistance to state and interstate agencies; and (3) substantial enforcement powers which have as yet been comparatively little used.

Present Organizational Arrangements. The Delaware River Basin Commission is the only interstate-federal compact agency in the United States and the only regional agency to be given such comprehensive powers. The central objective was to create a river basin commission that would devise and administer a comprehensive multipurpose water resources plan which would "bring the greatest benefits and produce the most efficient service in the public welfare."

The compact states that the United States "consents to, and joins . . ." an intergovernmental compact creating the Delaware River Basin Commission which is to be "an agency, an instrumentality of the governments of the . . . parties." The Commission has five members, one from each of the four member states and one from the federal government. The commissioners are the governors of the four basin states and the Secretary of the Interior representing the President of the United States. Each commissioner may specify a voting alternate. In each case, these have been men knowledgeable in the field of water management.

The Commission is charged with developing a "comprehensive plan . . . for the immediate and long-range development and uses of water resources of the basin" and a shorter-range "water resources program" based on the comprehensive plan. The Commission is granted the power to plan and implement the development of water resources by acquiring or building and operating and maintaining dams, reservoirs, and similar facilities to control and develop the water supply; to regulate the flows so as to regulate water quality; to control and abate existing pollution; to provide for flood protection; to institute sound practices of watershed management including prevention of soil erosion and promotion of land reclamation and sound forestry practices and fishing and wildlife conservation measures; to promote recreational uses of the river; to develop and operate facilities for the generation and transmission (but not for direct distribution to consumers) of hydroelectric power and to set rates and charges for such power; and to regulate and control withdrawals and diversions from the waters of the basin.

The Commission also has a wide variety of powers for implementing the plan including the authority to delegate certain of its powers to instrumentalities of signatory governments, to establish cost-sharing standards and formulas for the apportionment of costs among the different purposes included in multipurpose programs for the sharing of financial responsibility with the signatory parties, public bodies, groups, and private enterprise. The compact authorizes broad borrowing powers and the power to issue bonds. The parties agree to provide capital funds for the projects of the Commission in accordance with the cost-sharing provisions to be established by it. The compact provides for the apportionment of the annual expense budget among the signatories with all of them undertaking to include their portion in their respective budgets "subject to such review and approval as may be required by the respective budgetary processes." The Commission has the power of eminent domain and the state signatories agree not to undertake any development projects in relation to the Delaware River Basin unless the project is approved by the Commission and is in accordance with the comprehensive program. The federal government agrees to substantially the same terms.

The compact gives the Commission extremely broad power for the direct implementation of various measures affecting quantity and quality of water in the basin, both surface and ground. It is intended that the Commission shall exercise such powers only if another federal or state agency cannot or does not provide the same functions efficiently in accordance with the comprehensive plan.

Specifically with regard to water quality management, the Commission is given the powers to undertake investigations and surveys and acquire, construct, operate, and maintain projects and facilities to control potentially adverse waste discharges and abate or dilute existing waste discharges affecting quality of the water resources of the basin. It may invoke, as complainant against waste dischargers, the power and jurisdiction of water quality control agencies of the signatory parties. The Commission may assume jurisdiction to control future waste discharges whenever it determines after investigation and public hearings that the comprehensive plan requires it. The Commission, after public hearing, may also classify the waters of the basin and establish standards for treatment of municipal, industrial, or other wastes. It also has the power, after hearings, to amend and repeal rules, regulations and standards. The signatory parties also pledge themselves to pass whatever legislation may be necessary to control wastes in accordance with the comprehensive plan. The Commission also has direct enforcement powers and may, after investigation and hearing, issue orders to any persons or person or public or private corporation to cease any discharge which it determines to be in violation of the rules and regulations that have been adopted. The orders are subject to appeal in any court of competent jurisdiction.

To summarize, the Commission has far-reaching powers to plan, design, construct, operate, and finance facilities for water quality management if it can demonstrate that these are effective and efficient means for achieving the water quality objective and that the objective could not be so efficiently achieved by other units of government. The Commission also appears to have considerable scope under federal law to proceed as it deems best in the matter of standard-setting and control of discharges.

COMPARATIVE DISCUSSION OF
THE MANAGEMENT APPROACHES

In our earlier discussions, we suggested that if regional agencies were to be able to achieve economic efficiency they should have the power to: analyze and implement a wide range of alternatives; influence the pattern of land use as it relates to the water management program; and articulate private and local government decisions with their own operations through regulation or charges. We now look at the four cases outlined above in relation to these powers and in relation to the nature of the representation of, and the opportunity to influence decisions by, the affected parties. (The latter can probably enhance or hinder the achievement of economic efficiency.)

Ability to Evaluate and Implement a Wide Range of Alternatives. A regional agency is in a much better position to improve the efficiency of its water quality management system when it can make use of large-scale measures such as streamflow regulation, mechanical reaeration of streams, direct treatment of streams via oxidation lakes and other means, collection and treatment of municipal and industrial wastes in central plants serving entire regions, piping of wastes away from critical reaches of streams, and groundwater recharge. These measures will probably be most beneficial in highly developed basins, but they should be considered in others as well. In general, the regional approaches discussed in this chapter are cognizant of such opportunities, and the laws governing them make provision for their implementation. The only exception is England where the law establishing the River Authorities, the documents leading up to it, and discussions following it, all suggest that the River Authorities are not expected to undertake activities of this kind.

The *Genossenschaften* are a special case. They began with the idea of establishing integrated basin-wide systems and they have had a number of decades to implement them. The range of alternatives evaluated and implemented is wide, and virtually no possibility is ignored. Nevertheless, two factors may militate against the actual identification and implementation of an optimum system in the Ruhr. One is what appears to be an excessive separation of water quality and water quantity considerations. The other is that little or no use is made of formal systems analysis, despite the broad scope and responsibilities of the organizations and the utility of this mode of analysis for both planning and operating water quality management systems. This reflects a more general lag in the application of systems analysis to water resource engineering and economics in Europe. To what degree such techniques as computer simulation and more sophisticated analysis of hydrology might improve the systems must remain an open question. Limited information from U.S. research and practice suggests that these are important planning, design, and operating tools.

British practice has tended to place virtually complete reliance upon treatment at individual points of waste outfall. Efforts toward achieving scale economies in waste disposal have been few. The 1937 Drainage of Trade Premises Act authorized the discharge of trade wastes into public sewers subject to the approval of the local authority, and the Rivers (Prevention of Pollution) Act of 1951 encouraged the integration of separate local sewer systems and treatment plants. Up to this time, however, it cannot be said that there has been any systematic exploitation of the opportunities provided by collection and treatment of wastes on a regional scale (with the exception of some efforts by the Thames Conservancy), not to mention the array of other possible measures that might be implemented on a river basin basis. Even the new river agencies have no authority to implement a water quality management facility as such, although they can construct reservoirs and operate them for streamflow regulation.

The probable economies of broader regional scale measures has not gone unrecognized by many English water quality professionals, but neither the 1963 law nor the various available interpretations of it suggest that much emphasis will be placed on direct investment and operation of facilities for water quality improvement by any of the River Authorities. This contrasts strikingly with the emphasis placed upon the river basin development and management approach to water supply and the strong role assigned to the River Authorities. The situation probably reflects the long history of water quality control based on efforts to impose restrictions on individual waste dischargers, and the fact that several laws had not yet been fully tested at the time of the studies and debate on the River Authorities' legislation.

The French agencies, unlike some of the other regional agencies discussed in this report, seem to have an absolutely clear objective—economic efficiency in the full sense of the term. The aim is to establish a system in which the incremental costs of further improvement of water quality balance the incremental benefits, and in which the full range of alternative ways of improving water quality can be assessed and all measures brought into optimal balance. Current legislation does not give the river basin agencies authority for direct investment in regional-scale works, but they can make grants or negotiate contracts with private or public bodies to construct the facilities needed for an economically optimal system. There seems to be considerable sentiment to supplement the basic law by giving the basin agencies the authority to build and operate control measures.

The Delaware River Basin Commission has authority under the compact to plan, construct, operate, and finance measures for water quality improvement, but only if it can do so more efficiently than other agencies. The Commission seems particularly well-suited to undertake such measures although it would need a much larger staff for planning, economic evaluation, and program development. The Federal Water Pollution Control Administration study of the Delaware estuary (discussed in Chapter 11) went far in identifying and evaluating alternatives in terms of both combinations of measures to improve water quality and the objectives to be met. Although the study did not explore all the possibilities for realizing regional scale economies, its findings seem to justify direct action by the Commission in the construction and operation of works if it is to achieve the most efficient system for dealing with the water quality problems in the estuary. Moreover, in the matter of systems analysis tools the Commission is far ahead of any comparable regional agency in the United States or abroad. A board of consultants has strongly urged the Commission to use these tools and to proceed to implement a program of regional measures.

As each of the countries discussed makes at least some use of subsidies, it is worth pointing out again that financial aid of this kind—whether for streamflow regulation, municipal waste treatment plant construction, or industrial waste treatment facilities—may make an inefficient facility seem financially attractive and thereby distort the planning and implementation of alternatives. This suggests that a policy of subsidization would be more effective if the grants were not restricted to particular facilities but could be used by regional agencies where needed to implement an over-all regional plan for water quality improvement.

Ability to Integrate Related Water and Land Uses. As a rule there is a strong tie between considerations for water quantity and water quality. Streamflow regulation through reservoir storage not only influences the amount of water available for diversion, depletion, and in-stream uses but also affects the quality of water in the stream. Therefore, quality considerations should be taken into account in the planning, design, and operation of reservoirs. Furthermore, restrictions on water usage such as permits or charges for water supply withdrawal influence water quality. If an industrial enterprise is induced to recirculate its water, the waste load is more than likely to be reduced through internal treatment or waste recovery processes. Moreover, the residual waste load will be in a smaller volume and therefore less costly to treat.

Location patterns may greatly influence the costs associated with waste disposal along an estuary. For example, the establishment of a new industrial discharge immediately above a public water supply intake may impose a large enough burden to make it worthwhile for society to consider changing the pattern of development. Institutions for land and water management should be such that these interrelationships will be evaluated and properly taken into account.

In England, the Ruhr, and the Delaware Basin the interrelationships between water quantity and quality have been taken into account by putting them both under the authority of one agency. In France a separate agency will probably continue to be in charge of reservoir construction and operation. The law implies that releases for water quality improvement will be arranged on a reimbursable basis by the water quality management agencies and that they will participate in reservoir planning. It may be that an interagency relationship of this kind can achieve the same results as a single agency with the authority to internalize all direct interdependencies.

Because of the wide scope of their authority over water resources, the *Genossenschaften* are in a very good position to integrate all aspects of water management. The fact that institutional development has created a somewhat artificial distinction between water quality and water supply, may be of minor importance because the opportunities for flow regulation to improve water quality are so limited in the Ruhr. The Ruhrverband's charges for water withdrawal have caused industries to develop internal water recirculation systems, and the result has been a reduction not only in water intake but also in the volume of wastewater and the cost of treatment.

A certain amount of co-ordination with land-use development has been achieved by the staff of the Ruhrverband working with the Siedlungsverband, which is charged with general land-use planning in the industrial region of North Rhine-Westphalia. In devising its over-all plan for the region, the Siedlungsverband considers the impacts of land use upon water management. This is the only case among those considered here where there is a reasonably comprehensive and systematic co-ordination of land-use planning and water resources planning.

The English River Authorities have several potentially effective management controls at their disposal. They have the authority to regulate the withdrawal of water from natural watercourses, to regulate discharges of wastewater, to charge for the withdrawal of water, and to construct and operate water management facilities with primary emphasis on reservoirs for storage and flow regulation. While charging schemes are also possible, there seems to be a strong emphasis on direct controls, which, as was pointed out in earlier chapters, are often inferior to price-like devices as a means of achieving an economic optimum. Nevertheless, a number of critical interdependencies are clearly recognized and tools are provided to influence them. There is also some recognition of the influence of land use and development upon water quality management. Most of the River Boards had arrangements with local planning authorities for all planning applications involving new discharges of trade or sewage effluents to be referred to the River Board for review and advice. The River Authorities are expected to make similar arrangements. This system provides some protection against gross mistakes in the location of activities.

In sum, while most of the critical interdependencies appear to have been recognized in providing management tools to the English River Authorities, the heavy dependence on direct controls and failure to integrate water and land planning must be counted as deficiencies.

In principle, the French law provides for thoroughgoing management of both water quality and water quantity. The new law contemplates that charges will be levied upon water that is diverted and lost from the system, as well as upon effluent discharges. It is envisaged that two related but distinct fees will be paid by those who withdraw water and return waste to the system. It is also foreseen that the basin agencies will use grants, contracts, and subsidies to bring all elements in the water system into optimal balance. If, as is expected, the agencies are given the authority for direct investment, this power will be exercised in the same context. While these are only intentions at this point, it is fair to say that interdependencies between water quality and water quantity have been clearly and explicitly recognized.

On the matter of interrelationships between land use and the cost of water supply or waste disposal, the French law is largely silent. The same is true of various discussions of the law. The act does not go beyond providing for the setting up of protective zones around sources of public water supply.

The Delaware River Compact gives clear recognition to interdependencies between water quantity and quality, and in principle there is no reason why the Commission's authority to set standards, levy charges on effluents and on water withdrawals, and construct and operate facilities should not permit it to take optimal account of all interrelations between various water uses including waste disposal. It is somewhat doubtful whether this will actually be accomplished.

The matter of associated land use came up during the framing of the compact, but no action was taken on suggestions that the proposed commission be given open-ended authority and jurisdiction permitting other functions to be added later by the states. Apparently it was thought that opening the door to other government functions would bring forth complexities and political difficulties that would defeat the whole enterprise. As a result the compact is silent on the matter of relationships with land use. The Delaware Commission might have some influence on land-use patterns through its stream classification and charging powers, but in general the issue has not been confronted. Since location decisions should not turn upon water quality considerations alone, it may be that no appropriate consideration of this variable can occur until the basin has a regional land-use organization with regulatory as well as planning authority.

In summary, in each of the cases considered, interdependencies between water quantity and quality are explicitly recognized, and tools are provided for managing these interrelationships. Particular types of tools used or contemplated vary; some agencies place heavy emphasis on direct controls whereas others rely more heavily on indirect measures such as charges on water withdrawals and/or waste discharges. The only instance of reasonably systematic recognition of the interrelationships between emerging land-use patterns and water quality management problems is in the Ruhr. It may be significant that this is also the only region with an effective regional land-use planning agency.

Ability to Articulate Private and Local Government Decisions so as to Achieve an Efficient System. The extent to which co-ordinated action on a regional basis is achieved through direct planning, design, and operation of structural works by the regional authority will vary from case to case. In some instances, such as the operation of a reservoir or an in-stream treatment facility, it is in the interest of efficiency for the regional agency to provide and operate the facility because no other agency has the responsibility or capacity to do so. Major efficiency gains may also result from central operation of treatment plants at individual industrial and municipal outfalls. In the Ruhr area, the *Genossenschaften* operate all conventional treatment plants. Industries have frequently incorporated internal waste recovery and pretreatment processes, but it is one testimony to the efficiency of the *Genossenschaft* system that municipalities and industries have chosen to pay effluent charges rather than undertake treatment of their wastes.

In few cases, if any, could regional waste disposal considerations justify the direct design and operation of industrial processes by a regional agency, although internal process design, internal materials recovery, and by-product production can greatly reduce industrial waste discharges. The role of a regional agency should be to devise some method of causing industrial waste disposers to take account of the costs they impose on waste treatment facilities or successive users when they plan, design, and operate their production processes. Where the regional agency does not construct and operate treatment plants, it must use indirect means to induce optimal levels of waste load reduction at municipal and industrial outfalls.

Although the *Genossenschaften* do operate all conventional and some unconventional treatment devices, they still encourage industries to reduce their waste discharges. One incentive in this direction is the effluent charge which varies with the quality and quantity of waste discharged either to treatment plants or directly to the streams. The charge system, combined with technical and marketing assistance, has produced a substantial reduction in industrial waste loads. The effluent charges established in the Ruhr are not theoretically ideal, but they have had considerable practical effect in articulating the decisions of industrial waste disposers with the planning and operation of the regional works provided directly by the *Genossenschaften*.

The English authorities are equipped with a wide array of water management tools. They are authorized by laws passed in 1951 and 1961 to license all waste discharges in their areas. It is foreseen that each case will be decided on its own, and each license will specify permitted waste discharge. Since there is little or no evidence that the

English authorities will place much emphasis upon possibilities of exploiting economies of scale within their regions, it appears that these direct discharge controls will be the primary means for controlling water quality. In principle, it is possible to devise a system of direct controls tailored to conditions as affected by individual outfalls which would correspond to a regional economic optimum (considerations of regional scale economies aside). In practice, this technique requires more information and is less flexible than the effluent charges device. However, it may have the advantage of greater administrative ease. It does not, of course, provide a source of revenue for financing the activities of the regional agency, including the exploitation of economies of scale in water quality management.

The English law permits the River Authorities to devise and administer "charging schemes" under which "abstractors" will pay for water removed from surface or underground sources, and specifies that the rate may be adjusted to reflect differences in: (1) characteristics of the source of supply; (2) season of the year when water is withdrawn; (3) how the water is used; and (4) how it is disposed of after use. In principle, therefore, charges might be used as a flexible tool of management. The law might be interpreted to mean that the charge could be used to create an economic incentive for waste reduction activity by municipalities and industries and thus serve as a supplement to the administration of licenses for effluent discharges. At best, this would involve some problems. For example, some industries withdraw from the system of a water wholesaler but discharge directly to a stream. In this instance, it would be cumbersome for the River Authority, which can only levy charges on intakes, to devise a method that would provide the industry with an appropriate incentive to reduce its waste discharge. It must be said also that neither the law nor the associated literature suggests that charges be used as an incentive for waste control. The discussion is almost completely in terms of charges for withdrawals.

The French river basin agencies are expected to take cognizance of the economies inherent in regional action, and are authorized to promote the establishment of large-scale treatment plants for municipal and industrial waste, streamflow regulation, and other regional scale measures, when economic analysis reveals their desirability. Their water quality operations are to be financed by effluent charges, which are also intended to provide a way of inducing waste dischargers to take account of the costs they impose on the general economy when they make their waste disposal decisions. However, the law specifies that the rate schedules must be approved by the local river basin committees, and there is some doubt that the committees can be counted on to establish charges that actually reflect the external costs imposed on the general economy. Public and private users of the watercourse (municipalities, industries, recreational interests, etc.) have two-thirds of the seats on the committee and the central govenment has one-third. Nevertheless, it is intended that the effluent charges become the basic device for achieving control of effluents, particularly from industry. Moreover, the law specifies that all those affecting quality by their actions are subject to charges. Thus any action which reduces the waste assimilative capacity of the river— such as a deep impoundment might do, for example—is subject to charge under the legislation.

How the Delaware Commission will proceed on these matters is still unclear. The Federal Water Pollution Control Administration study of the estuary (reported in Chapter 11) found that minimizing the cost of treatment on a regional basis (even neglecting the possibility of large-scale measures) would be much less costly than following the usual administrative procedure of requiring that all dischargers meet a single effluent standard. In other words, given the water quality goal in the estuary, it is much less costly to remove wastes to a higher degree at some outfalls than at others. The savings stem from a number of factors including scale economies in treatment methods and the dynamics of waste assimilation in the estuary related to the spatial pattern of discharges. Savings in cost of 50 to 100 per cent are possible in the estuary area if a cost-minimizing procedure is adopted. Another study (reported in Chapter 8) found that effluent charges can be used to induce a pattern of treatment similar to that of the least costly treatment system, and that a charge of the necessary level (8¢ to 10¢ per lb. of oxygen-demanding material) was unlikely to disrupt the regional economy. The Panel of Consultants to the Delaware River Basin Commission has recommended that this approach be thoroughly explored. Whether it will prove politically feasible to implement the technique is still an open question.

Opportunity for Affected Parties to Influence Decisions. Achieving a supporting constituency and making sure that all relevant values are reflected in the decision-making process require some means of communication with the parties affected by the decisions. Knowledge of how the political power structure of institutional arrangements influences outcomes is too limited to permit linking it clearly to the economic efficiency objective. The matter of representation has nevertheless loomed large in the deliberations leading to the regional approaches considered in this chapter, and the laws establishing the regional agencies have all been quite specific on this point.

In drafting the plans for the Emschergenossenschaft, particular attention was accorded to the representation of interested parties because this was what had caused the failure of an earlier effort. The outcome was a political structure that seems highly unconventional from the perspective of the United States where it is unusual for private interests to be officially represented on public bodies with broad management authority.

Industrial interests were given a defined place in the assembly and on the board of directors of the *Genossenschaften,* and the Directors feel that this has given industry a strong sense of participation and reduced resistance to the provision of information and other co-operative services by industry. Communities are also represented in the assembly and on the board as a matter of legal right and are meant to speak for and promote the broader public interest. The direct representation accorded industry does not seem to have blocked attention to other values, and visitors to the Ruhr are impressed by the attention given to appearance and recreation opportunities. There is no way of knowing how the organizations would have fared if political power had been distributed in some other way, but the managers of the agencies believe that careful attention to the representation of affected parties has contributed to effective and efficient operation in the general interest of the area.

In England, the Proudman Committee recommended that the new river authorities follow the Ruhr pattern and have boards composed of representatives from user groups. However, a minority report favored continuation of the River Board pattern with members representing the local governments and the relevant ministries. The compromise which emerged specifies that the river authorities should range in size from twenty-one to thirty-one members, some to be appointed by local authorities and some by Ministers "because of their knowledge of particular aspects of the river authorities' work or interests affected by it." The various local taxing authorities are to be represented in accordance with the distribution of taxpayers in the area of each constituent local authority. The total number of members may vary, but local government representatives are to be a majority on each river authority.

To the extent that revenues are to be obtained from user charges, the specific users are not represented in accordance with financial contribution. However, local governments are answerable to the same clientele, and the water users and waste dischargers are represented through the local political process. Still, the distribution of power will be quite different than if industry were represented in some proportion to its water utilization or its role in the financing of the authorities.

The French public administrative establishments display still a third pattern, with half of the board members representing the central government, and the other half representing the local public and private users— communities, industry, agriculture, fishing, boating, etc. As the goal of the establishments is to achieve an economically efficient system, decisions will probably be guided by technical considerations at this level. The outcome may well be affected, however, by the actions of the advisory committees which are to be set up in each basin with water users, local communities and the administration each having one-third of the members. Charges are the critical financing and control measures in the French plan, but they cannot be levied until the rates are approved by the local committees. These committees may therefore play the central role in deciding how far-reaching water quality management actually will be. Since two-thirds of their members represent private and local government interests, the actual distribution of political power may not be unlike that of the *Genossenschaften* even though the organizational pattern is, at least superficially, quite different.

Representation takes a still different form on the Delaware River Basin Commission. The commission itself is composed of the state governors and their alternates and the Secretary of the U.S. Department of the Interior and his alternate. The alternates, at least so far, tend to be persons with a claim to technical expertise, and there is no direct political representation below the state level. The compact provides, however, that the Commission may appoint advisory committees "which may be comprised of representatives of the public and of federal, state, county, and municipal governments, water resource agencies, water using industries, water interest groups, labor, and agriculture." This is quite different from the situation in France where advisory groups are not only an integral part of the system, but they have certain critical powers of approval. Of all the regional agencies considered in this report, the Delaware Commission has the weakest links between itself and local governments and water users in the area. This may reflect the fact that the United States has three distinct levels of government whereas England and France have only two, and in Germany the federal government is not involved because all the *Genossenschaften* are within a single state.

The matter of an appropriate political structure for regional agencies is probably the least well understood aspect of water resources management. One of the most important issues seems to be the degree to which representation should reflect financial contributions. This has been a consideration in defining the structure of each of the regional agencies. However, in no case, except the Ruhr area, is there a one-to-one relationship between financial contributions and political representation. A separate but related issue is the matter of industry representation and its effect on the problems of implementing an effective water quality control program. The *Genossenschaften* seem to feel that direct industry representation can ease the problems, and their experience suggests that this approach should not be lightly dismissed.

This discussion should not be taken to imply that the authors feel that industry has not been well represented in previous decisions concerning water quality control—perhaps its views have been over-represented. What we are suggesting is that *responsible* representations may be worth trying, i.e., representations in which industry activities would be brought into the open and its representatives required to make clear what they favor as well as what they are against.

SELECTED REFERENCES FOR CHAPTER 13

General

Litwin, Joseph (General Rapporteur), *Control of River Pollution by Industry: Cases in Comparative Public Administration*, Brussels: International Association of Legal Science, International Institute of Administrative Sciences, 1965.

Malakoff, E. R., "Water Pollution Control: National Legislation and Policy," a comparative study done for the Food and Agriculture Organization of the United Nations, Rome, 1966.

World Health Organization, Expert Committee on Water Pollution Control, *Water Pollution Control*. Technical Report Series No. 318, Geneva, 1966.

English River Authorities

Central Advisory Water Committee, *Final Report*. London: Her Majesty's Stationery Office, 1943.

————, Sub-Committee on Growing Demands for Water, *First Report*, 1959; *Second Report*, 1960; *Final Report*, 1962. London: H.M.S.O.

————, Sub-Committee on Prevention of River Pollution, *Prevention of River Pollution*. London: H.M.S.O., 1949.

————, Sub-Committee on Water Charges, *Report on Water Charges*. London: H.M.S.O., 1963.

Craine, Lyle E., Unpublished paper on water resources management in England, prepared for the American Society for Public Administration Meeting, Washington, D.C., 1966.

Klein, Louis, *River Pollution II: Causes and Effects*. London: Butterworths & Co., 1962, p. 4.

————, "River Pollution in Industrial Areas: An Insoluble Problem?" *Journal of the Institute of Sewage Purification*, Part VI, 1961, pp. 503–11.

Lester, W. F., "Pollution Prevention," *Journal of the Institution of Public Health Engineers*, April 1958.

McNaughten, Sir George, "The Financial and Economic Aspects of Water Pollution Prevention" in *Aspects of Water Pollution Control*, Public Health Paper #13. Geneva: World Health Organization, 1962, p. 102.

Minister of Agriculture, Fisheries and Food and Minister of Housing and Local Government, "Water Conservation, England and Wales," presented to Parliament by both Ministers by Command of Her Majesty. Command No. 1693, London: H.M.S.O., 1962.

Natural Resources (Technical) Committee, Office of the Minister of Science, *Irrigation in Great Britain*, a Report of the Committee. London: H.M.S.O., February 1962.

Pugh, Norman J., "Water Supply," Chapter II, in *Conservation of Water Resources in the United Kingdom*, Proceedings of Symposium Oct. 30–Nov. 1, 1962. London: The Institution of Civil Engineers.

Turing, Harvey D., *River Pollution*. London: Edward Arnold & Company, 1952, pp. 72ff.

Water Resources Act, 1963. London: H.M.S.O., July 1963.

Wilson, H., *Final Treatment of Sewage Effluents*, The River Boards Association Yearbook for 1954, p. 85.

World Health Organization, Expert Committee on Water Pollution Control Working Paper No. 1, Geneva, 6–12 April 1965. Mimeo.

French Basin Agencies

Bigot, P., "Les problèmes de l'eau dans la région Rhône-Alpes," *Le Moniteur des travaux publics et du bâtiment*, 24 avril 1965, pp. 75–77.

Cheret, I., "La satisfaction des besoins en eau," *Annales des Mines*, juin 1966.

Colas, René, *La pollution des eaux*. Paris: Presses Universitaires de France, 1962.

Commission de l'Eau, *Atlas de la pollution des eaux en France métropolitaine*. Paris: La Documentation Française, septembre 1963.

————, *Recueil des travaux de la Commission de l'Eau*. 1959–1963.

Dondoux, Philippe, Note on the Water (Authorities, Classification, and Pollution) Act, 1964, in Michel Gentot, "France." See M. Gentot, below.

Eaux et Industries, Bulletin d'information de l'association française pour l'étude des eaux, décembre 1963, p. 2, and septembre 1964, p. 1.

Garcin, M., Assemblée Nationale—Document No. 571. Rapport de Garcin sur le projet no. 497.

Gentot, Michel, "France," Report by M. Gentot in Joseph Litwin (General Rapporteur), *Control of River Pollution by Industry: Cases in Comparative Public Administration*. Brussels: International Association of Legal Science, International Institute of Administrative Science, 1965, pp. 83–102.

Kempf, René, "Réglementation applicable à l'evaluation des eaux usées industrielles," *l'Eau*, avril 1965, pp. 173–77; mai 1965, pp. 243–52; juin 1965, pp. 293–300; juillet 1965, pp. 345–56.

Lalloy, Maurice, Sénat—Documents No. 155 I et II (Rapport de Lalloy, au nom de la commission spéciale), 1963–64.

"La protection des eaux contre la pollution dans le basin industriel de Longwy," *Bulletin français de pisciculture*, No. 187, 1957, pp. 37–47.

Le problème de l'eau en France, La Documentation Française, No. 3219, Paris, 1965.

Levy-Lambert, Hubert, Introduction to and concluding section of Allen V. Kneese, *Economie et gestion de la qualité des eaux*. Paris: Dunod, 1967. (*Economics of Regional Water Quality Management*, translated and adapted for French readers by Levy-Lambert.)

Martin, Yves, "Les problèmes de l'eau dans la Région du Nord," *Revue de l'Industrie Minérale*, mars 1966, pp. 167–81.

Ministère de l'Agriculture, Direction générale du génie rural et de l'hydraulique agricole. "Inventaire de l'assainissement des communes rurales," Situation au 1er janvier 1962.

Ministère de l'Intérieur, Direction générale des collectivités locales "Enquête sur l'alimentation en eau potable et l'assainissement des communes de plus de 2.000 habitants (Ville de Paris non comprise)," Situation au 1er janvier 1961.

Perrin-Pelletier, F., "Carte sommaire des pollution de surface existantes," *l'Eau*, mars 1962, pp. 60–64.

Régime et répartition des eaux et lutte contre leur pollution, Loi no. 64–1245 du 16 décembre 1964, *Journal Officiel* du 18 décembre 1964.

Ruhr Area Genossenschaften

Bucksteeg, W., "Problematik der Bewertung giftiger Inhaltsstoffe im Abwasser und Moeglichkeiten zur Schaffung gesicherter Bewertungsgrundlagen" (Problems in the Evaulation of Toxic Substances in Effluents and the Possibility of Obtaining Dependable Evaluation Standards). *Muenchener Beitraege zur Abwaesser, Fischerei- und Flussbiologie*. Band 6; Muenchen: Verlag von R. Oldenbourg, 1959.

———, "Teste zur Beurteilung von Abwaessern" (Tests for Judging Effluents), *Staedtehygiene*, Heft 9, 1961.

———, "Verfahren zur Bestimmung des Einwohnergleichwertes beliebiger Abwaesser" (Procedure for Determination of the Population Equivalence of Varied Effluents), Ruhrverband, Essen. Mimeo.

Fair, Gordon M., "Pollution Abatement in the Ruhr District," in Henry Jarrett (ed.). *Comparisons in Resource Management*. Baltimore: Johns Hopkins Press, 1961, pp. 142–71.

Fuenfzig Jahre Emschergenossenschaft 1906–1956 (Fifty Years of the Emschergenossenschaft). Selbstverlag der Emschergenossenschaft, Essen, 1957.

Husmann, W., "Die Abwaesser der metallverarbeitenden Industrien" (The Effluents of the Metal Working Industries), *Beseitigung und Reinigung industrieller Abwaesser*, Basel, 1958, p. 8.

————, "Einsatz neuerer Messmethoden auf dem Gebiet der Abwasserreinigung und Gewaesserkontrolle in Bereich der Emschergenossenschaft und des Lippeverbandes" (Institution of Newer Measuring Methods in the Field of Effluent Treatment and Water Control in the Area of the Emschergenossenschaft and Lippeverband), *Schweizerische Zeitschrift fuer Hydrologie*, Vol XXII, 1960, p. 461.

Kehr, Dieterich, and Möhle, Karl August, "Die Aufgaben der Abwasserreinigung in der heutigen Zeit," *Die Wasserwirtschaft*, May 1966, p. 148.

Knop, E., "Die Schaedlichkeitsbewertung von Abwaessern" (Evaluating the Damaging Effects of Effluents), *Technische-Wissenschaftliche Mitteilungen*, Heft 4, July 1961. Essen: Vulkan Verlag.

Koenig, H. W., "Wasserverbaende als rationelle Loesung fuer den Gewaesserschutz" (The Water Associations as a Rational Solution for Protection of Water Supplies), *Plan, Schweizerische Zeitschrift fuer Landes-, Regional- und Ortsplanung*, Zurich, September/October, 1960, p. 157.

————, "Die Wasserwirtschaft im Ruhrgebiet," *Die Wasserwirtschaft*, August, 1965, pp. 351–55.

Lippert, Fritz, "75 Jahre Wasserwirtschaftliches Verbandswesen," *Die Wasserwirtschaft*, May 1966, p. 40.

Moehle, Helmut, "Wasserwirtschaftliche Probleme an Industriefluessen" (Problems of Water Economics on the Industrial Streams), *Die Wasserwirtschaft*, April 1954.

Moeller, Ulrich, Referat ueber das Thema, "Wie werden in einem Flussgebiet die Beschaffenheit des Vorfluters, die Leistung der Klaerwerke und die entsprechenden Bau- und Betriebskosten aufeinander abgestimmt?" (How are the Characteristics of the Drainage Channel, the Capacity of Treatment Plants, and the Corresponding Construction and Operating Costs Articulated with One Another?), gehalten am 16.1, 1961, innerhalb des 25sten Siedlungs-Wasserwirtschaftlichen Kolloquims an der Technischen Hochschule Stuttgart.

Pruess, Max, "Der Ruhrverband und der Ruhrtalsperrenverein als Muster gemeinwirtschaftlicher Wasserwirtschaft" (The Ruhrverband and Ruhrtalsperrenverein as a Pattern for Collective Water Management), *Staedtehygiene*, Heft 9, 1954.

Ruhrreinhaltungsgesetz und Satzung für den Ruhrverband. June 5, 1913, reprinted 1964.

Ruhrtalsperrenverein, *Die Biggetalsperre, Einweihung und Einstau,* Essen, 1965.

Wasserwirtschaft in Nordrhein-Westfalen (Water Economics in North Rhine-Westphalia). Frankfurt/Main: Verwaltungsverlag G.m.b.H., 1960.

Zur, Maximilian, "Die Wasserwirtschaft der Hoesch-Westfalenhuette A.G., Dortmund" (The Water Economics of the Hoesch-Westfalenhuette, Incorporated, Dortmund), *Stahl und Eisen,* 1958. Heft 17.

Delaware River Basin

Delaware Basin Bulletin (published at irregular intervals by the Water Resources Association of the Delaware River Basin), various issues.

Delaware Conservationist (Quarterly issued by the Board of Game and Fish Commissioners, Dover, Delaware), Summer 1963.

Delaware River Basin Commission, "The Reciprocal Agreement for the Correction and Control of Pollution of the Waters of the Interstate Delaware River," undated. Mimeo.

———, *Annual Reports,* 1963, 1964, 1965.

Delaware River Basin Advisory Committee, *Annual Reports,* 1957, 1958, 1959.

———, Interstate-Federal Compact for the Delaware River Basin, February, 1961.

———, *Final Report 1956–1962.*

"Development of a Water Quality Management Program for the Delaware River Basin," Report to the Delaware River Basin Commission by a Board of Consultants, July, 1963.

Federal Water Pollution Control Administration, "Delaware Estuary Comprehensive Study," Report on Alternative Water Quality Improvement Programs, February 19, 1966.

Grad, Frank P., "Federal-State Compact: A New Experiment in Co-operative Federalism," *Columbia Law Review,* Vol. 63, pp. 825–55.

Keighton, W. B., "Delaware River Water Quality, Bristol to Marcus Hook, Pennsylvania, August 1949 to December 1963." Geological Survey Water-Supply Paper 1809-O, Washington: U.S. Government Printing Office, 1965.

Martin, Roscoe C., Birkhead, Guthrie S., Birkhead, Jesse, Munger, Frank J., *River Basin Administration and the Delaware.* Syracuse: Syracuse University Press, 1960. Particularly see the chapter "Travail on the Delaware."

Miller, William (General Counsel, DRBC), "Authority for Water Pollution Control and Abatement in the Delaware River Basin." Address at meeting of League of Women Voters, Inter-League Council on the Delaware River, March 25, 1965.

Phillips, Walter M., "Water Resources: The Delaware Basin," *Journal of American Institute of Planners*, Vol. 26, No. 3 (August 1960).

Report of Pennsylvania Water Resources Committee, February 1953, and *Delaware River Basin Report*, Pennsylvania Water Resources Committee and Engineer's Study Committee, January 1953.

IMPLEMENTATION AND MANAGEMENT

V

"A fundamental change has occurred in the national attitude toward the water pollution problem. The discussion has shifted from the issue of whether or not we should improve the quality of our water to the issue of how best to accomplish our objective."

Senator Edmund S. Muskie

A Policy for the Future

14

The fundamental task with respect to water quality improvement is how best to accomplish it. But it is also true that the task itself needs to be clearly defined. The job is not simply to "clean up" the nation's water bodies; rather, it is to manage continuously the quality of these waters over time in the dynamic context of a growing and affluent urban-industrial society. This dynamic context requires flexibility in adapting to changing circumstances if efficient management is to be achieved, which in turn has implications for the nature of the institutions needed for water quality management.[1]

In the following pages we outline an economic optimization approach to water quality management on a regional basis—an approach that reflects our interpretation of research over the past several years and that seems likely to provide a firm foundation for efficient progress. It is a distinct departure from the usual approach, which tends to see waste treatment as an end in itself and lays heavy emphasis upon enforcement actions against individual waste dischargers, perhaps supplemented by subsidies for selected means of reducing waste discharges.

As population grows, economic development proceeds, and interactions among uses and users of the country's water resources become ever more complex, the gain from such an economic systems approach will be even larger. A new initiative in policy appears needed at all governmental levels, but especially at the federal level, to permit the regional approach to evolve in an orderly way. New, broad-ranging, and responsible institutions will be needed for water quality management,

---

[1] Portions of this chapter build upon material developed by a panel of the National Academy of Sciences of which one of the authors was Chairman. The contributions of Irving Fox and David Smith to the panel report deserve special notice. See *Waste Management and Control*, Publication 1400 (Washington: National Academy of Sciences—National Research Council, 1966), App. 6 and 7.

but they must be consistent with the legitimate roles of our governments of general jurisdiction—local, state, and federal.

We believe that agencies should be established with powers to plan and implement management programs for an entire region, usually a river basin. These regional agencies would be responsible for planning, for the day-to-day operation of quality management systems, for the design and construction of appropriate management facilities and controls, and for data collection and research. With this combination of powers and geographical jurisdiction, the agencies should be able to:

1. Progress toward more systematic methods for reflecting the external costs associated with waste discharge in the waste disposal decisions of municipalities and the production and waste disposal decisions of private enterprises;

2. Search for, define, evaluate, and implement collective measures to reduce waste discharges, to reduce the adverse effects of waste discharges, and/or to improve or make better use of the assimilative capacity of watercourses;

3. Open the way for more efficient operation of reservoirs, treatment plants, and other components of a water quality management system through regionwide integration;

4. Adapt new knowledge and technology to the specific regional environment and incorporate them into a continuous management system at an optimal rate, because of their *continuous* responsibility for water quality management;

5. Give explicit consideration to the impacts of the spatial pattern of economic activities on water quality management and of the interrelationships between other aspects of environmental quality and water quality management.

Much of the discharge of water-borne wastes in this country is concentrated in a few river basins and bay and estuary areas. Most of these regions are sufficiently developed to support the expert staff and facilities a management agency requires.[2] Many other basins would benefit from collective measures such as flow regulation and in-stream aeration and from more systematic use of treatment and other measures, but they are not large enough or populous enough to support a separate management agency. Basins of this kind might be managed by the agency in charge of a contiguous river basin. Or a state might act as

[2] A number of "River Basin Commissions" have already been approved under the Water Resources Planning Act of 1965. These are not management agencies, since they have no construction or operating powers. Rather, they are planning and co-ordinating bodies which usually cover large areas (for example, one such commission covers the New England states). The planning activities of these commissions could be helpful in defining appropriate areas for water quality management.

the regional management agency if the basin lies within the state. The latter approach would require a substantial strengthening of the capabilities of the states in regard to water quality management—a matter to which we return subsequently.

In the following sections, we first state the criteria which research on water quality management suggests efficient regional management agencies (river basin or state) should meet. Then we describe what we feel are appropriate water quality management functions for the governments of general jurisdiction. They will still have an important role and without their leadership thoroughgoing regional water quality management cannot become a reality.

The final section addresses the question of the best means for internalizing the external costs imposed by the waste disposal activities of private enterprises and local governments. We conclude that an effluent charges system has major advantages over potential alternatives such as effluent standards and payments to reduce waste discharges, and at the same time it provides a needed source of funds to the regional management agency.

CRITERIA FOR REGIONAL WATER QUALITY MANAGEMENT AGENCIES

Given our broad definition of management, and assuming that the general goal of the regional agency is to foster the efficient use of resources, we suggest some criteria which regional agencies should meet. These criteria are based on technological and economic characteristics of efficient water quality management which we call determinants (see Table 16).

1. *The regional agency should internalize the major externalities associated with waste discharges to the watercourses of a region.* This does not necessarily mean that all external costs must occur within the territory under direct jurisdiction of the agency but that the major ones do and that any residual external costs which occur outside the area must be taken appropriately into account. Normally, the latter would occur through the activities of a higher unit of government. For example, an intensive management unit as large as the Mississippi Basin would probably be far from optimal in regard to administrative efficiency and the ability to involve the relevant publics in the decision-making process. Perhaps even the basin of the Ohio River with all its tributaries would be too large a unit for detailed water quality management, let alone over-all water resources management. But an Ohio Basin authority which controlled the quality of water from the tributaries by standards or charges at the points of confluence could articulate the

Table 16.   Determinants and Criteria for Regional Water Quality
Management Agencies

Determinants	Criteria
Existence of externalities.	Regional agency should be able to internalize the major externalities associated with waste discharges.
Economics of scale in various measures to handle wastes and to improve assimilative capacity of watercourses.	Regional agency should be able to implement measures of all types to improve water quality.
Inseparability of water quality from water quantity, interrelationships between water quality management and other outputs from water systems.	Regional agency should be able to take adequate account of the interrelationship between water quality and other aspects of water systems.
Interrelationship between spatial location of economic activities and water quality management.	Regional agency should be able to take into account through specific communication channels the interrelationship between water quality management and land use management.
Interrelationships between water quality management and impacts on other aspects of environmental quality, i.e., air, solid wastes disposal.	Regional agency should be able to take into account through specific communication channels the interrelationships between water and other activities having impacts on environmental quality.
Many of the benefits and costs associated with water quality are difficult to quantify in a generally acceptable manner.	Regional agency should: (a) delineate the wide range of choice possible—costs and consequences of different combinations of measures and of different levels of quality; (b) reflect or consider adequately the views of those affected by water quality management activities.

interest of the larger region with intensive management of water quality by tributary agencies.[3]

In many instances the states are in a good position to foster appropriate regional associations for watersheds or river basins within their jurisdictions. In a number of cases, conservancy districts and water authorities could be adapted to this purpose.[4] In these instances the state government should see that the river basin agencies consider the full costs associated with waste disposal in their regions. This could be done

[3] This idea was proposed by the staff of the Ohio River Valley Water Sanitation Commission. See Edward J. Cleary, *The ORSANCO Story* (The Johns Hopkins Press, for RFF, 1967), pp. 276–77.

[4] For example, "Proposed Procedure for Establishing and Financing the Miami Conservancy District as the Regional Water Resource Agency in the Great Miami River Basin (Preliminary)," The Miami Conservancy District, Dayton, Ohio (April 19, 1967).

by means of effluent standards or charges at the points where rivers discharge from such regions.

For interstate waters such as the Delaware, Hudson, and Potomac, interstate or interstate-federal agencies might well assume full and detailed water quality management functions. Under the program for federal initiative detailed below, the federal government would foster such organizations and insure that interstate and coastal effects of residual waste discharges are not overlooked.

2. *The regional agency should be able to implement all relevant measures to improve water quality.* Efficiency gains can often be achieved by implementing such collective measures as flow regulation, regional treatment plants, ground water recharge, effluent redistribution, and various measures to improve the waste assimilative capacity of watercourses. Accordingly, the regional agency should have the authority to see that such measures are implemented where economically justified. But the agency should also have the authority to acquire and operate more conventional treatment works where efficiency gains can be demonstrated. In some instances, the complexities of rather intricate system operation or the gains from more efficient use of technical and laboratory personnel may justify having the regional agency operate all treatment works in a region—even conventional ones at individual outfalls.[5]

3. *The regional agency should be able to take adequate account of the interrelationship between water quality and other aspects of water resource development and use.* The efficient use of watercourses for residual waste disposal cannot be disassociated from the development of water resources for other uses. Waste discharge imposes cost upon other water uses, and water quality may be improved or impaired by the way water bodies are managed for a variety of purposes. Controlled releases of stored water for hydroelectric power or navigation purposes may improve quality by augmenting low streamflows, thereby increasing the capacity of a stream to assimilate wastes. An irrigation development, on the other hand, is likely to have an adverse effect on water quality by reducing the flow of a stream and by contributing a return flow with a high concentration of dissolved solids. Thus water quality management is inextricably related to the total management of the hydrologic unit. Yet, it is generally treated as a separate activity.

How can water quality management be integrated with the over-all development and efficient use of an area's water resources? From an

[5] A proposal to do this has recently been put forward in the state of Maryland. ["A Program for Water Pollution Control in Maryland," by a Study Commission to Investigate the Problems of Water Pollution Control, mimeo, (February 1967).] Experience in the Ruhr area and in Ontario, Canada, suggests that major gains may accrue from centralized operations. We have no doubt that experimentation with this approach is merited elsewhere.

administrative standpoint, the simplest procedure would be to assign the responsibility for all aspects of water management to a single public regional agency. The Delaware River Basin Commission has such broad authority. This is also the approach used in the Ruhr area and contemplated under the water laws in France and England. This arrangement has much merit, but, again, experimentation would appear to be in order. For the most part in the United States, water quality responsibilities are now separated from other water development responsibilities at both the federal and state levels of government. And, in fact, water quality responsibility is itself divided among two or more agencies in many states.

An alternative to the integrated or broad regional agency is a separate regional water quality management agency that would buy services, such as the maintenance of minimum flow conditions, from the general water development agencies and charge other agencies whose activities have adverse effects on water quality. Such an arrangement would not be as simple to administer as the single agency, but in some instances it might be more practicable of attainment.[6]

4. *The regional agency should be able to take adequate account of the interrelationship between water quality management and land use management.* The location of an economic activity has a bearing on the costs of water quality management. The costs imposed by a major industrial operation with a potentially large residual waste discharge may be much larger in one location than in another. The economics of centralized waste treatment cannot be realized when development is scattered and waste collection costs are high. Furthermore, water-based recreation will not benefit from improved water quality unless the pattern of land use on areas adjacent to the water body facilitates the recreational activities.

The interrelationships between water quality management and land use management are perhaps less direct than those between water quality management and other outputs of water resources systems. Thus there is less reason for proposing that a single regional agency have jurisdiction over both water quality and land use management. What is essential, however, is that the water quality management agency have an explicit and formal relationship with the regional and local agencies responsible for planning and regulating land use, so that it will have ample opportunity to indicate how land use decisions would affect water quality

---

[6] In this connection, an ORSANCO staff memorandum may again be cited. The staff considered both the alternative of an entirely new compact to administer all aspects of water use and development, and the alternative of restructuring the existing compact to establish a regional authority for water quality management, roughly in accordance with the criteria here outlined. The staff favored and recommended the second alternative as offering more practical promise for political attainment. See Cleary, *op. cit.*

management. That opportunity should occur in the early phase of the land use planning process. (At the same time, it is essential that the activities of the regional water quality agency be reviewed with a view to their consistency with over-all land use planning.)

5. *The regional agency should be able to take adequate account of the interrelationship between water quality management and impacts on other aspects of environmental quality.* Removing waste materials from water streams does not destroy the wastes, it merely changes their form or location or both. Solid or gaseous waste materials may re-enter the productive cycle,[7] or they may present waste disposal problems of their own. Numerous examples could be cited. The kraft pulping process produces less waterborne waste than the sulphite process but it results in deterioration of air quality; if solids are removed from a wastewater stream and incinerated, gases and particulate matter are released to the air; disposing of sewage sludge as swampland fill reduces wildlife habitat; in one instance, underground disposal of a particularly difficult to treat waste stream is thought to have caused earthquakes.[8] Such environmental interrelationships are of sufficient importance that the regional jurisdiction and/or special agencies having responsibility with respect to other environmental quality problems must be involved in the process of decision making. There should be close working relationships between the staffs of the regional water quality management agencies and the agencies with responsibility for other aspects of environmental quality. Formal review procedures are also needed, and ways should be developed for the agencies to exchange funds to compensate for external benefits or costs conferred or imposed by one upon the other. These "market-like" devices can often allow much greater flexibility than the binary decision implicit in a permit.

6. *The regional agency should provide an opportunity for affected parties to have a voice in decisions.* The discussion of the Potomac and Delaware estuaries (Chapter 11) indicated the importance of benefits which are as yet difficult to quantify in monetary terms. This problem has two implications with respect to governmental organization for water quality management. First, the agency should delineate not only different ways of achieving a specified physical target but also alternative targets (including degree of certainty of achievement).

Second, those affected by water quality management activities should have a voice in decisions. Various techniques have been devised to meet

[7] As it becomes possible and necessary to weigh all the external costs associated with waste disposal—be it in liquid, gaseous, or solid form—techniques for holding materials in the productive cycle rather than "disposing" of them will become of greater significance relative to treatment.

[8] See Walter Sullivan, "How to Start an Earthquake," *New York Times*, March 27, 1966, p. 6E; D. M. Evans, "Man-made Earthquakes—A Progress Report," *Geotimes*, Vol. 12, No. 6 (1967), pp. 19–20.

this second problem. They range from the Delaware River Basin approach where only governments of general jurisdiction have direct voting power to the *Genossenschaften* of the Ruhr area where industrial representatives as well as governments are afforded voting rights on the governing board. As explained in Chapter 13, we can offer no hard criteria as to the appropriate arrangement.

One of the least understood questions in regard to water quality and over-all water resources management is how the agency's political structure can be arranged so that it is conducive to efficiency and equity. This is an area in which research is exceedingly difficult but badly needed.

We now turn to outlining a pattern of activities which we would regard as constructive initiative by the various levels of government to establish efficient systems of regional water quality management.

THE ROLE OF GOVERNMENTS OF GENERAL JURISDICTION

Establishing an optimizing system for water quality management in any region would involve essentially the following steps. The first—a political-legal one—would be to set up a new agency or restructure an established one with authority such that the criteria enumerated above are met. This could be done under state law for an intrastate region, under federal law for interstate regions, or through the mechanism of an interstate or interstate-federal compact. The second step would be to assemble a staff. This would include various kinds of engineers and natural scientists, and economists and other social scientists. The third step would be data collection and analysis—to illuminate alternatives available and to assess the benefits and costs associated with them. The studies of the Potomac and Delaware estuary areas reported in Chapter 11 are illustrative of this phase. The fourth step would involve formulating systems of physical measures and other control devices and policies (such as standards and charges) for water quality management in the region. The final step would be to construct and operate the first units of the agreed-upon system. Operation and further planning would then become a continuous process, with the system adapting to changing circumstances and the development of new information.

Federal Government

Water quality management is largely the province of state and local governments, and state governments are in a good position to encourage the establishment of appropriate management institutions in tributary basins that lie within an individual state. Federal leadership could be particularly important in dealing with interstate waters—with main-stem conditions on the larger river systems and with large groundwater basins. In such instances, interstate compacts establishing effective agencies are difficult to negotiate.[9] Also it might assist in various ways in the implementation of regional approaches in the smaller, intrastate basins.

The federal government could, of course, take direct action. It could set up regional water quality management agencies or regional water resource management agencies. These agencies could be separate entities such as TVA or regional units of a federal agency such as proposed by the First Hoover Commission. There has been so much opposition to arrangements of this nature, that it is questionable whether the federal government would be willing to move in this fashion.

An alternative would be for the federal government to establish incentives and guidelines for the organization and operation of regional management agencies either under state law or through interstate compact. An agency with adequate authority to plan and implement an optimizing system would be eligible for a grant of funds to support a portion of its budget (or expenditures) to help staff the agency and make the first data collection, analyses, and formulation of specific measures for water quality management. If the federal government is satisfied that the proposed program would meet reasonable optimizing objectives, the agency might be eligible for a grant to assist it with its actual construction and operating expenses. Such assistance might appropriately be limited to the early implementation period—say, five years. During this period, it would be necessary to work out longer-term arrangements for financing the agency, a point to which we return later.

The federal government might wish to approach the water quality management problem in the broader context of water resources development and management. In that event, the federal government could provide support of the type described above to regional water resources agencies having general water management responsibilities including quality management. In addition, the federal government could provide support through the regional agency for flood damage reduction, navigation, irrigation, power, and recreation on whatever terms such support is, or may be, provided for these purposes through federal agencies. Unless this were done, regional agencies would operate at a serious financial disadvantage, and it is doubtful that regions would willingly impose such disadvantages on themselves. A partial or complete alternative to the extension of subsidy arrangements to regional agencies would be a more

9 It is perhaps less difficult than in earlier years because: (a) the federal Water Quality Act simplifies obtaining consent of Congress for states to negotiate; (b) a fund of experience in writing compacts is now available; and (c) state legislatures have come to regard compacts as desirable means for co-operative action.

complete financing of federal water programs through user charges, which would produce greater efficiency in water resources use.[10]

Even with a regional agency as the primary device for effective and efficient water quality management, the federal government would have an important continuing role to play.

First, it should be prepared to intervene—in terms of data collection, analysis, and enforcement—if instances exist where it has not been possible to establish a duly constituted organization or state action, in significant interstate problem situations.

Second, the Federal Water Pollution Control Administration has begun to assemble teams of planners—scientists, engineers, and a few social scientists—to carry out its comprehensive surveys program. "Headquarters" teams of this kind could be retained to aid the regional and state agencies in their continuing planning and implementation functions. Joint studies by federal teams and local agencies, such as the study contemplated in the Houston-Galveston Bay area, might be undertaken. The federal teams should be in a position to bring a wider range of experience and expertise to bear on the regional problem than regional and state personnel.

Third, the federal government should expand its network of water quality monitoring stations, with respect to both surface and ground waters. Data from short-run sampling stations for specific investigations could then be related to the data from the base network.

Finally, the federal government should maintain a strong program of research on various aspects of water quality management, and make arrangements for the results to be passed on to the regional and state agencies. The headquarters planning teams might be particularly useful in this regard.

The Advanced Waste Treatment Research Program is an example of the type of research effort which can be extremely valuable. But the present research program should be strengthened in several directions:

1. More emphasis should be given to research on quality improvement measures such as reaeration of watercourses, flow regulation, groundwater recharge, regulated discharge of effluents, design of water and waste treatment plants for high-level intermittent treatment, and industrial waste reduction via process change, materials recovery, and by-product production. In the past, federal programs have focused on *treatment facilities* as independent entities rather than as potential components of a regional water quality management program.

---

[10] For good discussions, see Otto Eckstein, *Water Resources Development: The Economics of Project Evaluation* (Harvard University Press, 1958); and John V. Krutilla, "Is Public Intervention in Water Resources Development Conducive to Economic Efficiency?" *Natural Resources Journal* (January 1966).

2. More emphasis is needed on research in techniques of system planning, design, and evaluation, and on system operation.

3. More emphasis should be placed on research directed to defining water quality damage or loss functions.

4. Research on the interrelationships among liquid, solid, and gaseous wastes is badly needed and could logically be supported and stimulated at the federal level.

5. Continuous appraisal is needed of the technological changes in the major water-using industries and their effects on the generation, handling, treatment, and disposal of wastes. This would provide valuable information for regional water quality management.

The States

The states must establish much stronger organizations if the benefits of efficient regional water quality management are to be realized. A major function of the state governments should be to facilitate the organization of adequately financed regional management agencies of appropriate size and authority within their areas of jurisdiction. Probably most such organizations would be the creatures of state law. States must therefore assume a primary responsibility as governments of general jurisdiction to see that the previously stated criteria relating to regional agencies are met. In addition, the states should be in a position to offer technical advice and possibly financial aid to regional agencies, in much the same manner as proposed for the federal government vis-à-vis the states.

Furthermore, the states should be prepared to conduct appropriate water quality management programs in areas that have neither the size nor the development to justify a regional agency. A program of this kind has been proposed in Maryland.

In performing these functions, fragmentation of responsibility in state governments (as at other levels of government) may be a severe problem. Responsibilities for water quality and water resources management are, to various degrees, lodged in a variety of agencies in most states. A few states are almost in a position to perform the needed water quality management supporting functions, but most are very far from it.[11]

[11] The contention is often made that the states are financially incapable of carrying out their responsibilities along the lines suggested here. Such a contention is equally valid for many state activities in addition to water quality management, and results from the inadequate fiscal resources of the states in general. We believe that federal revenue-sharing plans of the type proposed by Walter Heller (formerly Chairman of the President's Council of Economic Advisers), and others, could materially aid the states in realizing their potential in this and other areas. (A good brief discussion of this concept is found in Walter Heller, "A Sympathetic Reappraisal of Revenue Sharing," in Harvey S. Perloff and Richard P. Nathan (ed.), *Revenue Sharing and the City* (The Johns Hopkins Press, for RFF, 1968).

Local Governments

The role of local governments in regional water quality management is a complex one primarily because the general government of metropolitan areas is itself often greatly fractionated. Nevertheless, these governments have extremely important functions in regional water quality management. They generally have the legal authority to regulate land use and, as the case study of the Delaware indicated, the pattern of land use and associated waste disposal can have an important bearing on the cost of regional water quality management programs.

Environmental problems are most apparent in the metropolitan areas; consequently metropolitan planning agencies must co-ordinate and integrate the activities of environmental agencies within their jurisdictions. It should also be their responsibility to see that proposed land-use patterns take adequate account of the environmental quality problems, including water quality, which may be associated with them.[12]

Local governmental units can influence regional water quality management through their water and waste disposal charges. Also, local governments can achieve major economies by organizing collective treatment and distribution works. This might be done with the help of the regional agency where the latter does not assume direct responsibility for instituting such works.[13]

Governments of General Jurisdiction and the Regional Agency

We have already noted the need for considerable flexibility and experimentation with respect to the composition of regional agency governing boards. In all instances, however, the governments of general jurisdiction in the region involved should be represented on the governing board.

CONTROLLING WASTE DISCHARGES
AND FINANCING THE REGIONAL AGENCY

Research has demonstrated that regional agencies capable of directly implementing collective facilities for regional water quality management could achieve major efficiencies. But equally important functions of management are to optimally control waste discharges from individual municipalities and industries and to appropriately influence industrial

---

[12] For a preliminary effort to analyze this connection, see *Waste Management* (Regional Plan Association, New York, March 1968). The report was prepared by B. T. Bower, G. P. Larson, Abraham Michaels, and W. M. Phillips.

[13] As indicated in Chapter 11, present federal grant arrangements provide an added incentive for metropolitan, area-wide collection and treatment systems. In several instances—Pittsburgh, Seattle, and St. Louis, for example—metro systems were installed or planned prior to the federal incentives program.

location decisions. These problems will confront regional agencies to differing degrees but will always be present.

At one extreme, an agency may do no more than induce the individual industrial plant or municipality to reduce its waste discharge to an appropriate degree, and not construct or operate waste handling facilities itself. In that case, it has only to decide how best to induce control of the waste discharges.

Near the other extreme is the approach used in the Ruhr area where the management agency provides both conventional treatment works and regional-scale facilities. Even there, however, industrial operations are encouraged to conserve the waste assimilative capacity of the stream via process changes, materials recovery, and specialized industrial waste treatment methods. Effluent charges are levied on industries discharging to the waste handling system and on those discharging directly to watercourses.

An intermediate case would be a regional agency that provided only facilities affecting the assimilative capacity of watercourses (reservoirs for flow regulation and facilities for stream reaeration, for example). Here, too, an appropriate means must be found to reflect the external costs[14] associated with waste discharges in the decisions which remain in the hands of industries and local units of government.

Direct regulation, payments, and charges are the terms used here to refer to the techniques for achieving this result. The alternatives are outlined below in general terms. Payments and charges, which were grouped in the analysis in Chapter 6 because they are in theory closely related, are treated separately here because they are very different in terms of administrative and institutional considerations. Furthermore, each of the techniques has different financial effects on the regional agency and on the amount of funds which would have to be obtained from taxes to support the activities of the regional agency.

Direct Regulation

This system would rely primarily upon direct public regulation of waste discharges by means of standards established in accord with laws and administrative orders. These standards would apply to discharges at individual (industrial and municipal) outfalls and to discharges from regional agency treatment plants. Such a system would constitute an extension or elaboration of existing policies and practices.

To be capable of optimizing under the regulatory system, the operating agency would have to be able to estimate not only the external costs associated with waste discharges but also the costs associated with in-

[14] Perhaps as represented by a stream standard surrogate; see the discussion in Chapter 7.

cremental reductions in waste discharges[15] by cities and firms through alternative means. It should be capable of taking into account possibilities for residual materials recovery and process changes, as well as conventional treatment.

Ideally, the standards would be varied to take into account the differing waste-assimilation capacity of the watercourse under varying flow conditions, the differing capacity at various locations, differing levels of demand upon the watercourse, and the differing incremental costs of waste reduction at various outfalls. This would mean different standards for different locations and for the same location at different times. The effluent standards would not only control the amount of existing discharges but, since they would vary geographically, would play a role in determining the location of industrial and municipal outfalls, and perhaps the location of industrial and even municipal activities. Optimum effluent standards might result in greatly different levels of required waste reduction at different outfalls, perhaps even at outfalls located close together.[16] This result raises major problems of equity which were explored in some detail in Chapters 7 and 8.

The success of a system of this kind would depend in large measure upon the ability of an agency to develop reliable data on the physical and economic effects of alternative waste reduction programs and then to enforce effluent standards that minimize waste management costs to society. The funds for establishing and operating such a system would presumably come from taxes because no prices or charges would be built into the system. This in itself presents a serious problem, since most taxes are not without distorting effects upon the allocation of resources.

Payments

This system would rely primarily on selective payments to waste dischargers to motivate them to restrict waste discharges to an optimum degree. A payment would be made for each unit of waste withheld. This arrangement would constitute a departure from existing policy and practice and would entail a major change in the kinds of subsidies already provided and proposed.[17]

On the basis of its estimate of the external costs, or of the incentive to achieve the stream standard surrogate, the operating agency would institute a schedule of payments for waste reduction to induce cities and firms to reduce their waste contribution to an optimum level. These

[15] Or to establish a stream standard surrogate for a damage function. See Chapter 7, Chapter 11, and the Appendix to Chapter 10.

[16] This was shown by the empirical investigation of effluent charges as they might apply to the Delaware Estuary area, as reported in Chapter 8.

[17] Variants of this system completely incapable of achieving optimum results but with considerable current political support have been discussed in Chapter 9.

payments should in principle be equivalent to the downstream costs imposed by increments of waste discharge. Payments would vary with water availability and with outfall locations, as well as with the quantity and quality of the effluent. Where the incremental costs associated with waste disposal can be reduced more efficiently by large-scale facilities than by payments, the agency would provide such facilities and reduce payments to reflect the efficiency gain. If the agency provided treatment plants and adhered to the payment scheme, it would pay industrial users to reduce discharge at least to the point where the marginal cost of a further reduction by internal measures began to exceed the marginal cost of treatment in agency plants.

No doubt some minimum direct regulatory measures would also be useful. For example, where a waterway is used for domestic water supplies and also has recreational and aesthetic values, it might be best simply to prohibit the discharge of toxic chemicals and/or particularly unsightly and odorous materials.

This system would require the expenditure of much larger sums, presumably raised through taxes, than the system utilizing effluent standards.

Charges

This system would rely heavily upon effluent charges to motivate firms and cities to cut back on discharges in such a way as to optimize waste discharge, (or to achieve a desired water quality level). The elements of such a system would be identical with the payments system except that instead of making payments to waste contributors to reduce effluent discharges to optimum levels (or setting standards to achieve the same purpose), charges would be levied on each unit of waste discharged. The schedule of charges would be based upon the external costs associated with increments of effluent discharge (or the agency's estimate of the incentive needed to achieve the stream standard surrogate). The charges system would take hydrologic variability into consideration. As with the system of payments, large-scale measures would be undertaken to the extent that their incremental costs were lower than the incremental individual outfall waste reduction costs and residual damages avoided by the measures.

Funds to finance the agency would be derived from the charges imposed on the waste dischargers.

Advantages and Disadvantages

Each of the three systems—direct regulation, payments, and charges— has certain advantages and disadvantages. The regulatory system, which in some ways is closest to present policy and practice, has proved reasonably effective in dealing with the grossest forms of water quality impairment. But it does not lend itself to balancing incremental costs and gains in a relatively precise manner. Moreover, it does not provide funds for the construction and operation of measures of regional scope, should these prove economical.

The payment and charge systems are in effect an application of the pricing system—on which our economic institutions rely so heavily to secure an appropriate allocation of resources—to the waste disposal field. But the payment system suffers from several major handicaps. The concept of paying a waste discharger for reducing the costs he imposes upon others is contrary to the popular concept of fairness—even if such a practice would assure greater economic efficiency. In addition, there would be the task of raising substantial funds through increased taxation. With so many urgent demands being placed upon government and the difficulty of framing taxes which themselves do not distort resources use, there are serious problems in obtaining the amounts required. Also, to be fully effective, payments must continue even after research produces lower-cost means of reducing effluent, or if a firm ceases manufacturing altogether in order to reduce its effluent contribution to the extent warranted by the payments. Even more of a problem is the matter of paying firms that would locate in a basin were it not for the social cost of waste disposal which they would impose; these firms would require payment even though they never locate in the basin. These amount to almost insuperable informational and administrative obstacles to a fully effective system of subsidies.

The charges system does not suffer from these handicaps, and it has the merit of providing funds to finance the construction and operation of quality management measures on a regional scale. If optimally applied, the charges system might be self-sustaining (see Appendix to Chapter 10).

The charges system might be opposed by waste dischargers who now avoid the external costs which they impose. However, the industry and regional examples reported in Chapters 4 and 8 have shown that for an individual firm the cost of an efficient waste reduction program— over realistic ranges—is not large compared with other costs of industrial production. Thus for the vast majority of industrial plants effective waste discharge control would hardly be a determining factor in the decision whether to operate the plant or not.

In a few instances, mostly in already depressed areas, plants may be capable of continuing operation only because they are able to shift all or most of that portion of production costs associated with waste disposal to other economic units. When this situation is coupled with one in which the plant is a major part of the employment base of a community, society may have an interest in assisting the plant to stay in business, while at the same time controlling the external costs it is imposing. This, however, does not suggest across-the-board subsidy for industrial waste control, but rather selective aid where a community might be seriously disadvantaged by the closing of a plant. Such aid might take the form of direct assistance to the plant for installing waste reduction equipment, or support to the community—retraining and preference in government contracts, for example.

LEADERSHIP IN INITIATION OF A CHARGES SYSTEM

There appear to be compelling reasons for favoring the effluent charges system as one of the cornerstones of regional water quality management.[18] But it may be difficult for particular states and regions to pioneer such a substantial departure from previous practice. The federal government's greater insulation from powerful local interests provides another opportunity for leadership. One approach would be for the federal government to levy a national effluent charge on all waste discharges above some minimum amount. The charge could be based on a formula similar to one of those used in the Ruhr area or one of those used by certain U.S. municipalities in levying sewer service charges upon industry. The charge might be set at a level which would approximately meet the cost of the federal program. Collection would depend on voluntary reporting and spot checks. The merits of this approach would be: (1) it would finance an important national program by means of a tax which would tend to improve the allocation of resources; and (2) it would hold an umbrella over regional agencies who wished to use the device for management and financial reasons. Once a regional agency was duly established, the authority and responsibility for levying the charges could be turned over to it. The agency could then refine the system of charges as a tool of management. The agency would be permitted

---

[18] We have emphasized the role of effluent charges because of the importance of water quality in water management currently and in the future. However, as has been indicated numerous times previously, water quality management is but part of over-all water resources management. In order to achieve optimal allocation of resources, it is essential to consider not only effluent charges but, where relevant, charges in relation to other components of water utilization. For example, another component of water utilization which a management agency must consider in the context of over-all water resources management is net depletion or consumptive use. Because different production processes (as well as different methods of waste treatment) may result in significantly different amounts of consumptive use, wherever water is relatively scarce it is relevant to consider possible incentives for the reduction in net depletion or consumptive use. In principle, charges should reflect the incremental external cost which a user imposes on the whole water resource system. Blair Bower has referred to such charges as "water utilization charges." See B. T. Bower, "The Economics of Industrial Water Utilization," in Kneese and Smith (ed.), *Water Research* (The Johns Hopkins Press, for RFF, 1966).

to raise the charge above the federal level but not lower it. It would be permitted to use the proceeds to operate and finance a regional water quality management system to the extent justified. Excess revenues, if any, would be made available for purposes of financing the federal program or turned over to other governments of general jurisdiction.

By taking this initiative and those discussed in earlier parts of this chapter, the federal government could lay the groundwork for effective and viable institutions for regional water quality management in the framework of over-all water resources management.

Index